A Course in Romance Linguistics

Volume 1: A Synchronic View

A comparative/contrastive description
of five modern Romance languages
—French, Spanish, Portuguese,
Italian, Roumanian—in terms of
an underlying grammar manifested
in surface similarities and differences

Frederick B. Agard

Georgetown University Press, Washington, D.C. 20057

Printed in the United States of America

Library of Congress Cataloging in Publication Data

Agard, Frederick Browning, 1907-
 A course in Romance linguistics.

 Bibliography: v. 1, p.
 Contents: v. 1. A synchronic view.
 1. Romance languages—Grammar. I. Title.
PC61.A3 1984   440   83-20817
ISBN 0-87840-088-5 (v. 1)

Contents

Adjectival structures

Adverbial structures

Verbal structures

Clausal structures

Clauses and discourse

Dependent clauses

Sentential structures

Part Two: Phonology

Foreword

This first of the two-volume *A Course in Romance Linguistics* is strictly descriptive (synchronic) as opposed to the second volume which is strictly historical (diachronic). Both embody the author's forty-odd years of experience in teaching this subject with never a fully satisfactory textbook at hand. The present manual is the first to set forth a concerted learning program designed to guide students through material organized in terms of up-to-date linguistic principles and at the same time to provide them with models of analysis and description on which to base exercises and projects of their own. In pursuit of this announced purpose, the stylistic register of the exposition and instruction is deliberately kept informal, without hesitating, for example, to use the personal pronouns *we* and *you* in order to achieve a pedagogical effect of teacher talking to learner.

The book deals with five standard languages—French, Spanish, Portuguese, Italian, and Roumanian—with but a minimum of attention to regional variation within each. Grammar—that is to say, morphosyntax as opposed to phonology—is presented first, with all examples given in conventional orthography. The presentation is built on a model which is deliberately eclectic, representing a descriptive approach developed by the author through long experimentation and admittedly tailored to the purposes of contrastive Romance statements in such a way as to make sense out of the surface similarities and differences between the five linguistic structures in terms of a single shared underlying structure (not 'deep structure' in any esoteric sense) at an appropriate level of abstractness.

While it is hoped that all five grammatical systems are comprehensively covered, no claim is made to exhaustiveness in the generative sense of formulations that will account for every possible sentence in each language. There being no corpus of speech acts to exhaust—how could there be, since no adequate corpus exists from which to extract the syntax of even one language?—the illustrative tokens are for the most part extrapolations by the author from three kinds of information source: (1) standard reference grammars and dictionaries of each language, descriptive of usage rather than prescriptive of correctness, (2) the author's own competence in each lan-

xii / Foreword

guage, limited of course and hence supplemented by (3) elicitation of utterances by native speakers.

As author, I wish to thank in particular the following persons who have generously shared their native-speaking intuitions with me: Irène Daly and Alexandra Littauer (French), Carlos Piera and Margarita Suñer (Spanish), Lúcia Helena Alves and Deborah Ravinowich (Portuguese), Pina Scaiola Swenson and Donatella Stocchi-Perucchio (Italian), Ileana Comorovski and Ioana Vornic (Roumanian). I add here also the expression of heartfelt gratitude to Milton Azevedo, Charles Carlton, Julia Herschensohn, Charles Hockett, Sanda Iliescu Huffman, Larry King, Clifford Leonard, Marilyn Martin, James Noblitt, Joseph Ricciardi, Carol Rosen, Donald Solá, and Dana Wheeler, my colleagues and/or former students who are also competent linguists, for the enthusiastic interest with which, over the years, they have discussed one or another Romance language with me and in so doing given me many an invaluable insight.

F.B.A.
Ithaca, New York

0. Introduction

0.1 Methodological orientation. In this fourth quarter of the twentieth century it may well be that Romance Linguistics, as a field of concentrated investigation and study, stands in danger of fragmentation if not of extinction. Why so? There would seem to be a twofold reason. On the one hand, Romance Linguistics has traditionally stressed the historical relationships among the various members of the family of languages known to be descended from Latin. On the other hand, in the wake of the third-quarter revolution which has pervaded the entire discipline of linguistics, we are now witnessing such a proliferation of synchronic studies as tends to crowd diachronic studies out of space and out of mind. Thus younger linguists, competing for space in scholarly journals and for the attention of deans and students alike, are coming out with articles or monographs on French causatives, or Spanish presentational sentences, or the like, a trend which means that there is more French Linguistics, or more Spanish Linguistics, or more Italian Linguistics, or whatever, being done, but commensurately less Romance Linguistics. Bits and pieces of a single grammar, not to mention two or more whole grammars compared and contrasted, seem to be the most that can be managed. For indeed, in terms of the in-depth analysis that has come to be generally considered de rigueur—an analysis which strives to account for many constructions which do *not* occur as well as for all those which do—the entire grammatical system of just one language is beyond most analysts' (and students') reach, while the comparison/contrast of two separate language systems (however closely related) is wholly unattainable and indeed well-nigh unthinkable. Neither our creative energies nor our brain capacities expand to keep pace with the new masses of data at our disposal.

Does this current 'state of the art' then signify that Romance Linguistics should be given up for lost? Or if not abandoned, should it simply go on being practiced within the comfortable, traditional mould of historical studies? One eminent Romance scholar[1] maintains that in the comparison of, say, French and Italian, diachronic considerations are in any case inevitable; but with this we must disagree. It is true that the languages of a given family are interrelated in certain formal ways precisely because of a common history

1

not shared with another family, and that we cannot come to understand that interrelationship completely without looking into that history. As for the Romance family, much of its past life is invitingly accessible through documents spanning two millennia, starting with an ample record of the parent language itself, Latin. On the other hand, the earlier stages of some groups of languages are much less abundantly attested; those of others, not at all. The point is that the interrelatedness of a set of languages is perceptible—visible to the naked eye, as it were—whether historically documented or not. Historical linguistics was in fact invented by nineteenth-century philologists on the basis of synchronic observation. It was their detection of similarities among linguistic forms of Latin, Greek, Gothic, Old Slavic, Old Persian and Sanskrit that led them to hypothesize a common source buried in history. Like archaeologists, they went on to reconstruct parts of that ancestral tongue (which they labeled Proto-Indo-European), and when it proved out that the reconstruction also of a Proto-Romance language tallied in most respects—mainly in phonology and morphology, to be sure—with Latin as it was known to have existed, the Comparative Method was validated once and for all.

There is no doubt that the Comparative Method profits from access to earlier, intermediate stages of any input language, e.g. 'French' of the thirteenth century and/or 'French' of the ninth century. The fact remains, however, that the method qua method rests first and foremost on the observation and manipulation of synchronic data; either Modern French or Old French has to be seen primarily as a language system existing at a given point in time, not as a system undergoing change before our eyes. And it is this indisputable fact that brings us around to the justification of the detailed synchronic analysis of intimately related languages. It is indispensable to compare and contrast whole grammatical systems and whole phonological systems, not mere bits and pieces of systems. We are about to examine the whole systems of five standard languages—French (Fr), Spanish (Sp), Portuguese (Po), Italian (It) and Roumanian (Ro)—and we are going to describe those systems in accordance with scientific linguistic principles which are up to date—not in the sense that the contemporary generativists' or stratificationalists' procedures are up to date, nor yet in the different sense in which the sociolinguists and the psycholinguists and the neurolinguists are up to date, but in terms of a descriptive model which nevertheless leaves well behind the conventional, prescientific, and wholly outmoded kinds of linguistic statement encountered in most full-scale treatments of Romance Linguistics thus far. We are going to compare and contrast first the grammatical systems of our five languages, and secondly their sound systems.

For the grammar we will follow a hierarchical phrase-structure model, from the morpheme up through the word, the phrase, the clause, and the sentence. Selectively, we will be drawing elements from American structuralism (including immediate-constituent and tagmemic theory), from early transformational grammar (TG) and even from the more recent relational grammar (RG), but without relying on the fancy visual trappings in vogue in all the new schools. Tagmemics will have us insist on the duality of form and function in syntax; TG and RG will allow us to posit more than one level of structure: basic, or underlying, structures and surface structures.

Our aim in comparing/contrasting the grammars of these five related languages is not, we emphasize, primarily historical. We seek at this point neither to add to nor to confirm our knowledge of their history, but rather to record information about the languages themselves and to observe in what particulars they are alike or similar, and in what ways they differ, both underlyingly and in their surface manifestations. The further inclusion of other Romance languages—e.g. Provençal, Catalan, Romansh, Sardinian— would doubtless refine our findings, but to work with more than five would overcomplicate the operation; any other(s) were better introduced in a separate study.

For the phonology (Part Two) we will provide concise sketches of both the systematic inventories and the autonomous phonemes, again based on a structural hierarchy from phoneme through syllable to word and phrase. Thus, the principal aim, in Part Two of this volume, is the same as with the grammar in Part One. In a second volume, we propose to utilize the phonological data as input for comparative reconstruction, but that will be a wholly separate operation with entirely different goals, to be explained in the introduction to *A Course in Romance Linguistics, Vol. 2: A Diachronic View.*

We are now ready for some more specific, substantive orientation to our immediate design.

0.2 Substantive orientation. A model proposed some years ago for potential use in contrasting languages looked essentially like Table 0.1.

In order to compare and to contrast any two language systems in any meaningful way at all, it is necessary to assume that these two share a number of fundamental properties and constraints, many of which will doubtless prove to be 'language universals' once theory has succeeded in identifying and defining the latter precisely. Proceeding on this assumption, we must further posit that the shared characteristics in question, being hidden from view—by virtue of the fact that no actual utterance is the same in the two languages—must reside in the source or 'deep' structure.[3] These assumptions allow us, it seems, to adapt and expand the model in Table 0.1 in such a way as to take account of the shared 'deep' structure versus the same-or-different 'shallow' shared structure of any two (or more) languages. This expansion would consist principally in splitting the right-hand half of the model into two (or more) sectors headed Language A, Language B, Language C . . ., minimally as in Table 0.2.

It seems necessary also to oppose 'deep' with 'shallow' rather than 'surface' structure, with a view to further subdividing the shallow into 'basic' or

Table 0.1 A suggested model for contrasting languages.[2]

Deep structure:

Experience → Sememes in semological space → Grammatical units in hierarchical arrangement → Transformational rules →

Surface structure:

Grammatical units in linear order → Phonemes in phonological space → Sound

Table 0.2 Expanded version of model in Table 0.1.

Deep structure:

Experience → Sememes in semological space → Grammatical units in hierarchical arrangement → Transformational rules / Transformational rules

Shallow structure:

Language A: Grammatical units in linear order → Language A: Phonemes in phonological space → Sound

Language B: Grammatical units in linear order → Language B: Phonemes in phonological space → Sound

'underlying' (terms usable interchangeably) structure and that which is manifestly 'surface' structure. Let us now proceed to interpret and flesh out this adapted model, moving from left to right.

We need not attempt to deal in any concerted way with the outer-left component of the deep structure, i.e. the semantic system with its particular units ('sememes' equate essentially with minimal semantic units), nor with the mechanisms whereby this system feeds into the grammatical system. For our purposes we need only to accept the notion (or at least the convenient fiction) of a uniform, cross-language semantic structure and to posit the existence of some set of realization rules that interlock the semantics and the grammar. We must, however, spell out one basic working assumption: that in any set of examples purporting to illustrate differences in surface structure among any of our five languages, meaning shall be held constant throughout the set in order to insure that we are not dealing with basic structures which are themselves different and therefore not validly contrastable. To illustrate: Fr *ce livre-ci est à moi* and Sp *este libro es mío* reflect the same basic structure, a fact corroborated by the meaninglessness of either Sp **este libro es a mí* or Fr **ce livre-ci est mien*, even though in other, different contexts Fr *à moi*/Sp *a mí* and Fr *mien*/Sp *mío* do coincide in meaning as well as in surface structure.[4]

The inner-left component of the deep structure represents the grammatical hierarchy which our particular languages have in common. We may posit their sharing of five interdependent levels of grammatical form, all but the first breaking down into the same internal constituencies as shown herewith.

Level 1. The MORPHEME, being the minimal unit of grammatical structure, distinguishable from all other morphemes in the language in form and/or meaning, and functioning as ROOT, AFFIX, INFLECTION, or MARKER at any of the higher levels.

Level 2. The WORD, composed of a root plus-or-minus ($\pm$) a DERIVATIONAL AFFIX, and functioning as HEAD at the next-higher level (Level 3).

Level 3. The PHRASE, composed of an obligatory head $\pm$ one or more attributes, and functioning as CONSTITUENT either at the next-higher level (Level 4) or at this same level (i.e. embedded in a larger phrase).

Level 4. The CLAUSE, composed of SUBJECT, MODALITY, PREDICATE and COMPLEMENTS and/or MODIFIERS, and functioning as constituent either at the next-higher level (Level 5), or at this same level (i.e. embedded in a larger clause), or at the next-lower level (Level 3) (i.e. embedded in a phrase).

Level 5. The SENTENCE, composed of a GRAMMATICAL CONSTITUENT and an INTONATION CONTOUR. The sentence is the maximal unit of grammatical structure in the present frame of reference, although in an extended framework it is not unusual to speak of 'discourse grammar' and the like.

We may now progress to the right-hand half of our model, mediated with the left half via another set of ORDERING RULES which are in principle different for each language, though many of them may overlap from language to language. We shall not be at pains to formulate these rules rigidly; suffice it that they are implicit in the descriptions that will be forthcoming as we compare and contrast the structures of our individual languages.

We are in a position to dwell at length, as we shall, on the inner-right, grammatical sector without first needing to consider the outer-right, phonological domain at all, and this for a practical and simple reason: since we will be examining and discussing linguistic forms on paper, we can, as it were, short-circuit directly to the shape they normally take when written down, namely, those graphic representations with which our visual perceptions are familiar and comfortable. In principle, of course, every stretch of language— every word and every construction—assumes a predictable phonemic form in order to issue forth as intelligible sound; and in our Romance languages (as opposed to, say, Chinese) it is the fleeting phonemic forms of speech that are themselves converted systematically to orthographic shapes in order to fix them on paper (or stone, or whatever). Analysts of any language, however, find orthographic representation ('spelling') less than adequate for capturing speech forms and hence devise phonetic and/or phonemic transcriptions to represent with fuller accuracy the linearly spoken output. Technically, therefore, we should be looking at our examples in phonemic notation, but in order to do so with proper awareness of their exact value in each language, we would have to know the phonemic systems on which the notations are based. To describe them, however, while also comparing and contrasting them, is a separate undertaking which we shall do well to postpone to later chapters (see Part Two: Phonology, Chapters 17-21). But, thanks to the short-cut of orthography, we may first proceed with our contrastive grammar and come later to 'phonemes in phonological space' and contrastive phonology.

0.3 Lexicon and grammar. Of preliminary relevance here are some considerations arising in connection with the lowest level (Level 1) in the hierarchy.

• Every dialect—that is to say, every standard, regional, or social variety of every language—has as one of its components a thesaurus of vocabulary items technically known as its LEXICON. The actual number of entries in any one lexicon is evidently finite at a given point in time but is theoretically open-ended all the time, since the speakers (the sum total of whose individual lexica go to make up that of the dialect) are both adopting new-fangled words and discarding old ones throughout their lives. The sum total of all the lexica of all the dialects constitute the lexicon of the language.

In theory, a basic lexicon will enumerate each and every morpheme of the language, whatever its function in the grammatical hierarchy. In practice a standard-type lexicon, i.e. a dictionary, is a surface lexicon which lists only those items which users of the language call 'words' and which we as linguists must qualify as LEXICAL WORDS.. These comprise what are often called also FREE STEMS. A free stem consists of a root morpheme ± one or more derivational affix morphemes, and is linguistically meaningful when spoken as an isolated utterance. In the French lexical word *internationaliser*, for instance, *-nation-* is root, *inter-* is prefix, *-al-* and *-iser* are derivational suffixes; *nation* is itself also a free stem, as are *international, national,* and *nationaliser*; but the affixes themselves are not.

• Lexical words are then to be distinguished at the surface from GRAM-MATICAL WORDS,[5] which are free stems ± INFLECTIONAL AFFIXES, i.e. grammatical affixes which signal number, tense, or the like. In addition to *internationaliser*, listed in the dictionary of French, there are the 'words' *internationalise, internationalisons, internationalisait, internationaliseront,* and so on through the forty-odd forms that make up the PARADIGM of the verb in view. Only the stem, or lexical word, appears in the lexicon.[6] But to every lexical word there corresponds either a single grammatical word (consisting of the free stem only, and not privileged to bear an affix, like (say) Spanish *aquí* or Italian *dopo*), or a paradigm of grammatical words depending for size on what class of words the item in question represents.

• While a lexicon is open-ended and theoretically infinite in size,[7] its storehouse of words is divided into a finite number of classes known as PARTS OF SPEECH, and for our five Romance languages we shall say that they all share the same four major classes: NOUNS, ADJECTIVES, ADVERBS, and VERBS. All four major parts of speech are defined by their privileges of occurrence in syntactic constructions; in addition, some of the nouns, most of the adjectives, and all of the verbs[8] are independently definable by their own distinctive paradigms. As to the lesser traditional parts: PREPOSITIONS we shall treat as a subclass of adverbs, namely, those which are TRANSITIVE, i.e. take OBJECTS; SUBORDINATING CONJUNCTIONS we shall collapse with adverbs also, for reasons to be made clear in due course, while COORDINATING CONJUNCTIONS remain a minor class, as do the very marginal INTERJECTIONS, e.g. Fr *zut*, Sp *olé*.

• We must now establish firmly the surface boundary between LEXICON and GRAMMAR. The latter term, although used somewhat imprecisely by nonlinguists, will subsume for us the MORPHOLOGY and the SYNTAX, as opposed to the lexicon, of a language.[9] Our first basic level, that of the morpheme, is technically the minimum unit of both the lexicon and the grammar, although in practice we tend to confine it to grammar and to take the lexical word as the basic unit of the lexicon. The grammatical word, while in one-to-one correspondence with the lexical word, is clearly in the realm of grammar where its paradigms are concerned; this is morphology.[10] All levels above the word are strictly grammatical in that they generate units larger than words—in short SYNTAGMEMES, or just TAGMEMES, for either of which we can comfortably use the more traditional term CONSTRUCTIONS.

The lowest level of construction (Level 3) is, then, the phrase. One indispensable element of the phrase functions as its HEAD; other elements, obligatory or optional as the case may be, function as ATTRIBUTES of the head. The actual form which occupies the central function slot—i.e. which serves as the head—is a unit from the level below, namely, a word; the part-of-speech subclass (or subsubclass, for such exist) to which the head belongs determines the type (or subtype) of phrase. Thus, a phrase with a noun as its head will be a noun phrase, a phrase with a verb as its head will be a verb phrase, and so on in one-to-one correlation.

The actual forms which fill the various attribute functions depend on the subtypes of attribute, which in turn differ by phrase types. We need therefore to analyze and illustrate each of the phrase types separately, beginning with the NOUN PHRASE (NP). However, just as 'noun' subsumes the three part-of-speech subclasses COMMON NOUN, PROPER NOUN, and PRONOUN, so also does NP subsume COMMON-NOUN PHRASE, PROPER-NOUN PHRASE, and PRONOUN PHRASE. Although the cover term is necessary for describing the composition of larger constructions, the internal structure of the NP is statable only in terms of its three subtypes. Consequently, as we move into Chapter 1 of Part One: Grammar, we shall take up these three NP subtypes in turn.

Notes for Introduction

1. D. L. Canfield in *An Introduction to Romance Linguistics*, 1975.

2. From W. G. Moulton, *'The use of models in contrastive linguistics'*. In: *Georgetown University Round Table on Languages and Linguistics 1968*. Edited by James E. Alatis. Washington, D.C.: Georgetown University Press. 27-38.

3. Current language-acquisition theory would have it that the shared basic structure is what makes it possible for speakers of Language A to learn Language B at all, while the differing surface features and arrangements are what makes it nonetheless very difficult for them to do so.

4. For example: Fr *A qui a-t-on dit cela?—A moi.* Fr *J'ai perdu le mien.* Sp *¿A quién le dijeron eso?—A mí.* Sp *He perdido el mío.*

5. Also frequently called MORPHOLOGICAL WORDS. Linguists identify also PHONOLOGICAL WORDS, though in a quite different frame of reference.

6. Actually, of course, the -r that adorns French (or Spanish) verbal stems in the lexicon is itself an affix, but this is a mere dictionary convention and beside the point.

7. Except for the inflectional affixes, which are indeed finite in number.

8. A trivial exception is Fr *voici* or *voilà*, It *ecco*, Ro *iată* or *uite*.

9. Many linguists now prefer to use the term MORPHOSYNTAX in this embracing sense.

10. More precisely, inflectional morphology. The grammar of roots and derivational affixes within the lexical word is also a branch of morphology for many descriptivists.

Part One: Grammar
Nominal structures
Chapter 1
The common-noun phrase

1.0 Internal structure of the common-noun phrase (CNP). This chapter discusses the internal structure of the common-noun phrase (CNP). Basically, this construction is the same in all our languages. It consists of a common noun as obligatory HEAD and of attributes divided into PLURAL-IZER, DETERMINER, and MODIFIER. The underlying linear order is shown in the formula:

CNP → (± pluralizer) (determiner) head (modifier)

The parentheses mean that the attribute is optional as against the unparenthesized constituents which are either obligatory (like the head) or, where preceded by the plus-minus symbol (±) constrained, i.e. occurrent in the environment of some heads, nonoccurrent in that of other heads. To take a very simple example: in the Spanish CNP *las lenguas modernas*, the head is the noun *lengua*, the determiner is *la*, the modifier is *moderna*, and the plural number is the *-s* suffixed to all three of the other constituents.

1.1 Common nouns as heads. The surface formula for the common noun as a grammatical word in all five languages is: CNoun → stem (± plural suffix). This is to say that a given noun may occur in singular or plural form. The singular form has no inflectional ending and the noun thus appears in its bare stem form.[1] The plural form acquires its inflection from the (optional) phrasal attribute of plural number, in the form of a suffix which 'hops' not only to the head noun but also to such attributes as are constrained by their form-class (e.g. adjectives) to add the suffix also and thus to AGREE with the

9

head noun. Again, the '±' means that the plural suffix can cooccur with some heads but not with others. In point of fact, all the languages have two types of common noun in their lexica: COUNTABLES and NONCOUNTABLES. The countables refer to discrete units of which there can be more than one (like Fr *un oeuf, des oeufs*), while the noncountables refer to substances in the mass (like Fr *du riz*). Many nouns belong to both types, e.g. Fr *du vin* vs. *un vin (domestique)* or *des vins (importés)*, or *du café* vs. *un café, deux cafés* . . ., where the countable means 'type of X' or '(served) portion of X'. The parenthesis in the formula means that the plural suffix is present in accordance with the optional presence of plural number in the phrase.

The MORPHOPHONEMICS of noun inflection must, of course, be stated in terms of the phonological structure of each individual language, and no relevant contrastive data emerge at this level.

[*Comment. Appendix A provides a brief description of common-noun inflection in Portuguese, on which those of the other languages can be modeled as regards method and presentation.*]

1.2 Gender of nouns. Every noun (common or proper) in every Romance language belongs to a GENDER class and there are just two of these: the so-called MASCULINE and FEMININE. Gender is a syntactic property of the noun, not a morphological one; there is no inflection in the paradigm of the noun that signals grammatical gender as such. There are, to be sure, certain derivational suffixes, such as Sp or Po *-esa, -ina*, and the like (cf. *duque* : *duquesa*) which refer semantically to an individual (person or animal) of the female sex; this includes the final single vowel (Fr *-e*, It/Sp/Po *-a*, Ro *-ă*) in pairs like Fr *chat* : *chatte* or Sp *amigo* : *amiga*. All the derived nouns built with these suffixes are in fact feminine, as are all simple-stem nouns denoting females, e.g. Fr *mère* or *vache*, Sp *madre* or *vaca*. Similarly, all simple stems designating males are masculine; there are no derivational suffixes for specific reference to a male individual. There are indeed many stems which designate either males or females with no variation in form, such as Fr *enfant* or *artiste*, Sp *reo* or *idiota*, It *cliente* or *indigena*. These simply belong to both genders at once, in correlation with the sex of the specific referent; or, in another view, they constitute wholly separate entries in the lexicon.

[*Query. Either position can be defended; which do you prefer, and why?*]

Nouns which denote inanimate objects, or abstractions, or living beings whose sex is (for whatever reason) not included among the noun's semantic features, belong arbitrarily to one gender or the other, e.g. Fr *fourmi* is feminine, while *ver* is masculine. Across our languages most cognate noun stems belong to the same gender; thus, for example, Fr *main*, It/Sp *mano*, Po *mão*, Ro *mînă* are all feminine. On the other hand, Fr *dent* is feminine while its cognates in the other languages are masculine. And even between similar languages we find such divergences as Sp *leche, miel, puente, sal, sangre*, all feminine, as against Po *leite, mel, ponte, sal, sangue*, all masculine. Each noun in each language is tagged for its gender within the lexicon, and no systematic comparisons are feasible.

What is more, only the grossest correlation exists in Romance between the gender of nouns and their phonemic shape. French exhibits the least, Portuguese not much more, Spanish and Italian somewhat more, Roumanian the most. It is true that most noun stems with final *-a* in Span/Port/Ital, final *-ă* in Roumanian, are feminine, and that most stems with final *-o* in Span/Port/Ital, final *-u* or no final vowel in Roumanian, are masculine; but there are exceptions both ways, e.g. Sp/Po/It *sistema* (m.) on the one hand, Sp/It *mano* (f.) or Po *tribo* (f.) on the other. It is possible to work out minor correlations between gender and stems with certain derivational suffixes; for example, Fr *-ité*, Sp *-idad*, Po *-idade*, It *-ità*, Ro *-itate* (as in Fr *densité* and so on) are all feminine. Two of the languages, namely Italian and Roumanian, have certain noun stems which are indeterminate as to gender in the lexicon, and only in the phrase grammar assume gender in correlation with number: masculine if singular, feminine if plural. In Italian there are a mere handful of such nouns (all being simple stems), for which the alternant of the plural suffix is always *-a*, as in *braccio* 'bras', pl. *braccia*, or *uovo* 'oeuf', pl. *uova*. In Roumanian there are a great many such noun stems, for which the plural suffix has either of the alternants *-e* or *-uri*, as in *braţ* 'bras', pl. *braţe*, or *corp* 'corps', pl. *corpuri*. This gender-switching group is characterized in traditional Roumanian grammar as 'neuter' nouns, but this assignment to a third gender does not bear scrutiny on formal, synchronic grounds; the singular members of the group have the same properties as other (nonswitching) masculines, and their opposite-number counterparts have the same syntactic properties as other plural feminines. A more appropriate label for the subset in view would be some adaptation of what French analysts call them: *les noms ambigènes* or *hétérogènes*.

Let us now turn to the remaining attributes in the CNP: the optional determiner and the optional modifier.

1.3 Determiners in the CNP. For our five Romance languages, the determinative function in the CNP is filled (1) by certain simple stems which as parts of speech are predominantly a subclass of adjectives (as evidenced by their inflectional paradigms), and here and there also a subclass of adverbs (uninflected stems identifiable by their primary function at the clause level; or (2) by certain two-adjective strings, or (3) by certain embedded CNPs; or (4) by certain determinative constructions of evaluation, result, or comparison.

1.3.1 Adjectival/adverbial words: articles, demonstratives, limiters, and quantifiers. In each language the adjectival/adverbial words which function as determiners constitute essentially a closed lexico-semantic set, although the exact number varies somewhat from language to language. Common to all are the same four functional subsets: ARTICLES, DEMONSTRATIVES, LIMITERS, AND QUANTIFIERS.[2] If we search out a common core of determinative words shared in the main by the five languages, we arrive at the array in Table 1.1. Those entries in Table 1.1 which are adverbial stems appear in italics, while those which are adjectival stems (the majority) are in plain type. The entire class of adjectives (not just the determiners) as grammatical words is characterized by the inflectional property of AGREEMENT (also known as CONCORD): that is to say, they add the plural suffix whenever the plural constituent of the CNP is present, in just the same way as does the noun with which they stand in construction. In addition, a large subclass of them also signals concord with the gender of the head noun, by inserting, ahead of the plural suffix, a gender-concord suffix whenever the head noun is feminine. Agreement with a masculine is by mere absence of inflecton, i.e. the bare stem, to which corresponds the form entered in Table 1.1. The formal aspects of adjective inflection are discussed briefly in 5.1, and only in that connection are sample descriptions of the morphophonemics (despite a higher degree of complexity in determinative than in other adjectives) of two individual languages given in the Appendices.

Many of the entries in Table 1.1 are keyed to a series of descriptive remarks immediately following the table;[3] the text proper resumes after these descriptive remarks.

Table 1.1 Common core of determinative words.

	French	Spanish	Portuguese	Italian	Roumanian
Articles					
Definite	le	el	o	lo	-l[1]
Indefinite[2]	un	uno	um	uno	un
Partitive[2]	du	. . .	. . .	dello	niste
Demonstratives					
Speaker-oriented	ce . . . (-ci)	este	este	questo	acest
Addressee-oriented	. . .[3]	ese	esse	cotesto[4]	. . .[5]
Other-oriented	ce . . . (-là)	aquel	aquele	quello	acel
Limiters[6]					
Definite	chaque	cada	cada	ogni	fiecare
	quel	cuál[7]	qual	quale	care
Indefinite	quelque	alguno	algum	alcuno	cîtva
	aucun	ninguno	nenhum	nessuno	nici un
	. . .[8]	qué	que	che	ce
	. . .[9]	cualquier	qualquer	qualunque	oricare
	tout	todo[10]	todo	. . .	. . .
Quantifiers					
Cardinal[11]	un	uno	um	uno	un
	deux	dos	dois	due	doi
	. . . *etc.*	. . . *etc.*	. . . *etc.*	. . . *etc.*	. . . *etc.*

Indefinite[12]	*beaucoup*	mucho	muito	molto	mult
	peu	poco	pouco	poco	puţin
	trop	demasiado	demasiado	troppo	*prea* mult[13]
	assez	bastante	bastante	*abbastanza*	destul
	combien	cuánto	quanto	quanto	cît
Comparative	*tant*	tanto	tanto	tanto	atît
	plus	*más*	*mais*	*più*	*mai* mult[13]
	moins	*menos*	*menos*	*meno*	*mai* puţin[13]

Remarks on Table 1.1

1. The Roumanian definite article in surface structure is suffixed to the first constituent in the CNP, most frequently the head noun as in *restaurantul român* 'le restaurant roumain' but occasionally another element in the determiner as in *primul restaurant* 'le premier restaurant'.[4] Its basic position in the phrase may be seen as that of any determiner, with the surface constraint that it is uniquely an ENCLITIC form and as such obeys a TRANSFORMATIONAL RULE which attaches it to the first element on its right. We shall encounter other CLITICS (EN- or PRO-) with similar behavior in all our languages in due course.

2. The indefinite article in this lexical form determines singular heads across the board. The possible occurrence of an indefinite article also with noncountable and plural heads must be looked at in conjunction with the partitive article. This entry—the French and Italian versions of which appear to be compounded of *de/di* plus definite article, but should not be so thought of descriptively—seems at first glance to be missing from the Sp/Po inventory. However, let us scan the following display.

	Noun-countable singular heads:		Pluralized heads:	
Fr	achète du miel	. . .	achète des oeufs	. . .
Sp	. . .	compra miel	compra unos huevos	≠ compra huevos
Po	. . .	compra mel	compra uns ovos	≠ compra ovos
It	compra del miele	≠ compra miele	compra delle uova	≠ compra uova
Ro	cumpără nişte miere	≠ cumpără miere	cumpără nişte ouă	≠ cumpără ouă

The available contrasts on the left side in Italian/Roumanian, and on the right side in all but French, are subtle but real; they are essentially tantamount to those existing between English *buy some honey, buy some eggs* vs. *buy honey, buy eggs*. We cannot therefore suggest that the determiner is 'omitted' or 'deleted' in the short versions because of some contextual factor, and we are led to posit a zero alternant of the indefinite article, in contrast to the partitive article, for all the languages except French. This zero alternant, occurring with noncountable singulars and countable plurals, is clearly in COMPLEMENTARY DISTRIBUTION with the overt form occurring with countable singulars. It then remains to point out that French neutralizes the indefinite ≠ partitive contrast completely, while Spanish/Portuguese neutralize it with noncountables. The zero alternant must above all not be confused with true absence of determiner, as with (usually) lone nouns occurring in expressions like Fr *avoir peur*, Sp *tener miedo*, or Fr *sans doute*, It *senza dubbio*, in which the nondetermined heads can even be singular countables.[5]

3. French lacks a specifically addressee-oriented demonstrative, and also freely neutralizes the two it does have by omitting the enclitic functor and saying simply *ce livre* rather than *ce livre-ci* or *ce livre-là*.

4. The addressee-oriented demonstrative of Italian, with its variant *codesto*, is fast becoming outmoded in current usage; *quello* is taking over.

5. Roumanian, like French, lacks an addressee-oriented demonstrative. It does have, on the other hand, informal variants of both its demonstratives: a speaker-oriented *ăst* and an other-oriented *ăl*.

6. Among the limiters and quantifiers, individual languages have one or more extra oddments unmatched across the board—e.g. It *qualche* 'quelque', which precedes countables when the underlying number is plural; this particular limiter itself conveys plural meaning to the phrase while blocking out the surface plural suffix, as in *qualche parola* (a shade different from *alcune parole*) 'quelques mots'. Other miscellaneous items: Fr *pas*, which is not restricted like *aucun* to singular countables—e.g. *pas de foi, pas d'illusions, pas de différence* (the latter a shade different from *aucune différence*); Fr *plusieurs*, occurring with pluralized heads only, and *autant* in special complementation with *tant*; It *ciascuno*, a mere stylistic synonym of *ogni*; It *parecchio* and *assai* (an adverb), both close semantically to *molto*; Sp *varios* and Po *vários*, with the meaning and constraint of Fr *plusieurs*; the Po adverb *demais*, in competition with *demasiado* and always extrapositioned to the end of the phrase, as in *tempo demais = demasiado tempo*.

7. Spanish can, and typically does, use the interrogative indefinite *qué* instead of *cuál* without sacrificing the definite feature immediately before a noun head; e.g. *qué niño* can also mean 'cuál de los niños'.

8. French, lacking this interrogative limiter, simply uses the available *quel* in a neutralization of the definite/indefinite feature.

9. French resorts to the phrasal *n'importe quel* for this limiter, or (in limited contexts) to *tout*. The semantically equivalent *quelconque* is strictly a post-head modifying adjective—e.g. *une solution quelconque*, syntactically parallel to *une solution excellente* or whatever.

10. Spanish and Portuguese alone use *todo* in contrast to *cualquier/qualquer*, and here too it is restricted similarly to Fr *tout*. Above all, one must note that this *tout/todo* is not to be confused with the all-inclusive specifier introduced in 1.3.2 (see Table 1.2), which is fully viable in all the languages.

11. Only the first two cardinal items are given here as tokens of this long sublist comprising a backlog of simple stems plus numerous items derived by suffixation (e.g. Fr *-ante*, Sp/Po *-enta*, It *-anta*) or compounding (e.g. It *ventuno, ventidue . . .* '21, 22 . . .', *duecento, trecento . . .* '200, 300 . . .', Ro *douăzeci, treizeci . . .* '20, 30 . . .'. The line of demarcation between derived items and phrasal items is quite tenuous, often not borne out by spelling, and determinable for each language separately on the basis of internal structural parameters. [*Comment. To do just this for one or more of the languages would make a worthwhile study project.*]

All these languages, of course, resort to special phrases in order to express the higher numbers. Typically, such phrases are constructions of two or more cardinal words conjoined by the word for 'and', as in Fr *trente-et-un*, Sp *treinta y uno*, Po *trinta e um*, Ro *treizeci și un*; or simply juxtaposed in an arithmetically determined order as in Fr *trente-deux* or *cent cinquante* (Sp *ciento cincuenta*, It *cento cinquanta*), or Fr *dix-neuf cent quatre-vingt quatre*, It *mille novecento ottantaquattro* '1,984', and so on. In either case these constructions cannot be said to consist of head plus attribute—which would be which?—and hence it may be preferable to say that they are generated in the lexicon rather than in the phrase grammar. [*Query. Can you think of other reasons as well, to support this preference?*]

A cardinal quantifier may be rendered less than totally precise in meaning by one or another of a lexically defined set of adverbials, preposed as in the following examples:

Fr   presque (seulement, environ, plus de, moins de . . .) deux cents pages
Sp   casi (sólo, cerca de, más de, menos de . . .) doscientas páginas
Po   quase (só, perto de, mais de, menos de . . .) duzentas páginas
It   quasi (sole, circa, più di, meno di . . .) duecento pagine
Ro   aproape (numai, vreo, peste, mai jos de) două sute de pagini

The same applies to the precise quantifying CNPs described in 1.3.3., e.g. Fr *presque un litre de vin*, Sp *casi un litro de vino*, etc.

12. All of the French indefinite quantifiers are adverbs, and all are characterized by use of the functor *de* to link determiner with head, as in *beaucoup de monde*, *peu de patience*, and so on.

As regards the cardinals, they are best classed as adjectives in all the languages because (1) the initial number shows gender concord across the board, e.g. Fr *une femme*, Sp *una mujer*, Po *uma mulher*, It *una donna*, Ro *o femeie*; (2) the second number also shows gender concord in Portuguese and Roumanian, e.g. Po *dois filhos*, *duas filhas*, Ro *doi fii*, *două fiice* 'deux fils, deux filles'; (3) the words for the hundreds agree in both gender and number (the latter redundantly, of course) in Spanish, e.g. *doscientas páginas*, and Portuguese, e.g. *duzentas páginas*; (4) French does not require *de* as with its other quantifiers; and (5) the entire subclass has no adverbial function elsewhere in the grammar.

13. The Roumanian quantifying word *prea* is an adverb like Fr *trop*, and Ro *mai* is an adverb like Fr *plus* and its cognates across the board. In Roumanian, adverbs cannot be directly attributive to noun heads, but only to adjective heads as in, for example, *prea lung* 'trop long' or *mai mic* 'plus petit', or the like. Hence the special determiner phrase built with Ro *mult* as second element, in which *prea mult timp* (cf. the ill-formed Fr **trop beaucoup de temps*, Sp **demasiado mucho tiempo*, and so on) is analogous to *prea puţin timp*, which does in fact have equivalent phrasal determiners in all the other languages (cf. Fr *trop peu de temps*, Sp *demasiado poco tiempo*, etc.). Except for the Roumanian case just noted, it seems that only *peu/poco/ pouco/puţin*, and not its antonym, can be preceded by one of the EVALUATIVE indefinites, as in It *troppo poco (tempo)* or whatever. We may now scan the following display which also brings in the derived determiner with suffix meaning 'très, extrêmement' in the three languages that possess it:

Fr	très peu	...	*très beaucoup	...
Sp	muy poco	↔ poquísimo	*muy mucho	↔ muchísimo
Po	muito pouco ↔	pouquíssimo	*muito muito	↔ muitíssimo
It	molto poco ↔	pochissimo	*molto molto	↔ moltissimo
Ro	foarte puţin	...	foarte mult	...

For other occurrences of *très/mucho/muito/molto/foarte*, see 5.2.1 under adjective phrases.

As for Fr *un peu*, Sp *un poco*, Po *um pouco*, It *un po'* (Ro *un puţin does not exist), it is a special CNP determiner of measurement, of the general type discussed in 1.3.3; used only with noncountables, it has a unique phrasal counterpart for use with plural countables in Spanish and Portuguese—e.g. Sp *unos pocos* (or *unos cuantos*) *minutos*, Po *uns poucos minutos*, as against Sp *un poco de tiempo*, etc. It seems clear enough that phrases such as Fr *très peu* (*de tempo*) have the second element as head while the first is a quantizing attribute of the determiner proper.

[*Query. Do the surface possibilities and constraints evident here suggest a neater underlying solution for this particular type of phrasal determiner? If you think so, then proceed to formulate it.*]

1.3.2 Two-adjective strings functioning as determiner. The first adjective is typically an article or demonstrative, and the second we shall designate as the SPECIFIER. This item simply serves to narrow yet further the delimitation already denoted by the initial item in its normal function. A common core of specifiers is displayed in Table 1.2, again with keyed-in remarks.

To the list given therein are to be added all the ordinal numbers, some of which are simple stems related only semantically to the cardinals (e.g. Sp *quinto*, only very awkwardly derivable from *cinco*) but most of which are, of course, lexically derived from the cardinals (e.g. Fr *huitième*, Sp *octavo*, Po *oitavo*, It *ottavo*, Ro *optulea*), plus all the possible ordinal phrases expressing '21st', '150th', '2086th', or whatever.

Table 1.2 Common core of specifiers in the determiner.

French	Spanish	Portuguese	Italian	Roumanian
seul	solo	só	solo	singur
. . .[1]	único	único	unico	unic
même	mismo	mesmo	stesso	acelaşi[2]
autre[3]	otro	outro	altro	alt[4]
tel	tal	tal	tale	cutare
certain	cierto	certo	certo	anumit
premier	primero	primeiro	primo	prim
dernier	último	último	ultimo	ultim
tout	todo	todo	tutto	tot
. . .[5]	ambos	ambos	ambedue	amîndoi

Remarks on Table 1.2

1. The French cognate adjective *unique* does not occur in the role of specifier. The first two entries across the board are essentially synonymous, but differ distributionally in minor ways: cf., for example, Sp *un solo remedio* vs. *el único remedio*.

2. The Roumanian item *acelaşi*, meaning simply 'le même' (not 'ce même') is derived from the demonstrative *acel* and therefore is, in its own right, a determiner word. Two suffixes are involved here: *-a*, elsewhere a function marker (see, for example, 1.5.1) but here hardly more than a mechanical adapter, and *-şi*, one of the reflexive clitics (see 11.3, and cf. the concept of 'self-same').

3. Corresponding to Fr *un autre livre, un tel livre, un certain livre*, Spanish alone shows just *otro libro, tal libro, cierto libro* with no visible article as head, while Portuguese hesitates between *um outro livro* and *outro livro*, etc. This seems a mere surface constraint related to the problem of the zero-shape indefinite article, which all the languages but French appear to use; see Table 1.1, Remark 2. This specifier alone is privileged to cooccur with limiting and quantifying determiners, and even with other specifiers as in Fr *aucune autre raison*, Sp *muchos otros lugares*, Po *cinco outros estudantes*, It *certi altri autori*, Ro *oricare alt motiv*; also Fr *tous les autres peuples*, Sp *todos los otros pueblos*,[6] Po *todos os outros povos*, It *tutti gli altri popoli*, Ro *toate celelalte popoare*.

4. In a Roumanian phrase consisting of definite article plus *alt*, each element has a surface alternant: the article takes the form *cel* (which occurs in other constructions as well; watch for it) and the specifier appears with a prosthetic *l* as *-lalt*, e.g. *cealaltă naţiune* 'l'autre nation' as against, say, *o altă naţiune* or *aceste alte naţiuni*. Though written as one word, with even a linking vowel in the uninflected form *celălalt*, it is difficult to justify characterizing this unique structure as a single lexical or grammatical word.

5. Across the board the two ALL-INCLUSIVE specifiers obligatorily precede, instead of follow, the article or demonstrative.

The first all-inclusive occurs in a singular NP—with the meaning of 'entier/entero' if the head is a countable common noun or a place name, as in Fr *toute la vie*, Sp *toda la semana*, Po *todo o verão*, It *tutto il giorno*, Ro *toată lumea* 'tout le monde'—or in a plural NP as in Fr *tous ces hommes*, Sp *todas esas cosas*, Po *todos os dias*, It *tutti quei paesi*, Ro *toţi acei copii* 'tous ces enfants-là'.

The second all-inclusive by its semantic nature occurs only in a plural CNP, e.g. Sp *ambas manos*, Po *ambas mãos*, It *ambedue le mani*, Ro *amîndouă mîinile*. The Span/Port/Ital forms in *amb-*, being obsolescent, are giving way to Sp *los dos*, Po *os dois*, It *tutti e due*, all comparable to the one available French phrase *tous (les) deux*.[7]

1.3.3 CNPs functioning as quantifying determiner. Various nouns denoting units of quantity or measure occur as head within an EMBEDDED CNP which serves to quantify the head of a HIGHER CNP, as for example in Fr *un litre de vin*, Sp *un litro de vino*, Po *um litro de vinho*, It *un litro di vino*, Ro *un litru de vin*. Nouns which operate in this way range referentially from those denoting a million (billion, trillion . . .)[8] through the various units of measure (Fr *litre, gramme* . . .) and the semiprecise derivatives of cardinal numbers (Fr *douzaine, vingtaine, centaine* . . .), through containers, portions, or servings (Fr *un verre de lait*), down to relatively imprecise expressions of number, amount, or mass (Sp *un montón de cosas, la mayoría de los hombres*).[9] In essentially all cases in all the languages, the quantifying CNP is linked to the higher head, in the surface structure, by the semantically empty functor (a preposition, traditionally) *de/di*.

1.3.4 Determinative expressions of evaluation, result, comparison.

• In the first of these, the head is one of the two evaluative quantifiers (*assez* and *trop* in French) and the attribute is an adverb phrase opened by the preposition used in all the languages to express goal or purpose. For example:

Fr	assez de pain pour le repas	trop de vin pour une jeune fille
Sp	bastante tiempo para la reunión	demasiado frío para octubre
Po	bastante calor para banhar-se	demasiadas festas para um mês
It	abbastanza soldi per te	troppa distanza per una
	'assez d'argent pour toi'	bicicletta
Ro	destul loc pentru maşină	prea multe lecţii pentru studenţi
	'assez de place pour la voiture'	'trop de leçons pour les étudiants'

It is to be noted that in this type of construction the phrasal determiner is discontinuous, i.e. split by the presence of the head of the CNP, whereas the interrupted stretch *assez . . . pour le repas* constitutes the determining attribute.

• In the second type, also discontinuous, the head is the indefinite Fr *tant* and its cognates, which acts as either a RESULTATIVE or a COMPARATIVE quantifier, and the attribute is an embedded clause denoting a consequence— obligatory material at the basic level, for Sp *tanto tiempo* or whatever is semantically incomplete without some such expansion as in (*tú gastas*) *tanto tiempo que nunca saldrás bien.* The context of discourse often permits deletion of the attribute, but that is a different matter.

• In the third type, also discontinuous, the head is one of the COMPARATIVE indefinites, including the above-mentioned *tant* etc. in a different semantic role and the attribute comprises material introduced by one of the various function words meaning 'than' or 'as', material obligatory at the basic level because Sp *más tiempo* (or *menos tiempo* or *tanto tiempo*) or whatever is meaningless without some expansion as in (*tú tienes*) *más tiempo que yo* or (*no hay*) *tanto tiempo como tú crees.*[10] (The context of discourse often permits deletion of the attribute.)

Inasmuch as either resultative or comparative determiners entail the embedding of (dependent) clauses, we relegate any further consideration of these structures to 12.7 and 14.

1.4 Modifiers in the CNP. These constituents are best seen as expansions of the basic phrase structure, their function being performed by one or another DEPENDENT construction, i.e. one which is shifted out of its primary, independent syntactic position in a higher construction and placed instead in a subordinate role as part of a construction of equal or lower rank in the syntactic hierarchy.[11] Dependent constructions thus embeddable within the CNP in our languages are:

(a) nouns or noun phrases (common or proper), and pronouns or pronoun phrases, all subsumable as NOMINALS

(b) adjectives or adjective phrases, subsumed as ADJECTIVALS

(c) adverb phrases of the type traditionally called PREPOSITIONAL

(d) clauses

Since we have not yet described the internal constituency of all the constructions just listed, and furthermore since their embedding in CNPs often entails in itself surface variations from their basic structure, we are not now in a suitable position to examine them in detail; this will be done in appropriate later sections devoted to dependent constructions. For the moment, transient examples of these various modifiers will have to suffice:

(a) Fr la maison de mon père
 Sp la casa de mi padre
 Po a casa de meu pai
 It la casa di mio padre
 Ro casa tatălui meu

(b) Fr une leçon très facile
     Sp una lección muy fácil
     Po uma lição muito fácil
     It   una lezione molto facile
     Ro o lecţie foarte uşoară

(c) Fr un musée d'art moderne
     Sp un museo de arte moderna
     Po um museu de arte moderna
     It   un museo di arte moderna
     Ro un muzeu de artă modernă[12]

(d) Fr une personne qui t'aime
     Sp una persona que te quiere
     Po uma pessoa que te quer
     It   una persona che ti vuol bene
     Ro o persoană care te iubeşte

1.5 The CNP and discourse factors: Substitution and reduction. Before going on to examine the structure of other types of NP, we must pause to consider two phenomena entailing the effect of surrounding context upon any and all nominal structures, namely, substitution and reduction.

It is a universal fact of language use that in sustained discourse—whether spontaneous or as a written text—constructions of all size-levels constantly recur by virtue of coordinations (X and Y; X or Y), subordinations (X because Y; X when Y; if X, then Y); or successive speech acts in either monologue (X. Then Y. So Z.) or dialogue ('X?'—'No, Y.'). When a topic of discourse has been established and we know that the talk (or writing) concerns a certain person, a certain fact, or whatever, we do not thereafter reinsert the lexical item first introduced (e.g. the common noun *livre* or the proper noun *Pierre*). Instead, we have recourse to certain avoidance strategies. One such we label SUBSTITUTION, i.e. the replacement of an original item, or indeed of the entire construction in which the item figures, with a SUBSTITUTE word. This serves the double purpose of avoiding tiresome repetition and confirming that the referent of the item is unchanged (it's still the same *livre* or the same fellow named *Pierre*). Most (though not all) substitute words in most languages belong to the subclass of nouns labeled pronouns (e.g. *lui* for *Pierre*), though (as Table 3.1 shows) not all pronouns are substitutes, and the process of replacement is called by some grammarians PRONOMINALIZATION. The substitutes are, of course, stored in the lexicon as all words are, but their selection is constrained by the above principle of lexical replacement. They will also vary in form/function in accordance with the form, function, or even property of the word or construction they replace.

A further avoidance strategy, more drastic than substitution, we shall call REDUCTION. This consists in playing down an original item (or even a substitute for an original item) wherever its recurrence in the discourse, though essential, yet furnishes no information not already implicit in the surrounding contextual clues, i.e. the rest of the phrase (or whatever) that contains it. In this case the item in question either is DELETED ('omitted as understood') or gives way to a special clitic form that contains some requisite formal trace signal but is minimal in size and inaccessible to distinctive stress or pitch.

To recapitulate the two avoidance measures with the simplest possible examples: starting with the Italian sentence *Giovanni ama Maria*, substitutions will yield *Giovanni ama lei*, or *lui ama Maria*, or even *lui ama lei*; while reductions will produce *ama Maria*, or *Giovanni la ama*, or simply *la ama*.

One of the most prevalent forms of reduction within a CNP is deletion of the head whenever that noun were to convey only old information already established by the context (and thus recoverable if 'thrown away') while retaining plural number and the determiner and such modifiers as contribute new and essential information. Let us examine some instances of head deletion in our languages, noting various constraints on the form taken by determiners in the environment of one or another modifier.

1.5.1 Where the determiner is an article. (i) If there is no modifier, no head deletion is possible since articles are syntactically bound forms incapable of bearing phrasal stress.[13]

(ii) If the modifier is an adjectival, reduction is as follows:

• After the definite article:

Fr le chien noir → le noir
Sp el perro negro → el negro
Po o cão negro → o negro
It il cane nero → quello nero
Ro cîinele negru → cel negru

We observe that the definite article remains intact, agreeing with the deleted head, in all but Roumanian. In this language the enclitic article -*l* (f.sg. -*a*, pl. -*i*, f.pl. -*le*) must, as we recall, be suffixed to the first constituent to its right, normally the head noun. Even when the head is deleted, it must be thought of as underlyingly present (it has triggered gender agreement on the determiner, and it is recoverable referentially) and hence as inhibiting suffixation of the article to anything else to its right. Thus stranded, the article alternates to the phrase-bound form *cel* (*cea, cei, cele*) in the regular determiner position.[14] By this device, incidentally, Roumanian alone readily distinguishes between the structure in view and an unmodified CNP with a lexically nominalized head: *cel negru ≠ negrul*, the latter having either the definite sense of 'le noir' (with plural *negrii* 'les noirs') or the generic sense of 'le noir (the color)' or 'ce qui est noir'.

French and Portuguese have no formal mechanism for distinguishing; Italian avoids the definite article in favor of *quello* without demonstrative force, as in *il cane nero* → *quello* [ ] *nero ≠ il nero*. Spanish alone has a contrast typified by *el negro* ≠ *lo negro*, the latter phrase (meaning only 'lo que es negro') being a true pronoun phrase with head *lo* plus adjectival modifier; see 4.3.

• After the indefinite article:

Fr un cheval blanc → un [ ] blanc = un blanc
Sp un caballo blanco → uno [ ] blanco ≠ un blanco
Po um cavalo branco → um [ ] branco = um branco
It un cavallo bianco → uno [ ] bianco ≠ un bianco
Ro un cal alb → unul [ ] alb ≠ un alb

Here again French and Portuguese fail to differentiate the structures analogous to those of the previous set, while Spanish and Italian share one mechanism, and Roumanian has another, for so doing.[15]

(iii) If the modifier is a dependent nominal or a relative clause (see 12.2):

Fr la maison du voisin → celle du voisin
   les produits qui se vendent → ceux qui se vendent
Sp la casa del vecino → la del vecino
   los productos que se venden → los que se venden
Po a casa do vizinho → a do vizinho
   os produtos que se vendem → os que se vendem
It la casa del vicino → quella del vicino
   i prodotti che si vendono → quelli che si vendono
Ro casa vecinului → a vecinului
   produsele ce se vînd → cele ce se vînd

Looking first at the Sp/Po examples, we note that in them the definite article[16] remains unperturbed upon head deletion, but that in the other languages it is obligatorily transformed, thus:

In Italian the alternant coincides in form with the demonstrative *quello* but has no more demonstrative force than in the reduction pattern illustrated in the preceding section, where we saw it in stylistic variation with the definite article.

In French the alternant likewise overlaps with that of the demonstrative determiner illustrated just below, and has the same irregular surface shapes in conformity with gender/number concord.

In Roumanian, if the nominal modifier is of the genitive subtype marked by the genitive/dative suffix (see 4.3), the alternation of the article is to the so-called 'genitive article' *al* (*a*, *ai*, *ale*); otherwise the definite article becomes the same *cel* we have already seen in the environment of an adjectival modifier.

1.5.2 Where the determiner is a demonstrative. (i) If there is no modifier:
Fr cet animal(-ci) → celui-ci
   cet animal(-là) → celui-là

Sp este animal → éste
    ese animal → ése
    aquel animal → aquél
Po este animal → este
    esse animal → esse
    aquele animal → aquele
It questo animale → questo
    quell' animale → quello
Ro acest animal → acesta
    acel animal → acela

In the environment of a deleted head, we note the following variations. In French, use of the enclitic demonstrative suffixes -*ci* and -*là*, neutralizable to zero after a head, are obligatorily retained; also the determiner proper exhibits irregular surface shapes in conformity with concord: *celui*, f.sg. *celle*, pl. *ceux*, f.pl. *celles*. In Italian, the rule shortening *quello* (and pl. *quelli*, see Appendix 2) cannot apply. In Spanish, the accent mark over the demonstrative is purely and simply a graphic device reflecting the syntactic, not the phonemic, situation. In Roumanian the suffixal marker -*a* is obligatory.

(ii) If there is an adjectival modifier, French cannot delete a noun head at all, as from e.g. *ce poète français*. Thus:

Fr ce poète français → *   ≠ ce français
Sp aquel poeta francés → aquel [   ] francés = aquel francés
Po aquele poeta francês → aquele [   ] francês = aquele francês
It quel poeta francese → quello [   ] francese ≠ quel francese
Ro acel poet francez → acela [   ] francez ≠ acel francez

In Italian and Roumanian, the alternation of the demonstrative serves to differentiate the two structures referred to in (ii) of 1.5.1. In Italian, however, the contrast is neutralized in the feminine forms: *quella francese* (f.pl. *quelle francesi*). In Roumanian the contrast obtains throughout the system by virtue of the enclitic marker -*a*, obligatorily suffixed whenever the demonstrative does not immediately precede a noun head at the surface level.

(iii) If there is a dependent nominal or clausal modifier, the rules are the same as in (i).

1.5.3 Where the determiner is a limiter.

Fr chaque personne → chacune
    quel médecin → lequel
    quelques souvenirs → quelques-uns
    aucun désir → aucun
    n'importe quel âge → n'importe lequel

Sp cada persona → cada una
    qué médico → cuál
    algunos recuerdos → algunos
    ningún deseo → ninguno
    cualquier edad → cualquiera

Po cada pessoa → cada uma
    qual médico → qual
    alguns recordos → alguns
    nenhum desejo → nenhum
    qualquer idade → qualquer (uma)

It ogni persona → ognuna
    quale medico → quale
    qualche ricordo → qualcuno
    nessun desiderio → nessuno
    qualunque età → qualunque

Ro fiecare persoană → fiecare
    care medic → care
    cîteva amintiri → cîteva
    nici un dor → nici unul
    oricare vîrstă → oricare

No head deletion is possible with the indefinite limiters *tout/todo* and *qué/ que/che/ce*. With regard to Fr *quel*, note also *quels médecins* → *lesquels*, where the alternant contains a prefixed element morphophonemically identical with the definite article. We might be tempted to state that in the cases of Fr *chaque* and *quelque(s)*, of Sp/Po *cada*, and of It *ogni* and *qualche*, straight deletion of the head does not occur and that we have here instead a replacement (pronominalization) of the head by a substitute homophonous (just as in the case of English *one, ones*) with the nonsubstitute pronoun *uno* of Spanish and Italian and indeed the cardinal quantifier of all the languages. However, not only would such a form of replacement be sporadic at best, but there is a valid counterargument: in a French clause like *Paul a lu quelques livres* → *Paul en a lu quelques-uns*, where the nominal is a direct object, the head *livres* is reduced to the clitic *en* (see 11.3.2 (2) and therefore cannot at the same time be replaced by *uns*; there is an exact parallel in Italian. Therefore we shall say that Fr *chacun* and *quelqu'un*, Sp *cada uno*, Po *cada um* and *qualquer um* (optional), It *ognuno* and *qualcuno* are in fact alternants of the respective limiters, used in the environment of a deleted noun head. The second element manifests gender concord—something which the first element never does in either alternant.

1.5.4 Where the determiner is a quantifier. Where the determiner is a quantifier there are no alternations, except, of course, that after one of the French adverbial quantifiers the functor *de* is absent when the head is deleted—e.g. *beaucoup d'amis* → *beaucoup*.

If a modifier of any type at all is present, it is not usual to reduce a limited or quantified head by deletion. In the rare instances where this does happen, the rules are simply the same as above. On the other hand, it is extremely common to reduce even CNPs which contain modifiers to just the determiner alone, provided, of course, that the latter is not a definite article (cf. 1.5.1). Thus, for example, Sp *muchos cursos de literatura española* can, as well as the modifierless *muchos cursos*, be reduced to just *muchos*.

1.5.5 Where the determiner is phrasal. (i) The only specifiers to undergo alternation with head deletion are Sp *primero* and *tercero* (technically also *postrero*, an archaizing synonym of *último*), which obey a general rule dropping stem-final -*o* under stated conditions but show the full form in absence of the head, e.g. *el primer día* → *el primero*. Compare the like behavior of the determiners *uno, alguno, ninguno, ciento*.

(ii) If an all-inclusive specifier is present, head deletion is possible even when the head of the determiner is the definite article, which in this case simply drops out—e.g. Fr *toutes les villes* → *toutes*, Sp *todos los países* → *todos*, It *ambedue le città* → *ambedue*; but cf. Sp *los dos países* → *los dos*, It *tutte e due città* → *tutte e due*.

(iii) It should go without saying that in the case of the various CNPs detailed in 1.3.3, head deletion is automatically accompanied by loss of the linking functor *de/di*, e.g. Fr *un million de francs* → *un million*, Sp *un poco de queso* → *un poco*.

Notes for Chapter 1

1. An alternative analysis takes the final vowel of an Italian noun like *casa* or *caso* or *mese* as an inflectional morpheme signaling singular number, parallel to and in contrast with the (also vocalic) plural ending. This would make the stem a BOUND FORM in an arrangement such as this:

Stem: cas- + sg. -a → casa   stem: cas- + sg. -o → caso
Stem: cas- + pl. -e → case   stem: cas- + pl. -i → casi

And in the lexicon homophonous stems like this would have to be indexed as cas-$_1$ and cas-$_2$. The same could be done for Roumanian, which also has vowel-final plurals. But it doesn't work for the other three languages with their pluralizing -*s* (which surfaces mostly as zero in French); and just as Sp stem *casa* + pl. -*s* → *casas*, so also—by a simple and straightforward morphophonemic rule which elides a stem-final vowel before a vowel-initial ending—It stem *casa* + pl. -*e* → *case*.

2. The so-called 'possessive adjectives' also unquestionably occupy a surface place among the determiners; but in the present analysis they represent reductions of genitive nominal structures which function primarily as modifiers and which are moved forward into the determiner slot when reduced. See 4.3.

3. It is questionable whether a valid matrix of binary semantic features

could be devised for differentiating these five-language determiner entries from one another on one and the same basis.

[*Comment. For each language separately it should certainly be feasible, and to do so would make a worthwhile project. A subsequent comparison of the five individual results could not fail to be illuminating.*]

4. In the present author's 1952 article 'Noun Morphology in Rumanian' (*Language* 29:2, reprinted in *Readings in Romance Linguistics*, J. M. Anderson and J. A. Creore, eds., 1972), as well as in his 1958 *Structural Sketch of Romanian* (Supplement to *Language* 34), the definite article is treated as an inflectional suffix on the noun or (secondarily) on the adjective, signaling 'definiteness' in a paradigm characterized by the formula: stem + plural + (definite + oblique case). The position here and now is, however, that the definite article belongs to the determiner function class in this language as in the others, by virtue of the syntactic properties it shares with the other determiners.

5. Thus in a Spanish clause like *ese hombre tiene coche*, the last constituent is in sharp contrast with *un coche* and implies that the fellow can afford to own a car.

6. Perhaps more common than Sp/Po *otro/outro* in this sort of plural context would be *demás/demais*, a specifier with a shade of semantic difference shared only by these two languages.

7. As regards other combinations of a definite article plus a quantifier (e.g. Sp *los cuatro generales* or *el mucho trabajo*), see 4.5.2.

8. In Roumanian alone, this includes also the equivalents of *cent* and *mille*, which are nouns rather than cardinal numbers, e.g. *o sută de persoane* 'cent personnes', *două mii de ani* 'deux mille ans'.

9. In this last range belongs the nominalized determiner *peu/poco/pouco* mentioned in Remark 3 to Table 1.1, as in Fr *un peu de pain*, Sp *un poco de pan*, Po *um pouco de pão*, It *un po' di pane*. (Roumanian alone does not nominalize *puţin*, but allows *puţină pîine* to mean either 'peu de pain' or 'un peu de pain', according to context.)

10. Semantically self-contained phrases like Fr *plus de courage* in the clause *Je n'ai plus de courage*, or It *(Non ho) più pazienza* would seem to embody an NP with comparative determiner; but in fact they represent a quite different construction; see negative clauses, 10.5.

11. For example, the primary function of an NP is that of subject or object within a clause. Contemporary generative grammar claims to derive dependent constructions from higher clausal origins by means of transformations. Thus if the Fr NP *la maison* is expanded to produce *la maison de mon père*, the modifier is viewed as stemming from a deep-structure clause, implied in the discourse, of the type *mon père possède la maison* (where *la maison* is direct object) transformed first to the relative clause *que mon père possède*, thence to *de mon père*. Needless to say, we could not, in a book of this scope, attempt to trace every type of dependent modifier back to its theoretical point of origin, even if it were thought useful to do so.

12. In Example (a), *de mon père* etc. is a NP despite the *de/di* introducing it in all but Roumanian; this surface preposition is underlyingly a function word marking the NP *mon père* as being of the genitive subtype of modifier; see 4.3.

13. Any NP with a semantically definite determiner, such as Sp *la chica* or *esta chica*, can be replaced by a substitute pronoun—*ella* in this instance. But that is not the same device as reduction through head deletion, despite the clear affinity and basis of complementation which exist between the definite article and the substitute pronoun—Sp *el* (*la, los, las*) vs. *él* (*ella, ellos, ellas*). (In Romance the two have the same historical roots, as we shall see in *A Course in Romance Linguistics*, Vol. 2: *A Diachronic View.*)

14. In Roumanian also, such a reduced NP as *cel negru* can itself function as modifier in a higher NP with equivalent head—e.g. *cîinele cel negru*, which presupposes a delimited field of dogs, the one referred to being 'the black one' and not another one.

15. We are restricted here to the overt form used with singular countable heads. For obvious reasons deletion is impossible after the zero alternant (cf. Remark 2 to Table 1.1). After the partitive article, deletion of pluralized countable heads is possible in Spanish and Portuguese only, e.g. Sp *unos caballos blancos* → *unos* [ ] *blancos*.

16. After the indefinite article, the rules are the same as when the modifier is adjectival, e.g. Sp *un reloj de oro* → *uno* [ ] *de oro*.

Chapter 2
The proper-noun phrase

2.0 Internal structure of the proper-noun phrase (PNP). This chapter discusses the internal structure of the proper-noun phrase (PNP). The structure of this noun phrase is the same in all our languages. It consists of a proper noun as obligatory head and of an optional modifier. The order of constituents is shown in the formula:

PNP → head (modifier)

It is immediately obvious that the PNP differs from the CNP in having no attributes of plural number or determiner. Neither is appropriate, because each and every proper noun head is underlying singular (or, in marginal cases of place names, underlyingly plural); further, it is inherently determined as definite and thus has a built-in feature [+ def] that corresponds to the definite article with a common noun. Other potential determiners (demonstratives, limiters, quantifiers) are simply not compatible semantically with proper nouns. One simple example: in the Spanish PNP *Ruy Díaz el Cid*, the head is the (compound) person name *Ruy Díaz* and the modifier is *el Cid*. Before going further it is necessary to distinguish between the two subtypes of proper nouns already hinted at: PERSON NAMES and PLACE NAMES.

2.1. Person names as heads. These nouns as morphological words consist of stem only; they are not inflectable for number like many of the common nouns. Their referent being the individual person (or animal) who has been given the name in question, they are inherently singular. Like common nouns with animate referents, they do have the syntactic property of gender in one-to-one correspondence with the sex of the named individual. Thus, for example, Fr *Jean*, It *Giovanni*, Sp *Juan*, Po *João*, Ro *Ion* name males and are masculine; Fr *Marie*, It/Po/Ro *Maria*, Sp *María* name females and are feminine. In Portuguese alone, masculine person names are optionally preceded by the definite article, though not in vocative use, in informal registers: *o Carlos, o Paulo, o Manuel* = *Carlos, Paulo, Manuel.* In Roumanian, the final **-a** of feminines like *Magda, Rodica, Sanda* is superficially the definite article, as evidenced by the potential addition of the genitive-dative suffix (see 4.3), e.g. **magda** + **y** → /mágdey/.[1] These strictly redundant articles are not to be seen as determiners in this case; they are noncontrastive and inseparable from the head.

All our languages, of course, have compound proper noun heads consisting of a person name followed by a surname, i.e. a 'family name', in this case a classifier and thus a kind of specifier rather than modifier. This surname 'satellite', as it were, has no gender itself, nor has it any way of copying the gender of the person name. Examples: Fr *Yves Montand*, Sp *Guillermo Vilas*, Po *Guiomar Novais*, It *Grazia Deledda*, Ro *Ilie Nastase*.[2]

[*Comment. A subject for investigation: the full grammar of person-naming in one or more Romance languages, including the modification of women's names when they marry.*]

2.2 Modifiers with person-name heads. Dependent constructions functioning as modifiers of a person name as head in our languages are:

(1) Adjectivals which characterize, and are therefore positioned left of the head in the surface structure (see 6.2), e.g. Fr *le pauvre Jean*, Sp *el pobre Juan*, Po *o pobre João*, It *il povero Giovanni*, Ro *săracul Ion*. Here we note, in every instance, the purely redundant surface presence of the definite article, which indeed is omitted in vocative expressions in all but Roumanian, e.g. Fr *Pauvre Jean!* but not Ro **Sărac Ioane!*

(2) Nominals which identify, e.g. Fr *Guillaume le Conquérant*, Sp *Juan Belmonte el torero*, Po *Henrique o Navegador*, It *Cicerone l'oratore*, Ro *Mihai Viteazul* 'Michel le Héros'. This modifier is limited to the appositive subtype of dependent CNP as described in 4.2.

Any further instances of common-noun-like syntactic behavior on the part of person names are probably attributable to actual common-nominalization in the lexicon, which alone seems able to account for such expressions as Fr *je connais plusieurs Jeans*, or Sp *ese otro Carlos a quien te refieres*, or It *quel Mario!* and the like. It may even be necessary to assume this sort of common-nominalization to explain certain types of appositive modifiers of personal name as heads. What, for example, is the structure of Fr *François Premier*, or of Sp *Juana la Loca*, or of Ro *Ştefan cel Mare* 'Étienne le Grand'? Clearly enough, in a phrase like Fr *Guillaume le Conquérant* or Po *Henrique o Navegador* the appositive modifier is a CNP, and no doubt it is simplest to say the same of Sp *Isabel la Católica* or Ro *Mihai Viteazul*, the head of the modifier being a nominalized adjective as described in 1.5.1. But a specifier like *premier* cannot be nominalized, and the adjective *mare* in *Ştefan cel Mare* is not. In these cases we seem therefore to be dealing with deletion reductions of *François* (= head) + *le premier François* (= appositive modifier) → *François Ier*, or *Alfonso* + *Alfonso número trece* → *Alfonso XIII*, in which the heads inside the appositive modifiers are in fact common-nominalized and so denote, rather than just 'X', 'individual named X'. There is no derivation of this sort for Ro *Ştefan cel Mare*, and therefore it seems to be a surface structure analogous to *scaunul cel mare* 'la grande chaise', which is derived as indicated in 1.5.1, note 14 from *scaunul* + *scaunul mare*.

2.3 Reduction of the PNP. Where the context allows for recovery, reduction of a PNP with person-name head may occur through deletion of a masculine person name, leaving just the surname, i.e. Fr *Jean Paul Belmondo* → *Belmondo*, Sp *Andrés Bello* → *Bello*. In normal usage, however, a feminine person name can be reduced in this way only in a larger construction. As may be seen under appositive modifiers (4.2), PNPs frequently fulfill this function in higher CNPs where the head noun denotes a social category or title,[3] e.g. Sp *el profesor Alberto Escobar* or Ro *Doamna Magdalena Petrescu-Dimitriu*. Now in all the languages it is very usual to reduce such larger PNPs by deletion of a head name of either gender, e.g. Sp *el profesor Alberto Escobar* → *el profesor Escobar*, or *la señorita Amada Segarra* → *la señorita Segarra*. And once this deletion has been made, it becomes possible to further delete a feminine title to achieve such surface contrasts with bare surnames of males as Fr *la Bernhardt*, Sp *la Segarra*, Po *a Novais*, It *la Fallaci*, Ro *Lupeasca*.[4] In Italian alone this same deletion is available with masculine titles as well, particularly in reference to males of general fame: *il Carducci, l'Ariosto*. Likewise it is common to delete a plural head and arrive at Fr *les Duval*, Sp *los González*, Po *os Lobo*, It *i Bocchino*, and Ro *Ilieştii* (again with the suffixed definite article transferred as in the case of the feminine singular).[5]

2.4 Place names as heads of PNPs. These proper nouns as morphological words consist, like person names, of stem only. Their referent being typically a single geographic (or geopolitical) entity from continent or ocean to village or stream, the majority are singular (e.g. *France, España, Portugal, Italia, România*), though some are inherently plural (*États-Unis, Antillas, Marche*), though never with a contrast of number in the same reference. Some are masculine, some feminine. Merely as a nonfunctional element of the head, rather than as a determiner, the definite article is overtly present with some, absent with others, always without contrast. The redundant article is typically present in the names of countries, states, provinces, as in Fr *la Chine, le Japon, les Pays-Bas* (but cf. *Haïti*);[6] always present with the names of rivers, as in It *l'Arno, il Tevere, la Volga*; typically absent from the names of cities or towns, as in Sp *Madrid, Roma, Buenos Aires* (but cf. *la Haya*).

2.5 Modifiers with place-name heads. Dependent constructions functioning as modifiers of a place name as head are characterizing adjectivals positioned left of the head, with the redundant definite article always present in the determiner position, as in Fr *la douce France*, Sp *la querida España*, Po *o pequeno Portugal*, It *la vecchia Italia*, Ro *frumoasa România* 'la belle Roumanie'. Further instances of common-noun-like syntactic behavior on the part of place names are probably attributable to actual common-nominalization in the lexicon as accounting for Fr *le Paris d'aujourd'hui est un Paris tout à fait différent* or the like. The common-nominalization of person names from 'X' to 'individual named X' is naturally more frequent than that of place names from 'Y' to 'place called Y', since there are indeed many individuals named X (especially without the surname added) but, generally speaking, only one place called Y.

Notes for Chapter 2

1. Roumanian person names also take a VOCATIVE suffix when the name is used in direct address and is thus not a constituent in any larger construction. The alternants of this suffix are **-o** with feminines, e.g. **rodika** + **o** → / rodíko/ *Rodico!* and **-e** ~ **-le** with masculines, e.g. **dan** + **e** → / dáne/ *Dane!* or **sandu** + **le** → / sándule/ *Sandule!*

2. A person name itself may be expanded to include one or more 'middle names' drawn from among given names, e.g. Sp *Juan Ramón* + *García* or Fr *Jean-Paul* + *Sartre*. Such expansion is best seen as taking place already at the lexical level rather than in the phrase structure; the same is doubtless true of the similar expansion of surnames, as in Sp *Juan* + *López Portillo* or Ro *Virgiliu Ştefănescu-Drăgăneşti*.

3. All our languages have one or more reverential titles, the one shared by all being Fr *Saint*, Sp/Po/It *Santo*, Ro *Sfînt*. Some are adjective-like in form, copying the gender of the person-name head, like the items just cited or like Sp *Don, Doña* and Po *Dom, Dona* (It *Don* occurs with masculine names only). Others are noun-like in form, e.g. Fr *Frère* and *Soeur*, Sp *Fray* and *Sor*, Po *Frei* and *Sóror*, It *Fra* and *Suora*. These phrase-bound items operate under a severe constraint. Their insertion into a PNP is not a syntactic process; only specific individuals are so referred to or addressed, and there is no optional deletion. Neither can the head name be deleted so as to leave only the title. Hence it may be preferable to claim that person names

like *Saint Pierre* or *Fra Giacomo* or whatever are generated in the lexicon rather than in the grammar.

4. Here Roumanian transfers the suffixed definite article from the head to the surname itself, i.e. **-a** + **lupesku** → /lupéaska/.

5. The Roumanian vocative suffix *-le* is also transferable to a surname in a headless PNP, e.g. *Bună ziua, Popescule!* 'Bonjour, Popescu!'

6. In Roumanian the final *-a* of feminine place names like *România, America, Dunărea* 'le Danube' is, like that of feminine person names, superficially the definite article suffix, though of course there is no contrasting form without it.

Chapter 3
The pronoun phrase

3.0 Internal structure of the pronoun phrase (ProP). This chapter discusses the internal structure of the pronoun phrase (ProP). This nominal construction in all our languages consists of a pronoun as obligatory head and of an optional modifier. The order of constituents is shown in the formula:

ProP → head (modifier).

Here, once again, there is no plural number or determiner attribute. Neither is appropriate, because every pronoun is underlyingly singular or plural; it is inherently determined as definite or nondefinite and thus has a built-in feature [± def] that corresponds to the definite or indefinite/partitive article with a common noun. As with proper nouns, other types of determiner would be semantically incompatible with a pronoun.

3.1 Pronouns as heads. Within the lexicon, the pronouns of a language constitute a small, closed class, finite rather than open-ended like the common or proper nouns. This is to say that the pronouns make up a subsystem which can be described in elements or terms differentiated from one another in accordance with a fully limited set of lexico-semantic features. As morphological words the common fund of pronouns shared by all our languages consist (like proper nouns) of stem only and are not inflected for number.

3.1.1 Personal, abstract and limiting pronouns. If we seek to represent the common core of Romance pronouns, shared in the main by the five languages and differentiable by one and the same gross matrix of binary features, we arrive at the arrays in Table 3.1. Many of the entries are also keyed to a series of descriptive remarks immediately following the table.

Table 3.1 Common core of pronouns.[1]

Pronoun type	French	Spanish	Portuguese	Italian	Roumanian
+personal[2]					
+local[3]					
+1st −pl.	moi	yo/mí	eu/mim	io/me	eu/mine
+2nd −pl.	toi	tú/ti	tu/ti	tu/te	tu/tine
+1st +pl.	nous	nosotros	nós	noi	noi
+2nd +pl.	vous	vosotros	vós	voi	voi
+substitute[4]					
−fem. −pl.	lui	él	ele	lui	el
+fem. −pl.	elle	ella	ela	lei	ea
−fem. +pl.	eux	ellos	eles	loro	ei
+fem. +pl.	elles	ellas	elas	loro	ele
+reflexive	soi	sí	si	sé	sine
+abstract[5]					
+anaphoric	ce	ello/lo	o	ciò	ceea
+demonstrative[6]					
+speaker-oriented	ceci	esto	isto	questo	aceasta ~ asta
+addressee-oriented		eso	isso	cotesto	
+other-oriented	cela	aquello	aquilo	quello	aceea ~ aia
+limiting[7]					
+indef. +human	(quelqu'un)	alguien	alguém	(qualcuno)	cineva
+indef. −human	(quelque chose)	algo	algo	(qualcosa)	ceva
+neg. +human	personne	nadie	ninguém	(nessuno)	nimeni
+neg. −human	rien	nada	nada	niente	nimic
+interrog.[8] +human	qui	quién	quem	chi	cine
+interrog. −human	quoi/que	qué	quê	che	ce
+all-incl. +human	tous	todos	todos	tutti	toţii
+all-incl. −human	tout	todo	tudo	tutto	totul
+distributive	chacun	cada uno	cada um	(ognuno)	(fiecare)

Remarks on Table 3.1

1. Gender. All of the pronouns except the substitute personals (see Remark 2) have inherent gender, just as nouns do. The local personals, and indeed also the reflexive substitute, are either masculine or feminine depending on the sex of the (always animate) referent. All the remaining pronouns listed are masculine.[1]

2. The personal pronouns. These are so specified not because they refer exclusively to persons (which they do not), but rather because they alone among the pronouns signal an opposition—traditionally three-way but here analyzed as two-way—between 'grammatical persons': the speaker-oriented 'first person' and the addressee-oriented 'second person' forms, subsumed here as the LOCAL PERSONAL PRONOUNS, as distinct from the other-oriented 'third person' forms subsumed here as the SUBSTITUTE PERSONAL PRONOUNS. For each and every Romance language the personal pronouns are cross-divided into a 'disjunctive' set (e.g. Fr *moi, toi, lui . . .*) and a 'conjunctive' set (e.g. Fr *me, te, le . . .*). However, neither the so-called 'conjunctive pronouns' of all our languages, nor the so-called 'subject pronouns' of French, qualify as true pronouns in the present frame of reference; they are rather clitic 'pro-phrases', or 'pro-complements', generated in the process of reduction, and as such are described in 11.

3. The local personals. The [−plural] entries for all but French display two basic alternants. The first occurs when the pronoun functions as subject, and the second when it functions otherwise, within a clause.

4. The substitute personals. Except for the [+reflexive] entry, these pronouns are strictly anaphoric. In accordance with formal requirements, any [+definite] nominal of any size having as its head a masculine singular noun (as in, say, Sp *el gran coche azul de la familia García* or Fr *Monsieur Valéry Giscard d'Estaing*) may be replaced in given context-determined situations by the corresponding masculine singular substitute (Sp *él*, Fr *lui*, etc.). Similarly, any [+definite] nominal having a feminine singular head may be replaced by the feminine singular substitute; and so on for nominals with masculine plural or feminine plural heads.[2] The substitutes are best viewed as having lexically derived feminine forms, like nouns (e.g. Sp *amigo, amiga*) rather than like adjectives inflected for agreement by copying; they are selected to match the gender/number of the head of the nominal which they replace. The above statements apply regardless of the function of the nominal being replaced, with one notable exception: if a nominal (other than a local personal ProP) functioning as subject in a clause recurs elsewhere within that same clause, then in all but French it is replaced by the reflexive substitute, e.g. **Juan habla para Juan → Juan habla para sí*. The French reflexive *soi* is not, as its cognates in the other languages are, a substitute for just any nominal; it is essentially restricted to reflexive replacement of a ProP with a limiting head such as *rien, chacun, tous, quiconque*, and including also the type of [+human] subject that does not surface at all, as in Fr *il faut penser à* *soi* or *on va rester chez soi.*[3]

5. The anaphoric abstract. This pronoun refers to an element of the discourse which does not necessarily have a surface manifestation at all, namely, a previously established or presupposed fact, act, state, situation, notion. In Spanish and Italian alone can this abstract pronoun occur with no modifier, as in Sp *pensar en ello,* It *pensare a ciò.* The other languages use instead a demonstrative with greatly reduced demonstrative force, e.g. Fr *penser à cela,* Po *pensar nisso.* All but the Spanish alternant *ello* and Italian *ciò* are in fact syntactically bound, functioning only as heads with certain modifiers, as exemplified in a pattern such as Fr *ce que tu dis,* Sp *lo que tú dices,* Po *o que tu dizes,* Ro *ceea ce tu zici.*

6. The demonstrative abstracts. These pronouns likewise refer to facts, acts, states, and the like, or to [−human] entities figuring in the discourse but not yet identified 'by name' as it were. French and Roumanian lack the addressee-oriented pronoun as well as the corresponding determiner, using either the speaker-oriented or the other-oriented item, principally the latter.[4] These demonstrative abstracts in Span/Port are traditionally designated as being somehow 'neuter' (as in Sp *ello/lo*), though this is inaccurate because there is no neuter gender in any Romance language. As regards adjective agreement—the sole criterion for detecting the gender of a noun or pronoun—they are strictly masculine, e.g. Sp *eso es nuevo,* Po *isso é novo,* like the corresponding items in the other languages.

7. The limiters. The parenthesized entries are to be seen as determinative adjectives which have undergone pronominalization, rather than as pronouns proper. The pronominalizing function of Fr *un,* Sp/It *uno,*[5] Po *um* extends to the limiting determiners Fr *chaque* (→ *chacun*), Sp/Po *cada* (→ *cada uno/um*), and It *ogni* (→ *ognuno*). Pronominalized also, without morphophonemic disturbance, are It *nessuno* and *ciascuno* and Ro *fiecare,* all masculine and all [+human] only.[6] The specifier item *tout/todo/tutto/tot* has as pronominal counterparts both a singular [−human] and a plural [+human] form, both masculine. French signals the [+human] plural with a final *-s* which is phonologically /s/, not /z/, hence never deleted. Portuguese signals the [−human] singular (redundantly?) by raising the root vowel in a pattern reminiscent of the demonstrative pronouns as against the determiners; Roumanian adds the appropriate form of the definite article suffix.

8. Among the interrogatives, Sp *quién* alone is inflected for number: plural *quiénes.* In the [−human] set, French uses *quoi* as an isolated utterance or as object of a preposition (as in *Quoi! De quoi s'agit-il?*), *que* as object in a clause (as in *Que sais-je?*). Portuguese in lieu of *quê* tends to use *o que,* with both components typically unstressed as in, say, *O que você sabe?*

Not included in Table 3.1 are certain quantifying pronouns and the honorific pronouns. Both sets are discussed herewith in 3.1.2 and 3.1.3.[7]

3.1.2 Quantifying pronouns. In all our languages the words of quantity which we have seen functioning as determiners may be pronominalized. Those of them which are adjectives have an overtly plural form in the lexicon, specified by the features [+ count] [+ human], while the singular form is specified by the opposing features [− count] [− human]. The French adverbs *beaucoup*, *peu*, and *combien*, though invariable in form, are either singular or plural syntactically,[8] being specified [± count/human], while the remaining French adverbs and all those of the other languages are singular only, thus [− count] [− human] only.

3.1.3 Deferential, or honorific, pronouns. We may now discuss the special pronouns which all our languages use in the direct addressing of persons either unknown to the speaker or known to be of a different social status than the speaker's. These DEFERENTIAL pronouns are of course integrated into the pronoun system of each language, but they share so few lexical and formal traits across languages that they are better excluded from the common core. They are also known to linguists as HONORIFICS, and we shall designate them with the lexical feature [+honorific]. In two of the languages, namely French and Italian, existing 2nd-plural locals are also used deferentially; the other three have separate personal pronouns marked [+hon] in the lexicon.

In French the 2nd-plural *vous* may refer to a single individual, in which case it is marked [+hon] and in semantic contrast with the always [−hon] *toi*; it is then grammatically singular for purposes of adjectival agreement, as noted in phrases like *vous seul* or *vous seule*, though not for verbal agreement with subject, e.g. *vous, vous allez* as against *toi, tu vas*. When *vous* has plural reference, the honorific feature is inevitably neutralized.

In Italian the substitutes *lei* and *loro* double as honorific personals (written *Lei* and *Loro*). When [+ hon], *Lei* is of either gender, as seen in *Lei stesso* ≠ *Lei stessa*, but despite its personal orientation it remains grammatically nonlocal for agreement in verbal inflection, e.g. *Lei se ne va* (like *lei se ne va*) as against *tu te ne vai* (see 9.6).

Spanish has one honorific, namely *usted*, plural *ustedes* (also typically written *Vd.*, *Vds.*) which, like It *Lei Loro*, is of either gender—as in *usted(es) mismo(s)* ≠ *usted(es) misma(s)*—but grammatically nonlocal despite its personal orientation, e.g. *usted se va* as against *tú te vas*.

Portuguese has two honorifics. One is *você*, plural *vocês* (occasionally written *V.*, *Vs.*), of either gender according to the sex of the referent but, like Sp *usted*, grammatically nonlocal. The other is historically the CNP *o(s) senhor(es)*, feminine *a(s) senhora(s)*, also grammatically nonlocal. Traditionally, *você* serves for respectful address of friends and social equals, while *o senhor* etc. is reserved for a higher degree of deference among strangers and social unequals.

[*Comment. For investigation: Present-day developments in deferential pronoun systems in the Spanish/Portuguese of the New World.*]

Roumanian has the most elaborate subset of honorific pronouns, both local and substitute, which may be displayed as in Table 3.2.

Table 3.2 Roumanian honorific pronouns.

Honorific pronoun	Singular	Plural
Local [+hon] (lower deference)	dumneata (D-ta)	
Local [++hon] (higher deference)	dumneavoastră (Dvs)	
Substitute [+hon]	{ dînsul, f.dînsa { dumnealui, f.dumneaei	dînşii, f.dînsele } dumnealor }

In the local forms there are two degrees of deference, neutralized, however, in plural address. Both locals are of either gender according to the sex of the referent(s). *Dumneavoastră* in singular reference is, like Fr *vous*, grammatically singular for adjective agreement (*Dvs singur* or *Dvs singură*), but not for verbal agreement, e.g. *dumneavoastră ştiţi* as against *dumneata ştii* 'vous savez'. The substitute *dumnealui* (f. *dumneaei*) has the less common alternant *dumneasa*, the same for either gender.

3.2 Modifiers in the ProP. As in NPs, we shall consider these constituents expansions of the basic phrase structure, their function filled by dependent constructions. Embeddable in this way within the ProP are the same four types of dependent construction enumerated in 1.4, but with more constraints. Only a few structures peculiar to ProPs alone are singled out in the present section. Treatment of certain other modifiers, including relative clauses, is deferred to appropriate later points where they are conflatable with modifiers of noun heads.

(i) All personal heads, including honorifics, may be modified by either of the following two special limiting adjectives in Table 3.3.

Table 3.3

Fren	Span	Port	Ital	Roum
seul	solo	só	solo	singur
-même	mismo	mesmo	stesso	însu-

Examples are Fr *moi seul(e)*, Sp *ellos solos*, Po *você só*, It *tu sola*, Ro *el însuşi*. We note that in Roumanian alone one of these modifiers is a different lexical item from the corresponding specifier in Table 1.3 under determiners. The oddment *însu-* not only copies gender/number agreement in the normal way, but also obligatorily suffixes a dative clitic in personal cross-reference to the head, thus: *eu însumi* or *eu însămi*, *noi înşine* or *însene*; see 11.3 for the forms of these clitics. A third limiting adjective, also matching one of the Table 1.2 specifiers, occurs uniquely after the [+pl] locals in Fren/Ital/ Roum but not in Span/Port: Fr *nous autres, vous autres,* It *noi altri, voi altri,* Ro *noi alţi, voi alţi.*

(ii) All the [+ pl] personals, including the honorifics, may be accompanied by the all-inclusive *tout/todo/tutto/tot,* also listed among the specifiers in 1.3.2. Basically, this element follows the head, as in Fr *nous tous, vous toutes, eux tous, elles toutes;* cf. also *nous deux* (and indeed *nous trois, nous quatre* . . .) instead of **nous tous (les) deux.* In Spanish *todo* may precede the head in *todos nosotros* (or *nosotros todos,* like *nosotros dos*), and it must precede in *todos ellos, todas ellas.* In Portuguese and Italian ordering of *todo/tutto* is the same as in Spanish. In Roumanian *tot* follows the locals and the local honorifics, as in *noi toţi, voi toate, dumneavoastră toţi,* and it may either follow or precede the substitutes as in *ei toţi* or *toţi ei, ele toate* or *toate ele.* The forms in *amb-* of the other all-inclusive do not occur in ProPs (thus Spanish has merely *nosotros dos,* Po *nós dois,* It *noi due*), but Ro *amîndoi* is available as in *noi amîndoi, ele amîndouă,* or whatever.

(iii) The abstracts may without exception be modified by the all-inclusive. Since both the anaphoric and the demonstrative abstracts are (redundantly) [−human], Portuguese by attraction uses the matching [−human] form with raised vowel, e.g. *tudo isto, tudo o* (*que tu dizes*).

(iv) Limiting heads are to some extent modifiable by the further limiting adjective *autre/altro* in French/Italian:

Fr quelqu'un d'autre, personne d'autre, rien d'autre
It nient'altro, chi altro, che altro

where Spanish/Portuguese instead adjectivalize the adverb *más/mais*:

Sp alguien más, algo más, nadie más, quién más, qué más
Po alguém mais, ninguém mais, quem mais, que mais

and Roumanian uses the lexically derived items *altcineva* 'quelqu'un d'autre' and *altceva* 'quelque chose d'autre' (cf. even *nimic altceva* 'rien d'autre'); as for *cine mai, ce încă,* as well as the exact parallels Fr *qui encore, quoi encore,* It *chi ancora,* etc., these phrases are best viewed as reductions of clausal structures in which the second items are underlyingly in an adverbial function.
This limiting set is also modified by characterizing adjectivals, in which case they are introduced by the marker *de/di* in French/Italian:

Fr quelque chose de nouveau, rien d'étrange
Sp algo nuevo, nada extraño
Po algo novo, nada extranho
It qualcosa di nuovo, niente di strano
Ro ceva nou, nimic straniu

(v) Modifiers of evaluation or comparison. With the first of these the head is one of the two evaluative quantifying pronouns (in Fr *assez* and *trop*) and the modifier is then an adverb phrase analogous to those illustrated in 1.3.4 as attributes in quantifying determiners of the evaluative subtype; with the second the head is one of the three (French has four: *plus*, *moins*, *tant*, and *autant*) comparative quantifying pronouns, and the modifier consists of material introduced by a functor meaning 'than' or 'as', also referred to in 1.3.4 under attributes of comparative quantifying determiners. Inasmuch as such modifiers entail the embedding of (dependent) clauses, we still relegate further consideration of comparative pronouns to Chapter 14.

Notes for Chapter 3

1. That includes Fr *personne*, a wholly different lexical item, synchronically, from the feminine noun *personne*; also Fr *quelque chose* and It *qualcosa* (or *qualchecosa*), even though the respective nouns *chose* and *cosa* are, in their own right, feminine.

2. Coordinated nominals such as Fr *la cigale et la fourmi* or It *San Pietro e San Paolo* are also replaceable by a [+pl] substitute.

3. For the place of *on* in the grammar of French, see 11.2.

4. Italian has certain additional pronouns related systematically to the main core. Thus among the substitutes, the variant *egli* is preferred to *lui* by many speakers as subject in a clause (*egli se ne accorge* rather than *lui se ne accorge*), though the same can no longer be said of archaizing *ella* as variant of *lei*. Further, *lui lei loro* are specified as [+human] only and there is a [−human] counterpart in the form of *esso -a*, plurals *essi -e*, unmatched (synchronically) in the other languages. In current usage there is considerable free variation in the plural between *loro* and *essi -e* for [+human] reference, perhaps because *loro* belongs to either gender and hence cannot, in itself, signal the sex of referents. This language is also alone in possessing a set of demonstrative substitutes:

	masc.	fem.	m./f.pl.
Speaker-oriented:	costui	costei	costoro
Other-oriented:	colui	colei	coloro

Obsolescent stylistic variants of the masculine forms are *questi* and *quegli* ~ *quei*, respectively, in which the final *-i* does not signal plurality but seemingly is analogical to the final vowel of *(co)lui* and *egli*, and indeed marking formal contrast with the masculine determiners *questo* and *quello* ~ *quel*.

5. Only in these two languages is *uno* not only a pronominalization of the corresponding determiner but also an item semantically like Fr *on*, Po *a gente*, Ro *omul* 'l'homme', though syntactically a pronoun in its own right.

6. Addable here, as a stylistic variant of *personne*, is Fr *aucun* and its near-synonym *nul*.

7. The so-called 'possessive pronouns' also occupy a place in traditional Romance grammars; but in the present analysis they form a single class with the 'possessive adjectives' as reductions of genitive nominal structures; see 1.3.1, note 1.

8. As shown by the person/number inflection on any verb of which they are subject in a clause, e.g. *beaucoup fait croire* . . . vs. *beaucoup croient* . . . Different in structure is the sporadic nominalization of the adjectives in view, as in Fr *un autre, aucun autre*, Sp *ningún otro*, Po *nenhum outro*, It *nessun altro*, where the first words are unmistakably determiners.

Chapter 4
Dependent nominals functioning as modifiers in larger nominals

4.0 Introduction. In 1.4 nominals were listed among the modifiers within larger nominal phrases. We are now in a position to examine such dependent, or embedded, nominals. They are divisible into four subtypes best treated separately: (1) CHARACTERIZING (4.1), (2) APPOSITIVE (4.2), (3) GENITIVE (4.3), and (4) DELIMITING (4.4). This chapter then concludes with a discussion of supercharged nominals (4.5), whether nominals with more than one modifier (4.5.1) or nominals with more than one determiner (4.5.2), and a discussion of coordinated nominals (4.6).

4.1 Characterizing modifiers: Nominals which characterize, or describe, the head. Examples to be taken into account here are of the following sort, occurring mainly in CNPs:

Fr une pièce de théâtre, une brosse à dents, des articles en bois, la fille aux yeux verts

Sp dolor de cabeza, sangre de toro, historia de ciencia

Po um relógio de ouro, café do Brasil, o museu de arte moderna

It i pozzi di petrolio, un abito da sera, spaghetti alle vongole, dei mulini a vento

Ro articole de lemn 'des articles en bois', hîrtie de scrisori 'du papier à lettres', un pahar de vin 'un verre de vin', haine pentru bărbat 'des habits pour homme', ţărani din Moldova[1] 'des paysans de la Moldavie'

In every case, in each language, the modifiers appear to be 'prepositional phrases' on the surface, and indeed they are structured exactly like the adverb phrases which we shall be discussing in 7.2.1, consisting of a transitive adverb (i.e. a preposition) plus a nominal object. However, here the preposition lacks any adverbial (i.e. spatial, temporal, or modal) meaning and is in fact no more than a function word serving to adapt the nominal to its role as modifier. In other words, at the underlying level it is *arte moderna* that answers what kind of *museu* is involved in the third Portuguese example, and the *de* is merely an obligatory element of the dependent nominal in the surface output. This no doubt accounts for the seemingly arbitrary selection of one lexical preposition as against another in this function, with no necessary cross-language correspondence.

The dependent nominal as characterizing modifier is, of course, readily associated with characterizing (i.e. descriptive) adjectives, and can often be replaced by one with little or no change in meaning, as It *pozzi di petrolio* = *pozzi petroliferi*. Many apparent nominals in this subfunction may well be already constituted at the lexical rather than at the phrasal level, particularly if they are idioms such as Fr *robe de chambre* or *cul-de-sac*.

[*Query. What, exactly, is an idiom anyway?*]

4.2 Appositive modifiers: Nominals which identify the head. Examples are the following:

Fr le capitaine Dreyfus, la ville de Paris, le mois de mai
Sp el rey Juan Carlos, la ciudad de Madrid, el mes de mayo
Po o presidente Vargas, a cidade de Lisboa, o mês de maio
It   il ministro Fanfani, la città di Roma, il mese di maggio
Ro doctorul Manuilă, oraşul Bucureşti, luna Mai

In order to be sure which is the head and which the modifier in such phrases, let us employ, as a discovery procedure, two cryptic dialogues:

A: — J'ai vu le capitaine.   A: — No conozco la ciudad.
B: — Quel capitaine?   B: — ¿Qué ciudad?
A: — Le capitaine Dreyfus.   A: — La ciudad de Madrid.

In the French exchange *capitaine* is the head of the nominal under scrutiny, which is tantamount to *le capitaine qui s'appelle Dreyfus*. This is the pattern for all titles in all the languages, including, for example, Fr *le sieur Durand*, Sp *el señor García*, Po *o senhor Lopes*, It *il signor Rossi*, Ro *domnul Popescu*.[2] That is to say, the title-word is the head, and the person name is the identifying, or appositive, modifier. Note that these title-phrases are determined by the definite article, which, however, is typically omitted (i.e. deleted) when directly addressing the person (*¡Buenos días, señora Gómez!*) in Sp/Po/It. In the Spanish dialogue above, *ciudad* is the head and the phrase is a reduction of *la ciudad que se llama Madrid*. This, then, is the same pattern as the preceding, with the minor constraint of marking the appositive modifier with *de/di* (a constraint to which Roumanian is not subject).

4.3 Genitive modifiers: Nominals which tell to whom (or to what) the head noun belongs or pertains. Since much more than mere 'possessive' relationship is involved, we shall use the term GENITIVE, primarily a label for the grammatical case which signals such relationships in languages like Latin or German. Typical examples of genitive relationships to consider are the following:

Kinship:
Fr le père de l'enfant
Sp una tía de Carlos
Po vários parentes dessa mulher
It la sorella di Mario
Ro copiii profesorului 'les enfants du professeur'

Property or attribute:
Fr le restaurant de la gare
Sp la historia del arte
Po a casa de Deus
It la proprietà dell'autore
Ro motorul automobilului

Products, activities, thoughts:
Fr l'opinion du doyen
Sp unos esfuerzos del maestro
Po as festas dos camponeses
It un capolavoro di Michelangelo
Ru poeziile lui Eminescu 'les poésies d'Eminescu'

Actions by the modifier:
Fr les prières des fidèles
Sp la caída de la lluvia
Po as contribuições dos ricos
It l'insistenza del capo

Ro moartea reginei 'la mort de la reine'

Actions upon the modifier
Fr l'éstablissement de la loi
Po o governo do povo
Sp el amor a los niños
It il lavaggio della macchina
Ro organizarea cursurilor 'l'organisation des cours'

In the last two sets the head nouns either parallel verbs (Ro *moarte : a muri*, Po *governo : governar*) or are actually deverbal nouns (Fr *établir → établissement*, Sp *caer → caída*), and the genitive modifier stands in either (1) verb-to-subject relationship (Fr *les fidèles prient*, Sp *la lluvia cae*, etc.) and is called SUBJECTIVE GENITIVE, or (2) a verb-to-object relationship (It *si lava la macchina*, Ro *se organizează cursurile*, etc.) and is called OBJECTIVE GENITIVE.

The function marker par excellence of the genitive modifier is *de/di*, with two minor exceptions and one major exception. The minor ones are the use of *à* in a French phrase like *une cousine à moi* (concerning which see 4.3.1) and of *a* in Span/Port for distinguishing an objective from a subjective genitive after certain heads such as *amor*; thus in Sp *el amor de los niños*, Po *o amor dos meninos* the children do the loving, while in Sp *el amor a los niños*, Po *o amor aos meninos* the children get the love.

The major exception is Roumanian, which instead of using *de*, puts the genitive modifier in the so-called 'genitive-dative case'. This term of course implies that the grammar of Roumanian has other cases too; and traditionally there is indeed one other, namely, the 'nominative-accusative'. This latter 'case', however, is inflectionally unmarked, which greatly weakens 'the case for case' in this language. In Agard (1952) and (1958) the 'oblique' suffix —which we will rename the genitive-dative (gen./dat.) suffix—is an element in the inflectional system of nouns, of pronouns, of adjectives located left of the head, and of numerous determiners. In that description partial paradigms are then as follows:

omul mare 'l'homme grand'	marele om 'le grand homme'	
omului mare 'de l'homme grand'	marelui om 'du grand homme'	
un om 'un homme'	acest om 'cet homme-ci'	acel om 'cet homme-là'
unui om 'd'un homme'	acestui om 'de cet homme-ci'	acelui om 'de cet homme-là'
celălalt om 'l'autre homme'	care om 'quel homme'	el 'lui'
celuilalt om 'de l'autre homme'	cărui om 'de quel homme'	lui 'à lui'

The one structure that does not occur here is bare stem plus gen./dat. suffix.[3] And since we now view the enclitic definite article as one of the determiners, we can very simply claim that the gen./dat. suffix attaches itself only to determiners. Yet its function is to adapt an entire nominal of any size or complexity to its role of genitive modifier within a higher nominal. This is exactly the function of de/di in the other languages and we may even say that both occupy the same position in the underlying structure, i.e. outside and ahead of the phrase proper. Thus the parallel is complete between Roumanian and (say) French:

Fr   de + le + homme → de l'homme
Ro   -i + lu + om → omului[4]

The morphophonemics of Roumanian gen./dat.-suffixation are extraordinarily complex and need not be spelled out here. Suffice it to add that the functor has two underlying shapes in morphological complementation: **-y** when the nominal is singular, **-or** when it is plural; thus, for example, **-y** + **ačəstu** + **dɔmnu** → /ačéstuy dómn/ as against **-or** + **i** + **ačəstu** + **dɔmnu** → /ačéstor dómny/.[5]

4.3.1 The replacement of genitive modifiers. In principle there are two patterns of substitution available, as shown in the following array of examples. In Pattern A just the inner nominal is replaced by a substitute pronoun while leaving the genitive functor intact, as can be done in any construction at all, e.g. Fr *c'est pour Pierre* → *c'est pour lui*, or It *cerco l'altra ragazza* → *cerco lei*. Pattern B entails replacement of the entire genitive modifier, including the functor, by a POSSESSIVE SUBSTITUTE, adjectival in form and copying gender/number concord with the head noun.

		Original full nominal		Pattern A: Replacement of inner nominal		Pattern B: Replacement of entire modifier
Main	Fr	un cousin à Marie		un cousin à elle		* . . .
det.	Sp	un primo de María		un primo de ella		un primo suyo
≠	Po	um primo de Maria	→	um primo dela	→	um primo seu
def.	It	un cugino di Maria		un cugino di lei		un cugino suo
art.	Ro	un văr al Mariei		un văr al ei		un văr al său
Main	Fr	le cousin de Marie		son cousin à elle		* . . .
det.	Sp	el primo de María		el primo de ella		el primo suyo
=	Po	o primo de Maria	→	o primo dela	→	o primo seu
def.	It	il cugino di Maria		il cugino di lei		il cugino suo
art.	Ro	vărul Mariei		vărul ei		vărul său

Certain observations on the display are relevant.

(1) The six Roumanian phrases illustrate an important constraint of that language, to wit: if a genitive nominal (in this case *Mariei*) as modifier is to follow the head directly, the latter must be determined by the definite article, as in the bottom frame. If the head is not thus determined, or if an adjectival modifier intervenes (as in, say, *vărul bogat al Mariei* 'le cousin riche de Marie', then the functor *al* is inserted as a mere 'adapter', semantically empty in this environment. Showing concord with the head, it is known to Roumanian grammarians as the 'genitive article' and does, in point of fact, function elsewhere as an alternant of the definite article proper.

(2) Definitely in Italian, and typically also in Spanish, Pattern A with its pronoun occurs under a contrastive/emphatic intonation with the force of 'I mean *her*, not someone else as you might be thinking', because the possessive substitute of Pattern B is ambiguous as regards the gender (and even the number, in Spanish) of the nominal being replaced.

(3) In Port/Roum, on the other hand, Pattern B is the preferred one when there is a reflexive connection involved—i.e. when the head of the genitive modifier is coreferential with the subject of the sentence, e.g. Po *João está com o primo seu*, Ro *Ion este cu vărul său*. In addition, however, Portuguese freely replaces the honorific genitives *de você(s), do senhor, da senhora* etc. with *seu*, regardless of reflexivity.

(4) French alone lacks Pattern B, and we may further note that *le cousin à elle* is ill-formed unless the definite article is replaced by a corresponding possessive article (more on the latter also under reduction). On the other hand, French alone can insert also a local pronoun after the functor *à*—i.e.,

un cousin à moi, . . . *à nous*, . . . *à toi*, . . . *à vous*, or *mon cousin à moi, ton cousin à toi*, etc., with adjustment of the possessive article for person, exactly parallel to *un cousin à elle* and *son cousin à elle*. In both of these environments the local pronouns in the other languages are obligatorily subject to a Pattern B replacement, as exemplified in a second display herewith:

		Original full nominal		Pattern B: Replacement
Main	Fr	mon cousin à moi		* . . .
det.	Sp			el primo mío
=	Po	(obligatory	→	o primo meu
def.	It	replacement)		il cugino mio
art.	Ro			vărul meu

Main	Fr	ce cousin à moi		* . . .
det.	Sp			este primo mío
is a	Po	(obligatory	→	este primo meu
dem.	It	replacement)		questo cugino mio
	Ro			acest văr al meu[6]

4.3.2 The reduction of genitive modifiers. In French the only genitive modifier susceptible of reduction is the type *à* + personal pronoun, with the further constraint that the determiner be the possessive article replacement of the definite article. Reduction is then effected by the simple deletion of the modifier, since its trace remains in the determiner, thus:

mon cousin à moi	→	mon cousin
ton cousin à toi	→	ton cousin
notre cousin à nous	→	notre cousin
votre cousin à vous	→	votre cousin
son cousin à lui/elle	→	son cousin
leur cousin à eux/elles	→	leur cousin

In the other languages it is the Pattern B replacement (lacking in French) alone that is subject to reduction. Where the main determiner is the definite article:

Sp	el primo mío →	mi primo
Po	o primo meu →	(o) meu primo
It	il cugino mio →	(il) mio cugino
Ro	vărul meu →	al meu văr

In Port/Ital, reduction is effected by moving the possessive adjective into the determiner slot, where it cannot come under phrasal stress. Its position relative to a specifier, if one is present, is somewhat fluid: cf. Po *um certo meu propósito*, It *un certo mio proposito* with Po *o meu único propósito*, It *il mio unico proposito*. One thing for certain is that the reduced possessive adjective is very tightly linked with the definite article, which is then obligatorily deleted without loss of the [+def] feature before certain lexically selected heads, principally nouns of kinship as in Po *meu pai*, It *mio babbo*. For Italian the deletion rule is quite stringent (for example, the phrase must not be pluralized); but Portuguese has an increasing tendency to delete the article variably before any head at all, e.g. *os meus livros* or just *meus livros*. In the cases of deletion the possessive is doing what it does systematically in Spanish as in French, namely, taking the place of the definite article as a [+ def] determiner; Sp *el primo* and *mi primo*, Fr *le cousin* and *mon cousin*, have exactly the same structure.

In constructions where no syntactic reduction is available, it is still possible to achieve the desired effect by moving the phrasal stress from the basic final position back to the head, as in Sp /un prímo mío/ → /un prímo mío/, or Ro /un vắr al mếw/ → /un vắr al méw/ (instances where the possessive cannot be moved), or even Ro /vắrul mếw/ → /vắrul méw/ instead of /al méw vắr/, which tends to be stylistically marked.

4.3.3 The few pronoun heads which may be followed by a genitive modifier. Not only noun heads, but also a restricted number of pronoun heads, may be followed by a genitive modifier. Thus:

• Indefinite and negative limiting pronouns specified as [−human]. The structure may be illustrated with *rien/nada* etc. as the head, including the possible Pattern A and Pattern B replacements:

	Original full ProP		Pattern A replacement		Pattern B replacement
Fr	rien à Pierre		rien à lui		* . . .
Sp	nada de Pedro		nada de él		nada suyo
Po	nada de Pedro	→	nada dele	→	nada seu
It	niente di Pietro		niente di lui		niente di suo
Ro	nimic al lui Petru		nimic al lui		nimic al său
Fr	rien à nous				* . . .
Sp					nada nuestro
Po	obligatory		→		nada nosso
It	replacement				niente di nostro
Ro					nimic al nostru

Of course, there can be no reduction of the genitive modifiers because there is no determiner slot to accommodate the possessive substitute.

• In Sp/Po/It but not Fr/Ro, certain of the abstract pronouns (which are redundantly [−human]). Examples with one of the demonstratives:

	Original:		Pattern A:		Pattern B:
Sp	aquello de Pedro		aquello de él		aquello suyo
Po	aquilo de Pedro	→	aquilo dele	→	aquilo seu
It	quello di Pietro		quello di lui		quello suo

Compare also, with obligatory Pattern B replacement, Sp *aquello vuestro*, Po *aquilo vosso*, It *quello vostro*, etc.

• Uniquely in Spanish, the anaphoric abstract in its stressless alternant *lo*, as in *lo de Carlos → lo de él → lo suyo*, and therefore also, in consequence of obligatory replacement, *lo mío, lo tuyo, lo nuestro*, and *lo vuestro*, with the meanings 'ce qui est à moi, . . . à toi', etc.[7]

4.3.4 Reduction/deletion of heads in nominals which contain genitive modifiers. Before leaving genitive modifiers, let us pause to consider the reduction/deletion of heads in nominals which contain genitive modifiers. In all the languages but ·French, the pattern is simply that already described in 4.3.2 (reduction through head deletion where the modifier is a dependent nominal), and is equally valid for Pattern B replacements as shown herewith:

Sp	un primo mío → uno mío	el primo mío → el mío
Po	um primo meu → um meu	o primo meu → o meu
It	un cugino mio → uno mio	il cugino mio → il mio
Ro	un văr al meu → *[8]	vărul meu → al meu

In French, on the other hand, in the absence of Pattern B replacement, reduction of the main head is possible only in that structure in which we have already observed reduction of the modifier—namely, where that modifier is *à* + personal pronoun. In this case the modifier is replaced by a possessive adjective uniquely reserved, in current usage, for this reduction. Thus:

mon cousin à moi → le mien   notre cousin à nous → le nôtre

ton cousin à toi → le tien   votre cousin à vous → le vôtre

son cousin à $\left\{ \begin{array}{l} \text{lui} \\ \text{elle} \end{array} \right\}$ → le sien   leur cousin à $\left\{ \begin{array}{l} \text{eux} \\ \text{elles} \end{array} \right\}$ → le leur

Traditional French grammar takes the two-word combinations *le + mien* etc. as 'possessive pronouns'; but since they signal a recoverable noun head, our principle of reduction precludes this. They are, by this reasoning, adjectives: *mien, tien, sien* copy the gender/number of the deleted head (*la mienne, les mien(ne)s*), but *nôtre, vôtre*, and *leur* copy only its number (*la nôtre, les nôtres*). We could also say that the possessive article, obligatory in the unreduced pattern (as opposed to, say, *le cousin de Pierre*), reverts to the expected definite article. However, the definite article and the possessive adjective being wholly inseparable,[9] it is equally feasible to posit that the definite article *le* and the possessive adjective *mien* together represent, as a single lexical item, a syntactic variant of the possessive article, in precisely the same relationship to *mon* as the interrogative adjective *lequel* is to *quel* (see 1.5.3).[10]

On the other hand, the adjectives in view can be lexically nominalized and function as CNP heads, as in *le mien* = 'ce qui est à moi, ce qui m'appartient' (semantically though not structurally equivalent to Sp *lo mío*), and this fact, of course, argues for consistent separation of the two elements. We therefore list the adjectives apart from the article in our cross-language display of Table 4.1.

Table 4.1 Possessive substitutes in the genitive modifier.

Original pronoun		French adj.	art.	Spanish adj.	art.	Portuguese adj.	Italian adj.	Roumanian adj.
Local	+1st—pl	mien	mon	mio	mi	meu	mio	meu
	+2nd—pl	tien	ton	tuyo	tu	teu	tuo	tău[11]
	+1st+pl	nôtre	notre	nuestro		nosso	nostro	nostru
	+2nd+pl	vôtre	votre	vuestro		vosso	vostro	vostru[11]
Substitute	—pl	sien	son				suo	său
				suyo	su	seu		
	+pl		leur				loro	*. . .[12]

[*Comment. A challenging exercise in data-handling: to state the morphophonemics of gender/number agreement for the possessive substitutes in one or more of the five languages.*]

4.4 Delimiting modifiers: Nominals which delimit the lexical field of the head. Let us first look at the following small array of minimally contrasting phrases:

Fr peu d'églises ≠ peu des églises
Sp pocas iglesias ≠ pocas de las iglesias
Po poucas igrejas ≠ poucas das igrejas
It poche chiese ≠ poche delle chiese
Ro puține biserici ≠ puține din biserici

The contrast in view, semantically identical in all the languages, entails opposing a CNP consisting of quantifying determiner plus noun, to a CNP made up of some sort of quantifying word plus functor plus definite article[13] plus noun. On the left side the noun is obviously enough the head. But on the right side it appears that the quantifying word—originally adjectival but nominalized here—is somehow the head and is modified by a [+def] CNP introduced by *de/di/din* and so delimiting the field of possible lexical nouns that *peu/pocas* etc. is narrowed to mean, in itself, 'peu d'églises'. However, since the word-for-word equivalents **peu d'églises des églises*, **pocas iglesias de las iglesias*, etc. never actually surface, it is not possible to claim that the head noun of the entire phrase is reduced through deletion. It is simply unrealized because it would be totally redundant, being lexically and referentially identical to the head of the delimiting modifier. Naturally, this head will be [—count] if the phrase is singular, as in Sp *un poco de ese queso*, or else [+count] if the phrase is pluralized as in our display examples. Further instances are:

Fr   quelques-uns des élèves, combien des livres, un de nos amis
Sp   ninguno de tus hermanos, algunos de los estudiantes, uno de estos días
Po   duas das igrejas, um pouco desse queijo, cada um dos reis de Portugal
It   troppe di quelle regole, ciascuna delle strade, uno dei miei figliuoli
Ro   cîteva dintre şcoale 'quelques-unes des écoles', multe din locurile astea 'beaucoup de ces places', unul din copiii voştri 'un de vos enfants'

We observe that the same functor marks these delimiting modifiers as marks genitive modifiers, except for Roumanian, which here uses *din* or *dintre* (cf. Fr *d'entre*).[14]

It is also of interest to note that the head-like constituent in this type of nominal alternates to the same form which it takes in a CNP which is truly reduced through head deletion. This alternant copies the gender of the head of the modifier, and, of course, plural number if present in the phrase. Subject to such alternation are Fr *quelque, chaque, quel,* Sp/Po *cada,* It *qualche,* Ro *un,* as illustrated in the following display:

	Reduced nominal	Nominal with delimiting modifier
Fr	quelques rois → quelques-uns	quelques-uns des rois
	quelques reines → quelques-unes	quelques-unes des reines
	chaque roi → chacun	chacun des rois
	chaque reine → chacune	chacune des reines
	quel roi → lequel	lequel des rois
	quelle reine → laquelle	laquelle des reines
Sp	cada rey → cada uno	cada uno de los reyes
	cada reina → cada una	cada una de las reinas
Po	cada rei → cada um	cada um dos reis
	cada rainha → cada uma	cada uma das rainhas[15]
It	qualche re → qualcuno	qualcuno dei re
	qualche regina → qualcuna	qualcuna delle regine
Ro	(nici) un rege → (nici) unul[16]	(nici) unul din regi
	(nici) o regină → (nici) una[16]	(nici) una din regine

Like any CNP, a delimiting modifier may be replaced in a Pattern A substitution, e.g.:

Fr   aucun des étudiants → aucun d'eux
Sp   ninguno de tus sobrinos → ninguno de ellos
Po   um ros reis de Portugal → um deles
It   ciascuna di quelle parole → ciascuna di esse
Ro   multe din ideile astea → multe din ele

What is more, as well as a substitute pronoun we can find a [+pl] [±hon] personal pronoun in the modifier, as in Fr *chacun(e) d'entre vous*, Sp *muchos de ustedes*, Po *uma de vocês*, It *alcune di noi*, Ro *cîţi dintre dumneavoastră.* This pattern lends further support to our claim that no noun has been deleted—for what nouns could have surfaced here to begin with? It is worth noting also that there occur a few scattered ProPs containing a delimiting modifier, e.g. Fr *rien de cela*, Sp *nada de eso*, Po *nada disso*, It *niente di quello*; cf. also Fr *qui d'entre vous, personne d'entre eux*, or Ro *cineva dintre ei, nimeni dintre voi*, types not exactly matched, however, in Span/Port.

[*Comment. A minor problem to solve: the phrase-structure of month-dates. Consider the following data:*

Fr   le premier juin, le deux (trois . . . trente-et-un) octobre
Sp   el primero de junio, el dos (tres . . . treinta y uno) de octubre
Po   primeiro de junho, dois (três . . . trinte e um) de outubro
It   il primo giugno, il due (tre . . . trentuno) ottobre
Ro   întîi[17] Iunie, doi (trei . . . treizeci şi unu) Octombrie

Can you propose one or more basic structural descriptions of these phrases in light of their surface similarities and differences? You will want to bear in mind also that when the name of the month itself is not mentioned, Sp día, *Po* o dia, *It* giorno, *Ro* ziua *are apt to be present before the number-word.*]

4.5 Supercharged nominals. The structural formulas which we have given for the three subclasses of nominal (CNP, PNP, ProP) are not intended to exclude the possible occurrence of two or more modifiers, or even of two or more determiners, in a single construction. We need to differentiate, however, between those phrases which contain more than one modifier and those which contain more than one determiner.

4.5.1 Nominals with more than one modifier. Let us take the following example:

	Det.	Adj. mod.	Head	Adj. mod.	Nominal modifier
Fr	la	belle	maison	blanche	des parents de Pierre
Sp	la	hermosa	casa	blanca	de los padres de Pedro
Po	a	formosa	casa	branca	dos pais de Pedro
It	la	bella	casa	bianca	dei genitori di Pietro
Ro	-a	frumoas-	casă	albă	a părinţilor lui Petru

We discern here two adjectival modifiers and one nominal modifier. The fact that *de Pierre, de Pedro* etc. is of itself a nominal is irrelevant, for it is a nominal within a nominal in a normal hierarchy of dependency which some call LAYERING. On the other hand, *belle* and *blanche* and *des parents de Pierre* are all independent of each other and do not stand in any structural hierarchy. Together with the head they constitute a string, and their order is set by positional constraints operating on the modifiers relative to one another in accordance with their subtypes. Thus, for example, an adjective like *beau* can precede a head, while one like *blanc* normally cannot; neither adjective can follow the nominal modifier; and so on. Although there may well be a hierarchy of new information within the message, with relative degrees of emphasis on the beauty, or on the color, or on the ownership of the house in view, the three modifiers are not involved in any syntactic hierarchy.

[*Comment. Before you accept this claim, however, examine numerous further examples of this overloaded sort from one or another of the languages.*]

4.5.2 Nominals with more than one determiner. Now let us take the following example:

	Def. art. det.	Quant. det.	Head	Clausal modifier
Fr	les	trois	plages	que nous avons vues
Sp	las	tres	playas	que hemos visto
Po	as	três	praias	que vimos
It	le	tre	spiagge	che abbiamo visto
Ro	cele	trei	plaje	pe care le-am văzut

In this pattern the first determiner must be the definite article or a demonstrative (i.e. [+def]), the second a quantifier.[18] We further note, at once, that if not a relative clause as illustrated, then at least a genitive nominal such as Fr *de cette île* etc., is an indispensable constituent of this sort of nominal; a mere *les trois plages* etc. is not semantically self-contained. Some essential element of the discourse context is unrecoverable without the modifier, which alone gives the necessary clue to an already expressed, or at any rate presupposed, locution containing just *trois plages*, such as *Nous avons vu trois plages* or *Cette île n'a que trois plages*. We therefore conclude that *trois* quantifies *plages* alone, while the definite article determines the entire phrase. There is thus some sort of hierarchical inner structure here, in view of which it may be best to take the NP *trois plages*, rather than just the noun *plages*, as the head in this type of complex, supercharged nominal having a head within a head.[19]

In all our languages the [+pl] personal pronouns, including the honorifics and the substitutes, may enter into construction with a following cardinal quantifier:

Fr   nous trois, vous cinq, eux sept
Sp   nosotros tres, vosotros cinco, ellos siete, ustedes diez
Po   nós três, vós cinco, eles sete, vocês dez
It   noi tre, voi cinque, loro (Loro) sette
Ro   noi trei, voi cinci, ei şapte, dumneavoastră zece

Since Sp *ellos*, say, is a substitute for any [+def] masc. nominal such as *los cuatro generales*, it seems to follow that *ellos cuatro* is a partial substitute for *los cuatro generales* and that, in consequence, any of the foregoing Pro + cardinal phrases are in fact supercharged nominals analogous to those described at the head of this section.

[*Query. Do you feel inclined to accept this analysis, or if not, have you a counterproposal?*]

4.6 Coordinated nominals. In all our languages, a device resorted to at every syntactic level—phrasal, clausal, sentential—is that of COORDINATION. Any two (or more) coordinated structures are independent of one another, as opposed to the subordination of one construction to another in the process of embedding. The prime means of coordinating given structures, at whatever level, is the minor part of speech we have labeled COORDINATING CONJUNCTION; since we shall not be using the term 'subordinating conjunction', we may safely speak simply of CONJUNCTIONS. The three all-purpose conjunctions which function at every level are:

Fr	Sp	Po	It	Ro
et	y	e	e	şi
ni	ni	nem	nè	nici
ou	o	ou	o	sau

These conjunctions serve to cordinate any type of nominal, in most cases regardless of the function of that nominal in a higher construction. We limit ourselves here to examples with the two conjunctions—the COPULATIVE and the ALTERNATIVE—which occur with complete freedom:

Fr   la lune et les étoiles, Marie et Joseph, vous et moi, du café ou du
     thé, toi ou elle
Sp   la luna y las estrellas, María y José, usted y yo, café o té, tú o
     ella
Po   a luna e as estrelas, Maria e José, você e eu, café ou chá, tu ou ela
It   la luna e le stelle, Maria e Giuseppe, voi ed io, caffè o tè, tu o lei
Ro   luna şi stelele, Maria şi Iosef, Dvs şi eu, cafea sau ceai, tu sau ea

Either copulative or alternative coordination may be reinforced/intensified by placing the same conjunction before both elements, e.g. Fr *et toi et moi, ou ceci ou cela*, Sp *y tú y yo, o esto o eso*, and so on.[20]
When more than two nominals are coordinated in a series, the conjunction is normally inserted before the last nominal only, as in Fr *le soleil, la terre et*

les autres planètes, or Sp *tú, yo o nadie*, and so on. The first two (or more) nominals in such a series, while no word intervenes between them, are nevertheless separated by a perceptible 'break', or pause, in the overall intonation, of a sort characterized in 16.2. Further references to coordination will be made as appropriate at the ends of subsequent chapters.

Notes for Chapter 4

1. As seen in this Roumanian example, the subtype can include PNPs with place names as heads, though PNPs with person names, as well as ProPs of any type, are excluded.

2. Even *Monsieur Durand, Madame Landré* etc. fit this pattern, with the possessive article replacing the expected definite article, even in direct address. For a description of possessive substitutions in the determiner, see 4.3. Roumanian employs the vocative suffix *-e ~ -le* for direct address with masculine titles only, e.g. *Bună ziua, Domnule Ionescu!*

3. We hold to this comprehensive label rather than 'genitive suffix' because it also serves to mark indirect complements (i.e. it has dative function) in the clause.

4. Both the gen./dat. suffix and the definite article 'hop' to the next-right element, the surface outcome being the same no matter which suffix be said to move first.

5. Although masculine person names (*Dan, Sandu, Grigore . . .*) as well as feminines not ending in the *-a* which is superficially the enclitic definite article, cannot directly receive the oblique suffix, they are nevertheless [+ def], for they can be 'obliqued' through preposing of the function-clitic *lui*, as in *ocupaţia lui Sandu*. Use of this clitic with the names of the months, as in *începutul lui Iunie* 'le commencement de juin' confirms the status of these items as masculine person names, grammatically speaking.

6. The Roumanian possessive adjective is subject to the same constraint as stated above regarding the use of the genitive article *al*.

7. The French gloss for Sp *lo mío* points to the equivalent phrases in the other languages, all using embedded (relative) clauses as modifiers of these pronouns: Fr *ce qui est à moi*, Po *o que é meu*, It *ciò che è mio*, Ro *ce este al meu*. We shall see that the superficially ambiguous Fr *le mien* is a different structure, as are also Po *o meu* and It *il mio* with their possible abstract meanings of 'ce qui est à moi' achieved through nominalization of the possessive adjective. As we shall have occasion to note, Spanish differs from the rest in its parallel use of adjectival modifiers—e.g. *lo viejo* as against Fr *ce qui est vieux*, Po *o que è velho*, and so on, again offset by the structurally different Fr *le vieux*, Po *o velho*, It *il vecchio* with the adjectives nominalized in reference to an abstract *quality*.

8. The expected **unul al meu* is not well-formed and gives way to the referentially similar *unul dintre ai mei*, a reduction of *unul dintre vării mei*.

9. A construction such as *un mien cousin*, embodying a hypothetical

reduction of a genitive modifier in *un cousin à moi*, is rejected by present-day speakers of French as old-fashioned; they prefer simply *un de mes cousins*; cf. the parallel existence, in Port/Ital, of *um meu primo* and *um dos meus primos* (etc.)—pairs embodying a minimal referential as well as structural contrast.

10. The fact that the article is written as one word with *quel* but not with *mien* has no bearing on the question; it is a mere accident of orthographic history.

11. *Tău* does not replace the honorific [+2nd−pl] personal *dumneata*, nor *vostru* the honorific [+2nd+pl] *dumneavoastră*; thus only the original obliqued forms of these honorifics function as genitive modifiers, e.g. *părinţii dumitale* 'tes parents', *adresa dumneavoastră* 'votre adresse'.

12. Traditionally, Ro *lor*, cognate to be sure of Fr *leur*, It *loro*, is included among the possessive substitutes. But *lor* is actually the obliqued form of the plural substitutes masc. *ei* and fem. *ele*, and it is therefore sounder to say that the Pattern B replacement is simply not available in this environment.

13. In Roumanian the definite article is deleted because of a surface syntactic constraint on nouns as objects of prepositions when they have no other attribute; cf. *puţine din bisericile astea* or the like.

14. It might be tempting to argue that delimiting modifiers are in fact a subtype of genitive modifier, for they do play a not dissimilar semantic role: in such a nominal as Sp *uno de mis amigos*, say, the *uno (amigo)* does somehow 'belong' in—or to, in the sense of forming part of—the whole group of *mis amigos*. It must be noted, however, that while *uno de mis amigos* is replaceable by *uno de ellos* but not reducible to *uno suyo* in this case, by contrast *un amigo de mis amigos* can reduce all the way to *uno suyo* but not, in this instance, to *uno de mis amigos* nor *uno de ellos*. On the other hand, [−animate] genitive and delimiting modifiers are accessible to one and the same form of clitic reduction in Fren/Ital, as we indicate in 12.1.5 [*Query. What is your view?*]

15. In addition, Portuguese optionally inserts *um* after *qualquer*, while Spanish adds the empty suffix *-a* to the corresponding determiner: Sp *cualquiera de Vds.*, Po *qualquer (um) de vocês*.

16. This Roumanian suffixal marker, although it has the surface form of the definite article, has neither its function nor its meaning.

17. Ro *întîi* is a specifier, basically interchangeable with *prim* but favored over it in certain expressions including this type.

18. Any cardinal works, but there are various constraints on the indefinites. Italian accepts *molto, poco, troppo,* and *tanto*; Span/Port the corresponding four. French is unique in allowing *quelque* (normally in a plural phrase) and otherwise accepts only *peu* (including indeed the DetP *quelque peu*), with the latter seemingly nominalized as in the DetP *un peu de* and therefore blocking the definite article's agreement with the head (thus always *le peu de* + any head). Roumanian accepts only *puţin*, which in turn takes

the definite article suffixally (*puţinele plaje . . .,*) as against a form of *cel* such as must occur when the following word (e.g. a cardinal) is not privileged to accept the suffix.

19. Just two of our languages, Span/ Roum, exhibit another type of nominal with two determiners, namely, the definite article and a demonstrative, e.g. Sp *el hombre ése*, Ro *omul acela*. Unlike the complex types just discussed, these are semantically self-sufficient and may appear to be transformations of the singly determined *ese hombre*, Ro *acel om* by a simple extraposition which puts the demonstrative into the modifier slot of a descriptive adjective while leaving the trace of the [+def] feature in the added definite article. This variant with both definite article and postposed demonstrative is stylistically marked in Spanish; but in Roumanian it is actually more current than the simpler phrase in the spoken standard, even when another adjectival modifier is also present, as in *maşina aceea veche* 'cette vieille voiture'. In any case the accent-mark over *ése* and the suffix -*a* on *acela* identify that variant of the demonstrative which occurs in the environment of a deleted head, and this suggests the possibility that instead of extraposition we are looking at an underlyingly nominal modifier reduced by deletion of an equivalent head, thus:

Sp el + hombre + ese hombre → el + hombre + ése [↓]
Ro omu + l + acel om → omu + l + acel + a [↓]

This analysis is supported by the incidence, in Roumanian alone, of a nominal construction of the type *omul cel bogat*, meaning the (specific) *rich* man within a delimited field of men and in opposition to mere *omul bogat* referring to either the rich man generically or else merely to the rich *man*. And here again, in view of the specific function of *cel* as a definite article variant in the absence of a head (see 1.5.1), the most likely derivation would seem to be: (head) *omu + l +* (mod) *omu + l + bogat* → *omu + l + cel +* [↓] + *bogat*. This derivation may also receive independent support from nominals with superlative adjectival modifiers, which contain two definite articles not only in Ro *omul cel mai bogat* but also in Fr *l'homme le plus riche*. Cf. 6.1.

20. When nominals with the same head but different attributes (e.g. Sp *esta mesa* and *esa mesa* or whatever) are coordinated, it is customary to reduce the (redundant) head of the second phrase by deletion, as in Fr *cette maison-ci et celle de mes parents*, or *la voiture noire ou la bleue*; Sp *esta casa y la de mis padres*, or *el coche negro o el azul*, etc.

Adjectival Structures
Chapter 5
The adjective phrase

5.0 Internal structure of the adjective phrase (AdjP). This chapter discusses the internal structure of the adjective phrase (AdjP). Basically, this construction is the same in all five languages and consists of an adjective as obligatory head and of attributes divided into optional QUANTIFIER and optional COMPLEMENT. The order of constituents is shown in the formula:

AdjP → (quantifier) head (complement).

To take a very simple example: in the French AdjP *trop plein de surprises*, the head is, of course, the adjective *plein*, the quantifier is *trop* and the complement is *de surprises*.

5.1 Adjectives as heads. Unlike the common noun with its optional morpheme of plurality, the adjective boasts no morphemic paradigm. Underlyingly it consists of stem only, and the suffixal inflections which it systematically displays cannot be characterized as morphemes in any strict sense, for they are totally devoid of lexical meaning. They are simply surface markers confirming, so to speak, the syntactic relationship of an adjective to the noun with which it stands in construction, whether intraphrasally (as within the same nominal) or extraphrasally (as in separate phrases within a higher, clausal construction). This manner of signaling is customarily termed either AGREEMENT or CONCORD.

The adjectives of each language fall neatly into two morphophonemic classes, in both of which concord with a masculine singular head is signaled only by the absence of any suffix at all. One of the classes takes just one ending, which matches (or 'copies', as many linguists now put it) only the number morpheme of the pluralized NP, regardless of the head noun's gender, as illustrated in Table 5.1 for Spanish.

Table 5.1

	Masculine	Feminine
Singular:	caso grave	cosa grave
Plural:	caso*s* grave*s*	cosa*s* grave*s*[2]

The second class, depending on the language, uses either a two-ending system, with a sibilant consonant to match plural number and a vowel to match feminine gender, as characteristic of Fr/Sp/Po and illustrated in Table 5.2 for Portuguese, or a three-ending system, all vocalic: one vowel for

Table 5.2

	Masculine	Feminine
Singular:	gato branco	*casa* branc*a*
Plural:	gato*s* branco*s*	*casas* branc*as*

fem. singular, a second for masc. plural, and a third for fem. plural, as characteristic of It/Ro as illustrated in Table 5.3 for Italian.

Table 5.3

	Masculine	Feminine
Singular:	padre buono	*madre* buon*a*
Plural:	*padri* buon*i*	*madri* buon*e*

Beyond these generalizations, the morphophonemics of concord inflection in adjectives must be stated in terms of the phonological structure of each individual language; no further relevant contrastive data will emerge. While for purposes of description it is convenient, perhaps even necessary, to segment off the concord endings, the fact remains that adjective stem and suffix are morphemically one. There is no contrast among, say, the French words *petit, petits, petite,* and *petites*: these are four surface alternants of one and the same basic morpheme, in complementation relative to the noun (or pronoun) with which they stand in construction.

[*Comment. Appendix 2 offers a brief account of those Italian adjectives which function as determiners in the CNP, and Appendix 3 provides an equally concise description of adjective inflection in French. These presentations will serve you as models for corresponding descriptions of adjective inflection in the other languages.*]

Of considerable lexical and syntactic import are the so-called participial adjectives, derived within the lexicon from verbs by suffixation. These come in two subsets, one of which may be designated as ACTIVE and the other by contrast as PASSIVE. Many grammarians label them, respectively, 'present participles' and 'past participles', but by synchronic criteria these are misnomers—not only because the former term is often applied alternatively to the deverbal adverb, or GERUND (see 13.3), but also because semantically the two forms do not stand in a tense-like present/past relationship at all: either one denotes an act or state unspecified as to its time of occurrence. Each is, however, specified for the semantic feature [±passive]. The [−passive], i.e. active, adjective is derived with the suffix Fr/Ro -*nt*, Sp/Po/It -*nte*, as in Fr *existant*, Sp/Po *existente*, It *esistente*, Ro *existent*, from the verb *exister/ existir* etc., and the process is restricted to relatively few verbs.[3] The [+passive] adjective, on the other hand, is derived with an ending phonologically identical to the function-suffix of the true PARTICIPLE that every verb has (although at the surface the adj. copies agreement), namely, one or another vowel in French, *-do* in Span/Port, *-to* in Italian, *-t* in Roumanian. Every transitive verb[4] affords this passive adjective, whether or not its active counterpart also exists—e.g. Fr *connu*, Sp *conocido*, Po *conhecido*, It *conosciuto*, Ro *cunoscut*, from the verb *connaître/conocer* etc.[5]

5.2 Quantifiers in the AdjP. The quantifying function in the adjective phrase (AdjP) is filled by (1) words of quantity (5.2.1), (2) an evaluative quantifier phrase (5.2.2), (3) a comparative quantifier phrase (5.2.3), (4) a superlative quantifier phrase (5.2.4), (5) adverbialized adjectives and derived adverbs in Fr *-ment*, Sp/Po/It *-mente* (5.2.5), and (6) nominals functioning as quantifiers for semantically measurable heads.

5.2.1 Words of quantity. The words of quantity are the same lexical items as the adverbs in French, and the adjectives or adverbs in the other languages, which function as quantifying determiners in the CNP, with the following variations—lexical, surface-syntactic, or merely morphophonemic—language by language.

• In French, *très* or *fort* supplants *beaucoup*, as in *très utile* or *fort étrange*; *si* takes the place of *tant*, and *aussi* that of *autant*, as in *si gentil*, *aussi récent*;[6] there is no counterpart to *combien*.

• In Spanish, *mucho*, *tanto*, and *cuánto* are apocopated to *muy*, *tan*, and *cuán*, respectively (though not if the head adj. is reduced by deletion), as in *muy amable*, *tan difícil*, *cuán estrecho*.[7]

• In Portuguese, *muito* is apocopated to *mui* before a polysyllabic head, as in *mui razoável* 'muy razonable'; and *tanto*, *quanto* are apocopated to *tão*, *quão* (unless the head is deleted), as in *tão comprido* 'tan largo', *quão estreito*;[7] *demasiado* is always excluded in favor of its post-head rival *demais*, as in *jovem demais*.

• In Italian, the adverb *così* is essentially interchangeable with the adjective *tanto*, as in *così debole* = *tanto debole* 'tan débil'; there is no counterpart to *quanto*.

• In Roumanian, *foarte* supplants *mult* as in *foarte greu* 'très pesant'; *prea* and *mai*, being adverbs in any case, do not require the adj *mult* to follow them, as in *prea tîrziu* 'trop tard' or *mai fericit* 'más feliz' (cf., however, *mai puțin fericit* 'menos feliz'); *destul*, *atît* and *cît*, being adjectives, require insertion of the functor *de* before the head, as in *destul de ieftin* 'bastante barato', *atît de bun* 'tan bueno', *cît de scurt* 'cuán corto'.[8]

Just as in the CNP (see Table 1.1, Remark 12), the item *peu/poco/pouco/puțin* can be preceded by one of the evaluative quantifiers, as in It *troppo poco sincero* or whatever. The adjectives of extreme degree derived with the Sp/Po/It suffix *-ísimo* (et al.) are not available for the present function. On the other hand, the CNP *un peu/un poco/um pouco/un po'* is much in use—without the *de/di* which links it to a noun head (cf. Fr *un peu de vin* vs. *un peu sec*)—except in Roumanian, where **un puţin* does not exist and *puţin* serves for either 'peu' or 'un peu', usually clear from the lexical collocation (e.g. *puţin sincer* as against *puţin bolnav* 'un peu malade') and frequently reinforced in the latter meaning by the adverb *cam*, as in *puţin cam scump* 'un peu cher'; *cam* also functions here in its own right, with the nonevaluative meaning 'assez/bastante', as in *cam delicat* etc.

5.2.2 Evaluative quantifier phrases. There is also the evaluative quantifier phrase within the AdjP, exactly analogous to the evaluative determiner phrase in the CNP (cf. 1.3.4), e.g.:

Fr	assez mûr pour comprendre	trop timide pour essayer
Sp	bastante pequeño para tu dedo	demasiado joven para casarse
Po	bastante duro para resistir	velho demais para estudar
It	abbastanza ricco per me	troppo difficile per gli studenti
Ro	destul de mare pentru cinci	prea complicat pentru un copil
	'assez grand pour cinq'	'trop compliqué pour un enfant'

5.2.3 Comparative quantifier phrases. As for the comparative quantifier phrase within the AdjP, it is wholly analogous to the comparative determiner phrase in the CNP (cf. 1.3.4); its description is deferred to Chapter 14 for the same reason—viz. Sp *más pobre* (or *menos pobre* or *tan pobre*), or whatever, is meaningless without some attribute, as in *(Juan es) más pobre que José*—the context often permitting deletion of the attribute.

5.2.4 Superlative quantifier phrases. The superlative quantifier phrase, on the other hand, has no analogue in the CNP. Its head is a two-word string consisting of one of the adverbs of quantity *plus/más* etc. or *moins/menos* etc. preceded by the definite article in a special nondeterminative rôle. Its attribute is either a prepositional phrase opened by Fr/Sp/Po *de*, It *di*, Ro *din*, as in for example:

Fr le plus beau de ma vie
Sp el más bello de mi vida
Po o mais belo da minha vida
It il più bello della mia vita
Ro cel mai frumos din viaţa mea

or a relative clause of the sort to be described in 14.

5.2.5 Adverbialized adjectives and derived adverbs in Fr *-ment*, Sp/Po/It *-mente*. In all but Roumanian, most adjectives qualifying as heads of AdjPs are also adverbialized in the lexicon with the suffix Fr *-ment*, Sp/Po/It *-mente*.[9] This sort of item, often semantically more of a 'qualifier' than a 'quantifier', functions as such in many an AdjP—e.g. Fr *extrêmement riche,* *horriblement laid*, Sp *extremamente rico, horriblemente feo*, Po *extremamente rico, horrìvelmente feio*, It *estremamente ricco, orribilmente brutto*. Roumanian, lacking this adverbializing suffix, simply uses the appropriate adjective itself, linked to the head in the manner of an adverb by the functor *de*, e.g. *extrem de bogat, grozav de urît*. Fr/Sp *bien*, Po *bem*, It *ben(e)*, Ro *bine*, and Fr/Sp/Po *mal*, It *mal(e)*, may be regarded as the adverbial counterparts of *bon/bueno* . . . and *mauvais/malo* . . ., respectively; the heads which they quantify include especially often the [+passive] adjectives touched on just above, e.g. Fr *bien construit*, Sp *bien construido*, etc.

5.2.6 Nominals functioning as quantifiers for semantically measurable heads. Nominals functioning as quantifiers in AdjPs may accompany heads which refer semantically to a measurable characteristic such as height or length. The nominal quantifier is itself quantified, i.e. its head denotes a unit of measure determined by its own (typically cardinal) quantifier, as in the following examples:

Fr haut de cinq mètres, long de plusieurs pieds
Sp cinco metros de alto, unos cuantos pies de largo
Po *
It alto cinque metri, lungo parecchi piedi
Ro înalt de cinci metri, lung de mai multe picioare

It is to be observed that in Fr/It/Ro but not Spanish[10] the quantifier is obligatorily moved into the complement position right of the head, and that in all but Italian the quantifier and the head are linked by the functor *de* regardless of the order.

5.3 Complements in the AdjP. Like modifiers in the CNP (cf. 1.4), these constituents are best seen as expansions of the basic structure, their function being performed by one or another dependent construction.[11] Such constructions embeddable within the AdjP in our languages are:
(a) adverb phrases of the type traditionally called prepositional,
(b) clauses.
For the same reason as given in connection with embedded constructions as modifiers in CNPs, transient examples must suffice at this point:
(a) Fr plein d'eau froide, certain de l'adresse, contraire à la nature, préparé pour la mort, détruit par les barbares, situé dans la ville
    Sp lleno de agua fría, cierto de la dirección, contrario a la naturaleza, preparado para la muerte, destruido por los bárbaros, situado en la ciudad
    Po cheio de água fria, certo do endereço, contrário à natureza, preparado para a morte, destruido pelos bárbaros, situado na cidade

It pieno di acqua fredda, certo dell'indirizzo, contrario alla na-
tura, preparato per la morte, distrutto dai barbari, situato
nella città

Ro plin de apă frigă, sigur de adresă, contrar la natură, pregătit
pentru moarte, distrus de barbari, situat în oraş

(b) Fr content de rester à la maison; sûr qu'il va pleuvoir

Sp contento de quedarse en casa; seguro de que va a llover

Po contente de ficar em casa; seguro (de) que vai chover

It contento di restare a casa; sicuro che pioverà

Ro bucuros să rămîn acasă; sigur că va ploua

Notes for Chapter 5

1. Determiners are deliberately excluded from these examples.

2. Cf. also *la cosa es grave* vs. *las cosas son graves*, where the adjective is outside the phrase containing the noun.

3. More than the other languages, Roumanian uses instead the suffix *-tor*, which matches Fr *-eur*, Sp/Po *-dor*, It *-tore*—primarily a nominalizing suffix but also potentially adjectivalizing as in, say, Fr *rêveur* (n. or adj.) or Sp *soñador*.

4. For the definition of a transitive verb see 9.3.

5. In a few Span/Port instances, where the typical [−passive] form is missing, the form derived with *-do* can be either [+passive] or [−passive], with the ambiguity resolved only by context—e.g. *divertido*, corresponding to both Fr/It *divertissant/divertente* and Fr/It *diverti/divertito*.

6. Note also Fr *il fait très froid (chaud . . .)* and *j'ai très froid (chaud . . .)*, as well as *j'ai très soif (faim, peur, sommeil . . .)*. *Froid, chaud* etc. are adjectives, and as such they are quantified by *très* rather than *beaucoup* even when nominalized as objects of *faire* when predicating weather, or of *avoir* when predicating a felt sensation. *Soif, faim, peur* et al. are, of course, bona fide nouns, yet as objects of *avoir* in this pattern they analogically take *très* instead of the expected *beaucoup*. Cf. also *j'ai si faim que . . .* rather than **j'ai tant de faim que . . .*

7. These Span/Port items, lacking counterparts altogether in Fren/Ital, are decidedly obsolescent though still available for use in certain elevated styles.

8. The adjective *atît* has an almost exact equivalent in the adverb *aşa*, which requires *de* (no doubt for symmetry) as in *aşa de elegant = atît de elegant*. Either *atît* or *aşa* may be preceded by the all-purpose *tot* to yield the distinction provided by Fr *si* vs. *aussi* (e.g. Ro *tot atît de urgent =* Fr *aussi urgent*).

9. The Roumanian lexicon does contain, in effect, a handful of adverbs like *generalmente* or *principalmente*, but they are not derived by a productive process from corresponding adjectives; they are simply independent

lexical items. None of them happens to qualify semantically for the function in view here.

10. Portuguese has only NPs such as *cinco metros de altura*, which Spanish also has, the AdjP in question being a resultant blend such that the quantifier stands in first position.

11. See the opening statement of 1.4, and especially note 11.

Chapter 6
Dependent adjectivals functioning as modifiers within NPs

6.0 Introduction. Dependent adjectivals function as modifiers within NPs. We are now in a position to examine these structures.

6.1 Basic position of modifier. Like all other modifiers in the CNP, an AdjP basically follows the head as in Fr *une leçon très facile*, Sp *una lección muy fácil*, Po *uma lição muito fácil*, It *una lezione molto facile*, Ro *o lecţie foarte uşoară*. If the AdjP is a superlative quantifier (see 5.2.4), the definite article in construction with the quantifying adverb also copies the gender/ number of the head noun in French and Roumanian, as in Fr *la leçon la plus facile . . .*, Ro *lecţia cea mai uşoară . . .*, whereas in the other three languages this definite article, rather than echo the article determining the matrix NP, is suppressed as in Sp *la lección más fácil . . .*, Po *a lição mais fácil . . .*, It *la lezione più facile . . .*[1] The attribute in a superlative quantifier often merely echoes the head noun of the matrix phrase, as in, say, Fr *l'étudiant le plus intelligent + des étudiants de la classe*, in which case the attribute may undergo partial deletion, leaving in place only the informationally important remnant *de la classe* or whatever.[2]

6.2 Extraposition of modifier. In all the Romance languages, on the other hand, many an adjectival modifier—either bare or with a superlative quantifier—when it carries old or presupposed or otherwise nonrestrictive information, may in the surface output be extrapositioned between the determiner and the head, in the slot (and even function?) of a specifier, as, for example, in Fr *une belle dame*, Sp *un famoso general*, It *la bianca neve*, or the like, though not **une moderne langue/una moderna lengua* or so; also, say, Fr *les plus beaux tableaux*, Sp *la más linda mujer*, Ro *cele mai înalte sentimente*, etc., but not, say, **les plus riches commerçants/los más ricos negociantes*.[3] The stylistic, semantic, or lexical factors and constraints, subtle and complex, which govern this sort of adjectival extraposition vary quite considerably from language to language; probably few across-the-board generalizations are valid.[4] Two, however, seem fairly safe:

• A handful of high-frequency adjectives that come in polarized lexical pairs of the sort illustrated by *bon ≠ mauvais*, or *grand ≠ petit*, or *jeune ≠ vieux* in French, very commonly surface left of the head when no contrast or association with the opposite sector of the range is implied. Thus Fr *une bonne idée* does not rely, for part of its message, on an association with *une mauvaise idée*, nor does *um grande abraço* in Portuguese suggest that a letter might alternatively be closed with '*um pequeno abraço*'. Some of these two-word combinations—a lone adjective plus a noun—may well be already constituted at the lexical level rather than at the phrase level; at least for French this is shown clearly enough to be the case because before them the partitive article is not reduced to *de* as is the rule when an adjectival modifier or a specifier precedes the head—e.g. *des jeunes filles* or *des petits enfants* as against *d'autres gens, de tels idiots, de jolies chansons*.[5]

• In PNPs, characterizing adjectivals are always lone adjectives and are always moved left because of the nonrestrictive principle—there is no other *Jean* than the one characterized as *notre pauvre Jean*, no other *Italia* than *la vecchia Italia*.[6]

Notes for Chapter 6

1. The deletion in question evidently takes place at the surface prior to any replacement of the matrix definite article by a possessive determiner in Spanish, as in *mis amigos más íntimos*.

2. On the other hand if the head noun is deleted for discourse reasons, the echo within the attribute tends to remain in place, as in Fr *[ ] le plus intelligent des étudiants (de la classe)*, or Sp *el [ ] más noble de (todos) los hombres*.

3. If a superlative AdjP thus precedes the head, such that in French or Roumanian the two definite articles involved would occur juxtaposed, then one of them is automatically deleted as in *les bateaux + les plus grands →
les + les plus grands bateaux → les plus grands bateaux. In the foregoing Roumanian example, the retained article is a form of *cel*, not because the matrix article is in fact the one suppressed, but because in any case the quantifier *mai* is ineligible to receive the definite suffix.

4. [*Comment. A worthwhile project would be to extract as much information as possible on 'adjective position' from a reference grammar of each language separately, in order to discover just how fully and deeply the tendencies are shared.*]

5. A few adjectives standing before the head are perhaps to be thought of as actually embodied in the determiner as specifier rather than as modifier at all (see 1.3.2). Thus in Sp *una nueva botella* the contrast is clear with *una botella núeva:* the former is not very different in meaning from *otra botella*

(más), whereas the latter implies that the bottle is the opposite of *vieja*. Fr *ancien* is the descriptive opposite of *moderne* in *l'histoire ancienne*, but has nothing more than the limiting notion of 'former' in *l'ancien régime*. [*Query. What about the adjectives Fr pauvre, Sp/ Po pobre etc., which in each of our languages means 'malheureux/infeliz' or 'pas riche/no rico' according to its position?*]

6. Adjectivals may be coordinated by a copulative or alternative conjunction, as in Fr *vert ou jaune, assez jolie et très aimable, plus court et plus facile*; Sp *verde o amarillo, bastante linda y muy amable, más corto y más fácil*, and so on, as well as by a third type of conjunction, the ADVERSATIVE— Fr *mais*, Sp *pero* (less usually *mas*), Po *mas*, It *ma*, Ro *însă* (also *dar* or *iar*)—as, for example, in Fr *beau mais très cher*, Sp *hermoso pero muy caro*, Po *formoso mas muito caro*, It *bello ma molto caro*, Ro *frumos însă foarte scump*.

Adverbial Structures
Chapter 7
The adverb phrase

7.0 Internal structure of the adverb phrase (AdvP). This chapter discusses the internal structure of the adverb phrase (AdvP). Basically, this is the same in all five languages, and consists of an adverb as obligatory head, of optional quantifiers, and of complements. The order of constituents is shown in the formula

AdvP → (quantifier) head ± complement.

The sign '±' means, of course, that some heads can or must be followed by a complement, others not. To take a very simple example: in the French AdvP *très loin de son pays*, the head is the adverb *loin*, the quantifier is *très*, and the complement is *de son pays*.

7.1 Adverbs as heads. Unlike the noun, the adjective, or the verb, the adverb displays no morphological paradigm at any level; both underlyingly and at the surface it consists of stem only. The adverbializing suffix *-ment(e)*, which is added to adjectives as already indicated in 5.2.5, is derivational rather than inflectional and operates in the lexicon, not in the grammar.[1]

In addition to what are universally recognized as 'adverbs' (e.g. Fr *maintenant*, Sp *ahora*, Po *agora*, It *adesso*, Ro *acum*), each of our five languages has in its lexicon a sizeable number of items traditionally classified as 'prepositions' and another considerable number labeled 'conjunctions', the latter subdivided into coordinating and subordinating conjunctions, or coordinators and subordinators. In reality, the two subclasses of 'conjunctions' have nothing whatever in common: coordinators make up a (minor) part of speech in their own right, while the subordinators and prepositions have so much in common syntactically with each other and with adverbs that they both may be included in the one part of speech we are labeling adverbs. The argument in favor of this option runs as follows.

An adverb in the traditional sense is not followed typically by a dependent construction in the way that a preposition is followed by a nominal or clause functioning as its 'object' (e.g. Fr *pour + le moment* or *pour + vivre en paix*) or that a subordinator is followed by a (finite) clause (e.g. Fr *pour que + l'on sache cela*). Nevertheless, adverbs, 'prepositional phrases' and 'subordinate clauses' (i.e. subordinators plus dependent, also called embedded, clauses) fulfill one and the same function—namely, that of complement or modifier within a higher phrase or clause. The fact remains, moreover, that most traditional subordinators consist precisely of (i) a preposition-like or adverb-like word followed by the functor Fr/Sp/Po *que*, It *che*, Ro *că* (or *ce* or *ca*)—be they written separately, as in Fr *pour que* or Sp/Po *para que*, or singly, as in Sp/Po *porque* or It *perchè*—or of (ii) just that functor alone. And since the presence/absence of *que/che/că* itself is syntactically conditioned—i.e. it introduces an embedded clause and nothing else—items such as Fr *pour* and *pour que*, Sp/Po *por* and *porque* are in complementary distribution. By this line of reasoning, 'subordinators' as a basic part of speech simply disappear. This leaves us with just 'prepositions' and 'adverbs', and indeed these also are in syntactic complementation: a 'preposition' is TRANSITIVE, i.e. it is followed by an object (be it phrase or clause); while an 'adverb' is INTRANSITIVE, i.e. it is not followed by an object. In line with this state of affairs we shall find it advantageous simply to subdivide adverbs as heads into three syntactic classes:

• Adv-1 will consist of traditional prepositions and subordinators, characterizable as transitive adverbs after which an object is required—e.g. Fr *pour*, Sp/Po *para*, It *per*, Ro *pentru*. There is nothing to be lost in continuing to label these adv-1s as prepositions in the surface structure, and this we shall in fact do.[2]

• Adv-2 will comprise those items which—like such verbs as Fr *chanter* or *manger*—may but need not take an object[3]—e.g. Fr *près*, Sp *cerca*, Po *perto*, It *presso*, Ro *aproape*.[4] We label these as adverb/prepositions.

• Adv-3 will consist of fully intransitive adverbs, i.e. adverbs 'proper' which we may label simply as adverbs. The nonderived lexical items resident in each class are a closed, finite list. Although the exact inventory of each class varies considerably from language to language, we nevertheless endeavor to represent the three common cores in Tables 7.1, 7.2, and 7.3. A double entry in one or another language column means that the semantic range of the set in question is somehow apportioned between the two variants, or that they are essentially interchangeable. It can also happen that a given item belongs to a class other than that in which it is tabulated; in such a case the item is flagged, as for example Fr *avec* (2) in Table 7.1 or Ro *după* (1) in Table 7.2.

Table 7.1 Common core of Class 1 adverbs (adv-1) (prepositions). (The French entry serves as gloss.)

French	Spanish	Portuguese	Italian	Roumanian
á	a	a	a	la
de	de	de	di, da	de
en, dans	en	em	in	în, din
avec (2)	con	com	con	cu
sans	sin	sem	senza	fără
par	por	por	per, da	prin, de
pour	para	para	per	pentru
sur	sobre, en	sobre, em	su	pe, despre
sous	bajo	sob	sotto	sub
dès	desde	desde	da	de
entre	entre	entre	fra = tra	între, dintre
jusque	hasta	até	fino = sino	pînă
vers	hacia	para	verso	spre, către
contre (2)	contra	contra	contro	contra

Morphophonemic alternations are undergone by certain of these adverbs in the environment of various complements—specifically, Po *de, em, por;* It *di, in, per, con;* Ro *în.* The processes involved are, however, independent of each other.

Table 7.2 Common core of Class 2 adverbs (adv-2) (preposition/adverbs).

French	Spanish	Portuguese	Italian	Roumanian
après	después	depois	dopo	după (1)
avant	antes	antes	avanti, prima	dinainte
devant	delante	diante	davanti	înainte
derrière	detrás	detrás	dietro	înapoi
au-dessous	encima[5]	encima[5]	sopra	deasupra
au-dessus	debajo	debaixo	sotto	dedesubt
dedans (3)[6]	dentro	dentro	dentro	înauntru
dehors (3)[6]	fuera	fora	fuori	afară
autour	alrededor	arredor	intorno	împrejur
au-delà	allende	além	al di là	dincolo
près	cerca	perto	presso, vicino	aproape
loin	lejos	longe	lontano	departe
à peine	apenas	apenas	appena	abia (3)

Table 7.3 Common core of Class 3 adverbs (adv-3) (adverbs proper).

	French	Spanish	Portuguese	Italian	Roumanian
Of time:	aujourd'hui	hoy	hoje	oggi	azi = astăzi
	hier	ayer	ontem	ieri	ieri
	demain	mañana	amanhã	domani	mîine
	toujours	siempre	sempre	sempre	totdeauna, mereu
	jamais	nunca = jamás	nunca = jamais	mai = giammai	niciodată
	déjà	ya	já	già	şi, deja
	souvent	a menudo	amiúde	spesso	des, adesea
	tôt	pronto	logo, breve	tosto	curînd
	tard	tarde	tarde	tardi	tîrziu
	de bonne heure	temprano	cedo	presto	devreme
(dem.)	maintenant	ahora	agora	adesso	acum
(dem.)	alors	entonces	então	allora	atunci
(Q)	quand	cuándo	quando	quando	cînd
Of place:	dessous	abajo	em baixo	disotto	dedesubt (2)
	en bas	"	"	giù	jos
	dessus	arriba	encima (2)	disopra	deasupra (2)
	en haut	"	"	su	sus
	ailleurs	--	alhures	altrove	aiurea
(dem.)	ici, ci, çà	aquí, acá	aqui, cá	qui, qua	aici = aicea
(dem.)	là	ahí, allí, allá	aí, ali, lá	lì, là	acolo, colea
(Q)	où	dónde	onde	dove	unde
Of manner:	bien	bien	bem	bene	bine
	mal	mal	mal	male	rău
	vite	aprisa	depressa	subito	repede
	ensemble	juntos	junto	insieme	împreună
(dem.)	ainsi	así	assim	così	aşa
(Q)	comment	cómo	como	come	cum
Residual	presque	casi	quase	quasi	aproape
	plus	más	mais	più	mai
	moins	menos	menos	meno	--
	aussi	también	também	anche, pure	şi, tot
	non plus	tampoco	tampouco	neanche, neppure	nici
	encore	aún, todavía	ainda, todavia	ancora	încă

[*Comment. A very challenging study project: to extract all the adverbs of one or more Romance language—excepting, of course, those which are derived from adjectives, or are merely adverbialized adjectives or nouns—and to subcategorize them according to present criteria, noting the types of complement taken by each in an AdvP, and making any relevant contrastive statements.*]

Tables 7.1, 7.2, and 7.3 enable us immediately to make the following observations:

• Adv-1s have the widest semantic ranges, some denoting either a temporal, a spatial, or some other relation according to the nature of the object; e.g. Fr *à* is temporal in *à cette heure-ci*, spatial in *à la maison*, and seemingly neither in *à mon avis*.

• Adv-2s are inherently temporal or spatial, necessarily so given their privilege of occurrence without an object; only the first two in Table 7.2 are temporal.

• Most of the adv-3s are conveniently subdivisible according as they contain semantic features of time, place, or manner. Certain members of each subset also carry a demonstrative feature, and in each there is one member of the cross-category of interrogative words (Q-words).

• The common core adv-3s of quantity does not include all the items first listed as determiners in the CNP (1.3) and again as quantifiers in the AdjP (5.2). While Fr *beaucoup, peu, trop, assez, (au)tant* and *combien* are all in effect bona fide adverbs, the corresponding words of quantity in the other languages are—except for It *abbastanza* 'assez/bastante' and Ro *prea* 'trop/ demasiado'—adjectives, not adverbs. All these adjectives can, nevertheless, be adverbialized in the syntax so as to function as modifiers in verb phrases (8.4) or clauses (9.4)—as in the simple example Sp *Juan duerme poco*, Po *João dorme pouco*, It *Gianni dorme poco*, Ro *Ion doarme puţin*. Whether the adjectives in view are also adverbialized en route to functioning as quantifiers is evidently debatable. [*Query. What is your opinion?*]

7.2 Complements in the AdvP. We shall do best to begin with these constituents, and to deal with quantifiers subsequently.

7.2.1 Complements with adv-1 (preposition) heads (transitive adverbs). After these fully transitive adverbs—still to be called prepositions with relation to surface structures, and the entire phrase to be called PREPOSITIONAL PHRASE (PrepP)—the obligatory complement is always an object. The slot is filled by the following constructions in a dependent rôle: (a) nominals, (b) adv-3s, (c) clauses. Random examples:

  (a) nominals:
    Fr   en tout cas, sans aucune trace, dès le début
    Sp   en una calle estrecha, hacia el horizonte, desde la Edad Media
    Po   com um grande abraço, até o fim do mês, sob o governo atual
    It   da tutte le parti, fra queste domande, per l'Italia
    Ro   la începutul anului, pe străzile astea, despre Ştefan cel Mare
        'au début de l'année, dans ces rues-ci, sur Étienne le Grand'
  (b) lone adv-3s of time/place, including the demonstratives and interrogatives:

Fr par-dessous, dès maintenant, jusqu'où
Sp hacia adelante, por allí, desde cuándo
Po para sempre, até logo, de aí
It per dopo, fin qui, da dove
Ro pentru azi, pînă acum, pe acolo 'pour aujourd'hui, jusqu'à maintenant, par là'

However, since some adverbials *are* privileged to fill this complement function, it seems reasonable to analyze such phrases as Fr *jusqu'au bout* or *jusque en France*, Sp *para con ustedes*, Po *para com os senhores*, It *fino a domani* or *sino d'allora*, and a plethora of Roumanian expressions (e.g. *pe lîngă aceea* 'outre cela', *pînă în prezent* 'jusqu'à présent') as constituted of *jusque + en France, para + con ustedes* etc. An alternative analysis would be phrasal head *jusque en* plus *France*, or *jusqu'à + le bout*, or *fino a + domani*, which takes the two as united in a single transitive head, perhaps already at the lexical level and as one word rather than two. [*Query. Which solution seems to you the better motivated, and why?*]

(c) clauses:

Fr sans que je m'explique, dès qu'ils seront rentrés, pour dire la vérité
Sp sin que yo quisiera, desde que te fuiste, por convencerte de esto
Po para que fossem seguros, porque não quero morrer, sem sabermos nada disto
It finchè vivremo noi, senza che essi vogliano, per comprare qualcosa
Ro pentru că eu nu vreau, fără să ştiţi nimic, pînă a primi un răspuns 'parce que je ne veux pas, sans que vous ne sachiez rien, jusqu'à recevoir une réponse'

The number of items privileged to take a clausal object is severely constrained in each language, though least so in Span/Port.[7] French permits them after *sans, dès, par, pour*, and *jusque*; Span/Port after *en/em, con/com, sin/sem, por, para, desde*, and *hasta/até*; Italian after *senza, per, da*,[8] and *fino*; Roumanian after *fără, pentru, pînă*, and *spre*. For more details see 12.6 and 13.6.

7.2.2 Complements with adv-2 (preposition/adverb) heads (partially transitive adverbs). After these partially transitive adverbs—which may be designated prepositions *or* adverbs, depending precisely on their (in)transitivity—an optional complement is always an object, with the slot filled by the same three dependent constructions as after adv-1 heads. Random examples:

(a) nominals:

Fr avant le déjeuner, devant l'école, près de Paris
Sp delante de la casa, dentro del jardín, lejos de ti
Po depois da guerra, detrás daquela igreja, perto duma praça
It prima dell'inverno, fuori le mura, vicino a me
Ro înainte de vacanţă, afară de oraşul acesta, aproape de noi 'avant les vacances, hors de cette ville, près de nous'

(b) adv-3s:
Fr avant d'aujourd'hui, après demain, loin de là
Sp antes de hoy, cerca de dónde, lejos de aquí
Po antes de hoje, perto daqui, longe de lá
It prima di oggi, dopo domani, lontano da lì
Ro înainte de azi, afară de aici, aproape de unde 'avant d'aujour-
    d'hui, hors d'ici, près d'où'
(c) clauses:
Fr avant que tu n'arrives, après avoir dîné, loin de mentir
Sp antes (de) que tú llegues, después de cenar, lejos de mentir
Po antes que tu chegues, depois de comer, longe de mentir
It prima che tu arrivi, dopo mangiato, lontano da mentire
Ro înainte să plecăm noi, după ce aţi mîncat,[9] departe de a minţi
    'avant que nous n'arrivions, après que vous aurez mangé, loin
    de mentir'

Again, the number of items which may take a clausal object is severely constrained across the board: only the first two items in Table 7.1 permit them.

7.2.3 Complements with adv-3 (adverb proper) heads (intransitive adverbs). After these intransitive adverbs, an optional complement is strictly a limiting type of attribute. Thus:

• The first three adverbs of time in Table 7.3 may be followed by a dependent nominal or adverbial specifying precisely the time of the day in question, e.g.

Fr demain matin, hier soir, aujourd'hui à dix heures
Sp mañana por la mañana, ayer por la tarde, hoy a las diez
Po amanhã de manhã, ontem de tarde, hoje às dez horas
It domani mattina, ieri sera, oggi alle dieci
Ro mîine dimineaţă, ieri seară, azi la ora zece

• The demonstrative adverbs of place may all be followed by a dependent adverbial functioning as a sort of appositive limiter, i.e. identifying more explicitly the locality referred to. Examples with adv-1 complements:

Fr ici à Québec, là sous les arbres
Sp aquí en la playa, allá por las nubes
Po aqui na praça, lá para o norte
It qui sulla spiaggia, lì da Giorgio
Ro aici pe pămînt 'ici sur la terre', acolo în ţara voastră 'là dans votre
    pays'

Examples with adv-2 or adv-3 complements (avoided in Roumanian):

Fr ici-bas,[10] là-haut, ci-dessous, là-dedans
Sp aquí dentro, allá adelante, acá arriba, ahí cerca
Po aqui arredor, cá fora, lá em baixo, ali encima
It qui presso, lì dietro, quaggiù, lassù[11]

• In the surface structure the three adv-3s which are also Q-words occur followed by a dependent clause, as in the following examples:

Fr quand nous sommes arrivés, où tu demeures, comme il est naturel
Sp cuando nosotros llegamos, donde tú vives, como es natural
Po quando nós chegamos, onde tu moras, como é natural
It quando noi siamo arrivati, dove tu abiti, com'è naturale
Ro cînd noi am sosit, unde tu locuieşti, cum e natural

In this type of phrase the adverb heads do not carry interrogative meaning. As constituents in higher constructions—e.g. Fr *quand nous sommes arrivés, il faisait déjà très chaud*, etc.—they state rather than ask a particular time, place, or manner and thus have an altogether different function from that in direct questions like Fr *Quand êtes-vous arrivés?* or embedded indirect questions like Fr *on ne sait pas quand vous êtes arrivés.* It seems clear, therefore, that the Q-words here are fulfilling their relativizing function, and this being so we shall analyze them in greater detail under relative clauses in 12.4 and 13.4.

7.3 Quantifiers in the AdvP. The quantifying function in the AdvP is filled by precisely the same set of structures, including the same lexical or morphophonemic variants, as we have listed in 5.2 for the AdjP. Examples:

(1) Fr très bien, fort mal, si tôt, aussi loin, assez souvent, trop en gris
Sp muy bien, tan cerca de ella, cuán lejos, poco despacio
Po muito bem, tão tarde, quão longe, cedo demais
It molto bene, così vicino a Napoli, abbastanza male, troppo lontano da me
Ro foarte bine, prea repede, atît de curînd, destul de aproape

Again here, the item *peu/poco/pouco/puţin* can be preceded in turn by an evaluative quantifier, as in It *troppo poco volentieri* or whatever; the NP *un peu* etc. is also available, as in Fr *un peu loin*, Ro *puţin cam departe*, etc.

(2) Evaluative quantifier phrases, e.g.
Fr assez tôt pour finir, trop tard pour le dîner
Sp bastante pronto para acabar, demasiado tarde para la comida
Po bastante cedo para acabar, tarde demais para o jantar
It abbastanza presto per finire, troppo tardi per il pranzo
Ro destul de curînd pentru a sfîrşi, prea tîrziu pentru masă

(3) Comparative quantifier phrase (description deferred to 14)

(4) Superlative quantifier phrases, e.g.
Fr le plus tôt (vite, clairement . . .) possible
Sp lo más temprano (pronto, claramente . . .) posible
Po o mais cedo (depressa, claramente . . .) possível
It il più presto (tosto, chiaramente . . .) possibile
Ro cel mai curînd (devreme, clar . . .) posibil

Since there is no nominal gender/number to be copied in an adverbial, all but Spanish use the unmarked (i.e. masculine singular) form of the definite article, while Spanish uniquely substitutes its article-like *lo*, in the only construction where this abstract pronoun is not functioning as head in a ProP. The attribute in one of these superlative quantifiers seems always to betray some sort of ellipsis, like the very frequent one exemplified above. Another would be *de tous/de todos* etc., as in, say, Fr *(c'est lui qui a parlé) le plus clairement de tous*; but here only French and Roumanian actually retain the superlative, Italian neutralizing it with the comparative quantifier (e.g. *lui ha parlato più chiaramente di tutti quanti*), and Span/Port normally recurring to some less awkward paraphrase.

(5) Adjectives adverbialized with *-ment(e)*—e.g. Fr *extrêmement mal*, Sp/Po *extremamente mal*, It *estremamente male*, and the Roumanian equivalent (with functor *de*) *extrem de rău*.

(6) NPs denoting time-spans quantifying time adverbs, e.g.

Fr   trois ans auparavant
Sp   tres años antes
Po   três anos antes
It   tre anni prima
Ro   trei ani înainte

Note also Fr *longtemps après*, with an adverb as quantifier.[12]

Notes for Chapter 7

1. Roumanian does employ the suffix *-e* to adverbialize (also in the lexicon) any adjective which is itself derived from a noun with the suffix *-esc*, e.g. *omenește* 'humainement', *firește* 'naturellement'. (The/sk ~ șt/ alternation is a pervasive trait of Roumanian morphophonemics.)

2. They are also known to some linguists as RELATORS, and their objects as AXES.

3. Some might prefer to claim that one of these items when occurring with a 'zero' object represents a reduced AdvP, i.e. a transitive head with actual deletion of a complement carrying merely old information already established by the context. However, the 'deleted' object is by no means recoverable in its exact form, and this is strong evidence for saying that it has no overt (lexical) form, even underlyingly.

4. A functor such as *de* linking an adverb of this class to its object is what has led traditional grammar to call the whole of Fr *près de* a preposition, but the *de* is merely a surface marker of the construction in view.

5. These Span/Port items point up as well as any a vexing descriptive problem. Inasmuch as the word *cima* exists as a noun, we cannot really determine whether *encima* is built out of *en/em* plus noun or whether it represents an independent adverb in the lexicon. However, in the absence of either phonological or syntactic contrasts between *encima* and a hypothetical *en cima/em cima*, it appears to be immaterial; in other terms, whether Sp/Po *encima*, or indeed Fr *au-dessous*, or It *al di là*, constitute one word or more than one word, they are by our criteria adverbials. Ideally, we should

like to represent them all consistently, and the most adequate way of doing so is as one word; otherwise, we should have to cull out all the minimal forms with separate existence in the lexicon, whether nouns or adverbs, and keep them separate in these as well as in innumerable Class 3 adverbials. Thus, even though it is clear *historically* that Fr *au-dessous*, say, derives from *à* + def. art. + *de* + *sous*, or Sp *adelante* from *a* + *de* + def. art. + *ante*, it is both awkward and unproductive to insist on this atomization synchronically. What, then, are the implications for such adverbials as Fr *à cause*, Sp/Po/It *a causa*, Ro *din causa*, or Fr *au lieu*, Sp *en vez*, Po *em vez*, It *invece* (exceptional in what *two* ways?), Ro *în loc*? Would you be influenced by the fact that some of the Roumanian items at issue, when followed by a nominal object, suffix the definite article and make the object genitive as in *deasupra norilor* 'au-dessus des nuages', or *împrejurul lacului* 'autour du lac'?

6. These two French items are in complementary distribution with the adv-1s *dans* and *hors*, respectively.

7. It is important to note in this connection that the first three sets of items in Table 7.1 double as functors in all the languages (except for Fr *dans* and Ro *la*), and it is only in this nonadverbial capacity that these (except for Sp/Po *en/em*) occur before dependent clauses; see 12.6. Function markers also, in the present description, are the battery of small items like Fr *que* (sometimes *ce que*, as in *par ce que je m'en vais*), Sp/Po *que*, It *che* (sometimes *-ché*, as in *perché, dacché*, etc.), Ro *că* and *ce*, all of which serve to mark (finite) embedded clauses in a higher construction of any sort. (Traditional grammar, of course, makes these functors constituent parts of subordinators as against prepositions, e.g. *parce que* as against *par*, Sp/Po *porque* as opposed to *por*.)

8. The cases of *per* and *da* may be arguable, if one should prefer to claim that the *per* which corresponds to Fr *pour* etc. is a mere homonym of the one that matches Fr *par* etc., or similarly that the *da* which corresponds to Fr *dès* etc. is a homonym of the one that matches Fr *par* etc. If such lexical separation is insisted upon, then the *per, da* which appear in the set with Fr *par* etc. are excluded from the items permitting a clausal object.

9. Technically, the second Roumanian example is not admissible here, since *după* is an adv-1, but it is included for the sake of analogy.

10. In French, the adverbs *en bas* and *en haut* alternate to just *bas* and *haut*, respectively, in the environment in view.

11. The writing of the Italian adverbials with *giù* and *su* as complement points to regarding them as single items formed in the lexicon. [*Query. But do you perceive an inconsistency in such a view? Does the use of the hyphen in the French examples seem to justify taking these as single lexical items?*]

12. Adverbials may be coordinated copulatively or alternatively, e.g. Fr *en France ou ailleurs*, Sp *arriba y abajo*, Po *quando e onde*, It *oggi o domani*, Ro *acasă sau în restaurant*; adverbialized adjectivals may be coordinated

adversatively as well. In Spanish and Portuguese, heads derived by means of *-mente* carry this suffix only on the last element in a coordination, e.g. Sp *rápida y cómodamente*, Po *rápida mas cômodamente*.

Verbal Structures
Chapter 8
The verb phrase

8.0 Internal structure of the verb phrase (VP). This chapter discusses the internal structure of the verb phrase (VP). Basically, this is the same in all five languages, and consists of a verb as obligatory head; and of optional attributes as follows: NEGATOR, PERFECTIVE ASPECT, MODIFIER.[1] The order of constituents is shown in the formula:

VP → (negator) (perfective aspect) head (modifier).

The parentheses mean that such constituents are optional as contrasted with the unparenthesized, obligatory head.

8.1 Verbs as heads. The surface formula for the verb as a grammatical word in all five languages is: Verb → stem (suffix), the parenthesis signifying that the bare stem may also occur. The suffixes are of three orders: (1) tense/ mode suffixes, which represent a basic constituent of the next-higher con- struction-level, namely, modality in the clause rather than in the VP itself; they will therefore be described at that level; (2) function-marking suffixes which, in complementation with the first order, indicate divers syntactic relationships either of the verb head to other material within the VP, or of the entire VP to outside material;[2] (3) concord suffixes which, whether added to the first order or to the bare stem,[3] mark a particular relationship between subject and predicate at the clause level and will be discussed in that connection.

The overall morphophonemics of verb inflection must, of course, be stated in terms of the phonological structure of each individual language. [*Com- ment. Appendix 4 offers a brief description of Spanish verb inflection, on which those of the other languages can be modeled.*] In the present descrip- tion of the VP, we shall cite verbs in their 'infinitive' form *as though* this were the actual stem, because it is conventional and comfortable to do so (dic- tionaries do it too), although in fact the infinitive in all but Roumanian is composed of stem plus a suffix containing the phoneme /r/, e.g. Fr *vendre*, Sp/Po *vender*, It *vendere*.[4]

We may now look at the attributes in the VP, all optional.

8.2 The negator. This function slot is filled by a unique NEGATIVE PARTICLE having the following forms:

Fr	Sp	Po	It	Ro
ne	no	não	non	nu

The French particle normally occurs only in correlation with another element of the VP or of the clause. Thus, although *ne* does occur alone with the head in a few atypical expressions, usually the negative adverb *pas* appears where in the other languages the negative particle is self-sufficient, as in, say, Sp *no cantar*, Po *não cantar*, It *non cantare*, Ro *a nu cînta*, as against Fr *ne pas chanter*.

8.3 The perfective aspect. The function of this optional attribute is performed by an AUXILIARY VERB (AuxV), i.e. a phrase-bound word having the morphosyntactic properties of a verb and also, elsewhere, the capability of functioning freely as head in a VP. The perfective AuxVs are:

Fr	Sp	Po	It	Ro
avoir	haber	ter	avere	a fi[5]
être			essere	

When the perfective AuxV is present, the head carries the participial suffix, morphophonemically complex in all the languages and shaped as follows for 'regular' verbs: Fr allomorphs *-é* ~ *-i* ~ *-u* by 'conjugation' class, Sp/ Po *-do*, It *-to*, Ro *-t*. In French and Italian, the AuxV is *avoir/avere* in the environment of all transitive verb[6] heads, and is *être/essere* in that of some intransitive (including all reflexive) verb heads. For the unpredictable intransitives, the selection is lexically determined: all those taking *être* in French correspondingly take *essere* in Italian (e.g. Fr *arriver* → *être arrivé* and It *arrivare* → *essere arrivato*), but many taking *avoir* in French take *essere* in Italian (e.g. Fr *pleuvoir* → *avoir plu* but It *piovere* → *essere piovuto*). A full set of examples:

	All transitive	All reflexive	Some intransitive	Other intransitive
Fr	avoir trouvé	s'être trouvé	être entré	avoir réussi
Sp	haber hallado	haberse hallado	haber entrado	haber logrado
Po	ter achado	ter-se achado	ter entrado	ter logrado
It	avere trovato	essersi trovato	essere entrato	essere riuscito
Ro	a fi găsit	a se fi găsit	a fi intrat	a fi reuşit

The adjective-like inflection of the participle in a VP perfectivized with Fr/ It *être/essere*, showing gender/ number concord with a nominal subject, is a marker of clause structure and is therefore examined in 9.6.

8.4 Modifiers in the VP. The form filling this slot at the VP level is an adverbial or (in certain restricted lexical collocations only) an adjectival. The modifier's basic position is following the head (i.e. closing the VP); it invariably refers to time, place, manner, or quantity. Some random examples:

Fr manger très bien, avoir commencé tout de suite, vendre cher
Sp comer muy bien, haber comenzado en seguida, vender caro
Po comer muito bem, ter começado logo, vender caro
It mangiare molto bene, avere cominciato subito, vendere caro
Ro a mînca foarte bine, a fi început imediat, a vinde scump

In certain patterns, however, varying by languages, a modifier consisting of a lone adverb occurs before the head, instead of closing the phrase. For example, in French and Italian, the negative adverbs *plus/più* and *jamais/mai*—which occur in negated VPs only—are positioned between the perfective AuxV and the head, as in Fr *n'avoir plus écouté, n'être jamais réussi* or It *non avere più ascoltato, non essere mai riuscito*. In French a few other adverbs of time, such as *déjà, souvent, encore* (e.g. *être déjà sorti, avoir toujours cru*), also precede in this environment, and in some styles the adverbs of quantity likewise follow suit, e.g. *avoir beaucoup (trop, assez . . .) bu*. In Roumanian the quantifying adverb *mai* always immediately precedes the head. In a negated VP the meaning of *nu . . . mai* is the same as that of Fr *ne . . . plus*, e.g. *a nu mai insista* or *a nu mai fi insistat*; but *mai* can also occur in a nonnegated VP where Fr *plus* must give way to *encore*—e.g. *a mai insista = insister encore*, or *a fi mai insistat = avoir encore insisté*.[7]

Notes for Chapter 8

1. The so-called 'conjunctive personal pronouns', which are clitic to verbs, also unquestionably occupy a surface place within the VP; but in the present analysis they represent reductions of structures which function primarily as other constituents at the clausal level and which are extraposed from without to within the VP when reduced.

2. These are the 'past participle', 'gerund' and 'infinitive' suffixes of traditional Romance grammar.

3. In Portuguese alone, this order may also be added to one of the function-marking suffixes, as we shall have occasion to observe in 13.1.2.

4. In Roumanian it is constituted by the proclitic functor *a* plus the stem, e.g. *a vinde* (like English *to sell*).

5. Forms of *a avea* which appear in perfective VPs—e.g. *Ion a cîntat* 'Jean a chanté'—are not, despite the surface correspondence, the perfective AuxV; rather, they represent an Aux in the tense/mode system.

6. See 9.3.1.

7. VPs may be coordinated, though not adversatively, e.g. Fr *lire et écrire*, Sp *comprar o vender*, etc. If the negator slot is filled underlyingly, the only viable conjunction is *ni/nem/nè/nici*, which effectively neutralizes copula-

tive and alternative coordination. It is required before both elements, thus paralleling Fr *et lire et écrire* or *ou lire ou écrire*, with the first occurrence replacing the regular negative particle: thus, for example, Sp underlying *no leer + y/o + no escribir* becomes *ni leer ni escribir*, and so on for all the languages.

Clausal Structures
Chapter 9
The clause: A general overview

9.0 Internal structure of the clause (Cl). This chapter discusses the internal structure of the clause (Cl) and presents a general overview of all clauses.

We recall that in our hierarchy of grammatical levels the PHRASE represents Level 3 in the range of grammatical forms, as well as the lowest of three construction levels. Having now completed our description of phrases (CNP, PNP, ProP, AdjP, AdvP, PrepP, VP), we are ready to move up to the CLAUSE, which represents Level 4 in the general hierarchy and the middle level of construction. The underlying structure of the clause is identical in the five languages: it consists of a SUBJECT, a MODALITY, a PREDICATE, one or more COMPLEMENTS, and an optional MODIFIER.[1] The basic order of constituents is shown in the formula:

Cl → ±subject ±modality + predicate ±complement(s) (modifier).

The sign '±' means as usual that certain clauses—as determined by factors such as the subclass of verb in the predicate—must contain a subject while others cannot, some a modality while others not, and some a complement while others not.

9.1 Verbals as predicates. The predicate slot in a clause—which as the foregoing formula states is the central constituent without which a clause cannot be constructed—is filled exclusively by a verbal, i.e. a verb or VP. Thus, for example, the Spanish verbal *llueve* or *ha llovido* can be functioning as predicate in a clause which has no subject, no complements, and no modifier, and therefore can of itself constitute a clause. The other slots are filled severally by various nonverbal forms, as we shall now observe.

9.2 Subjects. The subject slot in a clause is filled primarily by any type of nominal, secondarily by an embedded clause (see 12.1). Immediate full exemplification of subjects is not practicable at the present stage, because of numerous constraints upon their occurrence, linkage with the predicate, position, reduction, etc.—constraints which moreover vary according to the function of the clause itself. Consequently, we shall do better to treat subjects in detail at appropriate later points.

9.3 Complements. The complement function in a clause is filled primarily by a nominal, an adjectival, or an adverbial; secondarily by an embedded clause. Complements vary in both form and semantic function according to the lexical category of the verb in the predicate. There are three main categories of verb, two of which are subcategorized: transitive, copulative (or, should one prefer, linking), and intransitive. And, as determined severally by the verbal categories and subcategories, there are four distinct types of complement: object, dative, equivalent, and oblique. We may proceed to describe and illustrate the four under the several verbal headings.

9.3.1 Transitive verbs and their complements.

9.3.1.1 Transitive-1 verbs (trans-1). Many a lexical verb is semantically incomplete in itself, in that it denotes an action necessarily directed at (or toward, or against, or whatever) someone or something. The goal, or 'object', of the action as thus defined is then expressed by means of a complement traditionally called 'direct object', to be known here simply as OBJECT; and the verb is said to be TRANSITIVE. The form of an object is typically nominal, though it can also be an embedded clause (again see 12.1). Examples with nominals:[2]

Fr voir un film, prendre le train, admirer Michel
Sp ver un film, tomar el tren, admirar a Miguel
Po ver um filme, tomar o trem, admirar Miguel
It vedere un film, prendere il treno, ammirare Michele
Ro a vedea un film, a lua trenul, a-l admira pe Mihai

The last Spanish and the last Roumanian example show how, in these two languages alone, an object consisting of a person-name PNP, or of any [+ human] nominal denoting a specific person (or personalized creature, land, or the like) is marked with a functor: namely, *a* in Spanish,[3] *pe* in Roumanian.[4]

Most trans-1 verbs—e.g. Fr *prendre, jeter, garder* and their equivalents in the other languages—simply never occur without an object. There are, however, many trans-1s, such as Fr *chanter, manger, étudier* (and their equivalents), which need not always be accompanied by an expressed object, even though one is always implied and 'understood'.[5]

9.3.1.2 Transitive-2 verbs (trans-2). A number of transitive verbs (trans-2s) still remain semantically incomplete even with the expected object present, for they denote an action that entails not only an object but also a recipient or beneficiary thereof. The someone to or for whom the action is performed is then expressed by means of a complement traditionally called 'indirect object', to be known here simply as DATIVE (COMPLEMENT). The form of a dative is exclusively nominal, with [+animate] head, as in the following examples with the dative italicized:

Fr donner de l'argent *à Etienne*, ne rien dire *à personne*, demander *aux étudiants* de répondre

Sp dar*le* dinero *a Esteban*, no decir*le* nada *a nadie*, pedir*les a los estudiantes* que contesten

Po dar dinheiro *a Estévão*, não dizer nada *a ninguém*, pedir *aos estudantes* para responderem

It dare dei soldi *a Stefano*, non dire niente *a nessuno*, chiedere *agli studenti* di rispondere

Ro a-*i* da bani *lui Ştefan*, a nu-*i* zice *nimănui* nimic, a *le* cere *studenţilor* să răspundă

In all our languages a dative is marked: by the functor *à/a* in all but Roumanian,[6] and in the latter by the genitive/dative suffix attachable to the first constituent of a nominal, as described in 4.3.

The relative order of object and dative in the same clause is free and determined stylistically when both are nominals, with the shorter complement tending to precede the longer—e.g. Fr *envoyer un cadeau à chacun de nos amis* vs. *envoyer à Louise un paquet de jolis cadeaux.* However, any dative invariably precedes an object consisting of an embedded clause, as shown in the third example for each language.

Most trans-2 verbs—e.g. Fr *donner, envoyer, offrir* and their equivalents—simply never occur without their object overtly expressed, although their dative may be missing as in, say, Fr *donner du sang*, the unexpressed recipient being understood. With a small minority of items, however, either or indeed both complements may be zero, as in Fr *demander quelque chose à quelqu'un*, or just *demander à quelqu'un*, or just *demander quelque chose*, or just *demander.*

9.3.1.3 Transitive-3 verbs (trans-3).

A third group of transitives (trans-3s) remain semantically incomplete even with their expected object—which in this case cannot be zero—present, for they denote an action that entails not only an object but also the consequent location, situation, or activity in which the object finds itself. This further argument in the predication is then expressed by means of a complement traditionally called simply 'complement', and to be known here more precisely as an OBLIQUE (COMPLEMENT). The form of an oblique with a trans-3 verb is exclusively adverbial, as in the following examples with the oblique italicized:

Fr mettre les valises *dans la voiture*,[7] inviter des amis *au théâtre*

Sp poner las maletas *en el coche*, invitar a unos amigos *al teatro*

Po pôr as malas *no carro*, convidar uns amigos *ao teatro*

It mettere le valigie *nella macchina*, invitare degli amici *al teatro*

Ro a pune valizele *în maşină*, a invita nişte prieteni *la teatru*

The relative order of object and oblique in the same clause is free and tends to be determined pragmatically, i.e. by considerations related to the discourse.

9.3.1.4 Transitive-4 verbs (trans-4). Yet a fourth group of transitives (trans-4s) remain semantically incomplete even with their expected object— which, as with trans-3, cannot be zero—present, for they denote an action of somehow equating their object with some entity or characteristic. This further argument is then expressed by means of a complement traditionally called 'objective complement', to be known here as an EQUIVALENT (COMPLEMENT).[8] The form of an equivalent is either a nominal (for an entity) or an adjectival (for a characteristic). Examples with nominal equivalents (italicized):

Fr élire Jean *président*, considérer le capitaine *un scélérat*
Sp elegir a Juan *presidente*, considerar al capitán *un pillo*
Po eleger João *presidente*, considerar o capitão *um patife*
It eleggere Giovanni *presidente*, considerare il capitano *uno scellerato*
Ro a-l alege pe Ion *preşedinte*, a-l considera pe căpitan *un pungaş*

Examples with adjectival equivalents (italicized):

Fr rendre sa femme *heureuse*, laisser toutes les fenêtres *ouvertes*
Sp hacer *feliz* a su esposa, dejar *abiertas* todas las ventanas
Po tornar sua esposa *feliz*, deixar *abertas* todas as janelas
It fare *felice* sua moglie, lasciare *aperte* tutte le finestre
Ro a o face *fericită* pe soţia sa, a lăsa toate ferestrele *deschise*

9.3.2 Linking verbs and their complements. A few verbs (linking) are semantically incomplete in a totally different way from transitives: instead of an action directed toward an object, they serve merely to link, in the sense of equate, one entity with another or an entity with a characteristic. The first entity is expressed by the subject of the clause, and what the subject is (or becomes, or seems, or whatever) is expressed in the type of complement we have already identified as the equivalent occurring with trans-4 verbs. The form of an equivalent after a linking verb is, just as with trans-4, typically a nominal or an adjectival, though it can also be an embedded clause. Examples of nominal equivalents:

Fr être le professeur, devenir un héros, sembler une idée stupide
Sp ser el profesor, hacerse un héroe, parecer una idea estúpida
Po ser o professor, fazer-se um herói, parecer uma idéia estúpida
It essere il professore, diventare un eroe, parere una idea stupida
Ro a fi profesorul, a deveni un erou, a părea o idee stupidă

Examples of adjectival equivalents:

Fr être fou, être très connu, être médecin,[9] devenir plus faible, paraître mort, rester ouvert
Sp ser loco, ser muy conocido, ser médico, ponerse más débil, parecer muerto, quedar abierto
Po ser louco, ser muito conhecido, ser médico, tornar-se mais débil, parecer morto, ficar aberto

It   essere pazzo, essere molto conosciuto, essere medico, diventare più
     debole, sembrare morto, rimanere aperto
Ro   a fi nebun, a fi foarte cunoscut, a fi medic, a deveni mai slab, a
     părea mort, a rămîne deschis

The linking verbs simply never occur without their complement overtly
expressed. In certain limited contexts, they may be followed in addition by
an optional dative, as in the following examples:

Fr   être impossible aux élèves, sembler une horreur à ma tante
Sp   serles imposible a los alumnos, parecerle un horror a mi tía
Po   ser impossível aos alunos, parecer um horror a minha tia
It   essere impossibile agli allievi, sembrare un orrore a mia zia
Ro   a le fi imposibil elevilor, a-i părea mătuşii mele o groază

It is only with these linking verbs that dative complements are optional
rather than obligatory. [*Comment. Let us be sure we are clear on the difference between an optional constituent and one which, even if not overtly
expressed, is nonetheless implied and understood.*]

9.3.3. Intransitive verbs and their complements.

9.3.3.1 Intransitive-1 verbs (intrans-1). A sizeable number of verbs (in-
trans-1s), unlike either transitives with their required object or linking verbs
with their required equivalent, are nevertheless still semantically incomplete
to the extent of requiring an oblique, i.e. the type of complement already
identified under trans-3. Likewise, with these intrans-1s the oblique is typically adverbial in form, as in the following examples:

Fr   monter dans la voiture, consentir à un retard, s'occuper de cette
     affaire
Sp   subir al coche, consentir a una demora, ocuparse de ese asunto
Po   subir no carro, consentir a uma demora, ocupar-se desse assunto
It   salire in macchina, consentire ad un ritardo, occuparsi di quella
     faccenda
Ro   a se urca în maşină, a consimţi la o întîrziere, a se ocupa de lucrul
     acela[10]

All the so-called 'verbs of motion' (more precise would be 'locomotion')
are intrans-1, for goings and comings invariably imply destinations or starting points, however vague. Thus for example:

Fr   venir en ville, entrer dans la salle, sortir de l'école, aller chez Georges
Sp   venir a la ciudad, entrar en la sala, salir de la escuela, ir a casa de
     Jorge
Po   vir à cidade, entrar na sala, sair da escola, ir à casa de Jorge
It   venire in città, entrare nella sala, uscire dalla scuola, andare da
     Giorgio
Ro   a veni în oraş, a intra în sală, a ieşi din şcoală, a se duce la Gheorghe

Two semantically incomplete verbs, namely, Fr *coûter* and *peser*, and their
equivalents in the other languages, are complemented by a nominal denoting

a certain amount, as in:

Fr coûter mille francs, peser dix kilos
Sp costar mil pesos, pesar diez kilos
Po custar mil escudos, pesar dez quilos
It costare mille lire, pesare dieci chili
Ro a costa o mie de lei, a cîntări zece kilograme

We seem to have here a case of intrans-1 plus oblique, rather than of trans-1 plus object. And if this is so, then it is well also to take the complements in Fr *coûter trop, peser beaucoup*, and their equivalents as obliques filled by quantifying adverbs rather than as objects filled by pronouns.[11]

In all five languages the linking verb *être/ser/essere/a fi* operates also as an intrans-1 with an oblique, as in:

Fr	être de laine	. . . de Québec	. . . de Jean	. . . à la maison	. . . avec des amis
Sp	ser de lana	. . . de México	. . . de Juan		
Po	ser de lã	. . . do Brasil	. . . de João		
It	essere di lana	. . . di Milano	. . . di Gianni	. . . a casa	. . . con amici
Ro	a fi de lînă	. . . din Oltenia	[12]	. . . acasă	. . . cu prieteni

Note that the complements are adverbial in form and do not serve to equate as would the nominal or adjectival complements in Sp *ser lana, ser México* or *ser mexicano, ser Juan* or *ser el de Juan*, and so on, where *ser* is clearly enough a linking verb. The Spanish/Portuguese gap indicates that in these two languages *ser* does not accept an oblique denoting movable physical location,[13] condition, or the like, employing instead a different verb, namely, the intrans-1 represented by Sp/Po *estar*, It *stare*, Rou *a sta*—as in *estar en/em casa, estar con/com amigos*. Lacking an exact counterpart in French,[14] this verb takes not only obliques which are adverbial in accordance with the norm, as in:

Sp estar bien, mal, arriba, en pie, al sol . . .
Po estar bem, mal, là em cima, em pé, ao sol . . .
It stare bene, male, sopra, in piedi, al sole . . .
Ro a sta bine, rău, sus, în picioare, la soare . . .

but also obliques which are adjectival, including adjectivalized participles denoting body postures or states, as in:

Sp estar solo, junto, presente, contento, callado, sentado, acostado, . .
Po estar sòzinho, junto, presente, contente, calado, sentado, deitado, . .
It stare solo, zitto, allegro, fermo, seduto, coricato, sdraiato . . .
Ro a sta singur, cuminte, treaz, aşezat, culcat, îngenunchiat ('seul, sage, éveillé, assis, couché, agenouillé') . . .

In Spanish and Portuguese, a much wider range of adjectives can figure in obliques of *estar* than in Italian or Roumanian. Examples where Italian/Roumanian would not use *stare/a sta*: *estar frío/frio, delicado, gordo, bueno/bom, lleno/cheio, sucio/sujo, abierto/aberto*, etc. This being so, two semantic/syntactic contrasts are available to Spanish and Portuguese only:

• In, for example, *estar* vs. *ser delgado, estar* vs. *ser duro, estar* vs. *ser alegre*, *estar* vs. *ser callado/calado*, one and the same adjective denotes a condition, stage, or state, with no implication as to what is the norm (i.e. unmarked for norm), versus a normal, characterizing feature of the subject.

• In, say, *estar* vs. *ser escrito*, *estar* vs. *ser publicado*, *estar* vs. *ser escondido*, after *estar* the adjectivalized participle denotes *a state resulting from a previous action*, while *ser* plus (adjectivalized) participle is part of a passive clause denoting *the action itself*. In the other languages there is no surface distinction here, as in Fr *être écrit*, It *essere scritto*, Ro *a fi scris*, unless, of course, the participle is followed by the unambiguous agentive complement introduced by *par/por/da/de*; see 10.3.

9.3.3.2 Intransitive-2 verbs (intrans-2). A smallish number of intransitives (intrans-2s) are semantically incomplete in that they require a dative complement, as in the following examples:

Fr   plaire aux dieux, n'obéir à personne
Sp   placer a los dioses, no obedecerle a nadie
Po   prazer aos deuses, não obedecer a ninguém
It   piacere agli dei, non obbedire a nessuno
Ro   a le place zeilor, a nu se supune nimănui

Prominent among the intrans-2 subcategory is the highly frequent Sp *gustar*. Its Portuguese counterpart *gostar* is, however, an intrans-1 (e.g. *gostar deste país*). More on these verbs, as well as It *piacere* and Ro *a place*, in 13.1.

9.3.3.3 Intransitive-3 verbs (intrans-3). Finally, a very considerable number of verbs (intrans-3s), unlike either transitives or other intransitives, are semantically self-contained and therefore require no complement at all. Examples are Fr *naître, mourir, travailler, dormir, s'en aller* . . . Sp *nacer, morirse, trabajar, dormir, irse, despertarse* . . . Po *nascer, morrer, trabalhar, dormir, acordar-se* . . . It *nascere, morire, lavorare, dormire, andarsene* . . . Ro *a naşte, a muri, a lucra, a dormi, a se trezi* ('s'éveiller').

9.3.4 Feature summary of subcategories of verbs and their complements. If each subcategory of verb we have identified in the foregoing 9.3.1-9.3.3 is plotted in a binary feature matrix against the four types of complement found to cooccur with each subcategory, we arrive at the display in Table 9.1. And if we then take the further step of specifying each of the four types of complement in terms of the two binary features [±direct] and [±objective], we produce the matrix of Table 9.2. Whether the second differentiation is well motivated appears to depend on whether the equivalent complement can somehow be accepted as 'direct'; all else seems to follow.

Table 9.1 Verb categories and their complements.

	Object	Dative	Equivalent	Oblique
Trans-1	+	−	−	(+)[15]
Trans-2	+	+	−	−
Trans-3	+	−	−	+
Trans-4	+	−	+	−
Linking	−	(+)	+	−
Intrans-1	−	−	−	+
Intrans-2	−	+	−	−
Intrans-3	−	−	−	−

Table 9.2 The complement types by features.

	[direct]	[objective]
Object	+	+
Dative	−	+
Equivalent	+	−
Oblique	−	−

9.4 Modifiers in the clause. The form filling this slot is an adverbial denoting time, place, manner, extent, or circumstance; or a nominal expressing a point or period of time; or a clause denoting a circumstance. The basic position of the modifier is final in the clause, i.e. following the predicate and/or any complement, as in the following random examples:

Fr   partir demain matin, étudier la musique à Paris, parler français très
      bien, être allé en Europe l'été dernière

Sp   salir mañana por la mañana, estudiar música en París, hablar espa-
      ñol muy bien, haber ido a Europa el verano passado

Po   sair amanhã de manhã, estudar música em París, falar português
      muito bem, ter ido a Europa no verão passado

It   partire domani mattina, studiare musica a Parigi, parlare italiano
      molto bene, essere andato in Europa l'estate scorsa

Ro   a pleca mîine dimineaţă, a studia muzica la Paris, a vorbi româ-
      neşte foarte bine, a se fi dus în Europa vara trecută

As noted earlier (5.2.5), Roumanian does not adverbialize adjectives in the lexicon, but instead simply uses adjectivals freely in modifier function; so, for example, *a surîde trist* corresponds to Fr *sourire tristement*, Sp *sonreir tristemente*, etc. If the clause contains no complement, the functions of modifier at the VP level and at the clause level are seemingly neutralized and it is impossible to determine at which level a closing adverbial—provided it is privileged (like Fr *bien*) to function at either level—is in fact functioning. So, for example, the adverbial *très bien* is a constituent of the VP in *parler très bien le français*, but of the clause itself in *parler français très bien*; though in *parler très bien* alone it is indeterminate, and the same is true for the other languages.

9.5 Modality. As indicated by the formula for the clause, the underlying linearity orders the modality slot just ahead of the predicate slot. In our languages the modality slot is variously filled by suffixes and/or auxiliaries of tense/mode. In all but Roumanian, tense is obligatory and additional mode is optional;[16] in Roumanian tense and mode are mutually exclusive. In either case the following two ordered surface rules apply:

(1) Any Aux immediately precedes the predicate verbal, in which the first verbal element (i.e. exclusive of the negator)—be it the head verb or the perfective Aux—then takes the so-called 'infinitive' suffix merely as a marker.

(2) Any tense suffix hops to the first verbal element to its right, whether that element be the head of the predicate verbal, or the perfective Aux if present, or a modal Aux if present. To represent the structural description more graphically:

	Modality:	Predicate:	
Tense suffix {	――――――――		Head verb ↑
	――――――	Perf Aux ↑	Head verb
	Modal Aux- ↑	(Perf Aux)	Head verb

The actual morphophonemics of tense suffixation must be stated in terms of the verb inflection as a whole: see 8.1.

9.5.1 Tense and (mode) in Fr/Sp/Po/It. The tenses are three in number—conventionally labeled present, imperfect, preterite—and differentiable by a single pair of features, as follows:

	[Past]	[Fulfilled]
Present	—	—
Imperfect	+	—
Preterite	+	+

All three tenses are manifested by suffixes, as exemplified in the minimally simple illustrative clauses of Table 9.3, uncomplicated by the presence of complements or by any requirement of subject/predicate linkage.

As for the modes, the number varies slightly from language to language. All four have that PREDICTIVE, or PROJECTIVE, mode which in cooccurrence with the present tense produces the traditional 'future tense', while in the environment of the imperfect tense it generates the so-called 'conditional' form of the verb. We label this FUTURE MODE-1 (fut-1), and illustrate it in Table 9.4.

Table 9.3 Tenses in Fr/Sp/Po/It.

	[+tense] [−mode]	Clause
Fr	Present	Marie chante
	Imperfect	chantait
	Preterite	chanta
Sp	Present	María canta
	Imperfect	cantaba
	Preterite	cantó
Po	Present	Maria canta
	Imperfect	cantava
	Preterite	cantou
It	Present	Maria canta
	Imperfect	cantava
	Preterite	cantò

Table 9.4 Future mode-1 (fut-1) in Fr/Sp/Po/It.

	[+tense] [+fut-1]	Clause
Fr	Present	Marie chantera
	Imperfect	chanterait
Sp	Present	María cantará
	Imperfect	cantaría
Po	Present	Maria cantará
	Imperfect	cantaria
It	Present	Maria canterà
	Imperfect	canterebbe

While fut-1 is suffixal in form, modes other than fut-1 are expressed formally by means of certain verbs acting in a special auxiliary capacity. Thus Fr *aller* and Sp/Po *ir* (though not It *andare*) can convey a meaning of futurity (and not of locomotion) not very distant from, yet subtly contrasting with, that of fut-1. By virtue of this semantic affinity we label this FUTURE MODE-2 (fut-2), illustrating it in Table 9.5.

Table 9.5 Future mode-2 (fut-2) in Fr/Sp/Po.

	[+tense] [+fut-2]	Clause
Fr	Present	Marie va chanter[17]
	Imperfect	allait chanter
Sp	Present	María va a cantar[18]
	Imperfect	iba a cantar
Po	Present	Maria vai cantar
	Imperfect	ia cantar

These tables show that neither mode cooccurs with the preterite tense. It is indeed a general rule that the feature [+fulfilled] on a tense blocks any mode.[19] It is true that Fr *Pierre alla voter*, Sp *Pedro fue a votar*, Po *Pedro foi votar* and even It *Pietro andò a votare*—all with preterite tense—do occur, but here the first verb is specified for locomotion rather than futurity and is in fact the predicate verb, while the second verb is part of another, lower clause embedded as an oblique complement (13.2.3). In view of these two very different roles of *aller/ir*, present-tense or imperfect-tense clauses containing them involve a surface ambiguity resolvable only by context.[20]

In addition to *aller/ir*, modes to which we need not attempt to assign specific labels are expressed by:

• *avoir/haber/haver/avere*, as in Fr *Marie a* (or *avait*) *à chanter*, Sp *María ha* (or *había*) *de cantar*, Po *Maria há-de* (or *havia de*) *cantar*, It *Maria ha* (or *aveva*) *da cantare*;

• the recessive Sp *soler*, Po *soer*, It *solere*, missing from French;

• *venir*, uniquely in French, as in *Marie vient* (or *venait*) *de chanter*, like fut-2 *aller* [−locomotion] and standing in marked contrast to *Marie va* (or *allait*) *chanter*;

• *acabar*, uniquely in Spanish and Portuguese, as in Sp *María acaba* (or *acababa*) *de cantar*, with the same force as Fr *venir*.

When the verbal of a clause is perfective, only the tense and fut-1 suffixes can occur, as shown herewith:

Fr   Marie a (avait, eut, aura, *or* aurait) chanté
Sp   María ha (había, hubo, habrá, *or* habría) cantado
Po   Maria tem (tinha, terá, *or* teria) cantado
It   Maria ha (aveva, ebbe, avrà *or* avrebbe) cantato.

Here the cooccurrence of perfective and preterite is marginal, and found only in a few unusual embedded clauses (after *quand/cuando* or the like).[21]

Of special interest is the contrast between preterite tense + verbal and present tense + perfective verbal—e.g. between Sp *María cantó* and *María ha cantado*, etc. Both report an action or state as accomplished in past time;

but the preterite denotes absolute termination and fulfillment prior to the present moment, while the present perfective does not; the latter carries a notion of orientation to the moment of speaking, an as-of-now kind of relevance: something begun earlier but just ended, something still (or not yet) the case, something capable of happening again, or the like. In Spanish, the contrast in view is fully viable in all registers and styles, but not in standard French, Portuguese, or Italian. In French and Italian the preterite is a 'historical' past restricted to formal written narrative styles, while in general usage its meaning is taken over by the present perfective, thus essentially neutralizing the two structures at the surface level. So, for example, Fr *Charles est arrivé* or It *Carlo è arrivato* out of context is ambiguous, i.e. unmarked, as to present relevance. However, in Fr *Charles est déjà arrivé*, It *Carlo è già arrivato*, the present relevance is clear, and the Spanish equivalent would be *Carlos ha llegado ya*. And just as clearly in Fr *Charles est arrivé hier*, It *Carlo è arrivato ieri*, the present perfect is replacing the preterite and the corresponding Spanish would be *Carlos llegó ayer*.[22]

In Portuguese, contrariwise, it is the preterite which preempts most meanings of the present perfect in all registers and styles, likewise effecting a surface neutralization as in Po *Carlos chegou* corresponding to Sp *Carlos llegó* or *Carlos ha llegado*. Even when there is as-of-now relevance, Portuguese prefers the preterite—e.g. *Carlos não chegou ainda* as against Sp *Carlos no ha llegado todavía*—unless reporting progressive or recurrent actions oriented to the moment of speaking—e.g. *Carlos tem estudado muito = Carlos ha estudiado mucho*.[23]

9.5.2 Tense and mode in Roumanian. The tenses (T) are four in number, namely, present, imperfect, (simple) perfect, pluperfect. All four are manifested as suffixes, and generate, respectively, the verbals in *Maria doarme, Maria dormea, Maria dormi, Maria dormise*.

The modes (M), which do not occur with any tense, are four in number, all expressed formally by means of certain verbs acting in an auxiliary capacity. The four may be expressed as follows: first future (fut-1) *Maria va dormi*, second future (fut-2) *Maria are să doarmă ~ o să doarmă*, conditional *Maria ar dormi*, perfective *Maria a dormit*. The first-future AuxV *va* is in no way associated with the verb meaning 'aller', which is *a merge* or *a se duce* in this language. It is true that the second-future AuxV *are* is formally identical with the present tense of the verb *a avea* 'avoir', and indeed a case can be made for regarding the conditional and the perfective AuxVs likewise as positional variants of *a avea*, all in complementary distribution relative to the surface form taken by the predicate verb, which, however, is in turn determined by the modality itself.[24] [*Query. What arguments do you perceive, pro and con?*]

A clause with a perfective verbal accepts an Aux of mode but not one of tense. Thus from the verbal *a fi dormit* can be generated first-future *Maria va fi dormit*, second-future *Maria are să fi dormit*,[25] conditional *Maria ar fi dormit*, though not perfective **Maria a fi dormit*, wherein the two perfective elements (one in the modality, one in the predicate verbal) would be redundant.

Just as in three of our four other languages, so in Roumanian the contrast between the (simple) perfect tense and the so-called 'compound perfect' (i.e. what we are calling the perfective mode) is not fully viable in all registers and styles. The Roumanian simple perfect, like the French and Italian preterite, serves as a historical past limited to formal written discourse, while in general usage its meaning is preempted by the perfective mode in such a way that the two structures are neutralized at the surface level. So, for example, the clause *Ştefan a sosit* 'Etienne est arrivé' out of context is ambiguous as to present relevance; however, in *Ştefan a şi* ('déjà') *sosit* the present relevance is clear as against, say, *Ştefan a sosit ieri*, terminated and fulfilled.

In Roumanian the conditional mode has conditional meaning only, and thus never stands in a past-present relationship to the future as the two tenses of fut-1 often do in the other languages. Thus, for example, French says *Jean promet qu'il viendra* vs. *Jean promettait qu'il viendrait*, with the modalities of both embedded clauses expressing mere futurity (i.e. posteriority) to the moment indicated by the tense of the matrix-clause modality; Roumanian, however, says either *Ion promite că va veni* or *Ion promitea că va veni*, with the embedded future mode invariable regardless of the higher tense.

9.6 Subject-predicate linkage by person/number inflection.

All our languages exhibit a surface link between the subject and the predicate of a clause—a marking system which makes possible the widely resorted-to movement of subjects out of their basic position. The system comprises person/number (P/N) agreement suffixes which 'copy' the P/N of the subject onto the tense segment of the modality, wherever the latter is itself already suffixed to the predicate verbal in the surface structure (see 9.5). An actual overt P/N suffix occurs just if the subject is a local pronominal or a plural nominal, thus comprising a set of five.[26] Otherwise, including the case of an underlying subject which does not surface (10.1), or of a null subject (10.2), the linkage is marked by the very absence of a suffix (just as singular number is marked by the absence of the plural suffix in noun inflection). A token display:

P/N:	Loc. 1st sg.	Loc. 2nd sg.	Loc. 1st plural	Loc. 2nd plural	Nonloc. plural
Fr	je pleure	tu pleures	nous pleurons	vous pleurez	les enfants pleurent
Sp	yo lloro	tú lloras	nosotros lloramos	vosotros lloráis	los niños lloran
Po	eu choro	tu choras	nós choramos	vós choráis	os meninos choram
It	io piango	tu piangi	noi piangiamo	voi piangete	i bambini piangono
Ro	eu plîng	tu plîngi	noi plîngem	voi plîngeţi	copiii plîng[27]

If the predicate verbal is perfectivized, it is, of course, the AuxV that carries the tense/mode (T/M) and hence also the person/number (P/N) suffix—e.g. Fr *l'enfant a pleuré* vs. *les enfants ont pleuré* and so on. The head verb with its participial suffix remains invariable in all but French and Italian, but in these two languages after AuxV *être/essere* the participle inflectionally parallels an adjective in equivalent complement function, i.e. it copies the gender/number of the clause subject. Thus, for example:

Fr	la dame est restée	*-or-*	. . . s'est assise
	les hommes sont restés	*-or-*	. . . se sont assis
	les dames sont restées	*-or-*	. . . se sont assises
It	la donna è rimasta	*-or-*	. . . si è seduta
	i signori sono rimasti	*-or-*	. . . si sono seduti
	le donne sono rimaste	*-or-*	. . . si sono sedute

The widespread cooccurrence of two suffixes on a given Romance verbal stem—one representing the tense/mode (T/M) and the other manifesting person/number (P/N) agreement—makes for a complicated inflection describable, morphophonemically, only in terms of the phonological structure of each language. Once again *Appendix 4: Verb morphology in Spanish*, provides a model.

9.7 Extraposition of subjects. Let us recall once again that the basic, unmarked order of constituent slots in a clause is: subject ± modality + predicate ± complement(s) (±modifier). The modality + predicate order is never disturbed (other than by suffix-hopping in the surface output), and this sequence acts as a fixed, central unit around which the selective movement of other constituents revolves. We shall first examine movement of the subject, which is dislocated to the right of the predicate, i.e. extraposed, under two types of condition: one syntactic and obligatory, the other pragmatic. We are interested here in the former; the latter will be treated in 11.1.

The syntactic constraint on subject-predicate order relates to the incidence of an interrogative word—i.e. a lexical item of whatever part of speech, which carries the semantic feature [+ question]—hence what we are calling a Q-word—in any complement or modifier. When any Q-word is present, the constituent containing it moves to a location preceding the predicate and by so doing triggers extraposition of the subject. To illustrate:

- An object nominal either is a Q-pronoun or contains a Q-determiner:

Fr	Que sait le chien?	Quelle solution propose le chef?
Sp	¿Qué sabe el perro?	¿Qué solución propone el jefe?
Po	O que sabe o cão?	Que (*or* Qual) solução propõe o chefe?
It	Che sa il cane?	Che (*or* Quale) soluzione propone il capo?
Ro	Ce ştie cîinele?	Ce (*or* Care) soluţie propune şeful?

- A dative nominal either is a Q-pronoun or contains a Q-determiner:

Fr	À qui parle Jean?	À combien de votants répondra le président?

Sp	¿A quién le habla Juan?	¿A cuántos votantes responderá el presidente?
Po	A quem fala o João?	A quantos votantes responderá o presidente?
It	A chi parla Gianni?	A quanti votanti risponderà il presidente?
Ro	Cui îi vorbeşte Ion?	Cîtor votanţi le va răspunde preşedintele?

• An equivalent complement is, or contains, a Q-word:

Fr	Quelle est la différence?	Qui est ce monsieur-là?
Sp	¿Cuál es la diferencia?	¿Quién es ese señor?
Po	Qual é a diferença?	Quem é esse senhor?
It	Qual'è la differenza?	Chi è quel signore?
Ro	Care e diferenţa?	Cine e domnul acela?

• An oblique complement or a modifier is, or contains, a Q-word:

Fr	Où va notre ami?	À quelle heure part l'avion?
Sp	¿Adónde va nuestro amigo?	¿A qué hora sale el avión?
Po	Onde vai o nosso amigo?	A que horas sai o avião?
It	Dove va il nostro amico?	A che ora parte l'aereo?
Ro	Unde se duce prietenul nostru?	La ce oră pleacă avionul?

Now observe, also, the following situation in which three of the languages show a neutralization:

Fr	Qui voit le chien?	↔	Qui voit le chien?
Sp	¿Quién ve el perro?		¿A quién ve el perro?
Po	Quem vê o cão?	↔	Quem vê o cão?
It	Chi vede il cane?	↔	Chi vede il cane?
Ro	Cine vede cîinele?		Pe cine vede cîinele?

In French, Portuguese, and Italian a surface ambiguity makes it impossible to read which is the subject (for a subject can also be or contain a Q-word) and which is the object.[28] In consequence, in French the [+animate] *qui* is arbitrarily taken as subject, while the insertion of the question marker *est-ce que* immediately after the fronted object nullifies the subject-extraposition rule and averts the ambiguity noted, thus:

Underlying structure:	le chien + voit + qui
Fronting rule:	*qui + le chien + voit
Marker-insertion:	qui est-ce que[29] le chien voit[30]

When the [+animate] *qui* is in fact the subject (*que voit le chien* being then viable), the marker *est-ce que* is optionally available in the alternant form *est-ce qui* (*qui est-ce qui voit le chien*). On the other hand, when the [−animate] *que* is the subject, the marker in this alternant is obligatory (*qu'est-ce qui effraie le chien* and not **qu'effraie le chien*).

In Portuguese the question-marker *é que* is necessary to resolve the potential ambiguity, thus:

Underlying structure:	o cão + vê + quem	quem + vê + o cão
Fronting Rule:	quem + o cão + vê[31]	...
Marker-insertion:	quem é que o cão vê	quem é que vê o cão

When the predicate is a linking verb, the Fr/Po marker *est-ce que/é que* is unavailable[32] and extraposition must apply. Apart from this, however, both French and Portuguese make extensive use of the available *est-ce que/é que* after any fronted Q-word, the more so when the subject is short and the predicate long as in, say, *quand est-ce que Paul va se marier*. The arresting fact remains, however, that Spanish and Roumanian—both of which mark [+anim] objects overtly and hence never generate the sort of ambiguity we have observed (cf. Sp *¿A quién. . .?*, Ro *Pe cine . . .?*)—also lack any marker comparable to *est-ce que/é que*. As for Italian, which alone neither tags a [+anim] objects nor employs any counterpart of *est-ce que*, it can only resort when necessary to one or another pragmatic reordering of the sort available, for that matter, to any language.[33]

Notes for Chapter 9

1. Traditional grammar cuts a clause (or a sentence, without distinguishing the two consistently) into but two immediate constituents: a nominal subject and a verbal predicate; then again divides the predicate into verbal proper and complements, with modality (tense, mode, etc.) included under the former. However, there seems to be no compelling argument in support of intermediate nodes as against a straight four-way branching; the latter seems descriptively neater, as well as more realistic in the light of certain relational parallels between subjects and complements.

2. In the present context it is sufficient to cite the verbs as infinitives, subjects and modalities being irrelevant to the description in hand.

3. This *a* is not to be taken as the transitive adverb (preposition) *a*, which denotes motion toward any goal at all, as in *a la ciudad* or whatever; nor therefore is the entire phrase to be taken as an adverbial rather than as a nominal like any other functioning as an object. It is, on the other hand, the same functor as we shall see not only in Spanish but also in Fr/Po/It as ever-present marker of the complement type we shall be calling dative.

4. This *pe* is likewise not to be identified with the transitive adverb *pe* of an adverbial like *pe pămînt* 'sur (la) terre' or whatever. In this language, use of an object-marker extends to any NP with a deleted head, e.g. *a cumpăra maşina asta* 'acheter cette voiture-ci' but *a o cumpăra pe asta* 'acheter celle-ci' as against *a cumpăra asta* 'acheter ceci'. (The item *o* in the verbal will be explained later under the clitic copying of objects, in 11.3.)

5. Analysts of the persuasion referred to in 7.1, note 3 might prefer to claim that one of these items occurring with a 'zero' object represents a form of reduced clause, i.e. a transitive predicate with actual deletion of a complement carrying merely old or presupposed information; however, the 'deleted' object is by no means recoverable in its exact form, and this is strong

evidence for claiming that it has no overt (lexical) form, even underlyingly, despite the clear enough implication that *something* is indeed sung, eaten, studied, or what not.

6. As pointed out in 9, note 3, this *à/a* is not the transitive adverb (adv-1) *à/a*, though it is the same item as in a Spanish object referring to a person. The entire phrase, including the functor, is therefore to be taken as a (marked) nominal rather than as an adverbial. The apparent object/dative surface ambiguity existing in Spanish alone is resolved either by the very meaning of the (transitive) verb, so that, say, *a Carlos* in *prometer a Carlos* is naturally taken as a dative rather than an object; moreover, as in all the examples above, a Spanish dative is typically (though not obligatorily) duplicated by a clitic such as *le* or *les* in the predicate. Note the analogous clitics in the Roumanian examples as well; for a full discussion of all clitics in all the languages, see 11.2-3.

7. The location of the bags results from the action of 'putting'. We note also that *mettre les valises* without the second complement is essentially meaningless.

8. Our term is the broader in that it will cover also the traditional 'subjective complement' which accompanies a linking verb.

9. Lone items like Fr *médecin, ingénieur, avocat* etc., denoting professional status and lacking a determiner, are to be taken as lexical nouns 'adjectivalized' in this particular construction. On the other hand, items denoting nationality or place of origin, e.g. Fr *français, parisien* or the like, are already both nouns and adjectives in the lexicon.

10. As indicated by the last example for each language, the present analysis includes certain so-called 'reflexive verbs' among the intransitives, for they admit of no other complement than an oblique, provided, of course, that we do not take the clitic 'reflexive pronoun' *se/si* as the object in a transitive-plus-object string. The motivation against so doing—and indeed for taking 'reflexive verbs' as lexical items in their own right, with the clitic as a morphological property of the verb *as word*—will be given in due course; see 11.3.

11. By extension, Fr *coûter cher*, Sp *costar caro* etc. must be taken the same way. On the other hand, the verbs represented in French by *acheter, vendre*, and *payer* have quite a different status. [*Query: What sort of verbs are they?*]

12. The Roumanian gap could not be filled by *a fi al lui Ion*, which is rather the analogue of contrasting Fr *être celui de Jean*, Sp *ser el de Juan* and so on, where the verb is linking and the complement equivalent, i.e. a NP with head reduced by deletion.

13. In Portuguese but not in Spanish, an oblique denoting fixed (geographical) location may follow *ser*, e.g. *ser no Brasil*.

14. The intrans-1 *rester* comes close in some contexts, though it is basically nearer to Sp *quedar*, Po *ficar*, It *rimanere*, Ro *a rămîne* and readily

gives way to *être, se trouver*, or the like, e.g. *être à pied, se trouver loin d'ici*.

15. Optional oblique complements are limited to occurrence with a subset of trans-1s, namely, verbs of perceiving, as illustrated in 12.1.2.3.

16. Note that 'mood' (as opposed to 'mode') is not included among these basic constituents of the modality; in the present analysis the 'subjunctive', as opposed to the 'indicative', mood is a secondary inflection associated with tense and occurring only in embedded clauses where it is triggered by a certain semantic feature on an element of the higher construction. See 13.

17. As shown, in the three languages the tense is suffixed to the modal Aux (i.e. within the modality), while the predicate verb automatically takes the infinitive suffix *-r* as a marker of its function in the environment of a mode.

18. In Spanish alone, the predicate verb in this environment is redundantly marked by the functor *a*, obligatorily. [*Comment. Eventually, we will uncover a reason for this; can you anticipate it?*]

19. This being so, there must be good arguments for positing preterite as a mode rather than a tense. [*Query. What would they be?*]

20. Modes being mutually exclusive, there is no ambiguity in Fr *Marie ira* (or *irait*) *voter*, Sp *María irá* (or *iría*) *a votar*, where again the lead verb—with fut-1 attached—cannot itself represent fut-2 and therefore must be read as denoting locomotion only.

21. Once again, Fr *Marie est* (or *était*) *allée voter*, Sp *María ha* (or *había*) *ido a votar*, Po *Maria tem* (or *tinha*) *ido votar*, It *Maria è* (or *era*) *andata a votare* are, like the preterite and fut-1 instances cited above, unambiguously *not* cases of fut-2.

22. Another interesting example, with the contextual clue provided by a tense contrast in a clause embedded within the higher clause: Fr *Pierre a dit qu'il viendra*, Sp *Pedro ha dicho que vendrá*, It *Piero ha detto che verrà*, with present (+fut-1) in the embedded clause, as against Fr *Pierre a dit qu'il viendrait*, Sp *Pedro dijo que vendría*, It *Piero ha detto che sarebbe venuto*, with imperfect (+fut-1).

23. Portuguese has an inflectional suffix *-ara* ~ *-era* ~ *-ira*, as in *chegara, vivera, pedira*, which is traditionally labeled 'pluperfect tense'. Despite the patent analogy wherein *estudara* is to *estudou* as *tinha estudado* is to *tem estudado*, the two perfective past forms are semantically identical and offer a stylistic choice at best. Hence, if we take the suffixal form as a mere surface variant of imperfect tense + perfective *ter*, there is no need to posit an extra tense for this language.

24. After fut-1 *va* and conditional *ar*, the predicate verb automatically takes the infinitive form; after fut-2 *are* ~ *o*, it takes the *să*-form (for which see 13.1.1); and after perfective *a*, it takes the participle suffix, just as in a perfective verbal such as *a fi dormit*.

25. *Maria o să fi dormit* is well-formed but stylistically improbable, for the simple reason that the future variant with *o* is highly colloquial, a register in which the 'future perfect' combination of elements is rare.

26. If the subject is a coordinated nominal, its P/N is determined on the following hierarchical basis:

If one element is:	And the other is:	The P/N is as if the subject were:
local 1st sg. or pl.	any nominal	local 1st pl.
local 2nd sg. or pl.	any but local 1st	local 2nd pl.
nonlocal	nonlocal	plural

In addition, the required G/N agreement of an adjectival functioning as equivalent complement—or of the participial head of a perfectivized VP in Fren/Ital—is determined as follows. Regardless of number in either element:

If one element is:	And the other is:	The agreement is:
masculine	either gender	masculine plural
feminine	also feminine	feminine plural

[*Comment. Find examples in whatever language(s) you can to verify these P/N and G/N statements.*]

27. In Roumanian, where tense and mode are mutually exclusive, P/N is copied by a modal Aux as in fut-1 *copilul va plînge* vs. *copiii vor plînge, noi vom plînge*, etc.; further, as in fut-2 *copilul are să plîngă* vs. *noi avem să plîngem*, P/N is copied onto both the modal Aux and the head verb simultaneously, while in the alternant *copilul o să plîngă* vs. *noi o să plîngem*, the agreement is copied only onto the head and not onto the Aux. In certain embedded clauses, not only in Roumanian but also in Portuguese, agreement is copied by the head verb even where the modality of the clause is deleted; see 13.1.1-2.

28. Noting, however, that Fr *Qui voient les chiens?*, Po *Quem vêem os cães?*, It *Chi vedono i cani?* do *not* give ambiguous readings, see if you can formulate the exact conditions under which the ambiguity surfaces.

29. In some dialects of French, notably Canadian ones, *est-ce que* is reduced to just *que*, so that such outputs as *Qui que le chien voit?* or *Quel âge que tu as?* or the like are well-formed. After the [−animate] Q-pronoun *que*, however, the reduction is not permitted, so that *Qu'est-ce que le chien sait?* is not reducible to **Que que le chien sait?* [*Query. Can you hypothesize as to why this is so (see also note 32)?*]

30. For another surface version of this pattern—namely, *Qui le chien voit-il?*—with the subject left in place but with a cross-referring subject clitic following the verbal, see 11.2.

31. In some dialects of Portuguese, mainly Brazilian ones, postposition after fronting is not obligatory and such surface outputs as *Quem o cão vê?* or *Quantos anos você tem?* or the like are the norm, at least in popular or informal speech.

32. By exception in French, however, *est-ce que* is obligatorily inserted after *que* as equivalent complement, and as a further consequence the copula verb itself deletes, as in *que + est-ce que + un phonème + est?* → *Qu'est-ce qu'un phonème?*, thus leaving the subject final in conformity with the general

pattern. Here also the marker frequently takes the redundant variant form *est-ce que c'est que*, thus generating *Qu'est-ce que c'est qu'un phonème?* By exception in Portuguese also, *é que* is optionally inserted between *que* and the copula, after postposition has applied, e.g. *que* (+ *é que*) + *um fonema* + *é?* → *Que é que é um fonema?*

33. At the clause level, coordinations are possible with any one of the four conjunctions discussed thus far: Fr *et, ou, ni, mais*; Sp *y, o, ni, pero*; etc. A very simple example: Fr *Pierre s'en va mais Paul reste*, Sp *Pedro se va pero Pablo se queda*, etc. [*Comment. Again, find a few text examples in the language(s) of your choice.*]

Chapter 10
Special types of clauses

10.0 Introduction. This chapter accounts for five types of clausal construction, each distinguished by some one special characteristic: (1) clauses with indefinite underlying subject (10.1), (2) clauses with null subject (10.2), (3) passive clauses (10.3), (4) imperative clauses (10.4), and (5) negative clauses (10.5). As will be readily enough apparent, some of these special clause types are mutually exclusive, others not.

10.1 Clauses with indefinite underlying subject. In all our languages an action or state is often thought of as performed by a human agent so indefinite as to need no identification regardless of context. It is not a question here of such subject pronominals as Fr *quelqu'un*, Sp *alguien* etc., nor of the even vaguer Sp/It *uno*, Po *a gente* (which have no exact equivalents in French or Roumanian), but rather of a reference so totally indefinite as to preclude any lexical representation whatever. It is a question of an underlying subject specified only as [+human] [−def] and expressed at the surface, in the majority of instances, by means of a clitic on the predicate verbal which is formally identical to the reflexive clitic Fr/Sp/Po/Ro *se*, It *si*, though in this case wholly devoid of reflexive meaning. Further transformations and/or constraints vary with the subcategory of the verb in the predicate, as we now illustrate.

(1) With transitives and their objects (e.g. Fr *vendre les journaux* etc.), the object nominal typically switches function to become the surface subject, as is verified by the plural P/N concord in this first battery of examples:

Fr les journaux se vendent partout[1]
Sp los periódicos se venden en todas partes
Po os diários se vendem em todas as partes
It i giornali si vendono dappertutto[1]
Ro ziarele se vînd pretutindeni

We must note at once, however, that the likes of Fr *des journaux se vendent, Sp *periódicos se venden, etc., containing [−def] or undetermined nominals which convey wholly new information, are ill-formed; in such cases French resorts to the subject clitic on (see 11.2) and leaves the object as object—e.g. on vend des journaux—while the other four recur to the strategy of subject postposition, generating Sp se venden periódicos etc.[2]

Another constraint: the construction in view is not normally suitable for expressing an indefinite subject in the environment of a [+human] object nominal, because the nominal will be interpreted as the true agent, and the clitic se/si as reflexive or reciprocal, in such a clause as Fr les malades se soignent, Sp los enfermos se curan, etc. [Query. Can you think of marginal cases which would not be subject to the ambiguity in view here?] Avoidance strategies then are:

• Retention of the nominal as object at the surface. This is not infrequently done in Span/Port/Ital, though Roumanian disallows it, and it works very well for Spanish with its a-marked [+human] object—as in either se cura al enfermo or se cura a los enfermos—but in Port/Ital it disambiguates only with plural objects, e.g. Po cuida-se os doentes, It si cura i malati and is therefore used more sparingly.[3]

• Recourse to on in French, as in on soigne les malades.

• The alternative of a passive clause without agent in any of the five, as described in 10.3—e.g. Fr les malades sont soignés, Sp los enfermos son curados, etc.

(2) With transitives devoid of surface objects (cf. 9.3.1), with intransitives, or with linking verbs plus their equivalent complement (Fr manger, dormir, être content, devenir malheureux), se/si operates as in (1) in all but French, while the latter uses only on, as in this second set of examples:

Sp   se come bien, se duerme mal, se entra por aquí, se sale por ahí
Po   come-se bem, dorme-se mal, entra-se por aqui, sai-se por aí
It   si mangia bene, si dorme male, si entra di qua, si esce di là
Ro   se mănîncă bine, se doarme rău, se intră pe aici, se iese dincolo
But: Fr on mange bien, on dort mal, on entre par ici, on sort par là

Sp   se es rico, se es sabio, se está callado
Po   se é rico, se é feliz, se está sòzinho
It   si è ricchi, si è generosi, si sta bene
Ro   se devine un erou, se stă bine[4]
But: Fr on devient un héros, on est bien, on est riche

It can be tempting to take the clitic se/si as an actual (reduced) surface subject, either if there is no nominal present (as in Sp se duerme mal) or if there is a surface object (as in Sp se mató a los prisioneros), but there are valid arguments against this. [Query. What are they?]

(3) Lastly, all the languages but French (which must have a surface subject

of some sort) can alternatively express an indefinite and lexically unspecified subject by attaching the plural concord suffix to the verbal in contexts where there can be no question of a deleted plural nominal as subject—e.g. Sp *van a construir un puente* ⟷ *se va a construir un puente*, or Ital *qui fanno degli scavi* ⟷ *qui si fanno degli scavi*. In addition, Roumanian often attaches the P-2nd sg. concord suffix where there is no question of a deleted *tu* or *dumneata*, as in *nu ştii niciodată* ⟷ *nu se ştie niciodată* 'on ne sait jamais'.[5]

10.2 Clauses with null subject. These totally subjectless clauses have in their predicate a verb of the syntactic subclass traditionally known as 'impersonal', seemingly because they never have occasion to carry P/N concord suffixes. This means, in other terms, that there exists no subject whose P/N the modality can copy. There is, in fact, no underlying subject involved, and in all but French there is no syntactic subject; but since French requires clauses to have an overt subject, the clitic *il* is inserted as a 'dummy subject' at the surface. Verbs belonging to this subgroup—which we shall label Class [−S] verbs as opposed to Class [+S] verbs cooccurring with a subject (be it overt, reduced, or deleted)—are at least the following:

• Intrans-2s which, in themselves, denote actions of the weather, e.g. Sp *llueve, nieva* . . ., Po *chove, neva* . . ., It *piove, nevica* . . ., Ro *plouă, ninge* . . . but Fr *il pleut, il neige* . . . All of these are uniquely [−S].

• The trans-1s Fr *faire*, Sp *hacer*, Po *fazer*, It *fare*—which, together with an object, denote states of the weather—as exemplified by Fr *il fait beau, il faisait froid* . . . , Sp *hace calor, hacía viento* . . ., and so on.[6]

• Certain verbs which, together with an object complement, denote the mere existence of some entity. These are principally:

Fr y avoir,[7] *as in* il y a du café, il y avait beaucoup de femmes, y aura-t-il une invasion?

Sp haber,[8] *as in* hay café, había muchas mujeres, ¿habrá una invasión?

Po haver *or* ter,[9] *as in* há café ~ tem café, havia (~ tinha) muitas mulheres, haverá (~ terá) uma invasião?

It esserci,[10] *as in* c'è caffè, c'erano molte donne, ci sarà una invasione?

Ro a fi,[11] *as in* este cafea, erau multe femei, va fi o invazie?

[*Query: What evidence do you find that in Ital/ Roum the underlying object is promoted to syntactic subject in the surface output?*]

• Certain trans-2s which denote the need or necessity of what is named in the object, principally:

Fr falloir, *as in* il faut de l'argent, il fallait réfléchir, il a fallu que (+*embedded clause*)

It bisognare, *as in* bisogna fare presto, bisognava che (+*embedded clause*)

Ro a trebui, *as in* trebue bani 'il faut de l'argent', a trebuit să (+*embedded clause*)

The Spanish analogue here is [−S] *haber* of the foregoing set, though in restricted syntactic environments; in others Spanish uses a [+S] verbal, as Portuguese invariably does.

• Trans-1s which can, though do not always, denote an action not performed by an animate agent, but merely caused to happen by some impersonal force—whether man-made (say, a machine) or not (say, wind or heat). In this case the necessarily [−anim] object becomes the subject and the clitic *se/si* is added to the verbal, thus rendering these clauses indistinguishable from those of 10.1. Examples:

Fr	la porte s'ouvre automatiquement	la neige se fondait
Sp	la puerta se abre automáticamente	la nieve se derritía
Po	a porta abre-se automàticamente	a neve se derretia
It	la porta si apre automaticamente	la neve si fondeva
Ro	uşa se deschide automatic	zăpada se topea

[*Problem. Propose structural descriptions for the following clauses expressing time of day, day of the week, or the like:*

Fr	il est une heure, il était neuf heures, il serait midi, c'est jeudi
Sp	es la una, eran las nueve, sería mediodía, es jueves
Po	é uma hora, eram nove horas, seria meiodia, é quinta-feira
It	è l'una, erano le nove, sarà mezzogiorno, è giovedì
Ro	e (ora) una, era ora nouă ~ erau nouă, va fi miezul zilei, e joi]

10.3 Passive clauses. It has been widely contended in recent years that the passive construction is generated via the optional transformation of an underlying subject-plus-predicate-plus-object clause—that, for example, Fr *le pape a été blessé par un terroriste* is derived transformationally from *un terroriste a blessé le pape*—by reconstituting the object as subject, and the subject as an oblique complement, and by amplifying the transitive predicate verbal with a passive Aux. Stylistic and/or pragmatic factors aside, the two clauses do have essentially the same content. However, even though the passive is somehow the more marked of the two structures, it is difficult to justify positing either the active as underlying and the passive as derived, or vice versa.[12] We shall therefore claim here that while there is a definite semantic affinity between active and passive, neither is derived transformationally from the other in any Romance language. It then follows that a passive clause in our five has the following structural description: (1) a nominal as subject, naming an entity undergoing the action, (2) any modality, (3) a verbal containing the linking verb *être/ser/essere/a fi* as predicate, (4) an adjectival as equivalent complement, expressing the action and, optionally, its agent. The head of the adjectival equivalent is the [+passive] adjective derived from a transitive verb (cf. 5.1),[13] and its own agentive complement is a PrepP introduced by Fr *par*, Sp/Po *por*, It *da*, Ro *de*. In the following sets of examples, the referentially matched nonpassive clauses are displayed at the right, for comparison and in order to illuminate two further points to be made.

Fr	les timbres-poste sont vendus par les marchands de tabac	les marchands de tabac vendent les timbres-poste
Sp	los sellos son vendidos por los tabaqueros	los tabaqueros venden los sellos
Po	os selos são vendidos pelos estanqueiros	os estanqueiros vendem os selos
It	i francobolli sono venduti dai tabaccai	i tabaccai vendono i franco-bolli
Ro	mărcile sînt vîndute de tutungii	tutungiii vînd mărcile

Fr	les timbres-poste sont vendus	les timbres-poste se vendent
Sp	los sellos son vendidos	los sellos se venden[14]
Po	os selos são vendidos	os selos se vendem
It	i francobolli sono venduti	i francobolli si vendono
Ro	mărcile sînt vîndute	mărcile se vînd

Fr	le président a été élu	on a élu le président
Sp	el presidente ha sido elegido	han (~ se ha) elegido al pre-sidente
Po	o presidente foi elegido	elegeram o presidente
It	il presidente é stato eletto	hanno eletto il presidente
Ro	preşedintele a fost ales	l-au ales pe preşedinte

We may note that it would be even more cumbersome to derive the second set of passives from their nonpassive counterparts, for the following reason: while it is clear that nonpassives which use the clitic *se/si* are a surface output of clauses with either indefinite underlying or null subject, the null-subject type simply has no passive analogue because even in a passive with no complement in the equivalent, a [+anim] agent is always implicit there.

In the second set, all but the Span/Port entries are ambiguous out of context, for they can mean either that there is habitual stamp-selling (an action) or that the stamps are sold out (a state resulting from previous action); if the latter, the clause is simply not passive. Preterite tense in the modality makes for a passive interpretation only—Fr *les timbres-poste furent vendus*, It . . . *furono venduti*, Ro . . . *fură vîndute* are quite unambiguous. In addition, Italian alone has expanded the passive clause to allow use of two other verbs besides *essere*, namely, the intrans-1s *venire* and *andare*. Thus, *i francobolli vengono venduti*, with the adjectival as oblique complement, is the same as *i francobolli sono venduti* and unambiguously passive,[15] while *i francobolli vanno venduti* is equally passive, but with *vanno* meaning, additionally, 'doivent être/deben ser'. Span/Port, on the other hand, distinguish nonpassive from passive in this situation by using the intrans-1 *estar* instead of *ser* in the nonpassive clause; Sp *los sellos están vendidos*.[16]

10.4 Imperative clauses. Another recent claim of some linguists is that imperative structures are generated by means of a deletion transformation. In this theory, what surfaces as an imperative clause is what remains after (1) that clause has first been embedded as object in a higher clause, and (2) all but the embedded material itself has been thereafter deleted. So, for example, Sp *vaya usted con Dios* would be the output of an underlying subject (e.g. *yo*) + predicate (with, say, *querer* or *desear, decir* or *mandar* . . .) + object (→ the embedded clause [*usted va con Dios*]) producing *yo quiero que usted vaya con Dios* or whatever. Not only is this claim deficient from a pragmatic point of view—for how could we precisely identify what is to be deleted, and would the full version ever be uttered in just the context where the imperative clause is to be expected?—but also the mechanical details of the transformation would be extremely awkward to state for any of our languages. We shall find that the imperative clause in Romance is much more neatly accounted for as a unique type of independent clause having the following structural description: (1) a local pronoun as subject, (2) a null modality (an imperative cannot have tense!), and (3) a predicate with any [−stative] verb ± complement(s).

10.4.1 The subject in imperative clauses. As we have, of course, observed, the subject function in all clauses is filled basically by a nominal; but by the very nature of the imperative speech act, the only nominals available as subject in imperative clauses are the local pronouns, excluding, of course, the 1st singular. Including the honorifics, the list therefore comprises Fr *toi, vous, nous*; Sp *tú, vosotros, nosotros, usted(es)*; Po *tu, vós, nós, você(s)*; It *tu, voi, noi, Lei, Loro*; Ro *tu, voi, noi, dumneata, dumneavoastră*. In all the languages the person/number of the subject determines the choice of concord marker carried by the predicate—namely, a suffix which hops to the first constituent of the verbal.[17] When the subject is grammatically 2nd singular, concord is predominantly marked by the mere absence of a suffix and the verb then consists of bare stem only;[18] a certain number of French, Italian, and Roumanian verbs, however, add instead, as though by attraction, the same concord suffix as follows a tense/mode formative (see 9.6) in agreement with a 2nd singular subject. In all but French, a special suffix is added when the clause is negative (cf. 10.6).[19]

When the subject is one of the Span/Port/Ital honorifics which are grammatically nonlocal, the concord suffixes are peculiar to this pattern alone (cf. note 3). Observe the following matrix illustrating all the imperative variations existing for a verb like Sp *cantar*, with the different concord suffixes boldfaced. [*Problem. Then work out analogous charts for a Portuguese, Italian, or Roumanian verb.*]

Subject:	tú	vosotros	usted(es)	nosotros
Nonnegated:	canta	cantad	(no) cante(n)	(no) cantemos
Negated:	no cantes	no cantéis		

We have also noted that basically a subject stands in the opening position within a clause. It is a chief characteristic of imperative clauses that the subject-predicate order is transposed, as seen in, say, Sp *pide tú la cuenta* and not **tú pide la cuenta*. In this extraposition the subject is the more accessible to the intonational peak (and focus) of the utterance; for in an imperative speech act, the context of discourse is inevitably such that the subject either (a) receives contrastive/emphatic stress focusing on the addressee as opposed to someone else, or (b) is so obvious and redundant as to need no topicalization and to undergo full reduction through deletion.[20] Within the framework of this dichotomy, the French subjects *toi, vous, nous* (i) require reinforcement by the intensive *même* in order to receive the contrastive/emphatic focus—e.g. *écris toi-même la lettre* and not **ecris toi la lettre* like, say, It *scrivi tu la lettera*,[21] or (ii) are reduced fully to zero rather than to one of the stressless subject clitics occurring only in regular clauses (see 11.2)—thus, e.g., simply *écris la lettre, écrivez la lettre, écrivons la lettre.*

10.5 Negative clauses. By NEGATIVE CLAUSE is meant a clause whose predicate is constituted by a negative VP (cf. 8), as in the simple example

Fr Le moment n'est pas encore arrivé
Sp El momento no ha llegado todavía
Po O momento ainda não chegou
It Il momento non è ancora arrivato
Ro Momentul încă nu a venit.

In addition to the optional negator constituent of the VP, all five languages have in their lexicon a list of words characterized by the feature [+negative]. These items, which cut across the part-of-speech classification, are basically the [+neg] limiting adjectives (Fr *aucun/nul*, Sp *ninguno*, Po *nenhúm*, It *nessuno*, Ro *nici un*); the [+neg] [+hum] limiting pronouns (Fr *personne*, Sp *nadie*, Po *ninguém*, Ro *nimeni*); the [+neg] [−hum] pronouns (Fr *rien*, Sp/Po *nada*, It *niente/nulla*, Ro *nimic*); the [+neg] adverbs (Fr *plus* and *jamais*, Sp *nunca/jamás*, Po *nunca/jamais*, It *più* and *mai/giammai*, Ro *mai, niciodată*, and *nicăieri* 'nulle part'); the [+neg] conjunction (Fr/Sp *ni*, Po *nem*, It *nè*, Ro *nici*). The [+neg] words in view occur only in negative clauses as just defined.[22] Whatever be their function within the clause, i.e. as a constituent themselves (e.g. Fr *personne ne sait*, with the [+neg] pronoun as subject) or as part of a constituent (e.g. Fr *je n'ai aucune idée*, with the [+neg] adjective as determiner within the object NP); and regardless of whether the constituent precedes or follows the predicate, the basic negator in the VP remains present in the surface output of French and Roumanian. In the other three, however, the presence of a [+neg] word in a constituent which for any reason precedes the predicate, triggers deletion of the negator at the surface. This constraint may be illustrated with a Spanish clause containing three [+neg] constituents: *no le doy nunca nada a nadie*, with the modifier preposed, becomes *nunca le doy nada a nadie*; with the dative left-dislocated it becomes *a nadie le doy nunca nada*; or with the object similarly extrapositioned it becomes *nada le doy nunca a nadie*.[23]

In all five languages, constructions consisting of any element other than a verbal, plus the negator either preceding it or following it—as in Fr *pas moi* or *moi pas*, Sp *yo no* or *no yo*, and so on) are to be taken as reduced clauses functioning as sentential fragments, for the definition and description of which see 16.1.

Notes for Chapter 10

1. When the predicate is perfective, the clitic *se/si* in Fren/Ital entails selection of the Aux *être/essere* and consequent agreement of the participial verb head with the subject nominal—Fr *les journaux se sont vendus*, It *i giornali si sono venduti*.

2. Perhaps because of the object-becoming-subject involved in it, this type of *se*-clause has been characterized by some grammarians as an alternative passive construction, a 'pseudo-passive' or whatever, but this is misleading because *se*-clauses themselves have their regular passive counterparts, as we shall see (10.3).

3. What is more, in Italian a perfective predicate is not viable here: **si é curato i malati* is ill-formed.

4. Further assorted constraints: (a) Roumanian does not use *se* with the copula verb *a fi*, and Portuguese tends to avoid it; (b) in Italian, an equivalent adjectival arbitrarily carries a plural G/N concord suffix as a sign that in this language the underlying subject is specified as [+plural]; (c) in Italian alone it is possible to introduce *si* in addition to a *si* already present as the reflexive clitic, although the former *si* dissimilates morphophonemically in this particular environment, yielding, for example, *ci si difende bene* as the equivalent of Sp *uno se defiende bien* (**se se defiende bien* being ungrammatical); cf. Fr *on se défend bien*.

5. This last can be done even with a reflexive verb, e.g. *te scoli devreme* 'on se lève de bonne heure', in this language which alone lacks a match for Sp/It *uno*, Po *a gente*, where Spanish *uno se levanta temprano* is the only viable output here (**se se levanta* being ill-formed and *se levantan* being read as having a specific though deleted subject).

6. The Roumanian equivalent here is merely the existential [−S] *a fi* listed just below—e.g. *e cald = il fait chaud*, like *era loc = il y avait de la place*.

7. A separate lexical item from the [+S] or Aux *avoir*.

8. Here trans-1, but elsewhere an Aux, as in *él no ha llegado* or *Vd. ha de presentarse*. Present-tense *hay* and *ha* are alternants of one another, and

there are no variations in the other forms—e.g. *habrá tiempo, él no habrá llegado.*

9. Here trans-1, but elsewhere [+S] Auxs, as in *ele não tinha (~ havia) chegado, você há-de (~ tem de) se apresentar.*

10. A separate lexical item from the [+S] copula or Aux *essere.* Italian uniquely uses an analogous *volerci (≠ [+S] volere),* as in *ci vuole tempo, ci sono volute molte richieste,* with a meaning similar to that of *occorrere* and denoting required or desired existence.

11. Elsewhere the [+S] copula or Aux.

12. I.e., by reconstituting the oblique as subject, the subject as object, etc.

13. We may note that since only transitive verbs form passive adjectives, the Fren/Ital use of *être/essere* as the perfective AuxV as well occasions no ambiguity: thus Fr *s'être levé,* It *essersi alzato,* or Fr *être né,* It *essere nato* can only be perfective verbals, while Fr *être tué,* It *essere ucciso* can only be passive strings. In Roumanian, however, which perfectivizes all verbs with *a fi,* a string like *a fi primit* can correspond to either *avoir reçu* or *être reçu.* However, in perfective verbals the head signals no G/N concord and the AuxV no P/N concord, while passives always show G/N and, in *să*-clauses (see 13), P/N as well.

14. In all but French, the order in Sp *se venden los sellos,* etc., with subject extraposition, is very frequent here.

15. This is valid with any tense/mood and for ±perfective. Even with the preterite tense, *venire* may be preferred to *essere* in some registers.

16. Even with the preterite tense, *estuvieron vendidos* can contrast with *fueron vendidos* in certain embedded clauses, e.g. after *cuando* (cf. 12.4).

17. This is always a lone verb or, very marginally, a passive verbal; perfective verbals are semantically disqualified from figuring in imperative speech acts.

18. In one or another of the languages certain irregular verbs apocopate this form as only a bare stem could be apocopated—e.g. Sp *di, haz, ten, ven, pon, sal;* It *di;* Ro *zi, fă.*

19. Historically, this suffix in Ital/Roum is that of the infinitive form of the verb, while in Span/Port it is an amalgam of the present subjunctive tense/ mode formative and the 2nd sing. concord suffix, i.e. two elements cooccurring primarily in clauses with modality. [*Query. Synchronically, though, does it seem to make good sense to regard these imperative clauses as being, for some fortuitous reason, 'the same' as their 'doubles' elsewhere in the grammar? The same question applies to the next paragraph as well.*]

20. In Spanish, by exception, the subject *usted(es)* is retained even in the absence of contrast/emphasis in order to add a nuance of politeness to the imperative act; so, for example, *pase usted* is often preferred to just *pase,* in a situation where Portuguese would say just *passe,* or Italian just *passi.*

21. Also viable, of course, is *écris la lettre, toi* and so on, with the pronoun constituting a separate fragment, as evidenced by the intonation break, rather

than a part of the clause proper. However, this 'absolute' use of a personal pronoun as a fragment is nothing confined to cooccurrence with an imperative clause; it is a device used by all our languages, though more frequently in French for the very reason that the French personal pronouns do not occur as subjects or objects; cf. 11.

22. In a negative clause the regular adversative conjunction *mais/pero* etc. is replaced in Spanish by *sino*, in Portuguese by *senão*, and in Roumanian by *ci*. In most functions the reinforced Fr *et X et Y*, Sp *y X y Y*, etc. may be further intensified not only in negative clauses as *ni X ni Y* (cf. also 4.6), but also in nonnegative clauses with certain substitutes for the correlated conjunctions, viz.: Fr *non seulement X mais aussi Y*, Sp *no sólo X sino también Y*, Po *não só X senão também Y*, It *non soltanto X ma anche Y*, Ro *nu numai X ci şi Y*. (In this correlation, obviously, the negative particle does not make the clause itself negative.) Cf. also the substitutions in Fr *X ainsi que Y*, Sp *X así como Y*, Po *X assim como Y*, It *X così come Y*, Ro *X precum şi Y*.

23. Compare, on the other hand, with a [+neg] subject right-dislocated, normal inclusion of the negator: Sp *no ha venido nadie*, Po *não veio ninguém*, It *non è venuto nessuno*.

Clauses and discourse
Chapter 11
Movement and reduction transformations

11.1 Extraposition of subjects. In 9.7 it was stated that subjects are dislocated under two kinds of conditons: one syntactic, the other pragmatic. We now discuss subject extraposition under the pragmatic condition, with its constraints related to the discourse context of the clause.

• In all our languages except French, subject extraposition takes place whenever the subject (a) conveys information new to the discourse or (b) even if not new, is being singled out and focused upon in contrast to some other previously mentioned or presupposed entity. The extraposition serves to highlight the subject in the desired way by bringing it under the peak of the intonation contour, *whether declarative or interrogative.*

Table 11.1 illustrates the four-way variation.

Table 11.1 Extraposition of subjects.

		Without Extraposition:	With Extraposition:
Declarative contour:	Sp	El rey se ha muerto.	Se ha muerto el rey.
	Po	O rei morreu.	Morreu o rei.
	It	Il re è morto.	È morto il re.
	Ro	Regele a murit.	A murit regele.
Interrogative contour:	Sp	¿El rey se ha muerto?	¿Se ha muerto el rey?
	Po	O rei morreu?	Morreu o rei?
	It	Il re è morto?	È morto il re?
	Ro	Regele a murit?	A murit regele?

In simplest terms: on the left in Table 11.1, statement and question alike are about what happened to the king, while on the right both concern who has died. With the support of these data we can say that these four languages do not resort to extraposition in order to signal yes/no questions; that indeed they lack any syntactic device for this purpose and hence rely exclusively on intonation.

• French, on the other hand, does have a syntactic means of expressing yes/no questions; we shall see what it is in 16. For the pragmatic purpose in view here, however, French essentially has recourse to such transformations as *C'est le roi qui est mort* to signal the sort of focus achieved by extraposition in its sister languages.[1]

• Not infrequently in the four extraposing languages, whenever a subject conveying new information is to be fully highlighted by this device, any other constituent of the clause—i.e. a complement (be it object, dative, equivalent, or oblique) or any modifier—is necessarily displaced to the left of the predicate, i.e. *pre*posed, in order to bring the subject under the intonation peak. An example each from Spanish and Italian:

Spanish (underlying): Juan Ramón + recibió + el premio
→ (Subj. *post*posed): recibió + Juan Ramón + el premio
→ (Object *pre*posed): El premio lo recibió Juan Ramón.[2]

Italian (underlying): nessuno + non ha risposto + a Mario
→ (Subj. *post*posed): non ha risposto + nessuno + a Mario
→ (Dative *pre*posed): A Mario non ha risposto nessuno.

11.2 Reduction of subjects. At the opposite extreme from highlighting a subject as new and essential information stands the 'throwing away', or discarding, of a subject altogether as being fully established from the context and in no need of repetition. The principle of reduction as a discourse phenomenon has been expounded in 1.5. In that discussion we stated that when reduced, a given constituent either may be deleted or may give way to a special clitic trace form which is minimal in size and inaccessible to distinctive stress or pitch. Our examples of reduction in that section were confined to head deletion within a CNP; it was not yet practicable to illustrate reduction to clitics. Later, in 4.3.2, we illustrated the reduction of genitive modifiers in the CNP. But we were still not in a position to demonstrate in detail the reduction of entire nominals, adjectivals, or adverbials, because the manner in which such whole constructions are reduced correlates with their function in the clause of which they are inevitably a constituent. In the present context, we may now begin with the reduction of nominals functioning as subjects.

Any subject nominal eligible for reduction, being by definition specified as [+def], is fully deleted in all our languages except French, where instead it is reduced to a monosyllabic, unstressable clitic (also specified as [+def]) on the predicate verbal.[3] By way of illustration let us take the simplest of dialogues in each language.

Table 11.2 Reduction of subjects.

		Question:	Answer:
Sp		¿Qué hacen las mujeres?	Preparan la cena.
Po		Que fazem as mulheres?	Preparam a ceia.
It		Cosa fanno le donne?	Preparano la cena.
Ro		Ce fac femeile?	Pregătesc masa.
But:	Fr	Que font les femmes?	Elles préparent le souper.

In the answer there can be no doubt whatever as to who performs the act. However, as the examples make clear, in no one of the languages is the unexpressed subject lost without a trace. In all but French, the trace element is simply the P/N suffix on the verbal, which has been obligatorily added prior to the deletion and which provides at least the person and number of the reduced item.[4] In French, the subject clitic is selected in accordance with the head of the reduced subject nominal in terms of person, number, and gender, as displayed in Table 11.3. Belonging formally to this subject clitic system are also the items *on* (~ *l'on*) and *ce*. The former stands for a lexically unspecified referent, neutralized as to P/N/G and bearing only the semantic features [+human −def],[5] and already discussed in 10.1. The latter, like *il(s)* and *elle(s)*, is strictly anaphoric; but it occurs just with the linking verb *être*, in which limited environment it nevertheless has two distinct functions. In one of these it stands instead of *il* etc. for a reduced subject denoting an entity being named, identified, or characterized by the equivalent nominal, as in, for example, *c'est moi* or *c'est mon voisin* (in answer to *qui est . . .?*); *c'est un fruit* or *ce n'est rien* (in answer to *qu'est-ce que . . .?*); cf. also *c'est le moment, c'est une sainte, c'est un chef-d'oeuvre . . .*[6] In this function *ce* is marked (though not inflected) for the number of the reduced subject, so that agreement-copying operates to produce, e.g., *ce sont nos voisins, ce sont*

Table 11.3 French subject clitics.

Subject nominal to be reduced			Subject clitic
The local pronouns [±fem.]:	moi	→	je
	toi	→	tu
	nous	→	nous
	vous	→	vous
Any other nominal with	m.sg.	→	il
head that is	m.pl.	→	ils
	f.sg.	→	elle
	f.pl.	→	elles

des scélérats, ce sont elles,[7] etc. In the other languages all such subjects are simply deleted in the way already illustrated, e.g. Sp *es mi vecino, no es nada, es el momento, es una santa*, etc.[8] It appears to be this role of *ce* plus a surface equivalent complement that figures in the CLEFTING TRANSFORMA-TION highly favored in French for focusing on a particular clausal constituent, as when *Charles doit vous renseigner* becomes *c'est Charles qui doit vous renseigner*, or *on soupçonne Marianne → c'est Marianne que l'on soupçonne*. Cf. also the very high-frequency *c'est moi (toi, lui . . .) qui . . .*

In its second function *ce* stands for a lexically nonspecific and abstract referent being characterized by the equivalent complement (nominal or adjectival), and bearing only the semantic features [−anim +def], as in *c'est possible, c'est ridicule, c'est la vie, c'est dommage, c'est un fait, ce n'est pas la peine*, etc., denoting some act, fact, or situation already established by the discourse and figuring as the subject of a comment to be made. Once again, the equivalent mechanism in the other languages is simple deletion, as in Po *é possível, é ridículo, é um feito*, etc.[9]

In 9.7, note 29, we noted the French variant *qui le chien voit-il?*, which contains in addition to the subject nominal *le chien* the cross-referring subject clitic *il* following the verbal, i.e. in the position occupied by the subject itself when extraposition occurs.[10] This pattern may be regarded as an alternate (or secondary?) subject extraposition, which functions in parallel with the Q-marker *est-ce que*, not only in information questions containing a Q-word (*qui est-ce que le chien voit → qui le chien voit-il?*) but also in yes/no questions, e.g. *est-ce que la reine est morte? → la reine est-elle morte?* Thus, either introductory *est-ce que* or secondary extraposition constitutes, in fact, the French syntactic device we referred to, though without specifying it, in 9.7 for expressing yes/no questions.[11]

French also has special constraints on the use of personal pronouns as subjects—constraints not shared by our other four languages. The local pronouns do not, at least in careful standard speech, typically function as subjects in the surface output. Thus in the types of context exemplified by Sp *yo no acepto eso*, or *eso no lo acepto yo* (mutatis mutandis in Port/Ital/

Roum), French inserts the appropriate pronoun as a TOPICALIZER—phonologically isolated under a distinct intonational countour—either to left or right of the clause proper, and subsequently reduces the actual subject to a clitic in the usual way—as in *moi, je n'accepte pas ça* or *tu n'acceptes pas ça, toi?* In rapid colloquial, however, a preceding local is sometimes united phonologically to the clause proper, thus yielding *moi je n'insiste pas* (/mwaž-nɛ̃sistəpɒ/) or the like, and in this event we may argue that the pronoun itself is actually being promoted to the subject function. The corresponding clitic remains in cross-reference, though, for such a string as **moi n'insiste pas* is ungrammatical.[12] The substitutes *lui, eux, elle(s)*, on the other hand, are free to function as surface subjects, so that *lui n'accepte pas ça* etc. *are* grammatical, as well as *qu'est-ce qu'eux en pensent?* (kɛsköõpõs/). In careful speech, even so, these substitutes are also often topicalized in parallel with the locals to yield *lui, il n'accepte pas ça* or *ils n'acceptent pas ça, eux*.[13]

11.3 Reduction of complements. We are now in a position to observe the way in which complements may be 'thrown away' for the same pragmatic motives of discourse as are subjects. Typically in all the Romance languages, nominals functioning as objects or datives either reduce to monosyllabic stressless clitics on the predicate verbal, or delete altogether under certain conditions. We will best deal with the clitics first.[14]

11.3.1 [+def] objects. (1) In all the languages, object nominals specified as [+def] reduce to [+def] trace clitics on a selective basis of person, number, and to some extent gender, as displayed in Table 11.4. Also belonging formally and distributionally to this object clitic system is the item *se/si*, as either (i) the surface expression of an underlying [−def] subject (described in 10.1); or (ii) an essential formative in lexically/morphologically reflexive verbs such as Fr *se souvenir*, Sp *acordarse*, Po *lembrar-se*, It *ricordarsi*, Ro *a se aminti*; or (iii) as the trace clitic for an object which, being referentially identical with the subject of the clause, is normally unexpressed in the surface output.[15]

Table 11.4 Object clitics.

[+Def] object nominal to be reduced		Fr	Sp	Po	It	Ro
The local pronouns [±fem.]	1st sg.	me	me	me	mi	mă
	2nd sg.	te	te	te	ti	te
	1st pl.	nous	nos	nos	ci	ne
	2nd pl.	vous	os	vos	vi	vă
Any other nominal with head that is:	m.sg.	le	lo[16]	o	lo	l
	f.sg.	la	la	a	la (La)[17]	o[18]
	m.pl.	les	los[16]	os	li (Li)	i
	f.pl.	les	las	as	le (Le)	le

(2) Position of the object clitics. Upon the reduction of a nominal object, the resulting clitic is adjoined to the predicate verbal, normally being fronted to a slot immediately left of the first verbal element, thus even after a negator; in other words, it becomes *pro*clitic to the verbal, as illustrated by the simplest of dialogues in each language:

	Question:	Answer:
Fr	Quand vendez-vous la maison?	Nous ne la vendons pas.
Sp	¿Cuándo venden Vds. la casa?	No la vendemos.
Po	Quando vocês vendem a casa?	Não a vendemos.
It	Quando vendono Loro la casa?	Non la vendiamo.[19]
Ro	Cînd vindeţi Dvs casa?	Nu o vindem.[20]

There are, however, assorted restrictions on the fronting in view here: a major one reaching across the board, and minor ones peculiar to individual languages.

• In imperative clauses, which as we have seen lack the modality constituent, the adjoined clitic object is fronted to a spot *en*clitic rather than *pro*clitic (i.e. to the right, not left) to the verbal head. This enclisis seems basically connected with the highly frequent environment where, the subject being singular, the verb is a suffixless bare stem, though concord suffixes do also occur with plural subjects. When, on the other hand, an imperative clause is negated, and there is concomitantly some related suffix on the verb (except in French), the clitic seeks its regular proclitic position. To illustrate, then, the two complementary structures:

Fr	(J'achète les oranges?)	— Oui, achète-les (toi)./ Non, ne les achète pas.
Sp	(¿Compro las naranjas?)	— Sí, cómpralas (tú)./ No, no las compres.
Po	(Compro as laranjas?)	— Sim, compra-as (tu)./ Não as compres, não.
It	(Compro le arancie?)	— Sì, comprale (tu)./ No, non le comprare.
Ro	(Cumpăr portocalele?)	— Da, cumpără-le (tu)./ Nu, nu le cumpăra.

Exceptions to this predominant pattern are three: (i) In Italian, *pro*clisis whenever the subject is honorific—e.g. *Sì, le compri (Lei)*; (ii) also in Italian, enclisis in free alternation with proclisis when the clause is negated and the subject is *tu/voi*—e.g. *No, non compratele (voi)* ~ *No, non le comprate (voi)*; (iii) in Roumanian, proclisis whenever the subject is *noi*—e.g. *Da, să le cumpărăm (noi)*.

• Further constraints on clitic fronting are the following, most notably in Portuguese. In this language the incidence and degree of fronting is conditioned by the distribution of other elements in the clause. For one thing, an atonic clitic will not move to the left of a verbal which stands absolute-initial as a result of subject extraposition or deletion. Thus *Carlos escreve as cartas*, upon reduction of the object, results in *escreve-as Carlos* if the subject is moved, or in just *escreve-as* if it is deleted.[21] Secondly, even when the subject *is* deleted or extraposed, full clitic-fronting regularly occurs provided some other element of the clause is also located left of the verbal, thus providing an INTERTONIC spot for the clitic. Such elements are chiefly the negator *não* (actually *in* the predicate), a Q-word in any function, or a preposed modifier in any function (e.g. *já, talvez, então, nunca . . .*), as in *não as escreve, quem me acusará?, já nos têm convidado*, etc. In some dialects, including essentially all those of Brazil, speakers resistant to, or even fully unaware of, nonfrontings like *pediu-me* or partial frontings like *tenho-me levantado* or *conhecer-nos-iam*, will nevertheless conform to the absolute-initial constraint by leaving in place a discourse-deletable pronominal subject and will say, for example, *você me pediu* or *eu me tenho levantado* or *eles nos conheceriam*. In these same varieties, the complicated fronting rules tend to be side-stepped altogether through total deletion of any object nominal that if reduced would entail one of the clitic subset *o, os, a, as*. Thus the response to *onde você deixa seu carro?* can be simply *deixo na rua*.[22]

The other language in view here, Roumanian, has but one minor constraint on fronting: just the one clitic *o* remains unfronted when the verbal has two (or more) components, as in *Ion a văzut-o* 'Jean l'a vue', *cine ar crede-o?* 'qui le croirait?', *noi vom sfîrşi-o* 'nous le finirons', and the like.[23]

All other clitics, as treated in the following sections, obey the same rules of position as we have just detailed for the [+def] object clitics.

(3) We may now examine certain other assorted limitations on objects and their reduction.

● In French, the local pronouns cannot function as objects in the surface output. Thus in the types of context exemplified by Sp *no me aceptan a mí* (mutatis mutandis in Port/Ital/Roum), French introduces the appropriate pronoun as a topicalizer to either left or right of the clause proper, and subsequently reduces the underlying object to a clitic in the usual way—as in *moi, on ne m'accepte pas* or *on ne t'accepte pas, toi?* Likewise, the substitutes *lui, eux, elle(s)*, though free to function as surface subjects (as we noted in 11.2) cannot act as surface objects and are therefore topicalized in parallel with the locals to yield *lui (elle), on ne l'accepte pas* or *on ne les accepte pas, eux (elles)?*[24]

● In various environments in one or another of our languages, an object clitic is present in the predicate verbal even when the object nominal itself is unreduced. Thus, Span/Port/Roum require 'clitic copying' regularly with certain specific nominals, while all of them require it whenever the object is preposed for pragmatic purposes. The latter situation, however, is part of a broader picture we will look at in 11.5. As to the certain specific nominals:

In Spanish the local, honorific and substitute pronouns—all of which, being specified [+human],[25] join with all [+human] nominals in requiring the marker *a* when functioning as objects—are also obligatorily copied in the verbal via insertion of the corresponding clitic, as illustrated in *tú me ves a mí, yo te veo a ti, tú nos ves a nosotros, yo os veo a vosotros, lo veo a él* (or *a usted*), *los veo a ellos* (or *a ustedes*), *la(s) veo a ella(s)* (or *a ustedes*).

In Portuguese the locals are alone in requiring both marking with *a* and clitic-copying when functioning as objects, as in *tu me vês a mim, eu te vejo a ti, tu nos vês a nós, eu vos vejo a vós*. As for the substitutes, they may also be marked and copied if specified as [+human]—as in *eu o(s) vejo a ele(s), eu a(s) vejo a ela(s)*, but in many dialects (notably Brazilian ones) this is not required, so that *eu vejo ele(s)* or *ela(s)*, even when [+human], are as well-formed as *eu vejo você(s), o(s) senhor(es)*, etc. with the honorifics.

In Roumanian, *all* nominals marked by the functor *pe* as objects (see 9.3.1) are also obligatorily clitic-copied in the verbal, as in not only *tu mă vezi pe mine, eu te văd pe tine* (or *dumneata*), *tu ne vezi pe noi, eu vă văd pe voi* (or *dumneavoastră*), *îl văd pe el, o văd pe ea, îi văd pe ei, le văd pe ele*, but also *îl văd pe Mihai, nu le cunosc pe doamnele acelea* 'je ne connais pas ces dames-là' and even in *am cumpărat-o pe aceasta* 'j'ai acheté celle-ci' etc.

In all three, reduction thus consists merely of deleting the marked object and leaving the clitic intact, e.g. Sp *no me conocen a mí* → *no me conocen*, Po *não vos conhecem a vós* → *não vos conhecem*, Ro *nu le cunosc pe ele* → *nu le conosc*.

• When an underlying indefinite subject is expressed by means of the clitic *se/si* (as discussed in 10.1), and when an object nominal is *not* transformed to subject in the surface structure—an output permitted only in Sp/Po/It— the object nominal may be reduced to a clitic in Spanish or Italian, thus: Sp *se cura a los enfermos* → *se los cura*, It *si cura i malati* → *li si cura*.[26]

11.3.2 [−def] objects. Object nominals specified as [−def]—be they non-countable singulars or countable plurals—are reduced either (1) fully or (2) partially under appropriate pragmatic conditions of discourse.

(1) In Span/Port/Roum an undetermined object nominal is fully deleted under 'throw-away' conditions. Examples:

Sp	(¿Pescado?)	Sí, tenemos.	(¿Manzanas?)	Yo no compro nunca.
Po	(Peixe?)	Temos, sim.	(Mançãs?)	Eu não compro nunca.
Ro	(Peşte?)	Da, avem.	(Mere?)	Eu nu cumpăr niciodată.

In French there are no undetermined object nominals. One which is determined by the partitive article is fully reducible to the clitic *en*, as in:

Fr (Du poisson?) Oui, nous en avons. (Des pommes?) Moi, je n'en achète jamais.[27]

In Italian an object nominal which is either undetermined or determined by the partitive article is fully reducible to the clitic *ne*, as in:

It   (Pesce?)   Sì, ne abbiamo.   (Delle mele?)   Io non ne compro mai.[28]

(2) In all five languages an object nominal determined by a quantifier may 'throw away' the head noun (plus or minus a descriptive modifier) by total deletion in Span/Port/Roum (e.g. Sp. *visitaremos muchos puntos (intere-santes, de interés . . .)* → *visitaremos muchos*, and by cliticizing with *en/ne* in Fren/Ital as shown in the following display of examples, in all of which there could also be a descriptive modifier:

Fr   j'ai deux (quatre, plusieurs . . .) livres → j'en ai deux (quatre, plu-
       sieurs . . .)
       j'ai vu un autre (un tel, un seul) film → j'en ai vu un autre (un tel,
       un seul)
       vous avez beaucoup (peu, assez . . .) de talent → vous en avez
       beaucoup (peu, assez . . .)
       nous avons reçu beaucoup (peu, trop) de cadeaux → nous en avons
       reçu beaucoup (peu, trop)
       je n'ai aucune objection → je n'en ai aucune
       je n'ai plus de patience (d'illusions . . .) → je n'en ai plus[29]

It   ho due (quattro, parecchi . . .) libri → ne ho due (quattro, parecchi
       . . .)
       ho visto un altro (un tale, un solo . . .) film → ne ho visto un altro
       (un tale, uno solo . . .)
       Lei ha molto (poco, abbastanza . . .) talento → Lei ne ha molto
       (poco, abbastanza . . .)
       abbiamo ricevuto molti (pochi, troppi . . .) regali → ne abbiamo
       ricevuto molti[30] (pochi, troppi . . .)
       non ho nessuna obiezione → non ne ho nessuna
       non ho più pazienza (illusioni . . .) → non ne ho più

(3) Within an object nominal, dependent nominal modifiers of the genitive and delimiting types—typically though not necessarily [+def]—may them-selves be 'thrown away' by total deletion in Span/Port/Roum (e.g. Po *perdi a chave da casa* → *perdi a chave*; or *respondi a cada uma das cartas* → *respondi a cada uma*), and by cliticizing with *en/ne* in Fren/Ital, provided the modifier is [−human], as in the following arrays of examples:

• Reducing [−human] genitive modifiers:[31]
Fr   j'ai oublié le titre du livre → j'en ai oublié le titre
       j'ai perdu la clef de l'appartement → j'en ai perdu la clef
       on attend l'établissement d'une loi → on en attend l'établissement
It   ho dimenticato il titolo del libro → ne ho dimenticato il titolo
       ho perduto la chiave dell'appartamento → ne ho perduto la chiave
       si aspetta lo stabilimento di una legge → se ne aspetta lo stabili-
       mento

• Reducing [−human] delimiting modifiers:[32]

Fr nous avons perdu quelques-uns des documents → nous en avons
    perdu quelques-uns

je lirai chacun de vos essais → j'en lirai chacun

je voudrais une (trois, une douzaine . . .) de ces pêches → j'en
voudrais une (trois, une douzaine. . .)

on a retrouvé beaucoup (un peu, assez . . .) de l'argent → on en a
retrouvé beaucoup (un peu, assez . . .)

j'ai encore beaucoup (tant, trop . . .) de ces photos → j'en ai encore
beaucoup (tant, trop . . .)

il a écrit le premier (le deuxième, le dernier . . .) de ses articles → il
en a écrit le premier (le deuxième, le dernier)

It abbiamo perduto alcuni dei documenti → ne abbiamo perduto
    alcuni

leggerò ciascuno dei Suoi saggi → ne leggerò ciascuno

vorrei una (tre, una dozzina . . .) di quelle pesche → ne vorrei una
(tre, una dozzina . . .)

si è ritrovato molto (la maggior parte . . .) del denaro → se n'è
ritrovato molto (la maggior parte . . .)

11.3.3 [+def] datives. (1) In all our languages, dative nominals specified
as [+def] reduce to [+def] trace clitics on a selective basis of person and
number. For the local pronouns and for the reflexive,[33] these dative clitics
are formally identical to the object clitics in all but Roumanian, for which
see (2). The clitic reductions for all other dative nominals are shown in
Table 11.5.

Table 11.5 Dative clitics.

Dative nominal to be reduced	Fr	Sp	Po	It	Ro
With singular head:	lui	le	lhe	gli	i
With plural head:	leur	les	lhes	*[34]	le

(2) Just as object clitics are fronted so as to become proclitically adjoined
to the verbal, dative clitics behave in exactly the same way positionally, as
illustrated by simple dialogues in each language:

	Question:	*Answer:*
Fr	Qu'avez-vous dit à Jeanne?	Je ne lui ai rien dit.[35]
Sp	¿Qué le dijo Vd. a Juana?	No le dije nada.
Po	Que é que você disse a Joana?	Não lhe disse nada.
It	Cos'ha detto Lei a Giovanna?	Non le ho detto niente.[35]
Ro	Ce-i aţi spus lui Ioana?	Nu-i am spus nimic.

Portuguese has exactly the same fronting constraints as for object clitics, and
needs no further illustrations in that respect. We may therefore go on to
assorted limitations on datives and their reduction.

• In French, neither the local nor the substitute pronouns can function as datives in the surface output. Thus, in the types of context exemplified by Sp *no me contestan a mí* (mutatis mutandis in Po/It/Ro), French introduces the appropriate pronoun as a topicalizer to either left or right of the clause proper—unmarked if left, *à*-marked if right—and subsequently reduces the underlying dative to a clitic in the usual way, as in *moi, on ne me répond pas; on ne te répond pas, à toi?* or *lui (elle), on ne lui répond pas; on ne leur répond pas, à eux (à elles)?*

• In Span/Roum, a dative clitic *copy* is adjoined to the predicate verbal even when any dative nominal itself is unreduced. Thus in Spanish, e.g. *tú me dices a mí, yo te digo a ti, tú nos dices a nosotros, yo os digo a vosotros, le digo a él (a ella, a Vd., a José, a María, al señor, a la señora . . .), les digo a ellos (a ellas, a Vds., a los señores, a las señoras . . .).*[36]

• In Roumanian, as we have pointed out in 9.3.1, any dative nominal is marked as such by the gen./dat. suffix attached to the first constituent of the phrase. This suffix, regularly -*i* on singulars and -*or* on plurals,[37] gives way to fully or partially suppletive stem alternants in the personal pronoun paradigm, as follows:

Locals: *mie, ţie* (hon. *dumitale*), *nouă, vouă*; reflexive: *şie*
Substitutes: m.sg. *lui*, f.sg. *ei*, m.f.pl. *lor.*

The dative clitics corresponding to *mie, ţie, şie* are, respectively, *mi ţi şi*, thus in formal contrast with the object clitics *mă te se* in just these three items. Examples: *tu mi-ai spus mie, eu ţi-am spus ţie (dumitale), tu ne-ai spus nouă, eu v'am spus vouă (dumneavoastră), eu i-am spus lui* or *ei, eu le-am spus lor.*

In both Spanish and Roumanian, then, reduction consists merely of deleting the marked dative and leaving the clitic copy intact, e.g. Sp *no me gusta a mí* → *no me gusta, no les gusta a mis padres* → *no les gusta*, etc.; Ro *nu vă place vouă* → *nu vă place, nu le place părinţilor mei* → *nu le place*, etc.

(3) In 11.3.2 (2) we stated that within an object nominal, a [−human] modifier of the genitive type may be fully deleted in Span/Port/Roum and reduced in Fren/Ital to *en/ne*, and we cross-referred to the present section with regard to [+human] modifiers of this type. We may now add that within object nominals a clitic reduction of [+human] genitives is available in all five languages, as an alternative to the syntactically unconstrained reduction described above, in certain lexical contexts only. That is to say, when the possessor/possessed relationship that exists between a person and a part of himself (say, his hand) or an article of his clothing (say, his hat) or a common accessory (say, his watch) is presupposed as self-evident, the underlying genitive modifier is typically promoted to the status of dative complement and thence reduced to a dative clitic, as illustrated herewith:

Fr ils nous ont ôté les documents, l'enfant vous a cassé la montre, Jean se lavait les mains

Sp nos quitaron los documentos, el niño le ha roto el reloj, Juan se
 lavaba las manos
Po tomaram-nos os documentos, o menino lhe rompeu o relógio, João
 lavava-se as mãos
It ci hanno tolto i documenti, il bambino Le ha rotto l'orologio,
 Giovanni si lavava le mani
Ro ne-au luat documentele, copilul v'a rupt ceasul, Ion îşi spăla mîinile

As these examples show, the pattern is viable whether subject and possessor
are different persons or one and the same person.[38] The frequency and extent
of this promotion to dative varies from one to another of the languages,
being probably the least common in French and the most so in Roumanian;
cf. Fr *j'ai terminé mes études* or *Jean verra sa famille*, but not **je me suis
terminé les études* or **Jean se verra la famille*, as against Ro *mi-am terminat
studiile* or *Ion îşi va vedea familia*, which are effective reductions as compared with *am terminat studiile mele* or *Ion va vedea familia sa.*[39]

11.3.4 Equivalent complements. (1) Adjectivals (or adjectivalized nominals) functioning as equivalents are reducible only after linking verbs, mainly
the copula, this being the only contextual situation in which such complements are likely to constitute old information of the sort eligible for throw-
away. In Port/Roum the reduction of an equivalent is by full deletion, while
in the other languages it is to Fr *le*, Sp/It *lo*, a clitic unmarked for either
number or gender, as illustrated in the following very brief exchanges:

Fr Est-ce que ces familles sont très riches? — Oui, elles *le* sont.
 Êtes-vous acteur (actrice . . .)? — Je *l'*étais, mais je ne *le* suis plus.
Sp ¿Son muy ricas esas familias? — Sí, *lo* son.[40]
 ¿Es Vd. actor (actriz . . .)? — *Lo* era, pero ya no *lo* soy.
It Sono molto ricche quelle famiglie? — *Lo* sono, sì.
 Lei è attore (attrice . . .)? — *Lo* ero, ma non *lo* sono più.[41]

(2) On the other hand, when an equivalent nominal is serving to name an
entity already established by the context but not as yet identified—as in Fr
c'est un fruit, c'est mon voisin, ce sont nos voisins, c'est moi, etc. (cf. 11.2)—
it is, of course, the subject and hence not the complement that is reduced. In
all of the languages except French, after deletion of the underlying subject,
the equivalent nominal is transformed to surface subject as evidenced by the
P/N agreement on the verbal, e.g.:

Sp es mi vecino, son mis vecinos, soy yo, somos nosotros, es ella
Po é o meu vizinho, são os meus vizinhos, sou eu, somos nós, é ela
It è il mio vicino, sono i miei vicini, sono io, siamo noi, è lei
Ro e vecinul meu, sînt vecinii mei, sînt eu, sîntem noi, este ea[42]

11.3.5 Oblique complements. The only obliques eligible for reduction
under appropriate discourse conditions are, with trivial exceptions (cf. 11,
note 40) those filled by an adverbial. In Sp/Po/Ro the only available throw-
away is deletion, as in Sp *no me acuerdo de eso → no me acuerdo* or Po *você*

não estava em casa → *você não estava*; but in Fren/Ital reduction is to the clitics *en/ne* or *y/ci*, depending on the semantic role of the adverbial head.

(1) The preposition *de/di* selects the clitic *en/ne*, which obeys the same fronting rules as the other clitics. Examples:

Fr je m'occuperai de cette affaire → je m'en occuperai
    on m'a accusé de négligence → on m'en a accusé
    vous n'êtes donc pas sûr de l'adresse? → vous n'en êtes donc pas sûr?
    que pensez-vous de l'économie? → qu'en pensez-vous?

It mi occuperò di questa faccenda → me ne occuperò
    mi hanno accusato di negligenza → me ne hanno accusato
    Lei non è sicuro dell'indirizzo? → Lei non ne è sicuro?
    che pensa Lei dell'economia? → che ne pensa Lei?[43]

On the other hand, the prepositions Fr *à, en, dans, sur, sous, entre, parmi* and *chez*, and It *a, in, su, sotto, tra, fra*, and the *da* that equates with Fr *chez* but not the *da* that equates with Fr *de* or *par*, select the clitic *y/ci*.[44] Examples:

Fr nous sommes tous entrés dans la salle → nous y sommes tous entrés
    tu as mis les valises sous le lit? → tu y as mis les valises?
    je pense toujours à ton bien-être → j'y pense toujours
    ils vont tout de suite chez Georges → ils y vont tout de suite

It tutti siamo entrati nel salotto → tutti ci siamo entrati
    hai messo le valigie sotto il letto? → ci hai messo le valigie?
    penso sempre al tuo benessere → ci penso sempre
    vanno subito da Giorgio → ci vanno subito

The prepositions *à/a* and *en/in* are eligible for this reduction whether they are specified as [+place] or not (cf. Fr *j'y vais* or *j'y crois*, It *ci vado* or *ci credo*); but the other prepositions in view here qualify only when they are [+place]. As regards the item *chez/da*, it is unique in that it allows reduction even though its object is (exclusively) [+human]—e.g. Fr *je vais chez elle* is reducible to *j'y vais*, while *je pense à elle* is not reducible and *je pense à cela* is. Prepositions (other than *de/di*, of course) that are never specified [+place]— e.g. Fr *pour, après* . . ., It *per, dopo* . . .—are simply never reducible.

(2) Of the Class 2 and Class 3 adverbs, again only those specified [+place] are eligible for reduction, and they exclusively to *y/ci*. Examples:

Fr nous sommes restés derrière (la maison) → nous y sommes restés
    je vais laisser les bagages tout près (de la porte) → je vais y laisser les bagages
    vous gardez toujours votre auto ici (dans la rue)? → vous y gardez toujours votre auto?
    Jean ne descend jamais en bas → Jean n'y descend jamais

It noi siamo rimasti dietro (le quinte) → noi ci siamo rimasti
    lascerò i bagagli vicino (alla porta) → ci lascerò i bagagli

Lei tiene sempre la Sua auto qui (nella strada)? → Lei ci tiene sempre la Sua auto?

Giovanni non scende mai laggiù → Giovanni non vi scende mai

The parenthesized portions of the complements show how these adverbials are reducible either alone or with a complement of whatever type.[45]

11.4 Reduction of modifiers. The only modifiers typically eligible for reduction are, of course, those filled by an adverbial with a [+place] head. In Sp/Po/Ro, substitution of a given [+def] adverbial by one of the Class 3 demonstrative adverbs is normally possible—as, for example, Sp *yo trabajo en la ciudad* → *yo trabajo allí*—but reduction is not available. In Fren/Ital, on the other hand, there is reduction to the clitic *y/ci*.[46] Examples:

- With a preposition as head:

Fr   Pierre va étudier en Espagne → Pierre va y étudier
      on danse sur le Pont d'Avignon → on y danse
      j'ai cherché parmi les ruines → j'y ai cherché

It   Pietro studierà in Spagna → Pietro ci studierà
      non ballano mai sul Ponte Milvio? → non ci ballano mai?
      ho cercato fra le rovine → ci ho cercato

- With an adv-2 or an adv-3 as head:

Fr   l'avion vole au-dessus des nuages → l'avion y vole
      j'ai vu un étranger devant la porte → j'y ai vu un étranger
      il fait si froid là-dedans → il y fait si froid
      les enfants dorment toujours en haut → les enfants y dorment
      toujours

It   gli aerei volano sopra le nuvole → gli aerei ci volano
      ho visto uno straniero davanti alla porta → ci ho visto uno stra-
      niero
      fa tanto freddo lì dentro → ci fa tanto freddo
      i bambini dormono sempre giù → i bambini ci dormono sempre

11.5 Extraposition of complements. Within a clause the basic order of the constituents predicate + complement is transposed under the same two types of condition mentioned earlier (9.7) in connection with the opposite phenomenon, namely, the extraposition of subjects. The syntactic constraint is the same obligatory preposing of any complement containing a Q-element, as was amply illustrated in the previous connection. The pragmatic constraint—which normally applies to just one complement per clause—preposes a complement which is specified as [+def] and does not convey new information, in order to make it the theme of the clause while at the same time leaving the predicate (plus or minus some other constituent), or a simultaneously extraposed subject, as the case may be, under the intonation peak for the desired highlighting effect. When a complement thus becomes the theme it is copied within the predicate by the corresponding clitic, as we now illustrate:

- Preposed object:

Fr	ces livres-là, je les ai lus[47]	ça, je vais le faire tout de suite
Sp	esos libros los he leído	eso lo voy a hacer en seguida
Po	esses livros eu (os) li	isso vou (o) fazer já
It	quei libri li ho letti	quello lo farò subito
Ro	acele cărţi le-am citit	aceea o voi face imediat

- Preposed dative:

Fr	à Jean on ne lui a rien dit	à moi ça ne me paraît pas possible
Sp	a Juan no le han dicho nada	a mí no me parece posible
Po	a João não lhe disseram nada	a mim não me parece possível
It	a Gianni non gli hanno detto niente	a me non (mi) pare possibile[48]
Ro	lui Ion nu-i au spus nimic	mie nu-mi pare posibil

11.6 Extraposition of modifiers. Again we are dealing with the same two sorts of constraint: the incidence of a Q-element in a modifier triggers its preposing, as in Fr *à quelle heure commence le spectacle?*, Sp *¿a qué hora empieza la función?* etc.; also a modifier is very often preposed in order to pinpoint not merely the predicate happening, but the entire predication, including agent as well as action. Thus, for example, while Fr *le concert aura lieu demain soir* tells when, as opposed to some other time, a given event will take place, the left-dislocation *demain soir un concert aura lieu* sets the time for one event as opposed to some other event. In Italian but not normally in French, a place modifier thus preposed can (though need not) be traced in the predicate by the available clitic, as, for example, in *a Bologna ci studiano parecchi*.

11.7 Cooccurrent clitics. When for any reason two clitics cooccur in one and the same predicate, the rules for relative order differ substantially from language to language. Occasions for such cooccurrence are the simultaneous reduction of both an object and a dative, e.g.:

Fr	j'ai donné les instructions à Paul → je les lui ai données
Sp	le di las instrucciones a Pablo → se las di[49]
Po	dei as instruções a Paulo → dei-lhas
It	ho dato le istruzioni a Paolo → gliele ho date
Ro	i-am dat instrucţiile lui Radu → i le-am dat

or, in Fren/Ital, of both an object and an oblique or a place modifier, e.g.

Fr	as-tu mis les timbres sur la lettre? → les y as-tu mis?
It	hai messo i francobolli sulla lettera? → ce li hai messi?

as well as the reduction of one or another complement with (i) a lexically reflexive verb (e.g. Fr *je me souviens du passé → je m'en souviens*[50]) or (ii) in Span/Ital only, with the clitic *se/si* as marker of an underlying subject (e.g. Sp *se cura a los enfermos → se los cura*).

The morphophonemic behavior of clitics, including that of their cooccurrence, must, of course, be stated in terms of the phonological structure of each individual language.[51] [*Comment. Appendix 5 offers a description of Roumanian clitic alternations, on which those of the other languages can be modeled.*]

Notes for Chapter 11

1. By exception, however, extraposition does tend to occur when the subject nominal has a [−def] determiner, say the indefinite article, because such a subject almost always conveys new information—e.g. Sp *entró una mujer* or whatever. In this situation French does, in fact, allow a special form of extraposition, saying *il est entré une femme* etc. For discussion of the trace-form *il* occupying the original subject position, see 11.2.

2. For a discussion of the cross-referring clitic which typically appears on the verbal when a complement is preposed, see 11.3.

3. These are traditionally, though imprecisely, known as 'subject pronouns'. [*Query. Why is this a misnomer, strictly speaking?*]

4. In one or another language this trace mechanism is less than a fully airtight system—what is the person of the subject traced in Sp *hablaba despacio*, or the number of the subject in Ro *lucrează bine?*—but it actually does not need to be; it tolerates minor ambiguities easily enough because in most exchanges or discourses there are ample nonlinguistic clues to the identity of items to be understood even though unexpressed.

5. In some colloquial styles, however, *on* may be said to be [+def] and actually replace the subject clitic *nous*, as in, say, *quant à nous, on va rester ici*. (Cf. also the song title 'Heureusement que l'on ne s'aimait pas'.)

6. This excludes undetermined nominals (often consisting of head alone) which serve rather to categorize or classify (professionally, socially, etc.) and which are adjective-like in their lexical function; thus *M. Landré est professeur* reduces to *il est professeur*, analogous to *il est intelligent*.

7. But: *c'est vous*, whether *vous* is singular or plural; and, seemingly by analogy, *c'est nous*.

8. For the P/N-bearing verb in the other languages—as exemplified by It *sono i nostri vicini, sono loro, siamo noi*, etc.—see 11.3.4.

9. Even a specific inanimate thing, if not named earlier in the discourse, may be characterized by this reduction, as in *c'est neuf?* (speaking of a *voiture*) or *c'est sec!* (speaking of some *vin*); otherwise *elle est neuve* or *il est sec* is preferred, and in the case of plurals such as *elles sont petites* (of *maisons*) is required as against *c'est petit*. With any other verb than *être*, no reduction of abstract subjects is possible; they can only be replaced by one of the demonstrative abstract pronouns *cela* (= *ça*) or *ceci*, e.g. *ça ne m'intéresse pas*, which corresponds to Sp *eso no me interesa* etc. rather than to Sp *no me interesa* etc.

10. Be it noted, however, that in contrast to a full subject nominal, which when extraposed always follows the entire predicate verbal, a subject clitic splits any VP so as to come immediately after the modality-bearing element,

thus: *d'où est venu ce personnage?* as against *d'où est-il venu?*

[*Query. Morphophonemic aside: as regards the linking* /-t/ *which appears automatically between the (first element of the) verbal and the vowel-initial subject clitics* il(s), elle(s), on (*as in, e.g.,* /vwatil/, /vwatõ/, /parlǝtɛl/, /parlǝtõ/ *when extraposed, what alternative ways do you see of characterizing it? Which seems preferable, and why?*]

11. When in these interrogative contexts a subject nominal merits reduction, this is accomplished in the regular way just described in the case of primary extraposition or if *est-ce que* is present, while the subject is fully deleted in the case of secondary extraposition, with the cross-referring clitic simply remaining in place. To illustrate:

qui le chien voit-il? → qui voit-il?

la reine est-elle morte? → est-elle morte?

qui est-ce que le chien voit? → qui est-ce qu'il voit?

est-ce que la reine est morte? → est-ce qu'elle est morte?

12. This promotion seems indeed to be the rule when pre-subject material such as *est-ce que* is also present and the pronoun is under the intonation peak for contrastive emphasis—e.g. *qu'est-ce que toi t(u) en penses?* (/kɛskǝtwatõpõs/).

13. The pronominal compounds with *-même*, both local (*moi-même* etc.) and substitute (*elles-mêmes* etc.), have the special faculty of falling under the intonation peak and thus being unmistakably a constituent of the clause proper, there even being a contrast of meaning between *je n'en sais rien moi-même* (united) and *je n'en sais rien, moi-même* (isolated, as in *je n'en sais rien, moi*). This pattern is unique and seems to leave open the question of whether the compounds are promoted subjects in an extraposition peculiar to them alone, or whether they are, in fact, functioning as modifiers. [*Query. What is your opinion?*]

14. These items are known, traditionally, as 'conjunctive (as opposed to disjunctive) pronouns'. [*Query. Why, again, is this really a misnomer?*]

15. The object in question, if plural, may be either REFLEXIVE or RECIPROCAL. When it is the latter and the context of discourse fails to indicate this reciprocity clearly enough, a uniquely structured phrase may surface, as Fr *l'un l'autre*, Sp *uno a otro*, Po *um a outro*, It *l'uno l'altro*, Ro *unul pe altul*, all also pluralizable, as Fr *les uns les autres* etc. [*Query. How would you account for the form of such a phrase type, as well as for its function within the clause?*]

16. For the [+human] variants *le* and *les*, see 11.3.2.

17. The Italian clitic *La*, written with a capital, is the one and only reduction of the honorific *Lei*, even though that pronoun has either gender according to the sex of the referent. Honorific *Loro*, on the other hand, reduces to *Li* or *Le* in conformity with the general pattern.

18. By exception in Roumanian, the clitic *o* replaces the expected *l* as the m.sg. reduction of any abstract pronoun, or the trace of a discourse-estab-

lished fact, situation, notion. The abstracts themselves are m.sg. just as they are in the other languages (*aceea e frumos*, like Sp *aquello es hermoso*); hence the particular clitic in view is not exclusively in correlation with a f.sg. nominal, as Table 11.4 suggests.

19. A morphological note. Compare also, as other possible responses, Fr *nous l'avons vendue hier*, It *L'abbiamo venduta ieri*. In these two languages only, the participial suffix present on the head in a perfective transitive verbal (with Aux *avoir/avere*) exhibits adjective-like concord inflection—i.e. it copies the gender/number of any object nominal which is reduced to a clitic adjoined to that verbal. This rule also applies, naturally, to the clitic reductions of the locals (and, for Italian, honorifics) which switch gender according to the sex of the referent. Thus a female person might ask, in French: '*De quoi m'ont-ils accusée?*' and receive the response '*Ils ne vous ont accusée de rien.*' And analogously, in Italian, '*Di che mi hanno accusata?*'—'*Non La hanno accusata di nulla.*' (Let us not forget that while in Italian the agreement is always audible, in French it is phonologically erased at the surface, except with a handful of irregular participles such as *mis, écrit, fait* . . .).

20. In Roumanian, fronting is even to the left of the quantifying adverb *mai*, which (as we pointed out in 8) immediately precedes the head: thus, for example, *Nu o mai vindem = Nous ne la vendons plus*.

21. As indicated by the written hyphen, the clitic is here to be considered *en*clitic to the verbal. If, under this condition, the verbal has two components, the clitic will front to just the intertonic position between the two, as when *Carlos tinha escrito as cartas* becomes *tinha-as escrito (Carlos)*, or *Carlos escreverá as cartas* becomes *escrevê-las-há (Carlos)*. (In the case of either the intertonic *vai as escrever* (cf. Fr *il va les écrire*) or the unfronted *vai escrevê-las* (cf. Sp *va a escribirlas*), a different type of verbal structure (analogous to that with *quer escrever*) is involved; see 13.1).

22. This seems not surprising in view of the phonetic weakness of these particular clitics even when present in such strings as *deixo-o* or *deixa-a*, or *eu o vejo* or *ela a vê*, or the like. Relevant also is perhaps the Portuguese habit of answering questions by echoing the verb alone, as in *Q: Você comprou estas laranjas?—A: Comprei, (sim)*.

23. In the case of *eu am să-l (s-o, să te, să vă* . . .*) văd*, or of the equivalent *eu o să-l văd* etc., where any clitic at all fronts to just left of the head, a different type of verbal structure (analogous to that with *eu vreau să-l văd* 'je veux le voir' etc.) is involved. Similarly analogous to other Fren/Ital structures are cases like Fr *nous avons à le faire* (with partial fronting only) or It *noi abbiamo da farlo* (with no fronting at all). For all these, see 13.1.

24. [*Query. In the light of 11, note 13 on the pronouns with* -même *as subjects, what do you think about the possible status of these compounds as objects?*]

25. The substitutes can be [−human], but not as objects; only in strings like *trabajar sin ellos* or *cada uno de ellos* can the pronoun be replacing, say, *los libros*.

26. Cf. also Sp *no se me escucha nunca*, with a local pronoun, viable but considerably less favored in Italian. Portuguese here must resort to a passive clause with deleted subject, as in *(os doentes) são cuidados*, or a 3rd plural verbal as in *não cuidam os doentes* → *não os cuidam*—both of which variants are, of course, much more widely available across the board: cf. Sp *(los enfermos) son curados*, or *curan a los enfermos* → *los curan*, It *(i malati) sono curati*, or *curano i malati* → *li curano*. In French, clitic *on* and any object clitic are perfectly compatible, as in *on soigne les malades* → *on les soigne*.

27. This clitic being unmarked as to gender or number, there is no agreement-copying by the participle suffix in a perfective verbal containing *en*— e.g. *j'ai acheté des pommes de terre* → *j'en ai acheté*.

28. The clitic in view, though invariable in form like its French counterpart *en*, nevertheless does transmit the G/N of the reduced nominal—e.g. *ho bevuto (della) birra* → *ne ho bevuta*, or *avevano comprato (dei) libri* → *ne avevano comprati*. [*Query. How can we account for the reduction to* ne *in such Italian clauses as* non ci sono autostrade → non ce ne sono, *or si* vendono giornali → se ne vendono, *in which the reduced nominals, while [−def] to be sure, do not qualify as objects?* (*The last example here, incidentally, shows the clitics* si *and* ne *to be compatible, although* si *follows a clitic object (as seen in the earlier example) but precedes* ne *with a morphophonemic vowel adjustment occurring elsewhere in the two-clitic paradigm (cf. 11.7).*)]

29. Under negative clauses cf. also Fr *je n'ai pas de chance* → *je n'en ai pas*, as well as *je n'ai pas* (or *plus*) *reçu de lettres* → *je n'en ai pas* (or *plus*) *reçu*.

30. The clitic *ne* does not transmit G/N agreement on a participle when it is a reduction of only a part of the object nominal. [*Query. How can we account for reduction to* en/ne *in such clauses as* Fr il est arrivé un tas de lettres → il en est arrivé un tas, *or It* sono arrivate tre o quattro lettere → ne sono arrivate tre ó quattro, *in which the [−def] nominals with reduced heads are not objects?*]

31. For a parallel reduction of [+human] genitive modifiers, see under datives. [*Query: How can we account for the reduction to* en/ne *in such clauses as* Fr quelles sont les caractéristiques de cet élément? → quelles en sont les caractéristiques? *or It* quali sono le caratteristiche di questo elemento? → quali ne sono le caratteristiche? *in which the genitive modifiers are contained within nominals that are in effect not objects?*]

32. If [+human], substitution but not normally reduction is feasible—e.g. Fr *j'ai reconnu chacune des jeunes filles* → . . . *chacune d'elles*, It . . . *ciascuna delle ragazze* → *ciascuna di loro*, just like Sp . . . *a cada una de las chicas* → *a cada una de ellas*.

33. The dative clitic functions as the trace for a dative which is referentially identical with the subject of the clause and which, like the object clitic *se/si*, is either reflexive or reciprocal. When it is the latter, the phrase Fr *l'un à l'autre*, Sp *uno a otro*, Po *um a outro*, It *l'uno all'altro*, Ro *unul altuia* may

occur at the surface. [*Comment. Refer back to 11, note 15, including the query which has equal relevance to the present case.*]

34. The situation in Italian is rather complicated. In traditional grammar the dative plural slot is said to be filled by *loro* (hon. *Loro*), but this form is not a clitic; it is merely the substitute pronoun of Table 3.1, so that, for example, *questo dispiacerà ai tuoi genitori → questo dispiacerà loro* involves merely a substitution, not a reduction, even though *loro* does not happen to require the usual marking of a dative nominal with the functor *a*. Many users of the standard language do, in fact, practice reduction by using *gli* without distinction of number. Independently from this, the clitic in view alternates to *le* for the reduction of a fem.sg. (though not of a fem.pl.) dative nominal, as well as to *Le* for the sing. honorific *Lei*, either gender.

35. Fren/Ital participles in perfective verbals never copy agreement with a dative clitic.

36. It therefore turns out that in the case of the local pronouns, dative complements are wholly identical with objects in the surface structure of Spanish, as in *me dices a mí* vs. *me conoces a mí*—a formal ambiguity shared by all the languages except Roumanian whenever reduction takes place—e.g. Fr *tu me dis* vs. *tu me connais*, It *mi dici* vs. *mi conosci*, etc. In the case of the substitutes and the honorifics, there is surface contrast in *le digo a ella (a Vd.)* vs. *la conozco a ella (a Vd.)*, and in *le digo a él (a Vd.)* vs. *lo conozco a él (a Vd.)*—all with matching plurals—except that some prestigious varieties of Spanish, notably in and around Madrid and including careful written styles, reduce masc. [+human] objects and datives alike to *le, les*—a practice traditionally known as 'leísmo'—resulting in the identity of complements in *le digo a él (a Vd.)* and *le conozco a él (a Vd.)*; however, any formal ambiguity of this sort is immediately resolved in any case by the subcategory of verb: say trans-1 (e.g. *conocer*) vs. trans-2 (e.g. *decir*) in the predicate.

37. E.g. *eu i-am spus băiatului (acestui băiat, fetei, acestei fete . . .)* 'j'ai dit au garçon (à ce garçon, à la jeune fille, à cette jeune fille . . .)'; or *eu le-am spus băieților (acestor băieți, fetelor, acestor fete . . .)*.

38. In clauses like Fr *je ferme les yeux*, Sp *cierro los ojos*, Po *fecho os olhos*, It *chiudo gli occhi*, Ro *închid ochii*, no genitive modifier is present even underlyingly; the lexical collocation of itself implies a possessive relationship between subject and object.

39. It seems worth noting that precisely in this language is there no readily available syntactic reduction of a genitive (see 4.3); furthermore, Roumanian genitive modifiers and dative complements have very close formal affinity.

40. By analogy with *ser* in this pattern, the verb *estar* in Spanish allows for reduction of an adjectival having oblique rather than equivalent function in, e.g., *¿Están ustedes muy cansados?—Sí, lo estamos.*

41. Cf. Po *você é feliz?—Sou, sim*; or Ro *Dvs sînteți actriță?—Da, sînt.*

42. The transformation in view is perhaps modeled on such a clause as Sp *el profesor soy yo*, where *yo* is in effect the subject and *el profesor* an

equivalent, the two being a pragmatically transposed transform of *yo soy el profesor*, an equation rather than an identification. Here, incidentally, the equivalent nominal *can* be reduced (as in the exchange *¿Es Vd. el profesor?— Lo soy*, on the analogy of *¿Es Vd. profesor?—Lo soy*), provided, however, that the complement is singular, not plural.

43. If the object of *de/di* is [+human], reduction to *en/ne* is ruled out, as in Fr *que pensez-vous du président?* or It *Lei non è sicuro di Carlo?*

44. This Italian clitic is an entirely different lexical item from the local clitic *ci*; it has a variant *vi*, likewise different from the local clitic *vi*. Apart from minor syntactic constraints disallowing either *ci* + *ci* or *vi* + *vi* in the same verbal, the alternation is purely stylistic.

45. In Italian, but not in French, there exists the further possibility of reducing just the complement of an adv-2 (prep./adv.) whenever that complement is marked by the functor *a*. In this situation a [−human] complement is reducible to *ci*, while a [+human] complement reduces to the corresponding dative clitic—e.g. *noi stavamo vicino (accanto, intorno . . .) alla chiesa* → *noi ci stavamo vicino (accanto, intorno . . .)*, as against *noi stavamo vicino (accanto, intorno . . .) a Mario Saltarelli* → *noi gli stavamo vicino (accanto, intorno . . .)*.

46. Never to *en/ne*, because place modifiers exclude adverbials with the preposition *de/di (da)* (which alone selects *en/ne*) as head. Of course, in Fr *ils sont partis de Paris* → *ils en sont partis*, or It *sono partiti da Parigi* → *ne sono partiti*, the adverbials are indeed [+place], but their function is as oblique, not as modifier.

47. A subject that is not reduced is conjointly postposed, as in Sp *eso lo haré yo*, etc., except, of course, in French, which does not permit full subject-postposing and, indeed, tends strongly to avoid object-preposing in favor of clefting, as in *c'est moi qui ferai ça*. Even in the example given here, the object may well be topicalized under a separate intonation contour.

48. In Italian the copying of a preposed dative is not obligatory, and varies by dialect or style; a preposed oblique is more likely to be copied, as in *lì ci vanno sempre* (cf. Fr *c'est là qu'ils vont toujours*).

49. In Spanish or Roumanian, of course, two clitics can occur with no reduction of the dative, since datives are clitic-copied in any event—thus, e.g. Sp *se las di a José*, Ro *i-am dat lui Sandu*.

50. Cf. also Fren/Ital lexical items with two built-in clitics, such as Fr *je m'en vais*, It *me ne vado*.

51. The French forms *moi* and *toi* (cf. also *tais-toi*), as they occur in imperative clauses, must be taken as bona fide alternants of the clitics rather than as manifestations of the actual local pronouns, because: (a) even in this enclitic position they are inaccessible to contrastive/emphatic focus, and (b) they have their expected shape before the clitics *en* or *y*, as in *donnez-m'en* or (theoretically, anyway) *accompagnez-m'y*.

Dependent Clauses
Chapter 12
Dependent clauses
with unconditioned modality

12.0 Introduction. The function of subject, of complement, or of modifier at either the clause level or the phrase level may be filled transformationally by an embedded (i.e. dependent, or lower) clause, as we may now proceed to examine.

In the present chapter on dependent clauses with unconditioned modality, we shall illustrate only those environments in which an embedded clause is free to embody its own subject and to vary its own modality with regard to tense/ mode. In Chapter 13 on dependent clauses with conditioned modality, we shall observe how in a number of semantic environments, unrelated to the syntactic role of the lower clause, its subject must be deleted or its modality altered as conditioned.

This chapter discusses how clauses with unconditioned modality may function as subject, complement, or modifier in a clause, as modifier in a CNP, ProP, AdvP, or AdjP phrase, as object in a PrepP phrase, and as attribute within an expression of result.

12.1 As subject in a clause. The fairly frequent pattern of linking verb plus equivalent complement plus extraposed subject will serve as well as any to exemplify this construction and to point out its salient characteristics:

Fr Il est vrai (évident, clair, certain . . .) que les gens souffrent beau-
    coup
Sp Es verdad (evidente, claro, cierto . . .) que la gente sufre mucho
Po É verdade (evidente, claro, certo . . .) que a gente sofre muito
It È vero (evidente, chiaro, certo . . .) che la gente soffre molto
Ro E adevărat (evident, clar, sigur . . .) că lumea suferă mult[1]

The functor which introduces an embedded clause—called by some linguists a COMPLEMENTIZER—is regularly that shown here for each language: Fr/ Sp/ Po *que*, It *che*, Ro *că.*

In French, the subject clause is obligatorily extraposed and the subject position is filled by the clitic *il*, which in this case is not the surface reduction of some masc. sing. nominal, but merely a 'dummy' trace-form required by the syntactic rules of French. In the other languages extraposition is the norm, though Sp *Que la gente sufre es evidente* and its analogues are possible in highly marked styles.[2]

The equivalent complements here are typically adjectivals, although a few semantically appropriate nominals are possible also, such as Fr *un fait*, Sp *un hecho*, Po *um feito*, It *un fatto*, Ro *un fapt*. There are also a handful of intrans-3 verbs which may occur with a clausal subject—most of them associated with notions of happening, taking place, coming to pass, turning out, etc., such as Fr *arriver, survenir, se trouver, résulter* . . ., Sp *suceder, acontecer, ocurrir, acaecer, resultar* . . ., Po *suceder, ocorrer, acontecer, sobrevir, resultar* . . ., It *succedere, accadere, avvenire, risultare* . . ., Ro *a se întîmpla, a se petrece, a rezulta* . . . Whether to include here also the linking verbs Fr *paraître* or *sembler*, Sp/ Po *parecer*, It *parere* or *sembrare*, Ro *a (se) părea* is problematical, for a case can be made for taking a following clause as equivalent complement rather than as subject, as it almost certainly is after the copula (see next section), even when the underlying [+human] subject is lexically unspecified and does not surface. In any case, this potential ambiguity is often resolved in all our languages by an optional transformation which moves the subject of the embedded clause up to become that of the matrix clause as well, as for example:

Fr Il paraît que Jean travaille tout le temps ⇒ Jean paraît travailler
      tout le temps
Sp Parece que Juan trabaja todo el tiempo ⇒Juan parece trabajar
      todo el tiempo

and so on across the board. The surface construction in which the remaining constituents stand is one which will be first detailed in 12.2.3.

12.2 As complement in a clause.

12.2.1 As equivalent complement. Clausal equivalent complements may occur with the linking verb *être/ser/essere/a fi*, though only in lexically limited contexts where the subject of the higher clause is a CNP such as Fr *la vérité* or *le fait*, Sp *la verdad* or *el hecho*, Po *a verdade* or *o feito*, It *la verità* or *il fatto*, Ro *adevărul* or *faptul*. For example:

Fr La vérité, c'est que cela ne m'importe pas
Sp La verdad es que eso no me importa
Po A verdade é que isso não me importa
It La verità è che quello non mi importa
Ro Adevărul este că nu-mi pasă de aia

As shown in the French example, it is normal in this language to topicalize such a subject nominal paratactically in advance of the clause proper, while the anaphoric clitic *ce* fills the surface subject position. In French, Spanish, or Portuguese the underlying subject here can be merely [−human] and otherwise unspecified, surfacing in French as *ce*, in Spanish as the abstract pronoun *ello* or as zero, and in Portuguese as zero only—thus Fr *C'est que* . . .,[3] Sp *(Ello) es que* . . ., Po *É que* . . .

12.2.2 As object complement. Clausal objects may occur with numerous trans-1 and trans-2 verbs.

• The trans-1 eligibles are STATIVE verbs ranging from those of knowing through believing, hoping, and wishing to doubting, regretting, or fearing, on the one hand; and, on the other hand, PERCEPTUAL verbs, i.e. of seeing, hearing, understanding, or otherwise sensing. One example of each subtype will suffice:

Fr Tout le monde sait que la terre est ronde
Sp Todo el mundo sabe que la tierra es redonda
Po Toda a gente sabe que a terra é redonda
It Tutti quanti sanno che la terra è rotonda
Ro Toată lumea ştie că pămîntul este rotund

Fr Nous voyons que le café est terminé
Sp Vemos que el café está terminado
Po Vemos que o café está terminado
It Vediamo che il caffè è terminato
Ro Vedem că cafeaua e terminată⁴

• The trans-2 verbs which take a clausal object are the numerous verbs of communicating: on the one hand, the so-called PERFORMATIVES which introduce indirect discourse—verbs of saying, telling, declaring, reporting, announcing, asserting, denying, and so on; and on the other hand, certain AFFECTIVE verbs which entail not only communication but also a cause-and-effect relation, an influence upon the person named in the cooccurrent dative complement—i.e. verbs of asking, begging, urging, persuading, permitting, forbidding, advising, commanding, causing, and many more. We are in a position to exemplify only the performative subtype at this point:

Fr Le ministre a déclaré que les élections auront lieu
Sp El ministro ha declarado que las elecciones tendrán lugar
Po O ministro declarou que as eleições terão lugar
It Il ministro ha dichiarato che le elezioni avranno luogo
Ro Ministrul a declarat că alegerile vor avea loc

• It is to be noted that whenever the subject of the embedded clause is coreferent with the subject of the higher clause, it is obligatorily reduced by deletion, e.g.

Fr Moi je pense que j'ai raison
Sp Yo creo que tengo razón
Po Eu acho que tenho razão
It Io penso che ho ragione
Ro Eu cred că am dreptate

In embedded clausal objects the complementizer is the same in form as that noted for clausal subjects, with the following exception. After a certain few of the stative or perceptual trans-1s, a clausal object is capable of containing the interrogative feature [+Q]. In such so-called INDIRECT QUESTIONS, wherever [+Q] is embodied in an actual Q-word—fronted within its clause just as in any construction, regardless of its function therein—then the complementizer itself is zeroed out, as in:

Fr On ne sait pas quelle heure il est
Sp No se sabe qué hora es
Po Não se sabe que horas são
It Non si sa che ora è
Ro Nu se ştie cît e ceasul

If there is no actual Q-word present, the underlying yes/no [+Q] is conveyed by the alternative complementizer Fr/Sp *si*, Po/It *se*, Ro *dacă*, as in:

Fr Allons demander si le musée est ouvert
Sp Vamos a preguntar si el museo está abierto
Po Vamos perguntar se o museu está aberto
It Domandiamo se il museo è aperto
Ro Să întrebăm dacă muzeul e deschis[5]

12.2.3 As oblique complement. Clausal obliques may occur with numerous intrans-1 verbs and, optionally, with trans-1 verbs of perception. The first type must be held for treatment in 13.2.3. After a verb of seeing, hearing or whatever, we may find—following an object denoting the entity perceived—a clause reporting something performed or experienced by that entity. Underlyingly, then, we may posit a French predicate *vois* plus an object *les enfants* plus an oblique *les enfants sortent*, or a Spanish predicate *veo* + object *a los niños* + oblique *los niños salen*, and so on in all five languages. In the surface output the subject of the lower clause, being coreferent with the higher subject, is obligatorily deleted, as in:

Fr Je vois les enfants qui sortent de l'école
Sp Veo a los niños que salen de la escuela
Po Vejo os meninos que saem da escola
It Vedo i ragazzi che escono dalla scuola
Ro Îi văd pe copii că ies din şcoală

The complementizer is the regular *que/che/că* except in French, where the expected *que* plus any subject clitic (here *qu'ils*) is transformationally replaced by the appropriate RELATIVIZER, i.e. 'relative pronoun' in traditional parlance.[6] Actually, Sp/Po/It *que/che* are ambiguously either complementizer or relativizer, but Ro *că* rather than *ce* (or *care*) is unmistakably the former. Moreover, the fact that Fr *les enfants qui sortent*, Sp *los niños que salen* etc. is not an NP containing a head noun plus a clausal modifier is provided by reductions such as Fr *Je les vois qui sortent*, Sp *Los veo que salen*, etc.—for if it were, the result instead would be Fr *Je vois ceux qui sortent*, Sp *Veo a los que salen*, etc. Besides all this, an optional reduction of the embedded clausal oblique allows for deletion of the complementizer and of the modality tense as well, thus:

Fr Je vois les enfants sortir de l'école
Sp Veo a los niños salir de la escuela
Po Vejo os meninos sairem da escola[7]
It Vedo i ragazzi uscire dalla scuola
Ro Îi văd pe copii ieşind din şcoală

Here the modality slot is filled by the gerund suffix in Roumanian, and by the infinitive suffix in the other languages—either suffix being merely a semantically empty marker of the dependent construction. Neither the gerund nor the infinitive ever copies P/N agreement with the subject, with the notable exception of Portuguese, which under certain conditions does copy P/N onto the infinitive.[8]

The reduction in view is obligatory under one condition, namely, when the tense of the lower modality is the preterite, or its expected replacement in all but Span/Port, and is therefore exactly coterminous with the [+past] [+fulfilled] tense of the matrix modality. Thus, for example, Sp *Vi a los niños que salieron, or Fr *J'ai vu les enfants qui sont sortis . . . is not viable in the present context and must surface as Sp Vi a los niños salir, Fr J'ai vu les enfants sortir . . . It is also possible to transpose the infinitive and the object, as in Sp Vi salir a los niños . . . etc., and this is, in fact, the normal recourse whenever the object is a 'heavy' (i.e. long or supercharged) nominal. This transposition, in fact, constitutes, for at least two of our languages, a case of CLAUSE UNION conflatable with that first noted, though not so labeled nor fully explained, in connection with the verb paraître/parecer etc. in 12.1. In the unifying transformational process the matrix verb of perceiving moves, just as does paraître/parecer above, into the modal Aux position, while the lower verb becomes the head in the one and only predicate verbal (with paraît travailler etc. analogous to va travailler or vient de travailler etc.). Similarly here, the verb of perceiving moves into the modal Aux slot and the lower verb becomes the head of the one predicate verbal. Although here it is clearly not a question of moving the lower subject up, and although obviously enough je vois sortir is not exactly analogous to je parais sortir or je vais sortir in its derivation, both surface manifestations nonetheless reflect the process of clause union. And it is such clause union alone which accounts for, say, Sp se lo vi comprar as the ultimate reduction of vi a Juan comprar el vino, wherein the traces of both objects (Juan and el vino) are fronted to one and the same clitic position. Exactly parallel is It glielo ho visto comprare as a reduction of ho visto Giovanni comprare il vino. Note also that in both languages the object of the perceptual verb has been transformed to a dative. [Query. Why would this be so, and how does it lend further support to the analysis in view? Does the fact that French does not allow *je le lui ai vu acheter seem to have any bearing on the question?]

12.3 As modifier within a clause.

12.3.1 In a conditional clause. One type of embedded clause to function as modifier within a higher clause is the so-called PROTASIS (we will label it the CONDITION) of a CONDITIONAL CLAUSE (more traditionally 'conditional sentence')[9]—i.e. the clause which stipulates the condition, or circumstance, on which the truth value or relevance of the predicate happening (or of the entire predication) is contingent. The complementizer involved is Fr/Sp si,

Po/It *se*, Ro *dacă*,[10] and the condition can occupy the basic modifier position (i.e. last in the clause) or can be (and more often is) preposed so as to apply to the entire predication, as in the following examples:

Fr S'il pleut, personne ne sortira d'ici
Sp Si llueve, nadie saldrá de aquí
Po Se chove, ninguém sairá daqui
It Se piove, nessuno uscirà di qua
Ro Dacă va ploua, nimeni nu va ieşi de aici[11]

The modality of the condition and the CONCLUSION are necessarily congruent with respect to tense: both present, or both imperfect. As regards the futurity mode, the sample given (with fut-1 in the conclusion) shows that it is excluded from the condition in French and Spanish, is optional in Italian (*Se pioverà . . .* as well as *Se piove . . .*), and must be congruent like tense in Roumanian. We shall come in 13.3 to further types of conditional clause which we are not yet in a position to describe.[12]

12.3.2 Clauses with null subject. Also unmistakably identifiable as modifiers are Fr *il y a trois ans*, Sp *hace tres años*, Po *há três anos (atrás)*, It *tre anni fa*, Ro *acum trei ani* (lit. 'maintenant trois ans') in such clauses as Fr *le président a été élu il y a trois ans*, Sp *el presidente fue elegido hace tres años*, and the rest, and on the surface four of the five appear to be clauses with null subject (cf. 10.2) and with (transitive) predicate plus nominal object. There are, however, good reasons for not taking these constructions as underlying clauses at all. [*Query. If not as clauses, how else might they be accounted for? In your quest for a solution, consider also (i) such semantically equivalent constructions as Fr* il y a trois ans qu'il est (*or* qu'il a été élu) président, *Sp* hace tres años que es (*or* que fue elegido) presidente, *Po* há três anos que ele é (*or* que foi elegido) presidente, *It* sono tre anni che è presidente, *Ro* sînt trei ani de cînd a fost ales preşedinte; *(ii) the modifiers Fr* depuis trois ans, *Sp* desde hace tres años, *Po* desde há três anos, *It* da tre anni, *Ro* de trei ani *in such clauses as Fr* il est président depuis trois ans, *Sp* es presidente desde hace tres años, *etc., (iii) tense limitations on the modality of* il y a/hace/ há/fa.]

There is one other type of clausal modifier—that in which the predicate verbal is actually adverbialized grammatically, in a construction to be examined in 13.3.2. All other modifiers containing embedded clauses are themselves AdvPs and will therefore be treated as attributes at the phrase level.

12.4 As modifier within a CNP. Embedded clausal modifiers here are of two subtypes: (1) characterizing and (2) appositive. The first of the two, which serve to characterize the head of the NP, are those traditionally known as RELATIVE CLAUSES, a term which we shall have no reason to discard in reference to surface structures.

12.4.1 Relative clauses. Underlyingly, the characterizing clause repeats the head noun as one or another of its constituents—thus we might have, to take a random example from French, a head *femme*, determined by *la* and characterized (i.e. modified) by *la femme sourit*; or head *chien* determined by *un* and characterized by *j'ai vu le chien*.[13] In the surface output of all five languages, the string consisting of the repeated head plus its determiner (automatically [+def] at this point) plus any other modifier is reduced transformationally to one or another of the Q-words (traditionally called 'relative pronouns') which the language possesses; thus we get, in these instances, *la femme qui sourit* and *un chien que j'ai vu*. Table 12.1 displays the Q-words used by each language in each of the syntactic environments within the characterizing clause where the relativizing reduction can take place. Following Table 12.1 and keyed to the appropriate entries are some remarks on certain constraints applying within each functional area. The Q-word is always fronted, and thus serves typically to introduce the relative clause in the manner of a complementizer (cf. the formal overlap with it in the case of *que/che*). As will be observed, however, when the Q-word is inside an object of PrepP, it is the entire PrepP that is fronted and not just the Q-word.

Table 12.1 Relativizing Q-words.

Role in characterizing clause		Fren	Span	Port	Ital	Roum
Subject		qui	que	que	che	care[6]
Object		que				
Dative		à qui	a quien	a quem		căruia[7]
Object of prep (within oblique or modifier)	[+human]	qui	quien[2]	quem[2]	cui[2,3]	care
	[−human]	quel[1]	que	que		
Genitive modifier (in higher NP)		dont[4]	cuyo[5]	cuio[5]		cărui[7]
Oblique or modifier		où[8]	donde	onde	dove	unde

Remarks for Table 12.1.

1. When the head is reduced to *quel*, its determiner (automatically the definite article) must remain undeleted, as in *le crayon avec lequel j'écris*, or *une conférence à laquelle il faudra assister*. Note that the full PrepP *à laquelle* (⇐*à la conférence*) is itself an oblique complement to the intrans-1 verb *assister*, in which connection see also Remark **8.**

2. In Span/Port/Ital also, the head in an object of preposition, whether [+human] or [−human], may be reduced alternatively by Sp *cual*, Po *qual*, It *quale*, again with the definite article left undeleted, thus:

Sp   el lápiz con que yo escribo ⇒ el lápiz con el cual yo escribo
Po   o lápis com que eu escrevo ⇒ o lápis com o qual eu escrevo
It   il lapis con cui io scrivo ⇒ il lapis con il quale io scrivo[14]

3. Ital *cui* as dative complement need not be introduced by the marker *a*, e.g. *la donna cui ho dato le fotografie*. In a genitive modifier the definite article is left undeleted, as in *i bambini la cui mamma è scomparsa*.

4. Fr *dont* serves not only in a genitive modifier—e.g. *les enfants dont la mère a disparu*, but also it replaces *de* plus object in most any construction,[15] e.g. *les étudiants dont je vous ai parlé*, or *les livres dont ils ont besoin*. However, when a genitive modifier stands within an NP which is itself an object of preposition (as in, say, *avec les parents de l'élève*), then *dont* is unusable and replaceable by *quel* whether the head be [+human] or [−human]—thus *l'élève avec les parents duquel j'ai parlé*, like *l'article à l'auteur duquel je veux m'adresser*.

5. Span/Port *cuyo*/*cuio* are adjectival in form like the possessive adjectives described in 4.3.1 and function as determiners in the inner structure—e.g. Sp *la niña cuyos padres murieron* or *la niña a cuyos padres honraron*.

6. Ro *care* as object complement is uniformly preceded by the function-marker *pe*, which introduces nominal objects just when these are [+human]. The definite article, necessarily deleted when the head is reduced, nevertheless is traced by the appropriate object clitic on the verbal, again [±human]—e.g. *casa pe care noi o cumpărăm* 'la maison que nous achetons', like *candidatul pe care l-au ales* 'le candidat qu'on a élu', on the model of *l-au ales pe candidat* 'on a élu le candidat', despite the simple [−human] instance of *noi cumpărăm casa* 'nous achetons la maison'.

7. Ro *cărui(a)*—which is formally *care* plus the gen./dat. suffix—is adjectival in form, modeled on determiners like *acest(a)* (see 1.5.2), thus with fem.sg. *cărei(a)*, pl. *căror(a)*, the pronominalizing suffix *-a* being added whenever the Q-word in view functions as dative, as in *toţi cei cărora noi le-am spus asta* 'tous ceux à qui nous avons dit ceci'. When this word is functioning in a genitive modifier, it agrees with the outer head, while the definite article determining the inner head is retained as the 'genitive article' *al* (*a*, *ai*, *ale*) as in *copilul ai cărui părinţi au murit* 'l'enfant dont les parents sont morts'.

8. An oblique complement or a modifier, in the form of a PrepP whose object contains a noun denoting 'place where', may be and often is reduced to the Q-words Fr *où*, Sp *donde*, etc., as in Fr *la ville où* (as variant of *dans laquelle*) *nous sommes*, Sp *la ciudad donde* (as variant of *en que* or *en la cual*) *estamos*, etc. If locomotion *away from* a given place is involved, the appropriate Prep is inserted before the Q-word to produce Fr *d'où*, Sp *de donde*,[16] Po *de onde* (or *donde*), It *da dove*, Ro *de unde*. When an object contains a noun denoting 'time when', *quand*/*cuando* etc. are not the norm; Fr uses *où* here also (e.g. *le jour où* . . .), while the other languages tend to favor reduction to mere *que*/*che*/*ce* (e.g. Sp *el día que yo nací*).

We should note in passing that the head of a NP containing a relative clause can itself be reduced, in the context of discourse, by deletion—e.g. Fr *les plantes qui restent vives* → *celles qui restent vives*, Sp *las plantas que quedan vivas* → *las que quedan vivas*. In such a case the form of the determiner is affected in some of the languages, as shown in 1.5.1 (iii), but the relative clause itself is unaffected, the higher deletion being ordered to follow the relativizing reduction.[17]

When the antecedent subject, rather than being discourse-deleted, is [+human] but otherwise lexically unspecified at the underlying level (see 10.1), one version of the surface output is the same as just noted, with the definite article invariable as to gender and with everything [+def] merely by virtue of the relative clause which specifically defines and delimits someone otherwise unspecified. However, in this pattern an alternative surface structure is available, namely, one with no manifest antecedent at all and, in all but French, a concomitant variation in Q-word, as shown herewith:

Fr celui qui ne travaille pas ↔ qui ne travaille pas (ne mange pas)
Sp el que no trabaja ↔ quien no trabaja (no come)
Po   *[18]↔ quem não trabalha (não come)
It colui[19] che non lavora ↔ chi non lavora (non mangia)
Ro cel care nu muncește ↔ cine nu muncește (nu mănîncă)

It is to be noted, also, that It *chi* and Ro *cine* appear as relativizers in this structure only.

12.4.2 Appositive clauses. In this rather low-frequency construction the head noun is invariably one of a limited semantic set ranging over facts, beliefs, ideas, situations real or imagined. The head in question always occurs with a [+def] determiner, typically the definite article, as in:

Fr le fait, l'idée, la crainte, l'espoir, le danger . . .
Sp el hecho, la idea, el miedo, la esperanza, el peligro . . .
Po o feito, a idéia, o medo, a esperança, o perigo . . .
It il fatto, l'idea, la paura, la speranza, il pericolo . . .
Ro faptul, ideea, teama, speranța, pericolul . . .

The complementizer is the usual *que/che/că*, as in:

Fr le fait que les oiseaux volent
Sp el hecho de que los pájaros vuelan
Po o feito que os pássaros voam
It il fatto che gli uccelli volino[20]
Ro faptul că pasările zboară

and, as the Spanish example shows, in this language an appositive clause is further marked by the functor *de* (cf. also *la idea de que* . . . etc.). Portuguese has an optional *de* in this environment.

12.5 As modifier within a ProP. These are of just one type, namely, relative clauses. Pronouns which can act as head in a ProP containing a relative clause in all our languages are:

• the abstract pronouns, including the +demonstratives in all but French,

• the limiting pronouns, except those that are interrogative or all-inclusive,

• the quantifying pronouns, except the interrogative.

The roles of the relativizing Q-words in their clause are the first five among the six listed in Table 12.1 except, of course, that a relative as dative can occur only when the clause modifies a [+human] head. The majority of the potentially occurrent strings are without special interest, and we may content ourselves with a single set of examples in which, as is very frequent with relative clauses in ProPs, the antecedent is an abstract pronoun and the relativizing Q-word is functioning as subject or object:

Fr	ce qui m'intéresse	ce que tous désirent
Sp	lo que me interesa	lo que todos desean
Po	o que me interessa	o que todos desejam
It	ciò che mi interessa	ciò che tutti desiderano
Ro	ceea ce mă interesează	ceea ce toţii doresc

The Roumanian example embodies *ce* rather than *care*; the latter, though entered as the norm in Table 12.1, does not occur in this environment. There is one across-the-board deviation from the norm established above in connection with NPs, and that is that as object of Prep, Fr *quel* as well as the Sp/Po/It variants *cual/qual(e)*, are excluded because they require an undeleted definite article to determine them and none is available from within the underlying ProP. French therefore has to recur to a different Q-word altogether, namely, *quoi*, as in *ce à quoi (je pense), rien avec quoi, beaucoup sans quoi . . .* or whatever. The other languages make do here with *que/che*, as, for example, in Sp *eso en que, nada con que, algo sin que . . .*

12.6 As modifier within an AdvP. Again we seem to be dealing with the same two subtypes as in 12.4, and here we will first continue our description of characterizing, i.e. relative, clauses.

12.6.1 Relative clauses. We saw in 12.2 (and particularly in Remark **8** to Table 12.1, that the Q-adverb of place *où/donde/onde/dove/unde* also functions as a relative. This is equally true in the context of an AdvP, where the antecedent is any one of the demonstrative Q-adverbs of place, as in:

Fr	là où on cherche . . .
Sp	allá (allí, ahí) donde uno busca . . .
Po	lá (ali, aí) onde a gente procura . . .
It	là (lì) dove uno cerca . . .
Ro	acolo unde se caută . . .

What is more, the antecedent adverb in view can be deleted to produce an optionally variant construction parallel to that illustrated in 12.3; thus Fr *celui qui ne travaille pas* ↔ *qui ne travaille pas* is essentially analogous to *là où on cherche* ↔ *où on cherche* (*on trouve* or whatever). At the same time we noted that while French says *le jour où* or *au moment où* etc., the other languages favor the pattern of Sp *el día que* rather than **el día donde* etc. And this gives us a clue to the situation with the advs of time and manner as antecedents. French has *alors que* (or *lorsque*) and *ainsi que* rather than **alors quand* or **ainsi comme*; Italian has *allorché* and not **allora quando*, but it does have *così come*. For all the possible variations see Table 12.2.

Table 12.2 Relative adverbs of place, time, and manner.

	Place		Time	
Fr	là où →	où	*alors quand →	alors que ~ quand
Sp	allá donde →	donde	*entonces cuando →	cuando
Po	lá onde →	onde	*então quando →	quando
It	là dove →	dove	*allora quando →	allorchè ~ quando
Ro	acolo unde →	unde	*atunci cînd →	cînd

Manner	
*ainsi comme →	ainsi que ~ comme [21]
así como →	como
assim como →	como
così come →	come
aşa cum →	cum

All in all, it would seem justifiable to claim, then, that the three Q-adverbs in view function—despite the lack of direct evidence here or there—across the board as relativizers within AdvPs introduced, in the surface structure, by the several Q-words themselves.[22]

12.6.2 Appositive clauses. In any of our languages several of the adverbs—exclusive of the demonstratives, and of any adv of place—may be followed by a clausal modifier introduced by the standard complementizer, as, for example, in:

Fr maintenant que vous vous sentez mieux
Sp ahora que Vd. se siente mejor
Po agora que o senhor se sente melhor
It adesso che Lei si sente meglio
Ro acum că Dvs vă simţiţi mai bine

The overlap from language to language is slight, but a partial list of participating advs for each language separately looks something like this (including the complementizer):

Fr bien que, aussitôt que, afin que, maintenant que, puisque[23]
Sp ahora que, así que, luego que, siempre que, ya que, aunque
Po agora que, assim que, logo que, sempre que, já que, contudo que, ainda que
It adesso che, cosicchè, intanto che, sempre che, benchè, fuorchè 'sauf que', purchè 'pourvu que', subito che 'aussitôt que', affinchè[23]
Ro acum că, aşa că, măcar că 'quoique'[24]

There are two extensions, as it were, of this pattern, both entailing obligatory modifier clauses and, often, specialized (i.e. idiomatic, as in some cases above) meanings ranging over condition, concession, cause, purpose, result, etc. One involves the adverbialization (at the lexical level) of certain adjs (some of them derived from participles), as in

Fr   attendu que, pourvu que, vu que, sauf que, (étant) donné que
Sp   dado que, excepto que, puesto que, visto que, salvo que
Po   dado que, excepto que, posto que, visto que, salvo que
It   eccetto che, salvo che, visto che
Ro   fiindcă 'parce que'

while the other extension embraces numerous PrepPs such as

Fr   en attendant que, à condition que, à moins que, de sorte que, à mesure que, de façon que
Sp   con tal que, en caso de que, a fin de que, de modo que, de manera que, a menos que, a no ser que, en tanto que, a condición que
Po   (no) caso (que), a fim de que, ao passo que, de modo que, de maneira que, a menos que, a não ser que, a condição que
It   nel caso che, di maniera che, a condizione che, a meno che
Ro   în timp ce *or* cît timp 'pendant que', îndată ce 'aussitôt que', odată ce 'une fois que', cu toate că 'bien que', de vreme ce 'puisque', din cauză ce, cu condiţia ca 'à condition que'

12.7 As modifier within an AdjP. The number of adjs semantically suitable to occurrence with a clausal modifier being extremely limited, a single example will suffice at this point (but see 13.7). The complementizer is the usual *que*/*che*/*că*, as in:

Fr   sûr que la justice triomphera
Sp   seguro de que la justicia triunfará
Po   seguro (de) que a justiça triunfará
It   sicuro che la giustizia trionferà
Ro   sigur că justiţia va triunfa

and, again as the Spanish example shows, a clausal modifier is further marked by the functor *de*, seemingly by analogy with PrepP modifiers (e.g. *seguro de la fecha*); again Portuguese has an optional *de* here.

12.8 As object within a PrepP. Table 12.3 displays the adv-1s (preps) which may have an embedded clause as their object in all five languages, together with the complementizers which introduce the clause and which in certain cases vary from the usual *que*/*che*/*că*:

Table 12.3

	French	Spanish	Portuguese	Italian	Roumanian
Prep	parce que	porque	porque	perchè	pentru că
	pour que	para que	para que		pentru ca
	sans que	sin que	sem que	senza che	fără ca
	dès que	desde que	desde que	dacchè	de cînd
	jusqu'à ce que	hasta que	até que	finchè	pînă ce (*or* cînd)
Adv/ Prep	après que	después (de) que	depois que	dopo che	după ce
	avant que	antes (de) que	antes que	avanti che	înainte ce

The writings of the first item in all but Roumanian point to a lexicalization of these strings as some sort of 'subordinator'; but our description precludes such a part of speech, and we accordingly disregard the orthography and take Fr *ce que*,[25] Ro *ca* and *ce*[26] as simply conditioned variants of the complementizer.

In any one of the five languages there are a few other prepositions (some of them listed in the Table 7.1 common core, some of them not) which take a clausal object—e.g. Fr *à* (as in, say, *à ce qu'il paraît*), *depuis, pendant, selon*; Sp *a, con, en, mientras*; Po *a, com, de, em*; It *mentre*; Ro *pe (cînd)* 'pendant que/mientras'. For further details, see 13.8.

12.9 As attribute within an expression of result. The lone quantifying item *tant/tanto/atît* may be followed (discontinuously, if applicable) by a resultative clause embedded as attribute, whether the quantifying phrase is functioning as determiner in a CNP (cf. 1.3.4), or as a ProP (cf. 3.1.1), or as quantifier in an AdjP (cf. 5.2). Again the complementizer is the regulation *que/che/că*, as in the following assorted examples:

Fr J'ai tant de choses à faire que je ne peux pas t'attendre[27]

Sp Tengo tantas cosas que hacer que no puedo esperarte

Po Tenho tanta coisa para fazer que não posso te esperar

It Ho tante cose da fare che non posso aspettarti

Ro Am atîte lucruri de făcut că nu te pot aştepta

Fr Georges était si timide qu'il sortait très peu[27]

Sp Jorge era tan tímido que salía muy poco

Po Jorge era tão tímido que saía muito pouco

It Giorgio era così timido che usciva molto poco[28]

Ro Gheorghe era atît de timid că (*or* încît) ieşea foarte puţin

Fr Cela coûte tant que personne ne l'achète plus

Sp Eso cuesta tanto que nadie ya lo compra

Po Isso custa tanto que ninguém o compra mais

It Quello costa tanto che nessuno lo compra più

Ro Aceea costă atît de mult că nimeni nu o mai cumpără

As the first two sets of examples show, when the subject of the embedded clausal attribute is coreferent with that of the matrix clause, it is automatically reduced.[29]

Notes for Chapter 12

1. Here, as indeed in all the clauses enumerated in this entire chapter, the inner subject (*les gens* etc.) may be reduced for discourse purposes unconnected with any factor in the higher clause, just as though the lower clause were in fact independent (e.g. Fr *Il est vrai qu'ils souffrent beaucoup*, Sp *Es verdad que sufren mucho*, etc.). Underlyingly −S clauses (Fr *il pleut*, Sp *llueve . . .*) or clauses with indefinite underlying subject (Fr *on souffre*, Sp *se sufre . . .*) also occur freely.

2. In Fr *Que les gens souffrent beaucoup, c'est évident*, the *que*-clause is not embedded; it is syntactically independent of the clause *C'est évident*—thus related to it only paratactically—and furnishes the topic that serves as referent for the anaphoric *ce* as a true subject clitic.

3. It is the interrogativized form of this French string, namely, *est-ce que*, that becomes simply a lexicalized signal of Q, with the two clauses of the first cycle unified so as to eliminate the embedding process, e.g. *Est-ce + [que vous me croyez]?* ⇒ *Est-ce que + vous me croyez?* The Portuguese equivalent string for both *c'est que* and *est-ce que*, namely, *é que*, also functions as a Q-marker, as in *É que você vem?* like Fr *Est-ce que tu viens?*; also, in the environment of a Q-word, *Onde o senhor mora?* = *Onde é que o senhor mora?*, analogous to Fr *Où habitez-vous?* = *Où est-ce que vous habitez?* The structural relation between this pattern and the so-called CLEFT transformation—whereby Fr *Toi, tu me fâches* ⇒ *C'est toi qui me fâches* and Po *Você me enfada* ⇒ *É você que me enfada* or *Você é que me enfada* is too elusive for us to pursue here; it may involve a historically based blend of the two structures in view.

4. This last set of examples reports the perception of a fact. Predicating instead the direct perception of an act or state entails a different type of construction—namely, a nominal object plus an oblique modifier, as in, e.g., Sp *Yo vi + a Juan + que salía del teatro*. We shall examine this pattern in depth in 12.2.3.

5. Actually, the two complementizers are largely in noncontrastive distribution relative to the higher verbal, although rare contrasts do exist, as, for example, Fr *Savais-tu que Robert venait?* vs. *Savais-tu si Robert venait?*, with analogues in the other four languages.

6. A full discussion of relativization follows in 12.4 and 12.6.

7. Here the suffix *-em* added to the infinitive *sair* indicates agreement with the plural NP *os meninos* as the (deleted) lower subject. For a fuller discussion of this so-called 'personal infinitive', see 13.2.1.

8. The gerund suffix is also viable in Span/Port (e.g. Sp *Veo a los niños saliendo . . .*) but only as a reduction of something different which we will

take note of in 13.3.2.

9. It fits our definition of a clause rather than a sentence, because it can itself be embedded in a higher clause, which a sentence as we define it cannot.

10. Despite the across-the-board overlap with the complementizer mentioned just above as introducing clausal objects containing the yes/no [+Q], traditional grammars tend to distinguish *si* etc. meaning 'if' from *si* etc. meaning 'whether'. However, not only are the two in complementary distribution, but also the semantic distance between them is slight. [*Query. Do you sense the affinity?*]

11. Whenever the subject of condition and conclusion are coreferent, one or the other (typically the second) is obligatorily reduced, as, for example, in Sp *Si Juan estudia mucho, [ ] saldrà bien*, or *Si [ ] estudia mucho, Juan saldrá bien*, or *Juan saldrá bien si [ ] estudia mucho*, but not *[ ] Saldrá bien si Juan estudia mucho*.

12. Only then, also, shall we be ready to account for the Portuguese alternative *Se chover . . .* alongside *Se chove . . .*

13. As in, say, *un chien aveugle + j'ai vu le chien (aveugle)*.

14. In Spanish the definite article may, optionally, remain undeleted also with *que* as in *el lápiz con el que yo escribo*. Another Spanish alternative reduction within a [+human] object complement is *a quien* or *a . . .cual* instead of *que*, as in *el médico que he consultado = el médico a quien he consultado = el médico al cual he consultado*.

15. Exception: after an adv-2 (adv./prep.) such as *près*—e.g., a string like *près desquelles* cannot give way to **près dont*.

16. In Spanish the other adv-1 (preps.) also figure in this construction, according to their several meanings: thus *adonde, en donde, por donde, hacia donde, hasta donde . . .*

17. G/N agreement is obviously copied onto any occurrent Adj before even the inner head is reduced.

18. In Portuguese surface structure *o* modified by a relative clause is invariably the abstract pronoun (= Sp *lo*). Thus here, and even in the context of a deleted subject, *o* is not viable even though the G/N-agreeing *os, a, as*, being unambiguous, are. Either here or with a deletion, *o* itself may be replaced by *aquele* without demonstrative force (cf. It *quello + che . . .*).

19. The demonstrative substitute pronoun *colui* is preferred here to the demonstrative article *quello* required in the context of a deleted head.

20. The altered modality in It *volino* instead of the expected *volano* can be understood only in the general context elucidated in the forthcoming chapter.

21. Fr *comment* and *comme* are then syntactic alternants in complementation: *comment* in Q-clauses, *comme* in relative clauses.

22. If this claim is accepted, the role of the Q-adverb of manner becomes clear in such constructions as

Fr Jean parle comme hier (. . . comme un fou, . . . comme à un sourd)
Sp Juan habla como ayer (. . . como un loco, . . . como a un sordo)
Po João fala como ontem (. . . como um louco, . . . como a um surdo)
It Gianni parla come ieri (. . . come un pazzo, . . . come ad un sordo)
Ro Ion vorbeşte ca ieri (. . . ca un nebun, . . . ca unui surd)

in which an embedded clause introduced by the relativizing Q-adverb is
drastically reduced through deletion of contextually redundant constituents,
as, for instance, in Sp *Juan habla [así] como [hablo] yo*, or It *Gianni parla
[così] come [parlo] io* (although in this language the subjects *io, tu* become
me, te at the surface (*come me, come te*) as if *come* were a preposition—
which basically it is not—and the following nominal its object. Similar reductions will be noted in expressions of comparison as described in 14.

23. As indicated by the spelling, many of these items seem to be lexicalized
as 'subordinating conjunctions' in traditional grammar, sometimes with special semantic features. Cf. also the unique Fr *quoique*, in which, of course,
quoi is not an adverb at all yet parallels *bien que* in function and meaning.

24. Difficult to classify in the present framework are Ro *căci* 'parce que',
deşi 'bien que', and *de cînd* 'depuis que', all without complementizer.

25. [*Query. What, though, is to be done with the* à *in* jusqu'à ce que? (*See
7.2 for a clue.*)]

26. Although *ca* looks to be in contrast with *că* in the first pair of entries,
they are, in fact, in complementation relative to the modality of the embedded
clause, as we shall discover in 13.6.

27. Fr *autant* and *aussi*, respective syntactic alternants of *tant* and *si*,
occur only in comparisons of equality and so are not viable in the present
pattern. On the other hand, the quantifier *si* may be replaced stylistically by
the adverb *tellement* in the present pattern though not in comparisons of
equality.

28. Analogous to Fr *tellement* is It *talmente*, viable under exactly the same
conditions.

29. In Italian in this circumstance the resultative modality may also be
reduced to the infinitive suffix, with the functor *da* replacing *che* (. . . *così
timido da uscire* . . .) in a transformation shared by the other languages in
other environments but not here (cf. 13.4.1).

Chapter 13
Dependent clauses
with conditioned modality

13.0 Introduction. It was noted in 12.0 that embedded clauses, in any and all of the syntactic functions variously identified and exemplified in 12.1-12.8, are subject to an overriding semantic constraint on the modality and/or subject. The constraint in question is motivated by a binary semantic feature having its locus outside the embedded clause itself, that is to say, associated with one or another constituent of the matrix clause or phrase. What, then, is the feature we have to do with? It conveys a subjective attitude toward the true or potential reality of the proposition expressed in the lower clause. It is an attitude involving mental reservation on the part of the actor or experiencer—as either subject or complement (object or dative)—and it may range from total denial at one extreme, through doubt, uncertainty or mere indifference, anticipation of something as yet unrealized, to emotional reaction (surprise, pleasure, pain, rejection, or whatever) at the opposite extreme. One linguist[1] has termed the crucial feature [+reservation], or [+res] for convenience, and we shall do well to adopt this label for our purposes. And now, bearing in mind the existence of this feature and all the nuances of subjective attitude which it subsumes, we are ready to examine the effect of its presence on the surface structure of embedded clauses in our five languages. We shall recur to the same breakdown of the clauses by function, remembering that all strings analyzed and illustrated in Chapter 12 were unconstrained by the feature now in view—i.e. were [−res]—while all strings to be described in the present chapter entail the presence and effect of [+res].

13.1 As subject in a clause. (1) Also in 12.1, it was stated that in the pattern linking verb plus equivalent complement plus (extraposed) subject, the equivalent complements are typically adjectivals, although some nominals and a few intrans-3 verbs are possible too. With the adjs in the semantic range of Fr *vrai, évident, clair, certain*, and the like, [+res] is present only when the predication is negated or questioned, with the following surface result:

Fr   Il n'est pas vrai que le chef en *sache* trop (*or* Est-il vrai que . . .?)
Sp   No es verdad que el jefe *sepa* demasiado (*or* ¿Es verdad que . . .?)
Po   Não é verdade que o chefe *saiba* demais (*or* É verdade que . . .?)
It   Non è vero che il capo ne *sappia* troppo (*or* È vero che . . .?)
Ro   Nu e adevărat că şeful ştie prea mult (*or* E adevărat că . . .?)

In all but the Roumanian example,[2] the modality of the lower clause has an added constituent, i.e. it appears in a special marked form, the so-called SUBJUNCTIVE as opposed to the unmarked, or INDICATIVE, form. Morphologically, the subjunctive is one element in a modality suffix packaging also tense—a PORTMANTEAU followed, as the plain tense suffix is, by a P/ N agreement ending. There are thus, basically, two tense + subjunctive suffixes, as shown in the following minimal Span/ Port/ Ital paradigms:

Tense				+ Subjunctive	
Present (Sp/ Po/ It)	canta	$\Rightarrow$	$\Big\{$	(Sp/ Po)	cante
				(It)	canti
Imperfect $\Big\{$	(Sp)	cantaba	$\Rightarrow$	(Sp)	cantase ~ cantara
	(Po/ It)	cantava	$\Rightarrow$	(Po/ It)	cantasse

Although French has a comparable basic schema, the 'imperfect subjunctive' is obsolescent and is being replaced, in all but formal written registers, by the 'present subjunctive'—thus *Il n'était pas vrai que le chef en sache* (or perfective present *ait su*, but not *sût* or *eût su*) *trop.* Even in Span/ Port/ Ital—and in the formal registers of French that do exploit the imperfect subjunctive—the two suffixes in view are actually in complementary distribution relative to the tense of the matrix modality: the present subjunctive occurring when the matrix tense is present, the imperfect subjunctive when the matrix tense is imperfect or preterite (i.e. past). This means that when [+res] is on, the lower clause is NOT free to vary its own modality with regard to tense/ mode; rather it is conditioned from above, as it were, with tense essentially neutralized and mode essentially eliminated.[3]

As for Roumanian, it does have a subjunctive form, but the suffix manifesting it does not also contain a tense/ mode signal. In other words, there is just one subjunctive morph, and it largely coincides in shape with that of the present tense: totally so when a P/ N agreement suffix is appended[4] (as in, say, *noi cîntăm* or *noi facem*), and with a vowel contrast only where the subject is 3rd person and the P/ N suffix is zero or null (as in, say, *cînte* vs *cîntă* or *facă* vs *fac(e)*). However, what unequivocally marks the Roumanian subjunctive modality is the particle *să*—a functor which introduces any predicate verbal containing it—as we shall have ample occasion to observe henceforward.

(2) A different semantic range of adjectives in equivalent complements carry [+res] and hence trigger the subjunctive across the board. A representative list of such adjectives mostly shared by our languages might be the following:

French	Spanish	Portuguese	Italian	Roumanian
(im)possible	(im)posible	(im)possível	(im)possibile	(im)posibil
(im)probable	(im)probable	(im)provável	(im)probabile	(im)probabil
incroyable	increíble	incrível	incredibile	
douteux	dudoso	duvidoso	dubbioso	îndoios
facile	fácil	fácil	facile	uşor
difficile	difícil	difícil	difficile	greu
(in)utile	(in)útil	(in)útil	(in)utile	(ne)folositor
juste	justo	justo	giusto	just
naturel	natural	natural	naturale	natural
nécessaire	necesario	necessário	necessario	necesar
important	importante	importante	importante	important
mieux	mejor	melhor	meglio	(mai) bine
préférable	preferible	preferível	preferibile	
obligatoire	obligatorio	obligatório	obbligatorio	obligator
dangereux	peligroso	perigoso	pericoloso	periculos
triste	triste	triste	triste	5
étrange	extraño	estranho	strano	

The list is not intended to be exhaustive; there are doubtless many more shared items (cognate or not), as well as partially shared or individual ones. An example is now in order:

Fr   Il est nécessaire que les clients *paient*
Sp   Es necesario que los clientes *paguen*
Po   É necessário que os clientes *paguem*
It   È necessario che i clienti *paghino*
Ro   Este necesar ca clienţii *să plătească*

The Roumanian entry shows the complementizer in such a string to be *ca* rather than *că*. In case the subjunctive *să*-verbal for any reason stands first in the lower clause, so that the functors *ca* and *să* would be in juxtaposition, then *ca* is omitted and *să* assumes the dual function of complementizer and subjunctivizer—as for example in a subject extraposition or reduction: *Este necesar să plătească (clienţii)*.[6]

• If the matrix clause additionally embodies a dative, typically left-dislocated to the subject position and in fact coreferent with the subject of the dependent predication, then both the subject and the tense are obligatorily deleted as redundant, no complementizer occurs, and the modality slot is filled by the INFINITIVE suffix in all but Roumanian, as shown herewith:

Fr   Aux clients il est impossible de payer[7]
Sp   A los clientes les es imposible pagar
Po   Aos clientes é impossível pagarem
It   Ai clienti è impossibile pagare
Ro   Clienţilor le este imposibil să plătească

In Roumanian, where tense is already suppressed by the subjunctive, the infinitive transformation is not permitted. In this language—which allows of no tense in either one—infinitive and subjunctive are in strictly noncontrastive distribution although¯, of course, a subjunctive verb does copy P/N agreement while an infinitive does not.[8] In Portuguese, on the other hand, P/N agreement with a deleted subject is copied *even onto an infinitive*.[9] This unique pattern, already glimpsed in 12.2 and conventionally known in grammars of Portuguese as the 'personal infinitive', makes it feasible to suppress subjunctive modality in strings not permitting its omission in the other languages; thus the earlier example *É necessário que os clientes paguem* can be further transformed to *É necessário os clientes pagarem* or just *É necessário pagarem*, with the same surface result as with *Aos clientes é impossível pagarem, É impossível pagarem.*

• If the subject of the lower clause is underlyingly [+human] yet lexically unspecified, the subjunctive-to-infinitive transformation is the preferred norm, as in

Fr Il est dangereux qu'on fasse cela ⇒ Il est dangereux de faire cela
Sp Es peligroso que se haga eso ⇒ Es peligroso hacer eso
Po É perigoso que se faça isso ⇒ É perigoso fazer-se isso[10]
It È pericoloso che si faccia quello ⇒ È pericoloso fare quello

and indeed obligatorily with this or that adj in this or that language—e.g. Fr *Il est difficile qu'on décide ⇒ Il est difficile de décider*. [*Query. Why is there no Roumanian entry in the above set?*]

• Then, on yet another transformational cycle, it is possible to move an object in the embedded clause up to the role of subject in the matrix clause, while marking the left-over predicate with a language-specific functor, as shown herewith:

Fr Il est facile de convaincre les lecteurs ⇒ Les lecteurs sont faciles *à* convaincre
Sp Es fácil convencer a los lectores ⇒ Los lectores son fáciles *de* convencer
Po É fácil convencer os leitores ⇒ Os leitores são fáceis *de* convencer
It È facile convincere i lettori ⇒ I lettori sono facili *da* convincere
Ro Este uşor să-i convingi pe cititori ⇒ Cititorii sînt uşori *de* convins

Here the Roumanian entry indicates the possibility of moving directly from the expected *să*-clause (see 10.1 as to the 2nd-local P/N suffix) to an analogous transform entailing a *de*-marked participle (and not infinitive) in the final output.[11]

[*Query. What kind of complement do you take the remnant of the embedded clause to have become, at the surface, in each language?*[12]]

(3) Some equivalent nominals also carry [+res]—e.g. Fr *un miracle*, Sp *un milagro*, Po *um milagre*, It *un miracolo*—the most prominent single item perhaps being that in:

Fr C'est dommage qu'il n'y *ait* pas de lumière
Sp Es (una) lástima que no *haya* luz
Po É (uma) pena que não *haja* luz
It È peccato che non ci *sia* luce[13]

(4) [+res] verbals with clausal subjects are rather scarce, and the shared list is very small:

	Fren	Span	Port	Ital	Roum
Trans.	surprendre	sorprender	surpreender	sorprendere	(a surprinde) [14]
	fâcher	enojar	zangar		(a supăra)
	étonner	extrañar	estranhar		
	enchanter	encantar	encantar	incantare	(a încînta)
Intrans.	plaire	placer	prazer	piacere	a place
	convenir	convenir	convir	convenire	a se cuvine
	importer	importar	importar	importare	a importa
				bisognare	a trebui
				occorrere	

A random example with a transitive:
Fr Il m'étonne que personne ne soit venu
Sp Me extraña que nadie haya venido
Po Estranha-me que ninguém tenha vindo
It Mi sorprende che nessuno sia venuto
And with an intransitive:
Fr Il conviendrait que tous soient présents
Sp Convendría que todos estuvieran presentes
Po Conviria que todos estivessem presentes
It Converrebbe che tutti fossero presenti
Ro S-ar cuveni ca toții să fie prezenți
In this limited group belong It *bisognare* (and its near-synonym *occorrere*) and Ro *a trebui*, both meaning 'être nécessaire/ser necesario', e.g.
It Bisogna che i documenti ci siano restituiti
Ro Trebuie ca documentele să ne fie restituite

• If the dative complement of an intransitive is coreferent with the subject of the dependent predication, then both the tense and the subject are obligatorily deleted in favor of the infinitive (except, of course, in Roumanian):
Fr Il ne me plaît pas de répondre
Sp No me place responder
Po Não me praz responder
It Non mi piace rispondere
Ro Nu-mi place să răspund
Although the verb in this particular set functions identically across the board, its frequency in ordinary registers is far lower in Fren/Span/Port than in Ital/Roum, for the semantic range covered by the latter (to include the notion of liking as well as of pleasing) is divided between Fr *plaire* and *aimer*, Sp *placer* and *gustar*, Po *prazer* and *gostar*. Of these competitors, only Sp *gustar* is an intrans-2 like *plaire*; *aimer* is a trans-1, *gostar* an intrans-1 and

both will be mentioned again in later sections.

The same reduction operates if the dative and its coreferent lower subject are indefinite and lexically unspecified, as in:

Fr Il convient de se taire
Sp Conviene callar
Po Convem calar-se
It Conviene (or Bisogna, or Occorre[15]) tacere
Ro Se cuvine (or Trebuie) să taci

13.2 As complement in a clause.

13.2.1 As equivalent complement. In 12.2.1 we said that clausal equivalent complements occur after the copula, though in lexically limited contexts including, for Fren/Span/Port, that of a [−human] unspecified subject surfacing as *ce* in French, as zero in the others. When in this context the copula verbal is negated (though not when it is Q-ed; on this see especially 12.2.1, note 3), [+res] and its triggering effect are on, and this is viable also in Italian (though not in Roumanian), thus:

Fr Ce n'est pas qu'ils veuillent . . .
Sp No es que ellos quieran . . .
Po Não é que eles queiram . . .
It Non è che loro vogliano . . .

As for Q-ing the copula, on the other hand (nonoccurrent in Ital/Roum in this context), see again the same note 3 of 12.2.1.

In the marginal situation where two embedded clauses make up a copula-linked equation—the one functioning as subject and the other as equivalent complement—and both have the same (coreferent) [−human] but lexically unspecified subject, the modality of each clause is reduced to the infinitive:

Fr Voir, c'est croire [*Query. What is the* ce *doing here?*]
Sp Ver es creer
Po Ver é crer
It Vedere à credere
Ro A vedea este a crede[16]

13.2.2 As object complement. Here again, clauses may occur with both trans-1 and trans-2 verbals which embody the subjunctive-triggering [+res] as one of their own semantic features.

• A trans-1 example containing an extremely high-frequency stative verb:

Fr Ma femme ne veut pas que notre fille *habite* seule
Sp Mi señora no quiere que nuestra hija *viva* sola
Po Minha senhora não quer que nossa filha *more* sòzinha
It Mia moglie non vuole che nostra figlia *abiti* sola
Ro Soţia mea nu vrea ca fiica noastră *să locuiască* singură

A representative list of stative trans-1s:

Fren	Span	Port	Ital	Roum
vouloir	querer	querer	volere	a vrea
désirer	desear	desejar	desiderare	a dori
espérer	esperar	esperar	sperare	a spera
préférer	preferir	preferir	preferire	a prefera
aimer[17]				
croire	creer	achar	credere	(a crede)
penser	pensar	pensar	pensare	(a se gîndi)
nier[18]	negar	negar	negare	(a nega)
douter	dudar	duvidar	dubitare	(a îndoi)
regretter	sentir[19]	sentir		
craindre[20]	temer	temer	temere	(a teme)

Such verbs as Fr *croire* or *penser* and their counterparts trigger the subjunctive only when the predication is negated or questioned, and not with total consistency even then—for example:

Fr Personne ne croit que cela *soit* juste
Sp Nadie cree que eso *sea* justo
Po Ninguém acha que isso *seja* justo
It Nessuno crede che ciò *sia* giusto[21]

[+res] is likewise often present in, e.g., Fr *Croyez-vous que . . .?*, Sp *¿Cree usted que . . .?* and so on.[22]

• If the subject of the clausal object is coreferent with that of the matrix clause, that lower subject is obligatorily deleted and the modality reduced to the infinitive (except, of course, in Roumanian).[23]

Fr Nos amis espèrent vous revoir bientôt
Sp Nuestros amigos esperan verlos a ustedes de nuevo
Po Nossos amigos esperam ver os senhores de novo[24]
It I nostri amici sperano di rivedere Loro presto[25]
Ro Prietenii noştri speră să vă vadă pe Dvs din nou

• We are now ready to examine twó very small but very potent residues of trans-1 verbs, the first of which consists of the following list:

Fren	Span	Port	Ital	Roum
devoir	deber	dever	dovere	*26
pouvoir	poder	poder	potere	a putea
savoir	saber	saber	sapere	a şti

The third member of this list is not to be confused with its truly stative, across-the-board homonym illustrated at the outset of 12.2.2; here we are dealing with the unique verb of being capable in the sense of knowing how to do something, i.e. of [+human] capability as contrasted with mere ability.[27]

The presence of a cause-and-effect [+res] on these three affective verbs is confirmed by the Roumanian *să*-verbal in, e.g., *Nimeni poate să înceapă încă* 'Personne ne peut commencer encore', or *Dumneata știi să faci ski?* 'Tu sais faire du ski?'; but the semantics of all three are such that their own subject and that of a following clausal object are inevitably coreferent and therefore, in all but Roumanian, the object is obligatorily reduced to a subjectless infinitive clause. So for example:

Fr   Qui pourrait *se l'imaginer?*
Sp   ¿Quién podría *figurárselo?*
Po   Quem poderia *imaginá-lo?*
It   Chi potrebbe *immaginarselo?*
Ro   Cine ar putea să și-o închipuiască?

Fr   Cet homme sait *parler six langues*
Sp   Ese hombre sabe *hablar seis idiomas*
Po   Esse homem sabe *falar seis línguas*
It   Quell'uomo sa *parlare sei lingue*
Ro   Omul acela știe să vorbească șase limbi

Fr   L'avion devait *atterrir à midi*
Sp   El avión debía *aterrizar a mediodía*
Po   O avião devia *aterrissar a meiodia*
It   L'aereo doveva *atterrare a mezzogiorno*

In many grammars of French, Spanish, Portuguese, and Italian, the three verbs in view here—together with *vouloir/querer/volere*—are characterized as 'modal auxiliaries', such that the Aux plus a following infinitive constitute a unified VP. Structural proof of this unity resides in the fact that any clitic complement or modifier may be attached to either the first or the second verb without difference in meaning, as illustrated herewith for Spanish:[28]

Yo   [debo / puedo / sé / quiero]   hacerlo.   *or*   Yo lo   [debo / puedo / sé / quiero]   hacer.

In our present frame of reference we shall take the position that any one of the four verbs in question is eligible for an optional transformation in which the matrix verb moves into the main modality position, occupying the slot filled in the underlying structure by a modal Aux (predominantly *aller/ir*) as established in 9.5, while the dependent verb, once reduced to its infinitive form, moves up to the position of head verb, with the result that on this cycle two clauses have become united as one. Graphically, again using Spanish:

Yo + quiero + [hacer eso] $\Rightarrow$ Yo + quiero hacer + eso
(Cf. Yo + quiero + eso)   (Cf. Yo + hago + eso)
Yo + quiero + [hacerlo] $\Rightarrow$ Yo + lo quiero hacer

While this clause union can be detected at the surface in Span/Port/Ital just when a clitic is present, and in French not at all, it is in full view with Ro *a putea* because the lower verb reduces from subjunctive to infinitive precisely when it moves up, and this serves as independent motivation for positing the clause union at some level across the board. Clitic climbing applies as well, thus partially corroborating the evidence of the other languages. A Roumanian example:

Noi + putem + [să facem asta] ⇒ Noi + putem face + asta
(asta ⇒ o) Noi + putem + [s'o facem]   ⇒ Noi + o putem face

With *a vrea*, on the other hand, the unification is ruled out. [*Query. Shall we prefer to say that the union can occur, though with no surface change, with all three verbs in French, or that it is disallowed altogether in this language?*]

Our second minute residue list of trans-1s figures in all but Roumanian:[29]

Fren	Span	Po	It
faire	hacer	fazer	fare
laisser	dejar	deixar	lasciare

These are the verbs of CAUSATION, a prime type of affective verb and as such, of course, specified [+res]. By way of lead-in to the complicated syntax of these causatives, here is an example with subjunctive modality:

Fr   Qui fait que le soleil brille?
Sp   ¿Quién hace que el sol brille?
Po   Quem faz que o sol brilhe?
It   Chi fa che il sole brilli?

We must hasten to add that this construction is relatively infrequent in all our languages. What is generally preferred is a reduction of the lower modality to the infinitive (with P/N agreement in Portuguese). Perhaps through the intermediary of a pragmatic subject extraposition—i.e. Sp *¿Quién hace que brille el sol?* etc. (although French does not allow this)—the constituents of the infinitive clause are ordered as shown:

; Fr   Qui fait briller le soleil?
Sp   ¿Quién hace brillar el sol?
Po   Quem faz brilhar o sol?[30]
It   Chi fa brillare il sole?

at which stage the following unifying transformation has also applied: matrix verb to modal Aux, lower verbal to main verbal, and lower subject to object. Proof of this reading is in the fact that the subject-turned-object becomes a clitic if reduced, as in Fr *Qui le fait briller?*, Sp *¿Quién lo hace brillar?*, and so on. At this point a surface ambiguity also presents itself, for if an original lower clause containing an object but only an unspecified indefinite subject—e.g. Fr *?Qui a fait qu'on bâtisse ces hôtels?*—is reduced to the infinitive, the object remains the object and the result is *Qui a fait bâtir ces hôtels*, further reducible to *Qui les a fait bâtir?*

Only when the original lower clause contains an overt subject as well as an object is the ambiguity resolved, for then that subject becomes a dative instead of another object, as in Fr *Qui a fait que les enfants mangent les poires?* ⇒ *Qui a fait manger les poires aux enfants?* (in that order only). However, this very solution can give rise to another ambiguity whenever the lower clause contains a trans-2 verb with its own dative—e.g. when either Fr *Je ferai que l'on envoie l'argent à Jeanne* or *Je ferai que Jeanne envoie l'argent* become reduced to an identical *Je ferai envoyer l'argent à Jeanne.* This second ambiguity is resolvable when necessary as follows: instead of the subject becoming a dative, it becomes an oblique complement lifted from passive clause structure, i.e. a PrepP opened by *par/por/da*—thus Fr *Je ferai envoyer la lettre (à Jeanne) par Charles*, and so on.

Table 13.1 recapitulates the variously constituted clauses embedded as objects after a causative verb, together with the clause-union transformations they undergo in each language.

For consistency's sake, our causative examples have all been with Fr *faire* and its cognates, but in any of them the other causative we have listed could be used as well.[31] Some grammars list Sp/Po *mandar* among the causatives, perhaps because in some contexts it is closer semantically to *hacer/fazer* than to (say) *ordenar*; but in any of its meanings it belongs to the category of verbs we are now about to examine, namely, the affective trans-2s. A minimal but representative list of such verbs is the following:

Fren	Span	Port	Ital	Roum
dire	decir	dizer	dire	a zice *or* a spune
demander	pedir	pedir	domandare	a cere
	rogar	rogar	chiedere	
commander	mandar	mandar		a comanda
ordonner	ordenar	ordenar	ordinare	a porunci
conseiller	aconsejar	aconselhar	consigliare	a sfătui
défendre	prohibir	proibir	proibire	a opri

The first of these verbs is not to be confused with its performative across-the-board homonym, which belongs strictly among the trans-2s covered in 12.2.2; here it is feature-specified for giving an instruction rather than for reporting a fact.

Whenever, as often, the higher dative and the lower subject are different entities, a subjunctive clause is required as in, say, Fr *Le maître a ordonné à chaque parent que son enfant y prenne part*; and this is also the case where the dative is knowable from the context though unexpressed, as in Fr *Le maître a ordonné que chaque enfant y prenne part* (the order not being given directly to each child, but to someone understood from the context of situation). However, when dative and subject are coreferent, it is the latter which is obligatorily deleted, as in Sp *El maestro les mandó a todos que tomaran parte.* In this environment a subjunctive clause is viable in some of the languages while in others the modality is concomitantly reduced to the infinitive. The case is as follows for each individual language:

Table 13.1 Causative constructions.

Lower clause has:		Clausal object embedded	⇑	Modality reduced to infinitive, and union of clauses	⇑	Complements reduced to clitics
+subj	Fr	Je fais que Marie sorte		Je fais sortir Marie		Je la fais sortir
−obj	Sp	Hago que María salga		Hago salir a María		La hago salir
−dat	Po	Faço que Maria saia		Faço sair Maria		Faço-a sair
	It	Faccio che Maria esca		Faccio uscire Maria		La faccio uscire
−subj	Fr	Je fais qu'on écrive la lettre		Je fais écrire la lettre		Je la fais écrire
+obj	Sp	Hago que se escriba la carta		Hago escribir la carta		La hago escribir
−dat	Po	Faço que se escreva a carta		Faço escrever a carta		Faço-a escrever
	It	Faccio che si scriva la lettera		Faccio scrivere la lettera		La faccio scrivere
+subj	Fr	Je fais que Marie mange la poire		Je fais manger la poire à Marie		Je la lui fais manger
+obj	Sp	Hago que María coma la pera		Le hago comer la pera a María		Se la hago comer
−dat	Po	Faço que Maria coma a pera		Faço comer a pera a Maria		Faço-lha comer
	It	Faccio che Maria mangi la pera		Faccio mangiare la pera a Maria		Gliela faccio mangiare
−subj	Fr	Je fais qu'on écrive la lettre à Marie		Je fais écrire la lettre à Marie		Je la lui fais écrire
+obj	Sp	Hago que se le escriba la carta a María		Le hago escribir la carta a María		Se la hago escribir
+dat	Po	Faço que se escreva a carta a Maria		Faço escrever a carta a Maria		Faço-lha escrever
	It	Faccio che si scriva la lettera a Maria		Faccio scrivere la lettera a Maria		Gliela faccio scrivere
+subj	Fr	Je fais que Jean écrive la lettre à Marie		Je fais écrire la lettre à Marie par Jean		Je la lui fais écrire par Jean
+obj	Sp	Hago que Juan le escriba la carta a María		Le hago escribir la carta a María por Juan		Se la hago escribir por Juan
+dat	Po	Faço que João escreva a carta a Maria		Faço escrever a carta a Maria por João		Faço-lha escrever por João
	It	Faccio che Gianni scriva la lettera a Maria		Faccio scrivere la lettera a Maria da Gianni		Gliela faccio scrivere da Gianni

Fren: Obligatory infinitive, marked by the functor *de*, with all the
        verbs listed (e.g. *Le médecin m'a dit de ne plus fumer*)

Span: Optional infinitive with all except *decir, pedir* and *rogar* (e.g. *El
        médico me ha aconsejado que no fume*, or *El médico me ha
        aconsejado no fumar*; but *El médico me ha dicho que no
        fume*)

Port: Optional infinitive with P/N agreement with all except *dizer*
        and *rogar*, and marked by the functor *para* after *pedir* (e.g. *O
        gerente nos pedirá que venhamos*, or *O gerente nos pedirá
        para virmos*; but *O gerente nos dirá que venhamos*)

Ital: Obligatory infinitive, marked by the functor *di*, with all the
        verbs listed (e.g. *Abbiamo chiesto a Carlo di non farlo*)

Roum: Not applicable, since only a *să*-verbal is available (e.g. *Cine ţi-a
        cerut să pleci*? 'Qui t'a demandé de partir?'

We now come to the unique case of Fr *falloir* and It *bisognare*, which are
bona fide affective trans-2s although they are also specified as [−S] (see
10.2). Further, their semantic counterparts in the other languages belong to
other categories: Sp/Po *tener/ter* is a trans-1 and Ro *a trebui* is an intrans-1.
Let us first give an example in which there is no dative and the embedded
clause is, of course, subjunctive:

Fr   Il faut que la banque ferme ses portes
It   Bisogna[32] che la banca chiuda le sue porte
Ro   Trebuie ca banca să-şi închidă uşile

There simply exists no Sp/Po structural counterpart here, these two languages having to fall back on Sp *Es necesario* (or *preciso*) *que* . . . and its Po
equivalent.[33]

The lower modality is further reduced to the infinitive under two conditions:

(i) when the lower subject is specified only as [+human] (and there is, of
course, no dative in the matrix); here Span/Port do have a precise equivalent, as in:

Fr   Il faut fermer les portes
Sp   Hay que cerrar las puertas
Po   Tem que fechar as portas
It   Bisogna (*or* Occorre) chiudere le porte
(Ro   Trebuie să (se) închidă uşile)

Sp/Po *haber/ter* are [−S] like the others here, with the clausal object atypically marked by the complementizer *que* despite the fully reduced modality;

(ii) in French alone, when the matrix contains a dative coreferent with the
(deleted) lower subject, as in

Fr   Il leur a fallu vendre la propriété

Here, though, the other languages resort to other structures. Thus Span/
Port, using their [+S] *tener/ter* (which cannot have a dative), promote the
lower subject to main subject, move the verb into the modal position, thus

making the infinitive the head verb and uniting the two clauses into one:

Sp   Ellos tuvieron que vender su propiedad
Po   Eles tiveram que vender a sua propriedade

This transformation being impossible with *bisognare* (or *occorrere*), Italian again resorts to the modalization of *dovere*:

It   Loro hanno dovuto vendere la sua proprietà

while Roumanian simply promotes the lower subject to become that of *a trebui*, even though elsewhere it can have a dative:[34]

Ro   Ei trebuie să-şi vîndă proprietatea[35]

13.2.3 As oblique complement. Clausal obliques occur with both trans-3 and intrans-1 affective verbs embodying the subjunctive-triggering feature [+res]. A typical trans-3 example:

Fr   Aide Jeanne à terminer son travail
Sp   Ayuda a Juana a terminar su trabajo
Po   Ajuda Joana a terminar seu trabalho
It   Aiuta Giovanna a terminare il suo lavoro
Ro   Ajută-o pe Ioana să-şi termine lucrul

As in this example, and with the following minimal list of relevant verbs, the oblique complements do not surface with subjunctive modality (except, of course, in Roumanian) because the subject of the oblique is coreferent with the matrix object and is obligatorily deleted, while the modality is accordingly reduced to the infinitive:

Fren	Span	Port	Ital	Roum
aider	ayudar	ajudar	aiutare	a ajuta
inviter	invitar	convidar	invitare	a invita
prier			pregare	a ruga
encourager	animar	animar	incoraggiare	a încuraja
convaincre	convencer	convencer	convincere	a convinge
persuader	persuadir	persuadir	persuadere	a îndupleca
obliger	obligar	obrigar	obbligare	a obliga
forcer	forzar	forçar	forzare	a forţa[36]

In all but Roumanian the obliques are marked by the functor *a*, except for Fr/It *prier/pregare*, which like the trans-2 of the previous section, is marked by *de/di*. Now for a pair of intrans-1 examples:

Fr   Où avez-vous appris à parler français?
Sp   ¿Dónde aprendió a hablar español?
Po   Onde é que aprendeu a falar português?
It   Dove ha imparato a parlare italiano?
Ro   Unde aţi învăţat să vorbiţi româneşte?

Fr Mon mari est allé acheter les billets
Sp Mi marido ha ido a comprar los billetes
Po Meu marido foi comprar os bilhetes
It Mio marito è andato a comprare i biglietti
Ro Soţul meu s-a dus să cumpere biletele

Again here and with the following list of intrans-1s, the oblique complements do not typically surface with the subjunctive (except in Roumanian)—
this time because the subject of the oblique is usually coreferent with the
matrix subject and is deleted accordingly, while the modality is reduced to
the infinitive (without P/N in Portuguese).[37]

Fren	Span	Port	Ital	Roum
apprendre[38]	aprender	aprender	imparare	a învăţa
commencer	empezar	começar	cominciare	a începe
continuer	continuar	continuar	continuare	a continua
consentir	consentir (en)	consentir (em)	consentire	a consimţi
convenir	convenir (en)	convir (em)	convenire	a conveni
insister	insistir (en)	insistir (em)	insistere	a insista
cesser (de)	dejar (de)	deixar (de)	smettere (di)	a înceta
	atreverse	atrever-se[39]		
	olvidarse (de)	esquecer-se (de)		
	alegrarse (de)	gostar (de)[40]		
décider (de)	decidir	decidir	decidere (di)	a se hotărî
aller (none)	ir	ir (none)	andare	a se duce
venir (none)	venir	vir (none)	venire	a veni
	volver	voltar	tornare	

In all but Roumanian the obliques are marked by the functor *à/a*, except
as noted in parentheses following the entry.

13.3 As modifier within a clause.

13.3.1 In a conditional clause. To return to the topic of conditional clauses
(cf. 12.3.1), within which the condition itself takes the form of a clause
embedded as modifier, we may begin by recalling that the modality of the
condition and the conclusion are congruent with respect to tense. Under this
basic constraint, selection of the tense does not depend primarily on the time
of the actions relative to the moment of speaking. It depends, also, on the
attitude toward reality implicit in the complementizer. The example given at
12.3.1 in the present tense illustrates one of the two types of conditional
clause: the NEUTRAL as opposed to the HYPOTHETICAL.

• In a neutral conditional clause the complementizer *si/se/dacă* implies a
noncommittal attitude devoid of any presupposition as to the reality of the
stated condition—it is envisaged as being either true or not true, indifferently. The conclusion is typically projected as due to occur at some future
time, as the example in question demonstrates. It can also take place in the

present, as in Fr *S'il sait quelque chose, il ne dit rien*; Sp *Si sabe algo, no dice nada*, and so on. Such a neutral clause may also be in the imperfect tense, to depict a condition and conclusion both in past time, as in Fr *S'il savait quelque chose, il ne disait rien*; Sp *Si sabía algo, no decía nada*, etc.

• In a hypothetical clause, on the other hand, the complementizer hypothesizes that the stated condition is at best doubtful of fulfillment, or is actually contrary to established fact, as in the following example:

Fr   S'il savait quelque chose, il ne dirait rien
Sp   Si supiera algo, no diría nada
Po   Se soubesse algo, não diria nada
It   Se sapesse qualcosa, non direbbe nulla
Ro   Dacă ar şti ceva, nu ar zice nimic.

Such a hypothetical clause is invariably in the past tense, with the key addition of future-1 to the conclusion. There is thus no formal differentiation of time, and the example just given can denote occurrence in present, future, or past time. It is also very usual in all the languages, however, to perfectivize both verbals when past time is essentially involved, as in:

Fr   S'il avait su quelque chose, il n'aurait rien dit
Sp   Si hubiera sabido algo, no habría dicho nada
Po   Se tivesse sabido algo, não teria dito nada
It   Se avesse saputo qualcosa, non avrebbe detto nulla
Ro   Dacă ar fi ştiut ceva, nu ar fi zis nimic.

As both of our examples show, in Spanish, Portuguese, and Italian hypothetical clauses the semantic feature [+res] is also present in the complementizer, thus triggering the subjunctive mood in the condition. While French and Roumanian are free of this particular constraint, Roumanian obligatorily adds the futurity mode to the condition as well as to the conclusion, just as we saw it does in neutrals referring to future time.

In Portuguese alone, the subjunctive-triggering [+res] is also present, though optionally, in the *se* of a neutral condition referring to future time. Thus as an alternative to the 12.3 example (and cf. 12, note 12) *Se chove, ninguém sairá daqui*, there may occur also *Se chover, ninguém sairá daqui*.[41] The verb form thus generated is known in Portuguese grammar as the 'future subjunctive', a form with no morphosyntactic counterpart in the other languages.[42] We may analyze it as a mere alternant of present tense + subjunctive, for nowhere does it contrast syntactically with the 'present subjunctive' proper. Nonoccurrent is, for example, either **Se chova, ninguém sairá* or, say, **É possível que chover amanhã*.

13.3.2 Gerund clauses.

A completely different class of clausal modifier, stating the circumstances under which an action takes place rather than the condition on which it is contingent, is available provided that the subject in the modifier is coreferent with that of the matrix clause. In this construction the lower subject and tense are both obligatorily deleted as redundant, and the modality slot is filled by the GERUND suffix, which has the final shapes Fr -*nt*, Sp/Po/It -*ndo*, Ro -*nd*. This suffix may be said actually to adverbialize the lower verb, which nonetheless retains its property of taking whatever complement its category entitles it to. An example with the embedded clause in the basic modifier position (i.e. last in the matrix clause):

Fr Moi j'ai appris beaucoup en lisant ce livre-là
Sp Yo aprendí mucho leyendo ese libro
Po Eu aprendi muito lendo esse livro
It Io ho imparato molto leggendo quel libro
Ro Eu am învăţat multe citind cartea aceea.

It is to be noted that the gerund clause as modifier is marked in French by the functor *en*. This is automatic here, but cf. note 43.

This type of modifier is often preposed so as to apply to the entire predication, as in

Fr En entrant dans le magasin, nous avons rencontré Jean[43]
Sp Entrando en la tienda, encontramos a Juan
Po Entrando na loja, encontramos o João
It Entrando nel negozio, abbiamo incontrato Giovanni
Ro Intrînd în prăvălie, l-am întîlnit pe Ion

In a case of this sort the Span/Port or Roumanian embedded clause might prove ambiguous in the basic position, where the deleted subject can also be coreferent with the matrix object, as in Sp *Encontramos a Juan entrando en la tienda* or its Portuguese analogue, for the exact derivation of which see the paragraph which concludes this section.

In Spanish, Portuguese, and Italian only, an adverbialized gerund clause very frequently follows a predicate containing one of the verbs Sp/Po *estar, andar, ir, venir/vir, seguir*, It *stare, andare, venire*, as illustrated herewith:

Sp Los niños estaban (andaban, venían . . .) jugando en el jardín
Po Os meninos estavam (andavam, vinham . . .) brincando no jardim
It I bambini stavano (andavano, venivano . . .) giocando nel giardino

Rather than functioning as a modifier, however, the gerund clause here appears to be acting as an oblique complement, as confirmed by two facts: (i) the lower clause cannot be preposed as can a modifier—e.g. **Jugando en el jardín, los niños estaban* is ill-formed—and (ii) the verbs involved are intrans-1s (all but *seguir* exclusively so).[44] It so happens that in many grammars of these three languages, principally (though not exclusively) the verbs Sp/Po *estar* and It *stare* are characterized as 'progressive auxiliaries', such that the Aux plus a following gerund constitute a unified VP. Structural proof of 'progressive VP' unity is analogous to that adduced for modal Auxs in 13.2.2 relative to clitic climbing, again as illustrated for Spanish:[45]

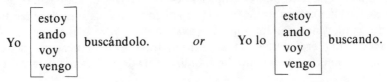

Yo $\begin{bmatrix} \text{estoy} \\ \text{ando} \\ \text{voy} \\ \text{vengo} \end{bmatrix}$ buscándolo.   *or*   Yo lo $\begin{bmatrix} \text{estoy} \\ \text{ando} \\ \text{voy} \\ \text{vengo} \end{bmatrix}$ buscando.

As before, we shall say that any of the intrans-1s in view may undergo an optional transformation whereby the matrix verb moves into the main modality position, occupying the slot filled in the underlying structure by a modal Aux, while the dependent verb, once reduced to its gerund form, moves up to the position of head verb, with the result that on this cycle two clauses have become united as one. Graphically, again using Spanish:

Yo + estoy + [buscando eso] ⇒ Yo + estoy buscando + eso
(Cf. Yo + estoy + aquí)   (Cf. Yo + busco + eso)
Yo + estoy + [buscándolo]   ⇒ Yo + lo estoy buscando

As for our earlier example Sp *Encontramos a Juan entrando* . . . and its Portuguese analogue, they structurally match *Vimos a Juan entrando* etc., which patterns with the *Veo a los niños saliendo* . . . mentioned in 12.3, note 7. In the present light it seems clear that *entrando* in this case represents a normal reduction of *que estaba entrando* to *estar entrando* (comparable to *que entraba = entrar*), with subsequent deletion of the progressive modal *estar* itself. As for Roumanian, the gerund would be as normal in *L-am întîlnit pe Ion intrînd* . . . as it is in *L-am văzut pe Ion intrînd* . . . with a verb of perception.

13.4 As modifier within a CNP.

13.4.1 Relative clauses. When the head noun in a CNP designates an entity characterized exclusively by the modifier and in all other respects unspecified and unidentified—i.e. someone or something anticipated or required that may or may not exist in reality—that noun carries the feature [+res] and so generates the subjunctive in the modality of the lower clause. Examples:

Fr Va chercher un garçon qui porte les bagages
Sp Vé a buscar un mozo que lleve el equipaje
Po Vá procurar um moço que leve a bagagem
It Va a cercare un ragazzo che porti i bagagli
Ro Du-te să cauți un băiat care să poarte bagajele

Fr Il nous faudra des personnes qui soient capables de servir
Sp Nos harán falta unas personas que sean capaces de servir
Po Precisaremos de umas pessoas que forem capazes de servir[46]
It Ci occorreranno delle persone che siano capaci di servire
Ro Ne va trebui niște persoane care să fie capabili de a servi

A considerable reduction in this pattern takes place when two additional conditions are met simultaneously:

(i) The Q-word is functioning as object (as in, say, Fr *un livre que je vais lire*);

(ii) The subject of the modifier clause is coreferent with either the subject or the dative in the matrix clause.

When all these conditions are met, both subject and modality are deleted from the relative clause, with such outcomes as the following:

Fr Je n'ai aucune question à poser
Sp No tengo ninguna pregunta que hacer
Po Não tenho nenhuma pergunta para fazer
It Non ho nessuna domanda da fare
Ro Nu am nici o întrebare de pus

Fr Prêtez-moi un livre à lire
Sp Présteme un libro que leer
Po Empreste-me um livro para ler
It Mi presti un libro da leggere
Ro Împrumutaţi-mi o carte de citit

As the examples show, the vacated modality slot is filled by the participle suffix in Roumanian, and by the infinitive suffix (plus P/N agreement in Portuguese) in the others. Spanish alone keeps the relativizing Q-word, while the others delete it in favor of one or another prep-like functor marking the construction.

13.4.2 Superlative phrases. As was indicated in 6.1, the attribute within a superlative quantifier (cf. also 5.2.4) typically undergoes a partial deletion because it echoes the head noun of the matrix NP. Just as Fr *l'étudiant le plus intelligent + des étudiants de la classe* normally surfaces as *l'étudiant le plus intelligent de la classe*, so also *l'étudiant le plus intelligent + des étudiants que je connais* will come down to *l'étudiant le plus intelligent que je connaisse*, i.e. with only a relative clause remaining and with the further result that *l'étudiant* as head of the matrix NP becomes the new antecedent of the relativizer, and in so doing acquires the feature [+res], thus triggering the subjunctive in the embedded clause. The subjunctive in fact appears here in all the languages but Roumanian, e.g. Sp *el estudiante más inteligente que conozca*, Po *o estudante mais inteligente que conheça*, It *lo studente più intelligente che conosca*. In all four, however, the subjunctive in this environment may be said to be variable at best; in the more colloquial styles it often fails to appear.

13.5 As modifier within a ProP. Again these are of just one type: relative clauses. Any of the pronouns eligible to act as head in a ProP containing a relative clause may, for the same reason as just given with regard to the head of a CNP (cf. 13.4.2), carry [+res] and so generate the subjunctive in the modality of the lower clause.[47] Examples:

Fr quelqu'un qui sache   ce que ce soit
Sp alguien que sepa   lo que fuera
Po alguem que saiba/souber   o que fosse
It qualcuno che sappia   quello che fosse
Ro cineva care să ştie

The same reduction as noted in 13.4.1 for a CNP is also available here under the same constraints and with the same surface outputs, as, for example, in:

Fr Ils n'ont rien à manger
Sp Ellos no tienen nada que comer
Po Eles não têm nada para (de, que) comer
It Essi non hanno niente da mangiare
Ro Ei nu au nimic de mîncat

Fr Vous m'avez laissé beaucoup à faire
Sp Vds. me han dejado mucho que hacer
Po Os senhores me deixaram muito para fazer
It Loro mi hanno lasciato molto da fare
Ro Dvs mi-aţi lăsat multe de făcut

13.6 As modifier within an AdvP.

13.6.1 Relative clauses. We have seen that the demonstrative adverbs are privileged to act as head in an AdvP containing a relative clause as modifier. When the head in such a phrase refers to an anticipated place, time, or manner that may or may not correspond to reality, it carries [+res] in Spanish and Portuguese but not in the other languages. Thus it is that, even with the head subsequently deleted as is normal, the subjunctive appears in the Sp/Po equivalents among the following examples:

Fr Nous descendrons où tu veux (*or* voudras)
Sp Bajaremos donde tú quieras
Po Desceremos onde você quiser
It Scenderemo dove tu vuoi (*or* vorrai)
Ro O să coborîm unde tu vrei

Fr Je verrai Pierre quand il arrivera ici
Sp Veré a Pedro cuando llegue aquí
Po Verei o Pedro quando chegar aqui
It Vedrò Pietro quando arriverà qui
Ro O să-l văd pe Petru cînd va ajunge aici[48]

In the present context, typically with a place adverbial and inevitably with a time adverbial, the action of the matrix clause is projected to take place at some future time; thus, after Fr/It/Ro *quand/quando/cînd*, future-1 is obligatory in the lower modality, and after Po *quando*, the future subjunctive. Note that even when the matrix clause is actually in the past tense, the lower clause will carry a future signal wherever [+res] does not apply:

Fr	Nous espérions voir Pierre quand il arriverait	(past + future-1)
Sp	Esperábamos ver a Pedro cuando llegara	([+res] ⇒ past + subj.)
Po	Esperávamos ver o Pedro quando chegasse	([+res] ⇒ past + subj.)
It	Speravamo di vedere Pietro quando arriverebbe	(past + future-1)
Ro	Speram să-l vedem pe Petru cînd ar ajunge	(future-2)

13.6.2 Appositive clauses. Section 12.6.2 enumerated certain adverbs followed by a clausal modifier, together with two extensions of this pattern involving adverbialized adjs (some of them participles) and PrepPs. It remains to point out here that several among these adverbials carry, either regularly or in given contexts, the subjunctive-triggering feature [+res]. Typically [+res] are such expressions of time, concession, proviso, condition, or purpose/result as the following:

Fr en attendant que, bien que, pourvu que, à moins que, à condition que, de sorte (*or* façon) que . . .

Sp luego que, así que, aunque, con tal que, en caso de que, a menos que, a no ser que, a condición que, de modo (*or* manera) que . . .

Po logo que, assim que, ainda que (*or* embora), contudo que, (no) caso (que), a menos que, a não ser que, a condição que, de modo (*or* maneira) que . . .

It subito che, benchè (*or* sebbene), purchè, a meno che, a condizione che, di maniera che . . .

Ro numai ca, cu condiţia ca *(the list is far smaller in this language)*

Among the foregoing, some of the time adverbials will carry [+res] whenever the time they specify is future relative to that of the matrix modality, though not when it is past and thus reports actual fulfillment rather than anticipation; so, for example, Sp *luego que ella se vaya mañana* with [+res] vs. *luego que ella se fue ayer* with [−res], or Po *assim que ela chegar amanhã* with [+res] vs. *assim que ela chegou ontem* with [−res]. Likewise among the foregoing, those adverbials of purpose or result (e.g. Fr *de sorte que*), Sp/Po *de modo que*, It *di maniera che*) are [+res] when they express (unfulfilled) purpose but [−res] when they express (fulfilled) result.

13.7 As modifier within an AdjP. A limited number of adjectives denoting an emotional attitude such as pleasure or regret are specified (except in Roumanian) as [+res] and consequently generate the subjunctive in a following clausal modifier, as in:

Fr Nous sommes contents que vous acceptiez

Sp Estamos contentos de que Vds. acepten

Po Ficamos contentes que os senhores aceitem

It Siamo contenti che Loro accettino ˙

Ro Sîntem fericiţi că Dvs acceptaţi

Whether [+res] is on the adjective head or not, if the subject of the clausal modifier is coreferent with that of the matrix clause, that lower subject is obligatorily deleted, and the modality is reduced to the infinitive, with the complementizer replaced by the functor *de/di*, as in

Fr Mon ami est très heureux d'accepter

Sp Mi amigo está muy contento de aceptar

Po O meu amigo fica muito contente de aceitar

It Il mio amico è molto lieto di accettare

Ro Prietenul meu este foarte bucuros de a accepta (*or* bucuros să accepte)[49]

13.8 As object within a PrepP. In 12.8 we listed certain adv-1 (preps) capable of taking an embedded clause as their object. Of those adv-1 (preps), the following embody [+res] by virtue of expressing denial, purpose, or anticipation, and therefore trigger the subjunctive in the modality of their clausal object:

Fr   sans, pour, jusque, avant
Sp   sin, para, hasta, antes, después
Po   sem, para, até, antes, depois[50]
It   senza, per,[51] avanti (or prima), dopo
Ro   fără, pentru[52]

A single example should suffice:

Fr   Moi, j'ai fait ceci sans qu'ils le sachent
Sp   Yo hice esto sin que ellos lo supieran
Po   Eu fiz isto sem que eles o soubessem
It   Io ho fatto questo senza che loro lo sapessero
Ro   Eu am făcut asta fără ca ei s-o ştie[53]

Whether or not an adv-1 (prep) is [+res], if the subject within its clausal object is coreferent with that of the matrix clause, that lower subject is deleted and the modality reduced to the infinitive, obligatorily in all but Roumanian and optionally even in this language after the Preps *fără, pentru* and *înainte*. Example:

Fr   Je vais parler avec eux avant de partir[54]
Sp   Yo voy a hablar con ellos antes de salir
Po   Eu vou falar com eles antes de sair[55]
It   Io parlerò con loro prima di partire
Ro   Eu voi vorbi cu ei înainte de a pleca[56] (or înainte să plec)

Notes for Chapter 13

1. J. J. Bergen in 'One Rule for the Spanish Subjunctive', *Hispania* 61:2 (1978). Although Bergen identifies and defines the feature in the framework of Spanish grammar alone, he hypothesizes its equal applicability to the other Romance languages—an assumption which our present analysis appears to corroborate amply.

2. It is possible to argue (a) that in the particular construction in view the lower modality is unconstrained despite the apparent presence of [+res] in the matrix, or (b) that somehow the [+res] attitude is lacking even in the denial or questioning of a truth. This latter claim is obviously difficult to substantiate, while the former one receives general support from the fact that in one or another construction in this or that language, alteration of the modality is not required (indeed not permitted) even when [+res] is patently present and the reality of the proposition cannot be taken for granted—as in e.g. Fr *Il me semble que tu as raison*, or Sp *Yo creo que Paco se equivoca*.

3. Fut-1 is totally blocked; fut-2 does occur marginally, in Fren/Span/Port, in a blending of the syntactic privileges of *aller/ir* as modal Aux with

those of the same verb as predicate.

4. A lone exception is the copula *a fi*, which has its basic stem throughout the subjunctive paradigm (*fiu, fii, fim, fiţi, fie*) as against the suppletive stems *sînt-* and *est-* of the present tense.

5. Roumanian has the cognates *trist* and *straniu*, but they are not included here because emotional rejection of a real proposition does not entail [+res] in this language.

6. Under a single minor condition *ca* and *să* do appear juxtaposed; for this, see 13.8, note 53.

7. The *de* of French alone can hardly be called a complementizer; its occurrence is strictly arbitrary.

8. Where besides in the phrasal future modes the infinitive actually occurs, we shall observe in due course.

9. The P/N suffix is clearly *-em* in the above example; if the subject were *nós*, deleted or not, the verb form would be *pagarmos*, and so on.

10. Just *fazer*, without the trace clitic *se* carried over as it is in Portuguese alone, would be taken as the 'personal infinitive' (reflecting a reduction of *é perigoso eu* (or *ele*) *fazer isso*, or whatever), even though the 1st and 3rd sing. P/N agreement allomorphs have zero shape.

11. The verb form in this type of construction is traditionally labeled 'supine'—a descriptively superfluous term.

12. Whatever it is here, it also turns up as equivalent complement in place of an adj in the likes of Fr *C'est à croire*, Sp *Es de desear*, Po *É de esperar*, It *È da aspettare*, Ro *E de preferat*, any of which predications may in turn have as their subject another embedded clause, e.g. Fr *C'est à croire que Jean viendra* or (with [+res]) *C'est à craindre que Jean ne vienne*. Roumanian favors the construction in view over certain adjs in the other languages—e.g. *de (ne)crezut* over '(in)croyable' etc., or *de dorit* over 'désirable' etc.

13. [*Query. Why not add also Ro* E păcat . . ., M-a surpris . . ., *with the same meanings?*]

14. The parenthesized items are taken in Roumanian as FACTIVE VERBS, following which any clause is complementized by *că* and the subjunctive is disallowed, whether or not [+res] is present.

15. As regards the equivalent Fr *Il faut se taire*, Sp *Hay que callar*, Po *Tem que calar*, they represent quite different constructions: watch for their mention further on.

16. Even in this construction, registers of Roumanian which avoid the recessive infinitive altogether will use the subjunctive in both halves of the equation, saying *Să vezi este să crezi*. [*A reminder. What does the suffix* -i *represent here?*]

17. While *aimer* here equates semantically with Sp/Po *gustar/gostar* and It/Ro *piacere/a place* (see 9.3.3), *aimer mieux* is about synonymous with *préférer* and its cognates.

18. This verb is actually performative rather than stative, though it patterns with the present set.

19. This Sp/Po verb does not fully match Fr/It *sentir(e)*. Italian uses the intrans-2 *dispiacere* or *rincrescere* in this meaning, while Roumanian recurs to *a pare* with the adv *rău* opposed to *bine*, as in *Îmi pare rău că nu puteţi* ('que vous ne puissiez pas') *accepta*, or *Îmi pare rău să nu pot* ('de ne pas pouvoir') *accepta*.

20. After this verb in French alone the predicate verbal containing a subjunctive modality is pleonastically negated, with *ne* corresponding to no negative adverbial modifier, e.g. *La mère craint que son enfant ne meure*.

21. By contrast with the other languages, It *credere* is normally [+res] even when *not* negated or questioned, e.g. *Tutti credono che ciò sia giusto*.

22. Contrariwise, [+res] is apt to be absent from a verb like Fr *douter* and its counterparts precisely when the predication is negated.

23. The reduction is obligatory with the affective subgroup (of wishing etc.) but optional with the others—as in Fr *Pierre ne croit pas qu'il réusisse = Pierre ne croit pas réussir*.

24. In this construction the Po infinitive never shows P/N agreement.

25. After most Italian verbs in this category the infinitive is further marked by the functor *di*, just as a few French ones (e.g. *regretter, craindre*) are flagged by *de*.

26. Roumanian offers only *a trebui*, an intransitive.

27. In Fr *Il se peut que . . .*, Sp *Puede que . . .*, Ro *Poate că . . .*, the verb is doubling as an intrans-3 triggering the subjunctive in a following clausal subject; these may reflect a special deletion of the copula as found in Fr *Peut-être que . . .*, Po *Pode ser que . . .*, It *Può essere che . . .* [*Query. How explain the surfacing of Fr* Peut-être que . . . *rather than the expected* *Il (se) peut être que . . .?*]

28. Present-day French lacks this syntactic variation which many linguists now label 'clitic climbing'. In Portuguese, where a 'conjunctive pronoun' can be either proclitic or enclitic to an infinitive, three orders are possible as in, say, *Não querem ver-me* or *Não querem me ver* or *Não me querem ver*.

29. The Roumanian cognates *a face* and *a lăsa* are never followed by an embedded clausal object; they belong among the trans-3 verbs treated in 13.2.2.

30. Portuguese alone tolerates also the order *Quem faz o sol brilhar?* or ([+pl]) *Quem faz os sóis brilharem?* Here, presumably, the lower subject is simply not transformed to object.

31. There is one minor wrinkle: Fr *laisser*, seemingly by analogy with the verbs of perception, permits (Table 13.1, col.2) *Je laisse Marie sortir* (like *Je vois Marie sortir*) as a variant of *Je laisse sortir Marie* (like *Je fais sortir Marie*).

32. The alternative *occorrere* is, like Ro *a trebui*, an intrans-1—cf. It *A me occorrono soldi* = Ro *Mie îmi trebuie bani*.

33. In other contexts Fr *falloir* and Ro *a trebui* express probability rather than necessity, as in Fr *Il faut que vous soyez fou* = *Trebuie ca Dvs să fiţi*

nebun. But here It *bisognare* is not viable; alongside Sp/Po *deber/dever*, It resorts to *dovere*, the 'modal' verb which expresses probability as well as obligation.

34. As in *Le trebuie vreme* 'il leur faut du temps'.

35. It is noteworthy that even in this $[-S] \Rightarrow [+S]$ promotion, *a trebui* does not copy P/N agreement when the promoted subject is a local pronominal—thus *Eu trebuie . . ., Noi trebuie . . .* etc. The P/N of a plural nominal *is* copied, however: the present-tense form *trebuie* happens to take a zero-shape suffix, but the agreement shows in the imperfect *Ei trebuiau . . .* as against *El trebuia*, or the perfect *Ei au trebuit . . .* vs *El a trebuit . . .* A passive clause embedded as subject of *a trebui* often undergoes a further reduction whereby e.g. *Proprietăţile trebuie să fie vîndute* becomes merely *Proprietăţile trebuie vîndute*. Italian offers an almost exact parallel in its transformation of the type *Le proprietà devono essere vendute* $\Rightarrow$ *Le proprietà vanno vendute*.

36. The Roumanian verbs *a face* and *a lăsa*, cognate with the causatives of the other languages, belong in this list along with *a pune* 'mettre/poner' and *a învăţa* 'enseigner/enseñar'.

37. Note, however, such possibilities as are illustrated by Sp *Yo me alegro de que tú lo sepas* or *Yo insisto en que ellos lo oigan* (with different subjects) alongside *Yo me alegro de saberlo* or *Yo insisto en oirlo* (with same subject).

38. In the sense of *enseigner* this verb is a trans-2. Both *apprendre* and *enseigner*, together with the latter's cognates Sp *enseñar*, Po *ensinar*, It *insegnare*, mark their clausal object with *a* instead of the *de/di* typical of this group (e.g. Fr *On leur enseigne à lire*, Sp *Se les enseña a leer*, and so on).

39. The semantic counterparts of these Sp/Po reflexive verbs—to wit, Fr *oser*, It *osare*, Ro *a îndrăzni*—are instead trans-1s, as are also Fr *oublier*, It *dimenticare*, Ro *a uita*. However, in all the languages numerous morphologically reflexive intrans-1s figure in the present group, e.g. Fr *s'opposer*, Sp *oponerse*, etc.

40. It was pointed out in 9.3.3 that Po *gostar* deviates syntactically from its Sp cognate *gustar* (as well as It/Ro *piacere/a place*) in the manner now exemplified (e.g. Po *Eu gosto de pescar* = Sp *A mí me gusta pescar*).

41. Since [+res] relates only to future time, an alternative **Se souber algo, não diz nada* would not be available for *Se sabe algo, não diz nada*.

42. Exception: Spanish does have an analogous 'future subjunctive' for marginal use in certain legal or bureaucratic styles only (*lloviere, supiere . . .*). It is not included in Appendix 4, however.

43. In this position the marker *en* is not obligatory, and its presence vs. absence conveys a difference in meaning. [*Query. What is it?*]

44. Cf. also the French equivalent *Les enfants étaient en train de jouer . . .*, where the PrepP *en train . . .* is clearly enough an oblique after *être* in its intrans-1 role.

45. Again in Portuguese, three orders are possible as in, say, *Não estão*

procurando-me or *Não estão me procurando* or *Não me estão procurando*.

46. Note the 'future subjunctive' here, in the context of a future-1 in the matrix modality.

47. In French even the interrogative pronouns *qui* and *quoi* as heads may be modified by a relative clause, as in *qui que vous soyez* or *quoi que je vous dise*. In Italian, [−human] *che* also qualifies marginally as in *checchè tu dica*; but apart from these oddments, comparable expressions in the other languages rely on one or another derivational affix attachable to a Q-word, be it pronoun or adverb—e.g. Sp/Po *-quiera/-quer* (as in, say, Sp *quienquiera* alongside *dondequiera*), It *-unque* (as in *chiunque* like *comunque*), Ro *ori-* (as in *oricine, orice* like *oricînd*). All these forms except the Roumanian carry [+res] and trigger the subjunctive (e.g. Sp *quienquiera que seas*).

48. [*Query. How would you account for the embedded clauses in:*

Fr   Jean crie comme s'il était fou
Sp   Juan grita como si estuviera loco
Po   João grita como se estivesse louco
It   Gianni grida come se fosse pazzo

Roumanian shows a quite different structure here: Ion strigă parcă (*or* ca şi cum) ar fi nebun; *to what extent does it fit with the others?*]

49. The optional use of the infinitive even in Roumanian is possible after the functor *de*—though, as here, the construction is stilted and old-fashioned. (Cf. also 13, note 56).

50. By exception, *depois* stands alone among Portuguese Preps in generating the future subjunctive: thus *depois que eles sairem* (at some future time) as opposed to *antes que eles saiam, até que eles saiam, para que eles saiam* etc.; *depois* evidently patterns instead with the time adverbials (*logo que eles sairem*, etc.), while the complementary distribution remains unperturbed.

51. It *per* is [+res] when expressing purpose but, of course, not when expressing cause.

52. The corresponding Roumanian Preps *pînă, după* and *înainte*, as well as Fr *après*, arbitrarily never generate the subjunctive.

53. When the subject is deleted from a *să*-clause, object of *pentru*, this preposition is replaced by *ca* in double function; thus: *eu am făcut asta pentru ca ei s-o ştie* reduces to *eu am făcut asta ca s-o ştie* and not **eu am făcut asta pentru s-o ştie*. This quirk alone accounts for the juxtaposition of *ca* and *să* hinted at in 13.1, note 6.

54. Fr *après* is unique in requiring that its clausal object when reduced to the infinitive also be perfectivized, as in e.g. *après être parti* and not **après partir*.

55. Regularly possible also in Portuguese after an adv-2 (prep/adv) is reduction to the infinitive with P/N agreement, even when the subjects are not coreferent, as in the alternative *Eu vou falar com eles antes de sairem*.

56. Note that where the functor *de* is required for linking an adv-2 (prep/adv) with its object, it fails to displace the Ro functor *a* which is inseparable from the infinitive form of the verb.

Chapter 14
Dependent clauses
in expressions of comparison

14.0 Introduction. At this point we may refer back to 1.3.4 as a point of departure. In all our languages the comparative quantifiers (see Table 1.1) have as attributes certain expressions of comparison. These structures are of two universally recognized semantic types: comparative and superlative. We have been able to deal with the superlative type already in 5, 6, and 13; but only now are we in a position to analyze and describe the comparative type, which subdivides structurally into what are frequently termed COMPARISONS OF INEQUALITY and COMPARISONS OF EQUALITY. Both of these attributive functions are performed by embedded clauses which, in the surface output, are drastically reduced through pragmatic deletions. The clausal attributes in question are equally indispensable whether the head word itself is functioning as quantifying determiner in a CNP (e.g. in Sp *más tiempo . . .*), as quantifier in an AdjP or AdvP (Sp *más fuerte . . .* or *tan rápidamente . . .*), as pronoun (Sp *saber más . . .*) or as adverb (Sp *reir tanto . . .*).

14.1 Comparisons of inequality. In these the comparative quantifiers are Fr *plus* or *moins*, Sp *más* or *menos*, Po *mais* or *menos*, It *più* or *meno*, Ro *mai* or *mai puțin*. In addition, either of the two may in turn be quantified itself by essentially any one of the indefinite quantifiers or by the special NP *un peu/un poco* etc., or by the adverb of increment *encore/aún* and its analogues, thus generating strings like the following:

Fr beaucoup (peu, assez, tant, un peu, encore . . .) plus/moins
Sp mucho (poco, bastante, cuánto, tanto, un poco, aún . . .) más/ menos
Po muito (pouco, bastante, quanto, tanto, um pouco, ainda . . .) mais/ menos
It molto (poco, abbastanza, quanto, tanto, un po', ancora . . .) più/ meno
Ro mult (puțin, cît, atît, și . . .) mai mult/mai puțin

Since these 'extra' quantifiers impose no noteworthy constraints, examples explicitly embodying them will not be included in the two subsections to follow here.

14.1.1 Symmetrical comparisons. In what we may characterize as SYMMETRICAL comparisons (the commonest subtype), one item is said to exceed, or fall short of, another item with respect to some specified property or behavior. The first item is a constituent of the matrix clause, the second item is a constituent of the embedded clause, and the two perform identical functions within their respective clauses. These constituents may be subjects, complements of any class, modifiers, even predicates and modalities.

Table 14.1, with examples limited for convenience to French and Spanish, displays the various underlying patterns with the compared items set in italic type.

In the surface output the following transformations take place:

• The comparative quantifier, if determining a noun (*argent/dinero*), or quantifying an adjective (*riche/rico*) or adverb (*souvent/a menudo*), moves to precede the item it quantifies,[1] while the attributive clause remains in final position in the matrix clause.

• A complementizer is inserted to introduce the attributive clause; see the following examples for its form (or forms) in each language.

• All material except the second item itself is obligatorily deleted from the attributive clause.

We may now record the surface forms of the Table 14.1 examples in all five languages:

Fr   Jean travaille plus que Paul
Sp   Juan trabaja más que Pablo
Po   João trabalha mais do que Paulo[2]
It   Giovanni lavora più di Paolo[3]
Ro   Ion muncește mai mult decît Petre[4]

Fr   Jean est plus riche que Paul
Sp   Juan es más rico que Pablo
Po   João é mais rico do que Paulo
It   Giovanni è più ricco di Paolo
Ro   Ion e mai bogat decît Petre

Fr   Jean a plus d'argent que Paul
Sp   Juan tiene más dinero que Pablo
Po   João tem mais dinheiro do que Paulo
It   Giovanni ha più denaro di Paolo
Ro   Ion are mai mulți bani decît Petre

Fr   Jean a plus d'ambition que d'intelligence
Sp   Juan tiene más ambición que inteligencia
Po   João tem mais ambição que inteligência
It   Giovanni ha più ambizione che intelligenza[3]
Ro   Ion are mai multă ambiție decît inteligență

Fr   J'écris plus à Jean qu'à Paul
Sp   Le escribo más a Juan que a Pablo
Po   Escrevo mais ao João que ao Paulo
It   Scrivo più a Giovanni che a Paolo
Ro   Îi scriu mai mult lui Ion decît lui Petre

Table 14.1 Underlying patterns of compared items in Spanish and French.

Function of compared items:	Matrix clause:	Embedded clause:
Subject	Fr *Jean* travaille + plus [ ]	→ [*Paul* travaille]
	Sp *Juan* trabaja + más [ ]	→ [*Pablo* trabaja]
	Fr *Jean* est riche + plus [ ]	→ [*Paul* est riche]
	Sp *Juan* es rico + más [ ]	→ [*Pablo* es rico]
	Fr *Jean* a de l'argent + plus [ ]	→ [*Paul* a de l'argent]
	Sp *Juan* tiene dinero + más [ ]	→ [*Pablo* tiene dinero]
Object	Fr Jean a de l'*ambition* + plus [ ]	→ [Jean a de *l'intelligence*]
	Sp Juan tiene *ambición* + más [ ]	→ [Juan tiene *inteligencia*]
Equivalent	Fr Jean est *ambitieux* + plus [ ]	→ [Jean est *intelligent*]
	Sp Juan es *ambicioso* + más [ ]	→ [Juan es *inteligente*]
Dative	Fr J'écris *à Jean* + plus [ ]	→ [j'écris *à Paul*]
	Sp *Le* escribo *a Juan* + más [ ]	→ [*le* escribo *a Pablo*]
Oblique or modifier	Jean dort *ici* souvent + plus [ ]	→ [Jean dort *là-bas*]
	Juan duerme *aquí* a menudo + más [ ]	→ [Juan duerme *allá*]
Predicate	Jean *dort* + plus [ ]	→ [Jean *étudie*]
	Juan *duerme* + más [ ]	→ [Juan *estudia*]
Modality	Je t'aime + plus [ ]	→ [je t'*aimais*]
	Te amo + más [ ]	→ [te am*aba*]

Fr Jean dort ici plus souvent que là-bas
Sp Juan duerme aquí más a menudo que allí
Po João dorme aqui mais amiúde que ali
It Giovanni dorme qui più spesso che lì
Ro Ion doarme aici mai des decît acolo

Fr Jean dort plus qu'il n'étudie[5]
Sp Juan duerme más de lo que estudia[6]
Po João dorme mais do que estuda
It Giovanni dorme più di quanto studia[3]
Ro Ion doarme mai mult decît studiază

Fr Je t'aime plus que je ne t'aimais
Sp Te amo más de lo que te amaba
Po Amo-te mais do que te amava
It Ti amo più di quanto ti amavo
Ro Te iubesc mai mult decît te iubeam[7]

14.1.2 Asymmetrical comparisons. In what we may characterize as ASYM-METRICAL comparisons, the compared item in the matrix clause lacks any offsetting item and is merely said to exceed the extent expected, apparent, or whatever. Again we may illustrate the underlying pattern with a pair of French and Spanish examples. The compared item may be in any function. See Table 14.2.

Table 14.2 Asymmetrical comparisons.

Matrix clause:	Embedded clause:
Jean est riche + plus [ ]	← [vous savez que Jean est riche]
Juan es rico + más [ ]	← [Vd. sabe que Juan es rico]
Jean est vieux + plus [ ]	← [Jean paraît vieux]
Juan es viejo + más [ ]	← [Juan parece viejo]

The surface outputs entail the same sorts of transformation as with symmetrical comparisons, yielding the following:[8]

Fr Jean est plus riche que vous ne le savez[9]
Sp Juan es más rico de lo que Vd. sabe
Po João é mais rico do que você sabe
It Giovanni è più ricco di quanto Lei non sa[10]
Ro Ion e mai bogat decît știți Dvs

Fr Jean est plus vieux qu'il ne le paraît
Sp Juan es más viejo de lo que parece
Po João é mais velho do que parece
It Giovanni è più vecchio di quel che non pare
Ro Ion e mai bătrîn decît pare

14.2 Comparisons of equality. In these the comparative quantifiers are Fr *autant*, Sp/Po/It *tanto*, Ro *atît*. In symmetrical comparisons of this type, one item is said to measure up to another with respect to a specified property or behavior; in asymmetricals a single item is said to measure up to the extent expected, apparent etc. As regards constituency and function, the structuring of the compared items is the same as in comparisons of inequality; hence displays of the underlying patterns could match exactly those given in Tables 14.1 and 14.2, *mutatis mutandis*—i.e. with the French quantifier *plus* replaced by *autant* and the Spanish *más* by *tanto*, and with the same three transformations to generate the surface output, together with certain further alternations manifested when the comparative word is quantifying an adj/adv:

• Fr *(au)tant* alternates to *(aus)si*;[11]

• Sp/Po *tanto* apocopate to Sp *tan*, Po *tão*, respectively;

• It *tanto* freely alternates with *così*, and Ro *atît* with *aşa*, both meaning 'ainsi/así' and both preceded by *tot* except in a negative clause:

Equality examples, both symmetrical and asymmetrical, paralleling those of inequality given above, are the following:

Fr Jean travaille autant que Paul[12]
Sp Juan trabaja tanto como Pablo
Po João trabalha tanto quanto Paulo
It Giovanni lavora tanto quanto Paolo
Ro Ion munceşte tot atît de mult ca (şi) Petre[13]

Fr Jean est aussi riche que Paul[14]
Sp Juan es tan rico como Pablo
Po João é tão rico quanto Paulo
It Giovanni è tanto ricco quanto Paolo[15]
Ro Ion e tot atît de bogat ca Petre

Fr Jean a autant d'argent que Paul
Sp Juan tiene tanto dinero como Pablo
Po João tem tanto dinheiro quanto Paulo
It Giovanni ha tanto denaro quanto Paolo
Ro Ion are tot atîţia bani ca Petre

Fr Jean a autant d'ambition que d'intelligence
Sp Juan tiene tanta ambición como inteligencia
Po João tem tanta ambição quanto inteligência
It Giovanni ha tanta ambizione quanto intelligenza
Ro Ion are tot atîtă ambiţie (pe) cîtă inteligenţă

Fr J'écris tant à Jean qu'à Paul
Sp Le escribo tanto a Juan como a Pablo
Po Escrevo tanto a João quanto a Paulo
It Scrivo tanto a Giovanni quanto a Paolo
Ro Îi scriu lui Ion tot atît de mult ca lui Petre

Fr Jean dort ici aussi souvent que là-bas
Sp Juan duerme aquí tan a menudo como allí
Po João dorme aqui tão amiúde quanto ali
It Giovanni dorme qui tanto spesso quanto lì
Ro Ion doarme aici tot atît de des ca acolo

Fr Jean dort autant qu'il étudie
Sp Juan duerme tanto como estudia
Po João dorme tanto quanto estuda
It Giovanni dorme tanto quanto studia
Ro Ion doarme tot atît de mult (pe) cît studiază

Fr Je t'aime autant que je t'aimais
Sp Te amo tanto como te amaba
Po Amo-te tanto quanto te amava
It Ti amo tanto quanto ti amavo
Ro Te iubesc tot atît de mult (pe) cît te iubeam

Fr Jean n'est pas si riche que vous le croyez[16]
Sp Juan no es tan rico como Vd. cree
Po João não é tão rico quanto você acredita
It Giovanni non è così ricco come Lei crede
Ro Ion nu e atît de bogat (pe) cît (o) credeţi Dvs

Fr Jean n'est pas si vieux qu'il le paraît
Sp Juan no es tan viejo como parece
Po João não é tão velho quanto parece
It Giovanni non è così vecchio come pare
Ro Ion nu e aşa de bătrîn cum pare

Notes for Chapter 14

1. When this happens, the comparative *plus/más/mais/più* in all but Roumanian fuses with a lexically restricted set of adjs/advs to yield irregular surface forms (which are lexical items in their own right), as shown herewith:

Fr plus + $\begin{bmatrix} \text{bon} \rightarrow \text{meilleur} \\ \text{bien} \rightarrow \text{mieux} \end{bmatrix}$ plus + $\begin{bmatrix} \text{mauvais} \rightarrow \text{pire} \\ \text{mal} \rightarrow \text{pis} \end{bmatrix}$

Sp más + $\begin{bmatrix} \text{bueno} \\ \text{bien} \end{bmatrix} \rightarrow \text{mejor}$ más + $\begin{bmatrix} \text{malo} \\ \text{mal} \end{bmatrix} \rightarrow \text{peor}$

más + grande → mayor   más + pequeño → menor

$$\text{Po} \quad \text{mais} + \begin{bmatrix} \text{bom} \\ \text{bem} \end{bmatrix} \rightarrow \text{melhor} \qquad \text{mais} + \begin{bmatrix} \text{mau} \\ \text{mal} \end{bmatrix} \rightarrow \text{pior}$$

$$\text{mais} + \quad \text{grande} \rightarrow \text{maior} \qquad \text{mais} + \quad \text{pequeno} \rightarrow \text{menor}$$

$$\text{It} \quad \text{più} + \begin{bmatrix} \text{buono} \rightarrow \text{migliore} \\ \text{bene} \rightarrow \text{meglio} \end{bmatrix} \quad \text{più} + \begin{bmatrix} \text{cattivo} \rightarrow \text{peggiore} \\ \text{male} \rightarrow \text{peggio} \end{bmatrix}$$

$$\text{più} + \quad \text{grande} \rightarrow \text{maggiore} \quad \text{più} + \quad \text{piccolo} \rightarrow \text{minore}$$

Several of the Sp/Po/It items occur also without the transformation, usually with semantic differences. Especially noteworthy is Sp *más bien* as opposed to *mejor*.

2. Portuguese complementizes with either *que* or *do que* (cf. Sp *de lo que*), a stylistic choice with no syntactic constraints.

3. Italian replaces the complementizer with the functor *di* when the compared items are subjects, and with *di* + *quanto* (or *quel che*) when they are predicates (or modalities). After the functor in view, the [−pl] local personal pronouns appear as their nonsubject alternants, e.g. *Giovanni lavora più di me* or *di te*.

4. Roumanian complementizes with either *decît* or *ca*, the latter being informal.

5. French inserts a pleonastic *ne* before the second of compared predicates (or just modalities). Being semantically empty (indeed contary to sense), this false negator tends to disappear from colloquial styles.

6. Before compared predicates (or just modalities), Spanish inserts *lo que* by way of offsetting, or balancing, the quantifying *más/menos*. Before this insert the regular complementizer *que* dissimilates to *de*. In this environment, if the predicates are accompanied by one and the same object nominal, the second occurrence of its head, while deleted at the surface, is nevertheless traced by the definite article *el* in the slot provided by *lo*, e.g. *Juan compra más libros de los [ ] que puede leer.*

7. Of course, it is not possible to delete all of an attributive clause except the modality, which is suffixal and hence requires repetition of the verb to which it is attached.

8. In this environment the complementizers are consistently as shown, the variations being free in Italian and Roumanian.

9. Instead of deleting an object or equivalent from the embedded clause, French reduces it to the clitic *le*.

10. Both French and Italian insert a pleonastic negator in the attributive clause, at least in formal styles.

11. The parentheses mean that *autant/aussi* is also in complementation with the shorter *tant/si*, the latter occurring when the matrix predicate is negated.

12. Cf. *Jean ne travaille pas tant que Paul.*

13. Other than after a negation, the insertion of *şi* 'aussi/también' before the second item (unless it is a VP) is very usual in this language.

14. Cf. *Jean n'est pas si riche que Paul.*

15. Whenever It *così* is selected rather than *tanto*, the complementizer is obligatorily *come* and not *quanto*.

16. Cf. 14, note 9, and note the optional clitic *o* in Roumanian.

Sentential structures
Chapter 15
The sentence

15.0 Internal structure of the sentence (S). Having disposed of the clause we have now reached the top of our hierarchy, namely, Level 5, the sentence (S), which also represents the highest level of grammatical construction in our frame of reference.[1] The basic constituency, not subject to ordering and with both elements obligatory, is shown in the formula:

$$S \rightarrow \left\{ \begin{array}{l} \text{segmental constituent} \\ \text{prosodic constituent} \end{array} \right\}$$

15.1 Clauses as segmental constituents. The segmental slot in a sentence is filled first and foremost by a clause, as in the French sentence *Je m'appelle Frédéric⌐* or in the Spanish sentence *Yo me llamo Federico⌐*. In typical conversational exchanges, however, and mainly in one speaker's response to another's question, the clausal constituent is very often pragmatically reduced to a mere word or phrase, namely, that word or phrase which conveys the expected new information; all the old information, redundant as it would be in a dialogue situation, is discarded via deletion. The indispensable remainder of a clause reduced under such circumstances may be defined as a SENTENTIAL FRAGMENT; whenever it is accompanied by a contextually meaningful prosodic component, it in fact constitutes one part of a sentence.[2] The fragment can be manifesting any one of the possible constituents of a clause (except, of course, a modality), as the display in Table 15.1 of examples from minimal dialogues in Spanish illustrates:

Table 15.1 Spanish questions and response fragments.

Question	Response fragment	Function in reduced clause
¿Quién te ha dicho eso?	— Don Paco.	Subject
¿A quién vio Vd. allí?	— A Don Paco.	Object
¿A quién le preguntaste eso?	— A Don Paco.	Dative
¿Quién es aquel caballero?	— Don Paco.	Equivalent
¿Adónde va Vd. ahora?	— A la universidad.	Oblique
¿Por qué vas a hacerlo tú?	— Porque quiero. ⎫	
¿Cuándo salieron Vds.?	— A las ocho. ⎭	Modifier
¿Qué tienes que hacer?	— Estudiar. ⎫	
¿Qué estabas haciendo?	— Leyendo. ⎭	Predicate (without modality)

Many a fragment will contain more than one clausal constituent, as, for example, *Leyendo un libro* (predicate plus object) or *A México con mis padres* (oblique plus modifier).

The words Fr *oui/si* or *non*, Sp *sí* or *no*, Po *sim* or *não*, It *sì* or *no*, Ro *da* or *nu* are not sentential fragments, for instead of representing any clausal constituent, they substitute for an entire clause and may be termed PRO-CLAUSES. Like any clauses, they may function as sentence segmentals or they may be embedded as objects in higher clauses—e.g. Fr *Je crois que oui (. . . que non)*, Sp *Yo creo que sí (. . . que no)*, Po *Eu acho que sim (. . . que não)*, It *Io credo di sì (. . . di no)*, Ro *Eu cred că da (. . .că nu)*. They may also constitute part of a sentential fragment by occurring after a word or phrase which echoes a clausal element from the foregoing context of discourse—i.e. a subject or a complement/modifier being singled out for a topicalization essential to keeping the discourse on track. Examples:

Fr Moi oui (*or* Moi si *if the previous clause is negative*), Ceux-là non
    (*or less emphatically* Ceux-là pas), Ici oui, Ici non (*or* Ici pas)
Sp Yo sí, Esos no, Aquí sí, Aquí no
Po Eu sim, Esses não, Aqui sim, Aqui não
It Io sì, Essi no, Qui sì, Qui no
Ro Eu da, Aceia nu, Aici da, Aici nu.

In this pattern the pro-clauses are functioning in exact parallel to the adverbs *aussi/también*, *non plus/tampoco* and their counterparts, as in

Fr Toi aussi, Ceux-ci non plus, Là aussi, Là non plus
Sp Tú también, Aquéllos tampoco, Allí también, Allí tampoco
Po Tu também, Aqueles tampouco (*or, more often*, Aqueles também
    não), Ali também, Ali tampouco (*or* também não)
It Anche tu, Neanche loro, Anche lì, Neanche lì[3]
Ro Şi tu, Nici aceia, Şi acolo (*or* Tot acolo), Nici acolo

Fragments of the foregoing sort formed with the negative pro-clause are inherently different from the type in which some element *new to the discourse* follows the negative item, as in

Fr Pas moi, Pas à Jeanne, Pas très bien, Pas tout à fait, Pas dange-
    reux[4]
Sp No yo, No a Juana, No muy bien, No enteramente, No peligroso
Po Não eu, Não a Joana, Não muito bem, Não inteiramente, Não
    perigoso
It Non io, Non a Gianna, Non molto bene, Non interamente, Non
    pericoloso
Ro Nu eu, Nu Ioanei, Nu prea bine, Nu întreg, Nu pericolos.

[*Query. How and on what grounds are we then to describe the construction in view?*]

15.2 Intonation contours as prosodies. The prosodic function in a sentence consists of an intonation contour, which is known to some analysts also as SUPRASEGMENTAL material. In our five languages, as indeed in all known human languages, an intonation contour is formed on the basis of distinctive PITCHES at certain points in the linear segment, plus a TERMINAL JUNCTURE (not posited by some recent theorists). The material functioning morphologically in this way is phonological rather than grammatical in nature, and consists of (1) phonemic differences of pitch, plus (2) fall, rise, or hold of the pitch whereon the voice fades before a pause. Complete and detailed intonational studies of our five individual languages have yet to be made, but meanwhile the following generalizations applicable to one and all at some underlying level seem reasonably safe on the basis of all having at least three phonemic pitch levels: low $/^1/$, mid $/^2/$, and high $/^3/$; and at least three terminal junctures: falling $/\downarrow/$, rising $/\uparrow/$, and sustained $/\rightarrow/$.

• There are at least three, and in complex contours more, significant PITCH POINTS along the linear segment, from ONSET pitch through PEAK pitch to FINAL pitch. The pitches at the three points can range from all the same to all different—e.g. $/^2...^2...^2/$, or $/^2...^3...^3/$, or $^2...^3....^1/$, or whatever; what counts is only that the pitch at each point be distinct from any other possible pitch at that point.

• The stressed syllable within a given word in the segmental—in Romance characteristically the last word but sometimes the first or indeed the only word—is not only a distinctive pitch but also receives extra loudness (and perhaps also extra length), and thus constitutes the peak of the intonation.

• There exist some compound contours overlaying a single segmental, each part having its three (or more) pitch points and its peak, and with the two parts separated by a special nonterminal juncture $/-/$ at which the voice pauses almost imperceptibly but does not fade to silence before resuming with the second part. This is evident, for example, within a series of coordinated phrases or clauses.

• Successive pitches are not discrete, as in music; one significant pitch flows smoothly into the next,[5] and except at the peak there is no correlation between the suprasegmental pitches and the segmental stresses. Thus, for example, the pitch may drop from a peak $/^3/$ to a final $/^1/$ either in the course of a single (stressed) syllable, as in the Spanish sentence $/^2$dáselo a jo^{3}sé$^1\downarrow/$ or over two or three syllables as in $/^2$yá se lo dí a ra^{3}móna$^1\downarrow/$ or $/^3$cuándo vá ustéd a ^{3}méxico$^1\downarrow/$.

A system of just three pitch points and three terminal junctures makes for 81 distinct contours of the shape $/^1...^2...^1\downarrow/$, or $/^2...^3...^3\uparrow/$; or $/^3...^2 ...^2\rightarrow/$, or whatever. By no means all of the potential contours are in use in any one of our languages, and a great many of them fail to occur in any at all. We simply do not know exactly which and how many any one of the five does make use of, though we do know that each occurrent prosodic contour is morphemically significant, i.e. that it conveys some meaning over and above the lexical and grammatical meanings contained in the linear segmental which it overlays—an expression of insistence, reservation, ingratiation, hostility, innuendo, disbelief, surprise—in short, a rich gamut of emotional reactions or involvements. What we also do not know is whether a given intonation which seems to be structured in precisely the same way, e.g. /3. . .2. . .3↑/ in, say, Spanish and Italian, has precisely the same meaning in those two languages. Before a contrastive study of Romance prosodies can be undertaken, the contours as they function in each separate language await investigation in much greater depth than has thus far been attained. The empirical data is not to be found in books, and probably not in field notes elicited directly from informants, but rather in voluminous tape recordings, mostly unavailable as yet, of spontaneous native conversation. The immensely challenging but very much worthwhile projects entailed in this largely unexplored domain await the efforts of a new generation of Romance linguists.[6]

Notes for Chapter 15

1. Even higher, of course, is a level generally identified with the term DISCOURSE GRAMMAR—a domain which in our present framework we make no pretense of describing in a concerted way. We have attributed certain syntactic phenomena to pragmatic factors present in 'the discourse'—i.e. in a dialogue or a paragraph of connected sentences, but outside the actual sentence under scrutiny; however, any systematic contrastive discourse grammar of the Romance languages lies beyond our present scope.

2. Any word, phrase or mere string uttered *without* a meaningful prosody would be taken at best as an unfinished sentence, at worst as nonsense.

3. Note, however, the opposite ordering in Ital/Roum. As current as *anche* and *neanche* in Italian, though more colloquial, are *pure* and *neppure*, which likewise take first position.

4. Since *pas* is also an adverb capable of functioning as quantifier (as in *pas de danger* or so), *pas* plus adjective appears analogical to *peu dangereux*, *trop dangereux*, or the like. The parallel has no relevance to the other languages, however.

5. The transition is not necessarily the most direct. In flowing, for example, from an onset to a peak, the actual (phonetic) pitch may rise perceptibly higher than either, as may be heard in varieties of (Brazilian) Portuguese or of Italian. Such deviation is, however, strictly nondistinctive since the rise is not located at a pitch point.

6. At the sentence level, coordinations are possible with not only the four conjunctions which operate at the lower levels, but also with numerous adverbial-type items such as the following:

Fr   alors, donc, ainsi, pourtant, cependant, néanmoins, d'ailleurs, de
là, de plus, du reste, en outre, ou bien, quand même, par consé-
quent, en tout cas, d'autre part, quoi qu'il en soit . . .

Sp entonces, así, pues, además, asimismo, empero, sin embargo, no
obstante, por lo tanto, por consiguiente, por eso (esto, aquello,
ello), por otra parte, sea lo que sea, en todo caso, por lo demás
. . .

Po então, assim, pois, contudo, todavia, portanto, porém, não obstante, por conseguinte, além disso, por isso (isto, aquilo), seja o que
for, em todo caso . . .

It allora, dunque, così, quindi, comunque, tuttavia, nondimeno, per-
tanto, però, eppure, oppure, inoltre, del resto, ciò non ostante, se
no, altrimenti, perciò, di più, in tutti i casi, contuttociò . . .

Ro atunci, deci, totuşi, oricum, iară, deasemenea, pe lîngă asta, aşa
dar, prin urmare, de aceea, pe de altă parte, în orice caz . . .

Located at the beginning (or occasionally after the first constituent) of a
given sentence, these items serve to link that sentence with a previous sentence in the discourse, by denoting that sentence Y is true by reason of, or in
light of, or in spite of, or in consequence of, or whatever, of sentence X.
[*Problem. Once again, search out some textual examples.*]

Chapter 16
The sentence as speech act

16.0 Introduction. Traditional grammar distinguishes three types of sentence: declarative, interrogative, and imperative, sometimes adding exclamatory as a fourth. Based on the internal structure of the sentence as we have
described it (segmental and prosodic constituents), however, there is no
formal ground for such a classification. The assignment of sentences to the
various categories in question depends rather on the function of the sentence
at a yet higher level—the discourse level. At this level, often also termed
PRAGMATIC, the immediate constituents of a dialogue, monologue, or whatever are UTTERANCES or, to use a newer and more precise term, SPEECH ACTS.
And it is the speech act, as a unit of discourse, that either (1) makes a
statement requiring no speech act in response, (2) asks a question requiring
another speech act in response, or (3) issues a request or order expecting
compliance in word (speech act) or deed (other act). It is in correlation with
these various pragmatic functions that the sentence as speech act possesses
certain formal properties, as we may now proceed to observe. The traits to
be looked for occur in one or in both constituents of the sentence: segmental
and/or prosodic.

16.1 Declarations and exclamations. Speech acts that require no speech
act in response subcategorize into those which are merely DECLARATIVE, and
those which are not only declarative but also EXCLAMATORY.

16.1.1 Purely declarative speech acts. Purely declarative speech acts have the feature [−Q] in the sense that the segmental clause contains no Q-word.[1] Prosodically, they are either unmarked or marked as the case may be. Unmarked declaratives carry a mere filler intonation (very typically /2. . .2. . .1↓/ in any of our languages) with no semantic overload. On the other hand, prosodically marked declaratives carry some intonation other than the neutral one just referred to—one which signals one or another shade of subjective coloring—e.g. approval, disapproval, surprise, insistence, concession, mental reservation, implication (as if to say 'More could be said about this, but I'm not saying it').

16.1.2 Additionally exclamatory declarative speech acts. Additionally exclamatory declarative speech acts are [+Q] only in the sense that some constituent of the segmental clause is, or contains, a Q-word. Although the particular Q-items eligible for use in exclamatory patterns are few, it may nevertheless be useful at this point to tabulate together the total inventory of Q-words in the lexicon of each language—items heretofore listed in three separate tables (Tables 1.1, 3.1, and 7.3) by reason of belonging to as many different parts of speech; see Table 16.1.

Table 16.1 Q-words.

Part of speech		Fren	Span	Port	Ital	Roum
Limiting	[+human]	qui	quién	quem	chi	cine[2]
pronoun	[−human]	quoi/que	qué	quê	che	ce
Adj as	[+def]	quel	cuál	qual	quale	care
limiter	[−def]		qué	que	che	ce
Adj/Adv as quantifier		combien	cuánto	quanto	quanto	cît
Adverb	[+time]	quand	cuando	quando	quando	cînd
	[+place]	où	dónde	onde	dove	unde
	[+manner]	comment	cómo	como	come	cum

Of the total stock, only the adjective as [−def] limiter, the adj/adv as quantifier, and the adverb of manner are available. Among these, the adjective *quel/que/che/ce*:

(i) determines the head in a CNP, as in:

Fr Quelle vie! Quelle vue magnifique!
Sp ¡Qué vida! ¡Qué vista tan (*or* más) magnífica!
Po Que vida! Que magnífica vista![3]
It Che vita! Che veduta magnifica!
Ro Ce viață! Ce privire minunată!

Such CNPs—with the Q-word unconditionally in first position—may function as subject or object in a clause, more often the latter as in, say, Fr *Quelle solution avez-vous proposée!*, but their commonest occurrence is in sentence fragments, as just illustrated. Fragments or not, they are distinguishable from interrogative speech acts by prosodic marking only—thus Fr *Quelle idée!* is under an exclamatory intonation contour while *Quelle idée?* is under an interrogative one. Spanish alone gives a segmental clue to the difference as well, provided the CNP contains a modifying adjective, as in the second Spanish example above with the adjective in turn quantified by either of the comparative quantifiers *tan* and *más*; the corresponding interrogative fragment would be simply ¿*Qué vista magnífica?*

(ii) quantifies the head in an AdjP or AdvP, as in:

Sp ¡Qué tonto eres tú!   ¡Qué bien canta esa mujer!
Po Que tolo es tu!   Que bem canta essa mulher!
It   . . .   Che bene canta quella donna!
Ro Ce prost eşti tu!   Ce bine cîntă femeia aceea!

Except in French and Italian, AdjPs of this sort function as equivalent complements, as shown in the first trio, but nowhere as modifiers in NPs. Fragments such as Sp *¡Qué hermoso!*, Po *Que formoso!*, Ro *Ce frumos!* are extremely common in conversation, and they do occur in Italian also (*Che bello!*), though not in French.[4]

(i) determines the head in a CNP, as in:

Fr Combien de fois as-tu manqué!   Combien d'excuses!
Sp ¡Cuántas veces has faltado!   ¡Cuántas excusas!
Po Quantas vezes faltaste!   Quantas escusas!
It Quante volte hai mancato!   Quante scuse!
Ro Cîte ori ai lipsit!   Cîte scuze!

(Including such fragments as may occur, these exclamatory speech acts are distinguished from their interrogative counterparts by prosody alone.)

(ii) is adverbialized to function as modifier in a clause, in parallel with the Q-adverb of manner itself, as in:

Fr   . . .   Comme tu mens, toi!
Sp ¡Cuánto os amo yo!   ¡Cómo mientes tú!
Po Quanto vos amo eu!   Como mentes tu!
It Quanto vi amo io!   Come menti tu!
Ro Cît vă iubesc eu!   Cum minţi tu!

It is to be noted that French, with *combien* not viable in this particular role, uses either *comme* (in a neutralization for purposes of quantification) or the elsewhere unavailable *que*—thus *Comme je vous aime, moi!* or *Que je vous aime, moi![5]* For the equivalent complements touched on above, French again here uses *comme* or *que*, while Italian resorts to either *quanto* or *come*, thus:

Fr Comme tu es bête, toi! *or* Que tu es bête, toi!

It Quanto sei scemo tu! *or* Come sei scemo tu!

Note also Fr *Que cette femme chante bien!*

16.2 Questions. Speech acts that ask a question requiring another speech act in response fall into two major subgroups: (1) yes/no questions and

(2) information questions.

16.2.1 Yes/no questions [−Q]. Yes/no questions expect a response which is minimally *oui/sí/sim/sì/da* or *non/no/não/nu*; these affirmative or negative MINOR SENTENCES (cf. 15.1) are in themselves declarative speech acts, prosodically marked or unmarked as the case may be. Any further response constitutes an additional speech act, of whatever sort.[6] In all five languages interrogatives of this type are [−Q] and are prosodically marked. The occurrent contours may vary from language to language, though all share a rising terminal / ↑ /, whatever the final pitch. This prosodic marking is actually redundant in French, which also signals interrogativity in the segmental clause either by secondary subject extraposition as in *Vos parents sont-ils partis?* or (more unusually) by the introductory *est-ce que* as in *Est-ce que vos parents sont partis?* (cf. 11.2), either of these contrasting syntactically with the segmental clause *Vos parents sont partis* of a declarative speech act.[7] In the other languages, however, subject extraposition takes place independently of the declarative-vs.-interrogative opposition, as already detailed in 11.1; hence, there being no other syntactic device at hand, yes/no interrogation depends entirely on prosodic marking for contrast with declaration.

Yes/no questions are very often mere fragments—e.g. Fr *Chez vous?*, Sp *¿Y después?*, It *Altro?*—and obviously they, too, are distinguished solely by their intonation, in French as well as in the rest.[8] A special kind of yes/no fragment is the so-called TAG QUESTION, which directly follows a declarative speech act and signals that the speaker expects his statement to be confirmed or agreed with. The tag question has just one basic form in each language, viz. Fr *N'est-ce pas?*, Sp *¿(No es) verdad?*, Po *Não é (assim)?*,[9] It *(Non è) vero?*, Ro *Nu-i aşa?*

16.2.2 Information questions [+Q]. Information questions require a declarative speech act other than a mere affirmation or negation. In all five languages interrogations of this type are [+Q] and are prosodically unmarked or marked as the case may be. Unmarked information questions carry a mere filler intonation (typically the same /2. . .2. . .1↓/ as over declaratives), with no semantic overload. On the other hand, prosodically marked questions of this subtype carry an interrogative intonation and constitute an *unrequired* response to a declaration. In this pragmatic situation the marked intonation, instead of being merely redundant in the presence of the Q-word, signals a desire on the respondent's part to have the preceding declarative speech act either repeated (perhaps because of misunderstanding) or reaffirmed (perhaps because of disbelief).

As has been made abundantly clear from 9.7 on, any Q-word—or any phrase containing one—is fronted to a position preceding the predicate, regardless of its function in the clause. It was also pointed out in 9.7 that after a (fronted) Q-element French and Portuguese frequently insert the marker *est-ce que/é que*, redundantly in the [+Q] environment but often preferred in French over subject extraposition, and in Portuguese seemingly as a conventionally tactful 'softener' of a questioning speech act.

A single illustrative information question should suffice at this point:

Fr Où avez-vous appris le français?—*or, more usually*—Où est-ce que vous avez appris le français?[10]

Sp ¿Dónde aprendió Vd. el español?

Po Onde o senhor aprendeu o português?—*or, more usually*—Onde é que o senhor aprendeu o português?[10]

It Dove ha imparato l'italiano Lei?

Ro Unde ați învățat Dvs limba română?

16.3 Commands/requests. Speech acts that issue a command, order, or request expecting compliance in word or deed are IMPERATIVE speech acts. They are [−Q] and, as a rule, unmarked prosodically, carrying merely the typical, semantically unloaded filler intonation. The clause which functions as their segmental constituent is, uniquely, the special type of clause described in 10.4 and identified already at the clause level as IMPERATIVE. Imperative speech acts are very often, though not necessarily, accompanied by a preceding or following fragment consisting of (i) a 'tactful softener' (Fr *S'il vous plaît*, Sp/Po *Por favor*, It *Per favore*, Ro *Vă rog*); or (ii) a proper nominal identifying the individual(s) to whom the request or order is addressed, and typically stripped to a lone person-name or reduced to a mere title such as *Monsieur/Señor/Senhor/Signore/Domnule*[11] or *Madame/Señora/Senhora/Signora/Doamnă*; or (iii) both a softener and an address form.[12] Since the essential syntactic trait of an imperative clause is its very lack of modality, there is no way to distinguish imperative from declarative fragments segmentally if they contain no predicate. While imperative fragments are in fact rare, they do exist and are recognizable in any of our languages by marked prosody, as, for example, in Fr *En garde!* or *Patience!*, Sp *¡Adelante!* or *¡Silencio!*

Notes for Chapter 16

1. This, of course, does not apply to the content of a syntactically embedded clause, which may indeed include a Q-word as in, e.g., Fr *Je ne sais pas que vous dire*, or Sp *No sé qué decirle*, and so on.

2. Ro *cine* plus the gen./dat. suffix *-i* are packaged as *cui*—e.g. *Cui i-ai spus aceea?* 'À qui as-tu dit cela?', or *A cui este mașina?* 'À qui est la voiture?'

3. In Portuguese a modifying adjective tends to precede the head noun and thus to follow immediately the Q-word, conceivably by analogy with AdjPs of the sort touched on in (ii). However, in any of the languages the high-frequency adjectives which move to the left of the head in any case (see 6.2) do so also here, e.g. Fr *Quel mauvais temps!* or It *Che brutto tempo!*

4. They have no interrogative counterparts, the Sp/Po Q-quantifier *cuánto/quanto* (truncated to *cuán/quão*) being exclusively exclamatory also,

essentially synonymous with *qué/que* (*¡Cuán peligroso!* = *¡Qué peligroso!*, etc.), and definitely confined to archaizing styles.

5. Informally, *est-ce que* may be inserted after *que* to yield *Qu'est ce que je vous aime!* Neither variant has an interrogative counterpart.

6. Portuguese habitually answers a yes/no question by echoing the modality of that question, together with the lone verb which embodies or carries it—negated if appropriate and with P/N agreement adjusted if necessary. The corresponding *Sim* or *Não* may also be added after the echo, optionally, as illustrated herewith:

O João vem amanhã?—Vem, (sim). *or* Não vem, (não).

Você deu os refrescos?—Dei, (sim).

O senhor quer começar já?—Quero, (sim).

Os rapazes estão estudando?—Estão, (sim).

7. *Vos parents sont partis?*—with interrogative intonation but with neither syntactic device—is also viable and is very close in meaning to *Vos parents sont partis, n'est-ce pas?*

8. The minor sentences (Fr *Oui* or *Non*, etc.) very frequently occur under an interrogative contour as yes/no questions in their own right, in unrequired responses to declarations.

9. The affirmative response to this Port tag is, as expected, the echo *É, (sim)*.

10. But cf. Fr *Comment allez-vous?* and Po *Como vai o senhor?*, both preferred to the longer forms.

11. In this function Roumanian person names and (masculine) common nouns are marked by a VOCATIVE suffix with allomorphs **-e** ~ **-le** ~ **-o**, resulting in such surface forms as *Domnule, Ioane* (← *Ion*), *Sandule* (← *Sandu*), *Mario* (← *Maria*). Cf. 12.1, note 17.

12. Address forms are not constrained to occur only with imperatives; they may also serve to attract someone's attention for purposes of speech interaction—in which case they are prosodically marked (Fr *Jules!* or *Monsieur!*, Sp *¡Julio!* or *¡Doctor!*), and they also, like certain other common nominals or adjectivals, often accompany other fragments, as in Fr *Merci, chérie*; Sp *Gracias, hija*; Po *Obrigado, Excelência*; It *Grazie, cara*; Ro *Mulţumesc, dragă*; or Fr *Bonjour, mademoiselle*; Sp *Buenos días, señorita*; Po *Bom dia, senhorita*; It *Buon giorno, signorina*; Ro *Bună ziua, domnişoară*. Each fragment evidently constitutes a separate speech act.

Part Two: Phonology
Chapter 17
Orientation

17.0 Introduction. Just as the left side of the contrastive model which we have adapted from Moulton (1968) (see 0.2, Figure 0.2) bespeaks a hierarchy of grammatical structures shared by related languages in contrast, so also does the right side imply a shared hierarchy of phonological structures. This chapter merely enumerates the five structural levels of phonology to be discussed in 18-21.

17.1 The five structural levels of phonology. As in the hierarchy of grammatical structures, so in phonology there are five interdependent phonological levels, all but the first breaking down into the same internal constituencies as follows:

Level 1. The phoneme, being the minimum unit of phonological structure, distinguishable in form[1] from all other phonemes in the language, and functioning as nucleus, onset, or coda at the level of the syllable.

Level 2. The phonemic cluster, composed of two phonemes and functioning in parallel with the unit phoneme as constituent at the syllable level.

Level 3. The syllable, composed of nucleus, onset, and coda and functioning as initial, medial, or final syllable at the word level.

Level 4. The phonological word, composed of one or more syllables and constituting the smallest link between the phonological and the grammatical component of a language, in the sense that every lexical or grammatical word, regardless of its internal structure, is in one-to-one correlation with a matching phonological word.[2]

Level 5. The phonological phrase, composed of one or more phonological words unified by an intonation contour—i.e. a sequence of prosodic features: pitches, stresses, and a terminal.

Notes for Chapter 17

1 Unlike a morpheme, a phoneme has no 'meaning'—that is, it has no semantic or grammatical signal to transmit.

2. The correspondence between smaller phonological and grammtical units—e.g. syllables or less versus morphemes—is not practicable, even though syllables and morphemes do tend to coincide fortuitously.

Chapter 18
Systematic phonemes
and autonomous phonemes

18.0 Introduction. At Level 1 are the phonological units which all languages are said to have, namely, phonemes. This chapter introduces both systematic phonemes (18.1) and autonomous phonemes (18.2), indicates how, according to the theoretical stance taken in the present treatment, both types of phonemes are requisite for adequate phonological statements (18.3), and presents an inventory of the systematic phonemes of French, Spanish, Portuguese, Italian, and Roumanian (18.4).

18.1 Systematic phonemes. In a theory of generative phonology these units are underlying representations, also called SYSTEMATIC PHONEMES, which are characterized in terms of a set of DISTINCTIVE FEATURES (binary, in the sense that any given feature can be [+] or [−]) postulated as valid for all languages, even though no one given language has all the features in the repertory. While some analysts define the distinctive features by acoustic parameters and in acoustic terms, and others in articulatory terms, the two essentially overlap except for the labels employed.[1] In line with the concept of phonemes in phonological space which our model requires, we are committed here to articulatory terminology, for the space in question is conceptually analogous to the three-dimensional, physical portion of the human anatomy delimited by the organs of speech. Generativists also hold that each systematic phoneme has a surface, or phonetic, manifestation within the actual flow of speech, and that these surface phones are conditioned either to switch from one to another distinctive feature (e.g. from [+high] to [−high]) or to add some nondistinctive feature (say, aspiration) in obedience to phonetic rules, i.e. rules which govern the behavior of given sounds under the influence of environing sounds in the speech stream.

18.2 Autonomous phonemes. In pregenerative phonologies which do not posit both underlying and surface levels of structure, each phoneme represents simply a class of phonetically similar sounds sharing certain characteristics (say they are labiodental fricatives and not bilabial stops) which in the particular language are functionally significant; the members of one phoneme class, called ALLOPHONES, may vary as to other characteristics (say one is aspirated, another unaspirated) which are not functionally distinct in that language. Phonological units defined in this way have come to be known as AUTONOMOUS PHONEMES.

18.3 The utility of both systematic and autonomous phonemes. The theoretical stance taken in the present treatment is that both underlying (systematic) and surface (autonomous) phonemes are requisites of phonological description if adequate statements are to be made about the interrelatedness of languages and dialects both synchronically (contrastively) and diachronically (comparatively). To put it as simply as possible, the phonological component of a given *language* is to be based on systematic phonemics, while that of each of its *dialects*—including, of course, the standard dialect—is to be based on autonomous phonemics. The underlying structure of a language is thus mappable into the surface structures of a dialect via the set of morphophonemic rules which begin to apply at Level 4, that of the phonological word. We therefore postpone further discussion of the problem in view until Level 4 is reached.

18.4 Inventory of the systematic phonemes of Fr/Sp/Po/It/Ro. The systematic phonemes of our five languages—qua languages—are inventoried in Tables 18.1 and 18.2, where they appear in matrices of universal distinctive features. Table 18.1 displays the vowel systems, all terms of which are specified as [+syllabic]; Table 18.2 the consonant systems, with all terms [−syllabic].[2] The branching feature trees at the top of each table represent the binary oppositions shared by all five languages; neither a plus nor a minus entry is to be regarded as MARKED. The bracketed features accompanying specific entries are peculiar to the individual language.[3] Every bracketed feature is posited as the marked term in a marked/unmarked opposition.

The structural unit on which to base the phonological description of a language is primarily the Level-3 syllable, which we may proceed to analyze in Chapter 19.

Table 18.1 Vowel feature matrix.

Tree structure:

```
                         [+syl]
        ┌──────────┬───────────┬──────────┐
   [+hi][-mid]  [+hi][+mid]  [-hi][+mid]  [-hi][-mid]
    ┌───┴───┐   ┌───┴───┐    ┌───┴───┐
  [-bk]  [+bk] [-bk] [+bk]  [-bk] [+bk]
```

	[+hi][-mid] [-bk]	[+hi][-mid] [+bk]	[+hi][+mid] [-bk]	[+hi][+mid] [+bk]	[-hi][+mid] [-bk]	[-hi][+mid] [+bk]	[-hi][-mid]
Fr	i [+rnd] ü	u	e [+rnd] ö	o	ε	ɔ	a [+bk] ɑ
					[+rnd] ɔ:		[+nas] ɑ̃
					[+nas] ɛ̃	[+nas] ɔ̃	
					[+r+n] ɛ̃ː		
					[+lng] ɛ̄		
					[+lax] e		
Sp	i	u	e	o		•	a
Po	i [+nas] ĩ	u [+nas] ũ	e [+nas] ẽ	o [+nas] õ	ε	ɔ	a [+nas] ã
It	i	u	e	o	ε	ɔ	a
Ro	i [-rnd] ɨ	u	e [-rnd] ə	o			a

Table 18.2 Consonant feature matrix.

	p	b	t	d	č	ǧ	k	g	f	v	s	z	š	ž	m	l	n	r	ʎ	ř	ñ	y	w
Fr	p	b	t	d			k	g	f	v	s	z	š	ž	m	l	n	r			ñ	y	w
Sp	p	b	t	d	č		k	g	f		s	z	x		m	l	n	r	ʎ	ř	ñ	y	w
Po	p	b	t	d			k	g	f	v	s	z	š	ž	m	l	n	r	ʎ	ř	ñ	y	w
It	p	b	t	d	č	ǧ	k	g	f	v	s	z	š	ž	m	l	n	r			ñ	y	w
Ro	p	b	t	d	č	ǧ	k	g	f	v	s	z	š	ž	m	l	n	r			ñ	y	w

Terminal feature specifications (left to right):
[−vc] [+vc] [−vc] [+vc] [−vc] [+vc] [−vc] [+vc] [−vc] [+vc] [−vc] [+vc] [−vc] [+vc] [−vc] [+vc] [+vc] [−ns] [+ns] [−ns] [+ns] [−ns] [+ns] [−bk] [+bk]

Branching node labels: [−syl]; [+res], [−res]; [+ant], [−ant]; [+ctn], [−ctn]; [−cor], [+cor]; [−bk], [+bk]; [−hi], [+hi]; [−cns], [+cns]

Additional annotations:
Sp: s̯ [+str]; ʎ [−lat], ř [−lax], ý [−lat]
Po: ř [−lax]
It: c [+str], z [+str]
Ro: c [+str]; h [+ctn]; ç [−hi]

Notes for Chapter 18

1. For example, 'high' vs. 'low' in articulatory terms, as against 'diffuse' vs. 'compact' in acoustic terms.

2. The feature [syllabic] is preferable to '[vocalic]' by reason of the SEMI-VOWELS—which, although not consonants, nevertheless differ from true vowels in respect to the property of syllabicity.

3. Or, exceptionally, to two in common: thus French and Portuguese in a sense share [+nasal] vowels; but, apart from the [−hi][−mid], i.e. LOW, vowel, not in the same column; in short, not systematically. Hardly systematic, either, are the [−strident] c's shared by Italian and Roumanian, or the [−lax] R shared by Spanish and Portuguese.

Chapter 19
The syllable

19.0 Internal structure of the syllable (Syl). Basically, this is the same in all our languages, and consists maximally of a NUCLEUS, an ONSET, and a CODA. The order of constituents is shown in the formula:

Syl → (onset) nucleus (coda)

The parentheses mean that either the onset or the coda is optional as contrasted with the unparenthesized, obligatory nucleus. To give the simplest of examples: in the syllable **bas-** of the Spanish or Italian word *basta*, the nucleus is **a,** the onset is **b,** and the coda is **s.**

19.1 Vowels as nuclei. The nuclear slot in a syllable is filled by a unit vowel phoneme or a vowel CLUSTER, typically a DIPHTHONG. Phonetically, a diphthong may be either ON-GLIDE (DESCENDING), consisting of a [−syllabic] glide[1] plus a [−syllabic] vowel; or OFF-GLIDE (ASCENDING), consisting of a vowel plus a glide.[2] Phonologically, however, each of our languages has, in addition to its stock of unit vowels, only on-glide diphthongal nuclei.[3] Although from a contrastive point of view the individual sets of diphthongs have little in common, we nevertheless enumerate them herewith.

• French has, unsymmetrically, **ye yɛ ya yɑ yö yɔ̈ yu yo yɔ** and **yɛ̃ yɑ̃ yɔ̃,** as in *pied, piège, fiacre, diable, mieux, sieur, pioupiou, miaule, pioche,* and *bien, viande, nation;*[4] also **wi wa wɑ** and **wɛ̃** as in *cuir, quoi, croix, coin.*[5]

• Spanish has symmetrical **ye ya yo yu** and **wi we wa wo,** as in *viejo, viaje, viola, viuda* and *suizo, sueco, suave, cuota.* The exclusion of off-glide diphthongs from nuclear function in items like *seis, baile, boina, feudo, causa,* further obviates the need for positing also triphthongal nuclei, as is traditionally done for this language.

• Portuguese has no phonological diphthongs. Words like *viela, viagem, viola, viuva* and *suíço, sueco, suave, suor* have a quite different syllabic structure, phonetically, from the similar Spanish items listed just above—for example, Po *viela, viuva, suíço, suave* are [vi'ɛ-lɐ], [vi'u-vɐ], [su'i-su], [su'a-vɨ], trisyllabic with medial stress setting in after the hiatus, as contrasted with Sp *viejo* ['bi̯e-xo], *viuda* ['bi̯u-d̯a], *suizo* ['su̯i-θo], *suave* ['su̯a-βe], disyllabic with initial stress-onset.[6]

• Italian has two symmetrically opposed diphthongs: yɛ and wɔ, as in *piede, lieto* and *buono, fuori.*

• Roumanian has four, without notable symmetry: ye, ya, ̦ea and wa, as in *piele, piatră, seară, soare.*

19.2 Consonants as onsets. The onset slot in a syllable is occupied by any consonant phoneme or by a consonant cluster consisting typically of a non-resonant plus a [−nasal] resonant. In addition to its consonant inventory proper, each of our languages has its own series of clusters, and these have considerably more in common than the diphthongs. Thus all have the clusters **pr br, tr dr, kr gr, fr vr**[7] and **pl bl, kl gl, fl;**[8] in additon, Italian has **py by, ky gy, fy vy,** and Roumanian has **ky gy;** Portuguese and Italian share **kw gw.**[9]

19.3 Consonants as codas. The coda slot in a syllable is also occupied by a consonant phoneme, but the inventory of coda consonants is not the same as that of onset consonants. While all the consonants displayed in Table 18.2 function as syllable onsets, only a restricted set of consonants operate as codas, and in the present analysis this excludes any clusters. Certain of the feature oppositions separating the full battery of onset consonants are simply neutralized in the coda position: for example, the features [anterior], [coronal], and [high], which serve to differentiate the Sp/ It onset nasals **m ≠ n ≠ ñ** (see Table 18.2), are redundant and nondistinctive in the coda position where [m], [n], and [ɲ] (as well as [ŋ]) are simply in complementary distribution relative to the onset consonant of the following syllable. With allowances made for such neutralizations, we may note that all five languages have as codas the resonants **l r y w** (though French lacks **w**), as well as the obstruents (= nonresonants) **p b, t d, k g, f,** and **s.**[10] As for the nasal codas, Fren/ Port essentially have none (as is usual when a language has phonemically nasalized vowels in its inventory)[11] while the other three have a mere undifferentiated **N**. In none of the languages do any of the aforementioned codas occur before onsets having exactly the same features as they. Uniquely in Italian, however—in which the obstruent codas other than **s** are extremely rare—there exists also a unique coda consonant which neutralizes absolutely all the features distinguishing onsets, in a complementary assimilation to the onset of the subsequent syllable. For want of a proper symbol we may adopt the arbitrary one =, and thus write *latte* as **la=te,** *mezzo* as **mɛ=ƶo,** *pioggia* as **pyɔ=ǧa,** *mamma* as **ma=ma,** *bello* as **bɛ=lo,** and so on.[12]

Notes for Chapter 19

1. The term GLIDE conveniently subsumes [+res] [−ant] [+hi] [−cns], i.e. chiefly **y** and **w**. Although these function as semivowels in diphthongs, and as semiconsonants in clusters, all glides are displayed with the consonants of Table 18.2 by reason of their overriding feature [−syl].

2. There exist also TRIPHTHONGS, with both an on-glide and an off-glide.

3. Off-glide diphthongs (and triphthongs) in any of our languages are more adequately characterized as consisting of simple nucleus plus semiconsonant as coda, as we shall have occasion to verify.

4. In words like *liaison* or *sciage*, there is a syllable boundary between the two vowels and each is a nucleus: **li-ɛ-zɔ̃, si-až** even though in normally rapid speech the **i** may be semivocalized, and the syllables telescoped, in surface forms such as /lyɛzɔ̃/ or /syaž/.

5. In words like *muet* and *fouet*, there is a syllable boundary between the two vowels and each is a nucleus: **mü-ɛ, fu-ɛ**, even though in normally rapid speech the **ü** or **u** may be semivocalized, and the syllables telescoped, in surface forms such as /mẅɛ/ or /fwɛ/. Similar modifications apply to items like *nuage* or *Louis*, thus ruling out the possibility of any contrast, at the systematic level, between [+back] and [−back] variants of the glide in view.

6. Spanish does have a handful of items syllabified like the Portuguese examples just given, e.g. *buhedo* [bu'e-ɗo], which, of course, confirm the diphthongal nature of the contrasting structure in *bueno* ['bu̯e-no]. In exactly analogous fashion items like Sp *gloria, tenue, mutuo* have one posttonic syllable (['glo-ri̯a] etc.), while their Portuguese counterparts have two (['glɔ-ri-ɐ] etc.). (Interestingly, the Spanish and Portuguese orthographic systems both recognize the difference here by their divergent use of the written accent-mark: Sp *suizo, tenue, gloria* vs. Po *suíço, tênue, glória*).

7. Except for Spanish, which has no **v** at all.

8. With the exception of the marginal French item *vlan*, Roumanian alone systematically includes **vl**, though in few items. Roumanian also has **hr, hl**, and **mr, ml**, and **kv gv**, all very marginally.

9. The choice of assigning a glide to an onset cluster or to an on-glide diphthong in a given language is based on distributional criteria within the economy of that language. We may illustrate this principle with the specific case of the clusters **kw gw**, posited here as occurring in Port/Ital but not in Fren/Span. Noting that **k g** are the *only* consonants which **w** follows in Port/Ital, while the **w** is in turn followed by any vowel (other than the like-featured **u**), we shall find it more economical to posit the clusters **kw gw** with near-total freedom of cooccurrence than to set up an entire series of on-glide nuclei, all limited to occurrence after just **k g**. On the other hand, French **w** freely follows any consonant (except **y**) but is in turn followed by only **i a ɑ ɛ̃**, and is therefore better assigned to just four diphthongal nuclei than to many onset clusters, all with very limited occurrence. Span **w**, on the other hand, freely occurs between any consonant and any one of the vowels **i**

e a o, and therefore more economically constitutes a small number of diphthongal nuclei than a large number of onsets.

[*Comment. A study project: To identify the distributional constraints that
point to assignment of the glide* **y** *to* **y**-*plus-vowel diphthongal nuclei rather
than to consonant-plus-***y** *onsets in Fren/Span, but half-and-half in Ital/
Roum.*].

10. Spanish codas include the same **s ≠ s̩** contrast as in onsets (e.g. *busco*
vs. *Cuzco*), and Roumanian has coda **š** as well as **s,** as does French aberrantly in just one item, namely, *fichtre* **fiš-trə.** The feature [voice] is fully
neutralized in the case of the continuants, notably with regard to the **s ≠ z**
contrast of Fren/Port/Roum; but not completely in the case of the stops (=
noncontinuants).

11. French and Portuguese, also atypically, have coda **m** before **n** only, as
in Fr *hymne* or *somnolent,* Po *límnio.*

12. An alternative solution here would be to take all coda-plus-onset segments of this geminate type as [+long] consonants, functioning strictly as
onsets in opposition to [−long] consonants. In this case we would write, say,
t: instead of **=t.** In determining which solution seems preferable, one must
also inquire how well each accounts for the Italian phenomenon traditionally described as 'syntactic doubling'; see 20.1.

Chapter 20
The phonological word

20.0 Internal structure of the phonological word. In each of our languages,
phonological words consist of one or more syllables. The great majority are
words of one, two, or three syllables, although there exist marginal (lexically
derived) items containing up to seven or eight.

20.1 Syllables and stress. However many syllables a given word has, one
and only one of those syllables bears the word stress, or structural stress, as
against the remaining syllables (if any) which bear no stress. In all our
languages the stress-bearing syllable may be the ultimate or the penultimate,
and in all but French it may also be the antepenultimate. In the languages
having all three possible stress locations, the unmarked position is the penultimate (or next-to-last, or pre-final); this pattern is by far the most prevalent
and hence qualifies as canonical. Thus it is that the systematic representations of the Spanish words *chico, alegre, trabajoso*—viz. **čiko, alegre, traba-
xoso**—require no notation of stress, so long as all items in which structural
stress is displaced to either right or left of the penult are, in fact, marked, as
in **kafé** for *café* or **páxina** for *página.*[1] Now the number of items requiring the

marking of right-displaced stress would be quite sizeable, particularly in Span/Port/Roum though less so in Ital, if consonant-final words (like Sp *igual, mujer, feliz*) were to be syllabicated (as they traditionally are) with the final consonant acting as coda of the last syllable, i.e. **i-gwál, mu-xér, fe-líṣ**, . . .[2] At the surface, however, the consonants in view are clearly enough onsets in inflected forms of such words (*iguales, mujeres, felices* are [i'ɣwa-les, mu'xe-res, fe'li-θes]), while in phonological phrases they may be either codas, as in [mu‚xer'lin-da] or onsets, as in [mu‚xe-rin-te-re'san-te].

We shall therefore be safe in saying that in the underlying structure of any phonological word, a final consonant is actually the undifferentiated onset/coda of a separate syllable which has a zero nucleus, in other words something we may label as MINOR SYLLABLE. On this principle, Sp *igual, mujer, feliz* are basically **i-gwa-l, mu-xe-r, fe-li-ṣ**, unmarked for word stress because stressed on the penult just as much as *chico* or *alegre*; in this way the number of words marked for right-displaced stress is drastically reduced for the lexicon as a whole. We may now look to the evidence of the other languages in support of this principle.

• Portuguese. The minor-syllable principle increases the stock of words unmarked for stress location—e.g. *igual, mulher, feliz* representable as **i-gwa-l, mu-ʎɛ-r, fe-li-z**—fully as much as in Spanish because although this language has no final **d** or **n**, it does show final **w** in far more words than Spanish has with **d, n**, and **w** combined: so, for example, Po *alemão* (**a-le-mã-w**), *lição* (**li-sã-w**), Sp *alemán* (**a-le-ma-n**), *lección* (**lek-ṣyo-n**). Note also such less-patterned differences as in Po *judeu* (**ž u-de-w**), *bacalhau* (**ba-ka-ʎa-w**), *irmão* (**ir-mã-w**) over against Sp *judío* (**xu-di-o**), *bacalao* (**ba-ka-la-o**), *hermano* (**er-ma-no**). Thus the frequency of minor syllables in the two languages tends to equalize.

• Italian. Superficially, this language has very few consonant-final words: apart from certain apocopated syntactic alternants (e.g. *far* of *fare* or *san* of *santo*), there are only *in, con, per* plus a handful of foreignisms (*autobus, film* . . .) and acronyms (*Fiat, Agip* . . .). However, apparent stress-displacement to the right in conventionally vowel-final items like *città* or *caffè* can be eliminated by the following descriptive device. Traditionally, according to the well-defined 'law of syntactic doubling', any consonant-initial word following a word with a final stressed vowel, e.g. *città bella*, surfaces with that initial consonant 'doubled', as in [čit‚tab'bɛl-la]. Consequently, if the first [t] is systematically the phoneme we have identified as coda =, then if so also is the first [b], and we can account for the syntactic doubling by positing **či=ta=** as the representation of *città*, the second = being then a minor syllable analogous to any other word-final consonant in any of our languages. For it *is* the word itself, and not the one which follows, that determines the cross-boundary gemination.[3]

• Roumanian. This language has innumerable consonant-final words, the vast majority of them substantives or adjectives which *could* be represented with underlying final -**u** (so *cal, copil, necesar* as **kalu, kopilu, nečesaru**) because that vowel does, in fact, surface when the definite article is suffixed, as in *calul* 'le cheval' etc. and *could* be taken as part of the stem rather than as part of the suffix; cf., precisely, *lucru* 'chose' and *lucrul* 'la chose'. However, given our minor-syllable principle whereby *cal, copil, necesar* are syllabifiable as **ka-l, ko-pi-l, ne-če-sa-r**, all thus unmarked for stress location, as against, say, *aşa* (**a-šá**) 'ainsi' or *suflet* (**sú-fle-t**) 'âme', marked for stress displacement, no economy is to be achieved by positing an underlying final -**u**.

• French. Finally, as regards this language, the position of word stress is fully predictable from the syllable structure and hence never marked. Again adhering to the minor-syllable principle, we may modify the traditional view by saying that words whose final syllable has either ə or zero as nucleus—e.g. *libre, voyage* (underlyingly **li-brə, vwa-ya-žə**) or *animal, public, chétif, hiver* (underlyingly **a-ni-ma-l, pü-bli-k, še-ti-v, i-vɛ-r**) are stressed on the penult, while words whose final syllable ends in a vowel other than ə are stressed on that syllable: e.g. *joli, quantité, bateau, bâtiment, fatras*, underlyingly **žɔ-li, kã-ti-te, ba-to, bɑ-ti-mã, fa-trɑ**.

20.2 Syllable syntax. In all the languages the strings of syllables which constitute phonological words obey certain constraints imposed by stress location and by the distribution of unstressed syllables relative to the stressed one. Thus in addition to stressed, or TONIC, syllables which can be initial, medial, or final, we uncover a distributional hierarchy entailing PRETONIC syllables both initial and medial, and POSTTONIC syllables both medial and final. The various distributional limitations to be noted are all statable in terms of nuclei, onsets, and codas. We shall now proceed to generalize the limitations to the extent possible, noting also certain ones peculiar to this or that language.

20.2.1 Nuclei. These are independent of their onset or coda satellites, being therefore limited only by TONICITY, i.e. the presence or absence of word stress. All nuclei occur in all types of syllable, except:

• French ə does not occur in a tonic syllable, and is the only nucleus to occur in a posttonic final syllable.

• Po/It [−hi] [+mid] ɛ ɔ, and the Italian and Roumanian diphthongs, do not occur in an atonic syllable, either pretonic or posttonic.

20.2.2 Onsets. These are constrained only by the nucleus of the syllable in which they function. All onsets, including zero (i.e. absence of any onset segment) occur in all types of syllable and before any nucleus, except: (1) nonanterior nonback onsets, including y-final clusters (e.g. **py**), because of the obvious redundancy involved do not occur before y-initial diphthongal nuclei; (b) Sp/Po r occurs only in a noninitial syllable following an open (i.e. zero-coda) syllable.

20.2.3 Codas. These are constrained only by the onset of the following syllable, except that Fr ə is never followed by any coda. No coda occurs before a zero onset, because any single consonant located between two nuclei is axiomatically an onset; that is, we have (say) **a-pa** but never ***ap-a**.[4] No obstruent coda occurs before a liquid or glide onset, mainly because any obstruent preceding a liquid or glide axiomatically forms an onset cluster (or is the onset before a diphthongal nucleus); thus we have, e.g. **a-pra, a-kwa** but never ***ap-ra, *ak-wa**.

There are no geminate segments of coda plus onset sharing an identical complex of distinctive features, e.g. ***p-p, *t-t**.[5]

Voiceless obstruent codas do not precede voiced obstruent onsets (e.g. ***p-d**), nor vice versa in French (e.g. ***b-t**).

No coda occurs before the onsets ʎ ñ. (Aberrant exceptions: **r-ñ** in Fr *borgne* etc., or **n-ʎ** in Sp *enllanta*. In Italian the one coda to precede ʎñ and š is =; furthermore, these three are never preceded by an open syllable; aberrantly, **s-č** does not occur in Italian either, but **s-ǧ** does (e.g. *disgelo*).

No coda occurs in a word-final syllable, tonic or atonic. Word-final consonants do indeed occur in all five languages, but they represent minor syllables, as we shall shortly illustrate.

No further generalization seems valid. There do exist a few disparate constraints in this or that language, but they seem to represent nothing more than haphazard minor gaps which could be filled without doing violence to the system; they are therefore devoid of contrastive interest.

20.2.4 Minor syllables in word-final position. For each language the list of minor-syllable consonants is lesser than that of onsets, but greater than that of codas—a fact that has implications for phonological phrase structure (21.2)—for not only do certain single onset types not figure, but also there are no clusters except in Roumanian, which has the largest overall inventory here: all the onset-type singles except ǧ (a fortuitous gap, seemingly), plus the clusters **ky gy**. Codas before minor syllables in Roumanian are also much more numerous than in the other languages; **p t, k g, f s š, l r** all occur, except before liquids and glides: the resonant codas freely, as in **kor-p** (*corp* 'corps') or **luN-g** (*lung* 'long'), but the obstruent codas in unpatterned distribution before obstruents with, however, both voiced or voiceless, as in **fap-t** (*fapt* 'fait'), **fik-s** (*fix* 'fixe').

The second-largest array of minor syllables is found in French: the list is **p b t d k f v s z š m n ñ l r y**. By no means all of these, however, figure in uninflected words or in substantives. The following do occur (the obstruents and nasals in few items, the resonants in many): **p** as in *cep*; **b** as in *club*; **t** as in *huit, zut*; **d** as in *sud*; **k** as in *avec, lac*; **f** as in *oeuf, chef*; **s** as in *ours, fils*; **m** as in *pensum, album*; **n** as in *hymen, albumen*; **r** as in *par, hiver*; **y** as in *oeil, travail*; **l** as in *sel, cheval*. All these are, of course, the items of which it is traditionally said that 'the final consonant is pronounced'. The linguistic fact is, however, that any 'final consonant' not heard in a singular substantive or uninflected word is simply *not there*; thus, for example, there is no **k** in *porc*, no **s** in *puis*, no **r** in *cahier*, and so on. It is claimed here, moreover, that there is no **p** in *champ* just because there is one in *champêtre*, no **t** in *part* by virtue of *partie*, no **n** in *raison* because of *raisonner*. In any Romance language (probably, indeed, any language at all), derivational morphology within the lexicon—i.e. the formation of lexical words out of roots plus affixes—is so diffusely spread over so vast a continuum of formal variation types that no reliable criterion seems discoverable for describing words in terms of underlying forms undergoing morphophonemic processes. In an item like *champêtre* it is doubtless feasible to posit a boundary between the segments **šãp** and **ɛtrə** and to assert that the root **šãp** underlies the word *champ* itself, assuming a rule which deletes a word-final minor syllable, in this instance (though not in all items) a **p**. It is next to impossible, though, in an item like *nocturne*, to proceed by rule from **nwi** to **nɔk** or **nɔkt** (or vice versa if one should prefer). In tracing the *history* of a language, it is, of course, necessary and indeed feasible to map the diachronic changes that in fact lead from Latin NOCTE- to Fr *nuit*, but it is folly to suppose that diachronic changes are perpetuated as synchronic rules, once the language (say Latin) has become another (say French or Spanish). There may well exist a semantic feature linking Fr *foliation* with *feuille*, but an analogous feature links Sp *foliación* with *hoja*, or for that matter English *foliation* with *leaf*. Neither a shared semantic feature, on the one hand, nor a similarity of form (either vague or precise), on the other, suffices to tell us whether or not a given item is describable in terms of derivation from a given root. Items with prefixes are especially resistant to clear-cut segmentations—for example, is the element *-tenir* in Fr *contenir, détenir, maintenir, retenir, obtenir, soutenir* . . . one and the same root, hence separable from the segments preceding it? What is the relation of *écrire* to *décrire*, and to *souscrire* with that intrusive **s**? Must we isolate a 'bound root' from *splendeur* and *splendide*? Whatever the answers to such questions, it is far more profitable to avoid the search for underlying forms subject to processes—a method indubitably valid when it comes to the inflection of morphological words—and to speak merely of variants and their arrangement, with (say) **nwi** and **nɔkt** equally underlying, equally basic. We are then free to insert formal boundaries between elements in a hypothetical derivation, and may go on to list alternants such as **šã** and **šãp** if we wish, though in the opinion of many linguists this would prove neither very enlightening nor very rewarding in terms of perception of the essential structure of the language under investigation.

The balance of the minor-syllable consonants we have listed for French occur quite freely in lexical items which constitute, unarguably in our view, the underlying stem forms of adjectives and verbs: so, for example, **d** as in **grãd** of *grand* or **vãd** of *vendre*,[6] **v** as in **aktiv** of *actif* or **swiv** of *suivre*, **z** as in **ɔ̈rɔ̈z** of *heureux*, **š** as in **frɛš** of *frais*, **ñ** as in **peñ** of *peindre*.

Codas before final minor syllables occur only sporadically in French: **k** or

s before obstruent, as in *strict, phénix, Brest, fisc*; liquid codas a bit more freely, as in *cobalt, talc, golf, parc, ours*, or **tɔrd** of *tordre*.

Spanish ranks in the middle of the five, with **d s ş n l r y̆** as final minor syllables, all occurring very freely, as in *merced, arroz, tres, jardín, árbol, dolor, buey*; **x** occurs marginally (*reloj*), as does **w** (*miau*). Codas do not typically occur before final minor syllables: unique by way of exception is the **k-s** of *fénix* or *tórax*.

Portuguese ranks next, with **z l r** as in *capaz, fácil, doutor*, and the glides **y w** in many items because occurring after nasal as well as oral vowels, for example in *pai* (**pa-y**), *erói* (**e-rɔ-y**), *europeu* (**ew-ro-pe-w**), *céu* (**sɛ-w**), *mau* (**ma-w**); also *mãe* (**mã-y**), *porém* (**po-rẽ-y**), *põe* (**põ-y**), *então* (**ẽ-tã-w**), *órgão* (**ɔ́r-gã-w**). As in Spanish, codas occur only aberrantly in such oddments as *tórax* (**tɔ́-rak-s**).

Italian, lastly, has just **n** and **r** from among the onset types, as in *con, in, per*; but, by virtue of our claim in 20.1, we include the coda-type 'all-feature' consonant (=) in the underlying form of any lexical item that induces syntactic doubling—thus *così* (**ko-si-=**), *me* (**me-=**), *età* (**e-ta-=**), *ciò* (**čɔ-=**), *vertù* (**ver-tu-=**), and so on. A final minor syllable is never preceded by a coda in Italian.[7]

20.2.5 Minor syllables in nonfinal position. If the notion of the minor syllable is indeed a structurally valid one, it may be extended to cover the occurrence of certain consonants in pretonic and posttonic position in all five languages. Let us begin with word-initial segments. In three of the five (Fren/Ital/Roum), most onsets (including the clusters) occur preceded by an initial sibilant (=[+ant+cor±vc]) in Fr/Ro *strict*, It *stretto*. Traditionally, such sequences as **tr, st**, or **str** have all been lumped as onset clusters. The patterning of the continuants in Fren/Ital/Roum, however, is exactly parallel to their manifestation as codas, specifically in (a) the assimilative neutralization of voicing before the subsequent consonant—phonetically then [sp st sk] as against [zb zd zg], pointing to a single phoneme as distinct from the **s ≠ z** contrast in onsets; and (b) the occurrence of contrasting **s** and **š** in both distributions in Roumanian, again with voice neutralized. Consequently, if these continuants are classed underlyingly as 'codas in minor syllables', we not only avoid an awkward proliferation of onset clusters, but also account for the transformation of the continuants into 'true' codas in phonological phrases such as Fr *c'est stupide* [sɛs-tü'pid] vs. *s'estimer* [sɛs-ti'me], or It *fra stati* [fras'ta-ti] like *Frascati* [fras'ka-ti].[8] Let us then follow up, language by language, on this description of word-initial minor syllables.

• In French, the **s** occurs very freely before voiceless obstruents (e.g. *stage, splendide, scruter, sphère*), less so before voiced obstruents (where it is redundantly voiced, as in *sbire, svelte*) or before resonants (where it is voiceless, as in *smille or slave*).

• In Italian the **s** patterns almost exactly with coda **s** elsewhere, with just one sequence not found internally, namely, the **s-r** of a few (derived) items like *sradicare* or *sregolato*.

• In Roumanian, both **s** and **š** precede onsets in essentially the same distribution pattern as elsewhere, with unsystematic gaps and with only one sequence not found in the other environments (for good morphophonemic reasons, actually), namely, the **s-č** in a handful of items like *scenă* or *scelerat*.

• As for Spanish and Portuguese, it is common knowledge that neither permits any initial surface sequence of **s** plus consonant. However, nothing runs counter to our positing an underlying initial minor syllable for these languages as well as for the others, realized in the surface structure with a nucleus as [es]; this seems justified for two independent reasons: (i) if the stem of the Sp/Po verb *estar* is taken as **sta** rather than ***esta**, it then patterns with other one-vowel 'short stems' such as **da** with regard to stress placement (i.e. present tense [es′ta] rather than the expected [′es-ta]); (ii) the **s** can also figure as a *non*initial minor syllable in such items as Sp *instinto, obstante, extraño* (as **in-s-tin-to, ob-s-tan-te, ek-s-tra-ño**), or Po *adscrito, obstante, substituto*.[9]

A propos of this phenomenon of wider distribution, the other three languages likewise have words with noninitial **s** plus obstruent onset: French in the sequences **p-s, k-s** (as in *obscur, extrait*), It **n-s** (rather rarely, as in *constare, instabile*), Ro **p-s, k-s, n-s** (as in *substanță, extrem, construcție*). It is true that the **s** in this medial position can never become either the onset or the coda of a surface syllable in a phonological phrase, as final minor syllables regularly do and as initial ones often do; this constraint does not, however, appear to justify setting up numerous 'coda clusters' solely to account for this medially 'trapped' **s**.[10]

Finally, we must note that other coda consonants than sibilants can occur as initial minor syllables in certain specialized, technical words which, though absent from the lexicon of most native speakers, must nevertheless not be ignored in a full description of the language. Examples are **p, k, g, f, m,** as in Fr *ptérodactyle, psychologie, pneumonie, cnémide, gnome, phthysie, mnémonique*; Po *pterodáctilo, psicologia, pneumonia, gnomo, mnemônico*; It *pterodattilo, psicologia, pneumonia, gnomo, mnemonico*; Ro *psihologie, pneumonie, ftizie*.[11]

We may now resume our discussion, begun in 18.2-3, of systematic vs. autonomous phonemes.

20.3 Autonomous phonemes and allophones. The underlying structural units (i.e. the systematic phonemes) in the phonological component of a language are manifested in the surface structure of each variety of that language as autonomous phonemes best describable as articulatory units occupying phonological space. These units form a network of contrasting sound-signals by virtue of some, but not all, of the perceptible feature differences between them. The phonemic distinctions, or contrasts, are those which, in one and the same phonetic context, signal a semantic difference between two otherwise identical segments.[12]

The subphonemic, or allophonic differences, on the other hand, are those which do not signal a semantic difference. It is in the light of these two kinds of differences that the sound-units of a given dialect of a given language are sortable into a set of sound-types or classes, each embodying one particular, significant combination of features which it shares fully with no other class. Each class may contain, though it need not, phonetically similar yet discretely different noncontrastive variants. The network of contrasting sound-classes constitutes the phonemic system of the dialect.

20.4 Autonomous phonemes and their correlation with underlying phonological units. The terms of the system, i.e. the phonemes themselves, do not stand in absolute one-to-one correlation with the underlying phonological units of the language, though very nearly so. For example, in the standard educated Spanish of Latin America there is no phoneme $/\theta/$. For a speaker of this variety of the Spanish language, the words *pasa* and *plaza* simply have the same medial onset; and yet that same speaker will pluralize *tesis* as $/$ tésis$/$ and *lápiz* as $/$ lápises$/$. Thus his language competence somehow embraces two structural types of sibilant which in the inflection of certain nouns obey different rules. But only if he is literate or bidialectal does he consciously know that one of those structural sibilants corresponds precisely to the underlying $[-str]$ $\underset{\sim}{s}$.

Whether or not we wish to hypothesize that a speaker, in *en*coding a message, somehow goes through a process of mapping a sequence of systematic units into a corresponding stretch of surface phonemes, in any case it is the surface stretch alone that is available to the hearer for *de*coding. In doing so, he attends only to the phonemic signals and disregards the allophonic variations.

In languages like our five, in which syllable structure overrides word boundaries within phrases (cf. Sp *con otros amigos* syllabified as [ko͵no-tro-sa'mi-ɣos]), the hearer does not count on perceiving all actual boundaries between lexical items, although there are overt clues to some of them, as we shall see under Level 5, the phonological phrase (Chapter 21).

20.4.1 The autonomous phonemes of the standard languages. In Table 20.1 are separately displayed the autonomous phonemic inventories of the standard speech of educated inhabitants of Paris (France), Madrid (Spain), Lisbon (Portugal), Rome (Italy), and Bucharest (Roumania). The inventory of each appears in an independent tabulation, for at this level each is sui generis and does not lend itself to meaningful comparison/contrast of the sort feasible at the systematic level and presented in an overall distinctive feature matrix in Tables 18.1 and 18.2. The present two-dimensional diagrams reflect, to the extent possible, the useful concept of phonological

Table 20.1 Autonomous phonemes

French (Paris Standard)

	Lb	Al	Pa	Ve	PV
Oc	p/b	t/d		k/g	
Fc	f/v	s/z		x	š/ž
Na	m	n			ñ
La		l			
Vi		r			
SC			y̆	ẅ	

	F	C	B
SV	y/ẅ		w
H	i/ü		u
HM	e/ö		o
		(ə)	
LM	ɛ/ɛ̃	ɔ̃/ɔ̃	
L		a/ã	

Spanish (Madrid Standard)

	Lb	Al	Pa	Ve	PV
Oc	p/b	t/d	č	k/g	
Fc	f	θ	s	x	š/ž
Na	m	n	ñ		ñ
La		l	ʎ		
Fp		r			
Tr		R			
SC					

	F	C	B
SV	y		w
H	i		u
M	e		o
L		a	

Portuguese (Lisbon Standard)

	Lb	Al	PV
Oc	p/b	t/d	k/g
Fc	f/v	s/z	š/ž
Na	m	n	ñ
La		l	ʎ
Fp		r	
Tr		R	

	F	C	B
SV	y		w
H	i/ĩ		ũ/u
HM	e/ẽ		õ/o
LM	ɛ		ɔ
L		a/ã	

Italian (Rome Standard)

	Lb	Al	PV
Oc	p/b	t/d	k/g
Af		c/z	č/ž
Fc	f/v	s	š
Na	m	n	ñ
La		l	ʎ
Vi		r	

	F	C	B
SV	y		w
H	i		u
HM	e		o
LM	ɛ		ɔ
L		a	

Roumanian (Bucharest Standard)

	Lb	Al	Pa	Ve
Oc	p/b	t/d		k/g
Af		c	č/ǧ	
Fc	f/v	s/z	š/ž	x
Na	m	n		
La		l		
Vi		r		

	F	C	B
SVH	y		w
SVM		ę̆	i̯/u
H		i	ɨ/u
M	e	ə	ə/o
L		a	

Abbreviations:

Af	Affricate	HM	Higher mid
Al	Alveodental	L	Low
B	Back	La	Lateral
C	Central	Lb	Labial
F	Front	LM	lower mid
Fc	Fricative	M	Mid
Fp	Flap	Na	Nasal
H	High	Oc	Occlusive
Pa	Palatal	Tr	Trill
PV	Palatovelar	Ve	Velar
SC	Semiconsonant	Vi	Vibrant
SV	Semivowel		

space. According to this notion each vowel matrix represents a spatial continuum of front-to-back tongue position and spread-to-rounded lip position simultaneously along the horizontal axis, and of high-to-low tongue position and closed-to-open lip position simultaneously along the vertical axis. Similarly, each consonant matrix represents a horizontal continuum of front-to-back point of articulation along with a vertical mapping of divergent manners of articulation. The locus assigned to the symbol for a given phoneme does not imply its spatial accuracy for all allophones of that phoneme. For example, the voiced obstruents of Spanish all have allophones with FRICATIVE ([+ctn]) rather than OCCLUSIVE ([−ctn]) manner of articulation. In every case the class symbol for the phoneme is merely the appropriate one for the canonical allophone, i.e. the allophone which is not merely a positional variant conditioned by its environment. Pairs of symbols separated by a slant line stand for phonemes occupying the same space, as it were, but distinguished by a co-articulatory feature difference of nasality among vowels, or of voicing among obstruent consonants.

In all five sets, most of the vowels may cooccur with the SUPRASEGMENTAL feature designated as STRESS, and in all but French the presence vs. absence of stress on a particular vowel is phonemically relevant and hence must be included in the phonemic notation, despite the constraint that there can be but one stress per phonological word. Thus, for example, Sp /término/, /termíno/, and /terminó/ signal three grammatically and semantically different entities.

A necessary part of the phonological description of any variety of any language is a phonetic characterization of each phoneme in terms of the articulatory features which separate it from the other phonemes, as well as the redundantly nonsignificant features of its allophones, if any. Accordingly, in Appendix 6 we present a brief run-down of the phonemes of standard Bucharest Roumanian, designed to provide a model in terms of which any variety of French, Spanish, Portuguese, or Italian can be similarly described by a student in a work project.

20.4.2 Principal differences between the European and American standards of Fr/Sp/Po. Although each and every dialect has its own stock of autonomous phonemes, each of these inventories is fully congruent with the systematic inventories of the language to which the dialect belongs. By definition, every systematic phoneme has its exact counterpart in at least one of the dialects. This dialect may have just one phoneme corresponding to two in the language, or that dialect may have two phonemes representing just one in the language, but there is a predictable correlation in either direction. The dialect most likely to match *all* the units of the language is the educated standard of the capital region, on which the official and literary idiom everywhere is based, including its written representation and its orthoëpic aspects, i.e. preoccupation with 'correct pronunciation', a social norm. However, the three Romance tongues spoken in both hemispheres of the world have slightly different regional standards on either side of the Atlantic: the standard French of North America, the standard Spanish and the standard Portuguese of Latin America, as well as the respective standards of the French, Spanish, and Portuguese capitals in Europe. We shall give brief attention to the principal differences between the hemispheric standards.

• French. In American French, centered on the major cities of Quebec Province in Canada, all the nuclei in the language inventory are native to the average speaker, including the ɛː ≠ ɛ and **a** ≠ ɑ oppositions orthoëpically prescribed by educators but largely neglected by even the most prestigious Frenchmen in everyday speech. The inventory of the Parisian standard simply omits the (marked) correlates of ɛː and ɑ; but the language-to-dialect mapping, in terms of the underlying representations of identical lexical items as phonological words, may be formalized by the rules ɛː → /ɛ/ and ɑ → /a/—rules which say, respectively, that in Paris, (i) an item like **frɛːlə** (*frêle*) is /frɛl/, with the same nucleus as **sɛlə** (*selle*); and (ii) that items like **šasə** (*châsse*) and **šasə** (*chasse*) are both /šas/, and so on. Canadians, on the other hand, clearly distinguish the low vowels **a** and ɑ in *patte* [−bk] vs. *pâte* [+bk], while in the place of the ɛː they use the off-glide diphthong [ɛi]; and since this nucleus is the same as that in, say, *soleil*, it is phonemically /ɛy/ in the dialect: *maître* is then /mɛytr/ as against *mettre* /mɛtr/, while in fact *père* is /pɛyr/, *neige* is /nɛyž/, *rêve* is /rɛyv/ etc., even in the environments where there are no contrasts and where even Parisians lengthen the nucleus phonetically 'by position', as in [nɛːž] rather than *[nɛž] for *neige*.[13]

Furthermore, increasing numbers of contemporary European French speakers reflect no phonemic opposition between the [−hi] [−mid] nuclei **e ö o** and the [−hi] [+mid] nuclei ɛ ö ɔ; they merely use higher vocoid phones in phonetically open syllables and lower ones in closed syllables, in this way extending the already partial complementation existing between [−bk] e and ɛ, with the ɛ occurring only in phonetically closed syllables. The fully generalized neutralization may be formalized in the rule ɛ ö ɔ → /e ö o/, which states that Fr **byɛ** (*biais*) is /bye/, like **pye** (*pied*); that **nɔsə** (*noce*) is /nos/ [nɔs], just as **fosə** (*fosse*) is /fos/ [fɔs]; that **žönə** (*jeûne*) and **žönə** (*jeune*) are both /žön/ [žön], and so on.

• Spanish. In American Spanish standards, radiating out from the various national capitals from Mexico City and Havana to Santiago de Chile and Buenos Aires, there is no autonomous phoneme /s̩/ and no /ʎ/;[2] the s̩ of the language is replaced in lexical items by /s/, which also matches **s**, and the ʎ by /y̌/, which also matches **y̌**. Formal language-to-dialect mapping rules for these neutralizations are simply s̩ → /s/ and ʎ → /y̌/, which mean respectively that, in the specified dialects, Sp **bras̩o** (*brazo*) is /bráso/, like **paso** (*paso*), or **as̩teka** (*azteca*) is /astéka/, and that Sp **gaʎo, poʎo** (*gallo, pollo*) and **gayo, poyo** (*gayo, poyo*) are both /gáy̌o, póy̌o/, and so on.

• Portuguese. In American Portuguese, more usually termed Brazilian

Portuguese, centered on the two metropolises of Rio de Janeiro and São Paulo, there is no coda or minor-syllable /l/; in either function the l of the language is replaced in lexical items by /w/, so that the language-to-dialect relation is formalized by the rule l → /w/ __C or #, meaning that Po **altu** (*alto*) and **awtu** (*auto*) are both /áwtu/ in Brazil, or that **kanal** (*canal*) is /kanáw/, ending like **kinaw** (*quinau*), and so on.

Notes for Chapter 20

1. It must be noted that in illustrating stress location we necessarily restrict our examples to the phonological representation of lexical words as we originally defined them. Grammatical words composed of stem plus inflectional affix (e.g. *chicos, alegres, trabajando*) also have matching phonological words, but their surface formation is subject to morphophonemic rules which entail, in many instances, relocation of stress, as in *trabaja* vs *trabajamos*.

2. The hyphens we sometimes insert to flag the syllable boundaries are merely a graphic convenience, not essential to the phonological representation.

3. Many superficially monosyllabic Italian words also have this same property of triggering syntactic doubling, e.g. *ma, se, più, lì* . . . These can as well be represented as **ma=, se=, pyu=**, etc. With respect to the alternate long-consonant theory suggested in 19, note 12, a relevant question to ask is how words like *città* or *più* could be represented systematically so as to project the 'lengthening' of initial consonants which succeed them.

4. This is based on actual phonetic evidence, clear enough when the second syllable is tonic (e.g. [a'pa]) and not countered in other sequences— e.g. [a-pa] with neither syllable stressed, or ['a-pa] with the first one stressed, even though in the latter two cases nothing more than an undifferentiated 'interlude' may be audible.

5. See 20.1 for so-called geminates in Italian.

6. The underlying form of many French verbs is the shape occurring in the present tense when the plural P/N agreement suffix is also present: cf. also **dɔrm** of *dormir*, **finis** of *finir*, **rɔ̃p** of *rompre*, **mɔ̃r** of *mourir*, **val** of *valoir*, etc.

7. Foreignisms are generally unmanageable and therefore deliberately excluded from our account of this language, because (along with acronyms) they are very easy to identify; they include even the words for the cardinal compass points—*nord, sud, est, ovest*—which are fully assimilated to the phonological structure of the other languages. Cf. also, incidentally, the assimilated item *clube* of Portuguese as against *club*, strictly a foreignism in Italian and, presumably, in French and Spanish as well.

8. In Italian the **s** in view, in careful speech at least, develops its own syllabic nucleus [i] if the previous word ends in a consonant (other than =), e.g. **in spagna** → [i-nis'pañ-ña] written *in Ispagna*.

9. Many speakers of standard Spanish, in fact, pronounce no [k] in words written with -x-, saying simply [es'tra-ño] etc. But for the language as a whole the **s** must be counted as preceded by **b d k n,** whereas Portuguese has only **b d.**

10. Even one or two *pos*tonic medial minor syllables must be noted for Roumanian, as in *text* (**ték-s-t**) or *punct* (**pún-k-t**). And how would you syllabicate Fr *absorption,* Ro *absorpţie*?

11. Spanish optionally spells many of these words in comparable fashion (e.g. *psicología ~ sicología*), but only the **g** has phonological reality, being realized as true coda **g** [γ] in a phrase like *de gnosticismo* (cf. the word *agnosticismo*), though as zero elsewhere.

12. To illustrate: In a hypothetical dialect of some language, if ['a-sa] means one thing and ['a-za] another, then these forms differ by virtue of the difference of voicing between [s] and [z]; the two sibilants therefore represent two classes of phones, i.e. two phonemes. If, on the other hand, ['a-sa] and ['a-za] mean exactly the same thing even though pronounced in one or the other way, then the sibilant phones are not separate phonemes—they are merely noncontrastive variants, or ALLOPHONES, of one and the same phoneme. Likewise, while ['a-sa] and ['az-na] differ in meaning by reason of the presence versus absence of the nasal onset, the sibilants are not necessarily phonemically distinct, for the voiceless one is an onset between nuclei, while the voiced one is a coda between a nucleus and an onset. Again they are allophones in COMPLEMENTARY DISTRIBUTION, which is also called COMPLE-MENTATION.

13. Cf., even, the Canadian matching diphthongization of ɔ and ŏ wherever long by position, e.g. in *sort* /sɔwr/ and *soeur* /sŏ̈wr/.

14. This is equally true of Southern Spanish standard as based on the speech of the urban centers of Andalucía, chief among them Sevilla.

Chapter 21
The phonological phrase

21.0 Internal structure of the phonological phrase. A phonological phrase is a string of one or more phonological words bound together by a prosodic unit, i.e. an intonation contour. This suprasegmental constituent, character-ized by a sequence of distinct pitches plus a terminal, as already detailed in Chapter 16.2, thus functions at two levels: not only at the phonological level as now stated, but also at the syntactic level, where it serves as the indispensa-ble prosodic constituent of a sentence. Thus, while a phonological phrase and a sentence segmental are in one sense fully coterminous, their consti-tuency is analyzable from two distinct viewpoints, leading, on the one hand, to breakdown into clauses, phrases, and grammatical words, and on the other hand, to breakdown into phonological words. At this point, of course, we are concerned only with the latter analysis, i.e. with the mechanisms whereby phonological words (P-words) combine to make up phonological phrases (P-phrases).

21.1 Stress. In French, only the stress of the last word in the phrase is perceptible; this is automatic and unconnected with the prosodic contour. The so-called *accent d'intensité* is in itself not a word-stress, and it may or may not coincide with the stressed syllable of this or that word; it is rather a feature of the intonation peak typically characterized by an extra-high pitch.

In the other four languages, the inherent stress of *most* of the words making up the P-phrase is audible: the stress which coincides with the intonation peak—typically though not obligatorily the last in the phrase—is invariably the strongest while the others, though still unmistakable, are comparatively reduced in intensity. The minority of words which manifest no stress at all, ever, are certain monosyllabic items which, syntactically, are strictly phrase-bound—viz. all of the adv-1s (prepositions), certain determiners (the articles), AuxVs, and, in the surface structure, clitics, complementizers, and functors—and which, by their very nature, are barred from occurring under the peak of the intonation contour.[1] If these small items are in fact matched by P-words in one-to-one correspondence, then it is impossible to determine the number of P-words in a given P-phrase: how many are there in Sp *He visto la película por la tarde* (/ebístolapelíkulaporlatárde/)? If they are *not* P-words, then they must be fragments of P-words, so that either Sp *desunido* or *de su nido* counts as a single phonological word, namely, /desunído/.

In any case it seems clear that the listener/decoder does not[2] attend to the number of P-words contained in a P-phrase he hears, not only because of the indeterminacy just observed, but also because the boundary between any two P-words is, in the majority of instances, imperceptible in the stream of speech. Thus, even though the concept of the P-word seems reduced to a mere descriptive unit for the convenience of the linguist, we may usefully take note of various phonological processes associated with word boundaries and known in some circles as EXTERNAL SANDHI.[3]

21.2 Word boundaries. No more than the final syllable of one word and the initial syllable of the next word are ever involved at boundaries. The configurations to be discussed in this frame of reference are:[4]

			Final	*Initial*
(1)	[V+C]	=	+Nucleus	+Onset
(2)	[V+V]	=	+Nucleus	−Onset
(3)	[C+C]	=	−Nucleus	+Onset
(4)	[C+V]	=	−Nucleus	−Onset

(1) In the [V+C] case the basic syllable structure is, save for two important exceptions, unperturbed and therefore affords no clue to the presence or absence of a boundary in any of the five languages. Verify this for yourself with strings like Fr *merci bien* or *entre nous*, Sp *otra vez*, Po *agora mesmo*, It *due volte*, Ro *astă seară*. As you multiply the examples you will realize that the incidence of stress on one or the other, or on neither, of the crucial syllables is immaterial; but that stress on *both* syllables, as in Sp *aquí dentro*, or Po *está frio*, or Ro *ceva scump*,[5] does provide one bit of boundary information, albeit imprecise. [*Query. What is it?*]

• The first important exception here entails the standard reduction of the systematic French nucleus ə to phonemic zero at the autonomous level. Within a phrase-final P-word this happens (i) regularly in *jeune, faute, branche, digne, drôle . . .*, (ii) regularly also in *force, borgne, halte, luxe . . .*, (iii) variably in *titre, simple, marbre, filtre . . .* When the word is nonfinal, however, the reduction occurs only in words of the first subtype. In that group, then, a postnuclear open syllable such as -nə is transformed into the minor syllable -n, so that *une jeune fille* ünə žönə fiyə → /ünžönfiy/, and the surface result is the boundary configuration [C+C], which is to be dealt with in (3).[6]

• The second important exception entails the surface reduction of the systematic Roumanian nucleus -i in a word-final open syllable: to phonemic zero after a palatal onset (as in reǧ+i → /réǧ/), and to the semi-vowel /y/ elsewhere (as in an+i → /ány/ or ka+i → /káy/). When another word follows, a postonset /y/ is in turn deleted,[7] so that *cîţi ani* is /kícány/ or *cîţi copii* is /kíckopíy/. Thus, a second word that is onset-initial generates the boundary configuration [C+C], to be discussed in (3).

(2) In the [V+V] case also, the basic syllable structure is unperturbed, save for certain noteworthy deviations. Apart from these, especially in French and Roumanian, numerous [V+V] sequences occur across a boundary that are never found within a word, and hence reveal the existence of that boundary, as in Fr *peu honnête* /-öɔ-/ or in Ro *vremea umedă* /-ęaú-/. Again, in all but French and Italian, stress falling on both syllables—e.g. Sp *qué hora* /-éó-/, Po *será útil* /-áú-/, Ro *tu afli* /-úá-/ does give away one bit of information, in this case precise; cf. 21.2.(1).[8]

• The first noteworthy deviation here is that French final schwa (ə) is invariably reduced to phonemic zero before a vowel-initial word, as in *votre enfance, chère amie, l'ennemi, d'accord, s'asseoir . . .*[9] No other final nucleus is ever elided except the feminine suffix -a of the definite article/clitic *la*, and this is in conformity, rather, with an M-rule (cf. *va ouvrir*, unelided), just as much as is the occurrence of *mon, ton, son* instead of the expected *ma, ta, sa* before a vowel-initial feminine noun or adjective.[10]

• A special situation in Spanish: wherever one of the nuclei is an unstressed high vowel and the other is not, the two fuse into a diphthong and the two syllables thus become one, concealing the word boundary. So, for example, $i+e \rightarrow$ /ye/ in *si entras* (the same as in *sientas*), or *casi entero*; $i+a \rightarrow$ /ya/ as in *mi alma* (like *miaja*), $u+i \rightarrow$ /wi/ as in *su hijo* (like *suizo*), $u+e \rightarrow$ /we/ as in *su época* (like *suegra*), and the rest; conversely, e.g. $a+u \rightarrow$ /aw/ as in *la unión* (like *laurel*), $o+i \rightarrow$ /oy/ as in *no insistas*, and so on.

• In reference to Roumanian, we have already pointed out that a word-final i is first semivocalized and then, after an onset, is elided so that *mulţi ani →* /múlcány/, or *vezi aceasta →* /vézačásta/. In addition, when neither V_1 nor V_2 is stressed: (i) V_1 ə is elided before a nonhigh V_2 as in *cîntă aşa →* /kíntašá/ or *încă o dată →* /ínkodátə/; (ii) conversely, V_2 i is elided *after* any V_1, as in *lucrează împreună →* /lukrҽázəmpreúnə/, *o doamnă înaltă →* /odwámnənáltə/, *vino în casă →* /vínonkásə/; (iii) V_1 e fuses into a diphthong with V_2 a, as in *vine acasă →* /vínҽakásə/, though it is elided instead if preceded by i or a palatal consonant, as in *o soţie americană →* /osocíamerikánə/ or *se duce acolo →* /sedúčakólo/.

• Above and beyond the foregoing deviations, the following applies to all the languages but French. Whenever V_1 and V_2 are identical and neither is stressed, the two nuclei are fused into one, the two syllables telescoped and the word boundary obscured. Examples: Sp *dónde está →* /dóndestá/, *para acá →* /paraká/, *casi iguales →* /kásigwáles/; Po *onde está →* /ődestá/, *casa aberta →* /kázabérta/, *muito urgente →* /mũyturžéte/; It *qualche elenco →* /kwálkelénko/, *senza amore →* /séncamóre/, *molto onore →* /móltonóre/; Ro *spre exemplu →* /spregzémplu/, *arta americană →* /ártamerikánə/.

(3) In the [C+C] case, C_1 starts as a minor syllable, as defined in 20.2.4, and when followed by a C_2 onset it becomes the coda of the preceding syllable. From this it follows that wherever a given coda-plus-onset sequence is one which also occurs word-internally in the particular language, the boundary involved is not disclosed as such unless, of course, C_1 and C_2 are identical in any but Italian. There are, however, special situations in each of the languages as the underlying patterns are manifested at the surface.

• In French, the final minor syllables in the basic structure of the word comprise all the simple onsets with the trivial exception of ž. In the conversion to surface phonemics, however, there are two noteworthy wrinkles: (i) before a C_2, certain C_1s are regularly deleted as in *pətit livrə →* /ptilivr/[11] (as against *pətit ɔmə →* /ptitɔm/), or in *me+z fiyə+z →* /mefiy/ (as against *me+z ãfã+z →* /mezãfã/);[12] on the other hand, (ii) the final ə → ∅ rule cited in (1) apropos of [V+C] swells the list of minor syllables occurrent in the surface structure to the entire repertory of onset consonants. Thus it is that although, say, minor-syllable t, z, or r displays a certain variability in its deletion as C_1, absolutely any onset which is converted to a minor syllable by ə-loss is certain to constitute a coda in the [C+C] pattern. Those of them which have no coda counterparts word-internally, of course, betray the word-boundary, as in *Garage de France* → /garaždəfrãs/, or *la rive gauche* → /larivgoš/, or *à la bonne femme* → /alabɔnfam/.

• In Spanish, final minor syllables are **d ṣ s x y̆ n l r**. Of these, (i) C_1 y̆ becomes /y/ and fuses with the preceding nucleus to form a diphthong, as in **un ʀey̆ kruel** → /unʀéykruél/; (ii) C_1 **s, ṣ**, and **r** delete before C_2 ʀ, as in *todos los ríos* → /tódosloʀíos/, *diez refranes* → /dyéʀefránes/, *alcázar real* → /alká-ṣaʀeál/; (iii) C_1 **n** behaves like the nasal coda N and thus surfaces as /m/, /n/, or /ñ/ in feature assimilation to the C_2 onset, as in *un beso* → /umbéso/, *un dedo* → /undédo/, *un chico* → /uñčiko/.[13] Thus, apart from geminations like *un niño* → /unníño/ or *más severo* → /mássebéro/, boundaries are for the most part undetectable.[14]

• In Portuguese, final minor syllables are **z l r y w**. Of these, C_1 **r** deletes before C_2 ʀ, as in *quer receber* → /kéʀesebér/; but the only behavior of systematic interest is that of C_1 **z**, which behaves like the coda **s** and thus surfaces as /s/ or /z/ in [α voice] assimilation to the C_2 onset, as in *duas vezes* → /dúazvézes/ as against *duas filhas* → /dúasfíʎas/, etc. This coda normally deletes before onset **z** or **s**, as in *os meus zelos* → /uzméwzélus/ or *os meus selos* → /uzméwsélus/. Thus, apart from the trivial gemination in e.g. *mal ligado*, boundaries in this language are essentially undetectable.[15]

• In Italian the only final minor syllables are **n, r**, and the all-feature **:** of 20.1 and 20.2.4. In addition to the prepositions *in, con,* and *per,* certain apocopations result in the onset **l** becoming, along with the other two resonants, a surface minor syllable in just a [C+C] phrase, e.g. *a tal punto* or *dolce far niente* with stylistic apocope, or *il mondo, del vino, un giorno, capirlo* etc. with M-rule apocope. Before a word-initial onset **š, c, ʐ**, or minor-syllable **s**, no apocopation is permitted and therefore no [C+C] is generated.[16] When **=** becomes a coda, it acquires all the articulatory features of the C_2 onset, the surface result being a cross-boundary gemination as in *che sciagura* **ke=šagura** → /kéššagúra/ or *così sicuro* **kozi=sikuro** → /kosíssi-kúro/; if, however, C_2 is the minor syllable **s**, gemination is impossible, the **=** is absorbed, and the **s** becomes C_1, as in *più strano* **pyu=strano** → /pyústráno/.

• In Roumanian, final minor syllables comprise all the simple onsets (with the trivial exception of **ğ**) plus the clusters **ky gy**. The only systematic limitations on these minor syllables as codas are: (i) C_1 **n** behaves, just as in Span/Ital, like the undifferentiated nasal coda N and thus surfaces as either /m/ or /n/ (there being no /ñ/) in assimilation to the C_2 onset, as in *un porc* → /umpórk/, *un cîine* → /unkɨyne/;[17] (ii) there is something of a tendency for a [−voice] C_1 —particularly a fricative—to become [+voice] in assimilation to a voiced C_2, as in *am ales doi* → /amalézdóy/ or *m-aș gîndi* → /mažgɨndí/. Those C_1s which have no counterparts word-internally, or which comprise coda-plus-onset sequences not extant word-internally, of course give away the word boundary, as in *joc puţin* → /žókpucín/ or *ochi frumoşi* → / ókyfrumóš/. Although there are more of such instances here than in the other languages, the comprehension of spoken Roumanian is still far from dependent on this sort of data.

(4) In the [C+V] case, C starts as a minor syllable just as in the [C+C] configuration, but when followed by a nucleus-initial word that minor syllable (including any secondary one resulting from deletion of final schwa as described in 21.2 (1), e.g. Fr **frɔmažə** → /ˈfrɔ-ma-ž/), becomes the onset of the following syllable. From this it follows that wherever a given onset-plus-nucleus sequence is one which also occurs within a word in the particular language, the boundary involved is not identified as such. A couple of random examples from each language should suffice here, with the syllables deliberately separated by hyphens in the phonemic notation: Fr *dans un instant* / dã-zɔ̃-nẽs-tã/, *comme une étoile* / kɔ-mü-ne-twal/; Sp *diez horas antes* / dyé-ṣó-ra-sán-tes/, *dos o tres años* / dó-so-tré-sá-ños/; Po *por um tal amigo* / po-rũ-tá-la-mí-gu/, *dez anos atrás* / dé-zá-nu-za-trás/;[18] It *con essi* / ko-nés-si/, *per un attimo* / pe-ru-nát-ti-mo/; Ro *cam elegant* / ká-me-le-gánt/, *mă duc în oraş* / mə-dú-kɨ-no-ráš/. Roumanian alone shows a systematic departure from the word-internal CV norm, as in e.g. *aici în ţară* / a-í-čɨn-cá-rə/, where the syllable / čɨn/ is nonoccurrent word-internally because the palatal onsets č ǧ š ž y are never followed by ɨ or ə, *except* across a boundary.[19] Also noteworthy is the mere deletion of the special Italian minor syllable = before an initial nucleus,[20] as in *chi arriva* / kíarríva/ or *città aperta* / čittáapérta/, thus generating the [V+V] configuration (2) in the surface structure.

A final generalization is in order here at the conclusion of our description of the phonological phrase. If any of the foregoing statements on transitions across word boundaries prove inaccurate in one or another instance, this reflects the speaker's insertion of a DISJUNCTURE (also called 'plus juncture') between a given pair of words with the express purpose of marking the boundary.[21]

Notes for Chapter 21

1. A seemingly trivial exception is that of isolating one of these items strictly for the purpose of citation, as in, say, Sp *No he dicho 'le'; he dicho 'te'*. Now a small minority of disyllabic prepositions, such as Sp/ Po *para* or *sobre*, It *fino* or *verso*, Ro *către* or *pentru*, when thus singled out for citation and so placed under the intonation peak, clearly emerge with penultimate stress (e.g. Sp [ˈpa-ra], never [paˈra]), and this fact seems a reasonably strong argument for crediting all the words in the language with inherent stress and thus giving the small items in view legitimate status as P-words as well as grammatical words. A counter-argument would be that the mere citability of these (or any) entities is linguistically irrelevant, that they in fact lack inher-

ent stress and therefore fail to qualify as P-words at all. [*Query. What do you think?*]

2. Recall also that a speaker of French *cann*ot.

3. In this exercise we shall assume that *all* grammatical words, including the small phrase-bound residue discussed above, have their one-on-one phonological counterparts.

4. For simplicity's sake we shall limit our examples to two words each.

5. [*Query. Why can there be neither a French nor an Italian token here?*]

6. Note also that a ə in the initial syllable of a noninitial word also reduces to ∅ under certain conditions—e.g. in *à demain* /admɛ̃/ as against *pour demain* /purdəmɛ̃/, though never in *la première* /laprəmyɛr/. [*Query. Can you explain how none of this has relevance, however, to the boundary question?*]

7. This is not the case where /y/-final clitics are involved; these words (if words they are) obey instead morphophonemic rules (M-rules), as set forth in Appendix 5.

8. It *che ora* or *sarà utile* seem analogous, but in fact they are surface manifestations of [C+V], q.v. at 21.2(4).

9. Orthographic recognition of the elision is, of course, limited to the monosyllabic ə-final items.

10. How shall we explain the spurious /t/ which appears in *reste-t-il* or *va-t-il*, where we would expect **restə+il** → */restil/ or **va+il** → */vail/?

11. The failure of **t** to delete from *sept* in, say, *sept fois* → /sɛtfwa/ is due to a special set of M-rules applying also to other cardinal quantifiers (*cinq, six, huit, neuf, dix*) as well.

12. In the inflectional process a given final C is deleted before the pluralizing suffix **-z**, so that **pətit+z** → /pətiz/ before deletion reapplies in *petits livres* → /pətilivr/ as against *petits hommes* → /pətizɔm/. How does, say, the surface form of the plural noun *oeufs*, namely /ö/ rather than /ɔ̃f/, confirm the ordering of the deletions as stated? (Take account also of *oeuf d'or* → /ɔ̃fdɔr/.)

13. Exactly the same is true of Italian **n**, and need not be pointed out again in connection with that language.

14. Fortuitously discernible are those in, say, *reloj bueno* because **x** is not a basic coda, or *diez pesos* or *libertad ganada* because **ş** and **d**, codas of very limited distribution, do not happen to occur before this or that onset word-internally. Obviously enough, the detection of word-boundaries is by no means essential to the comprehension of a Spanish P-phrase.

15. In standard Brazilian speech, either minor-syllable or coda **l** maps to surface /w/ (*mal ligado* → /máwligádu/), thus eliminating the possibility of gemination totally from the system, for while **w** and **y** do occur as codas, they do not also occur as onsets.

16. After *in, con*, or *per*, a minor-syllable **s** becomes coda in the initial syllable /is-/ and the surface result is the configuration [C+V], q.v. at 23.2 (4).

17. The analogous behavior of the labial **m** can also be observed, though it is much less frequent in the standard language.

18. In Portuguese, since **y w** do not occur word-initially, the boundary is revealed as located after rather than before the C in *não é* /nãwé/ or *quem é* /kẽyé/. It is, in fact, debatable whether these two semiconsonants ever do become surface onsets. [*Query. What is your thought?*]

19. By exception to the exception, in word-final position only the open syllables **šə** and **žə** do exist, as in *mătuşă* or *grijă*.

20. By an M-rule applied variably at best, it does surface as /d/ in the monosyllabic items **a=**, **e=**, and **o=**, as in *ad esempio, tu ed io, ieri od oggi*.

21. For example, if Fr *petits trous* and *petites roues* do not sound identical despite the difference in syllabication, there must be a disjuncture at the word boundary in one or the other (or both) renditions.

Appendix 1
Noun morphology in Portuguese

0. Noun stems are here classified according to the location of stress, which is taken as inherent rather than assignable in dependence on the linear sequence of phónemes. There is no advantage to classifying stems by gender, which correlates only very grossly with phonemic shape and is, for that matter, a property rather than a constituent of the noun. The plural suffix is underlying **-z**, realized as surface / z / ∼ / s / except where, as noted below, the phonological structure of the standard language requires an adjustment rule.

1. The great majority of stems carry stress on their penultimate, or next-to-last, syllable. If we take this canonical shape of word as inherently unmarked for stress, then there is no need to include stress in the basic notation of the stem.[1]

1.1 In most such stems the final (unstressed) syllable ends in one of the nuclei **-a** or **-ã**, **-u** or **-ũ**, **-e** or **-i**, as in the following samples:

casa	**kaza**	*livro*	**livru**	*vale*	**vale**
janela	**žanɛla**	*oceano*	**oseanu**	*saúde*	**saude**
fotografia	**fotografia**	*paraíso*	**paraizu**	*continente*	**kõtinɛte**
órfã	**ɔrfã**	*álbum*	**albũ**	*juri*	**žuri**

• Stem alternants: a RADICAL-CHANGING VOWEL. Many stems ending in **-u** show a surface alternation between / ó / and / ɔ /: the higher vowel in the singular form, the lower vowel in the plural form, as in / žógu : žɔgus / *jogo(s)*. Since there are other stems which show only / ó /, we can use underlying ɔ with a rule which raises the vowel in the bare form, thus: **žɔgu+#** → / žógu /, or ɔʎu+# → / óʎu / *olho*, etc., as opposed to, say, **mosu** *moço* or **bolu** *bolo*, unchanging. [*Query. Does the alternation in view reflect a phonological rule (P-rule) or a morphological rule (M-rule)?*]

• Suffix alternants: none.

1.2 In addition, many penultimate-stressed stems end in a minor-syllable consonant, i.e. in **-l**, **-r**, **-z**, **-y**, or **-w**, as in the following examples:

sol	**sɔl**	*vez*	**vez**	*céu*	**sɛw**
fusil	**fuzil**	*mês*	**mez**	*pau*	**paw**
paúl	**paul**	*deus*	**dewz**	*mãe*	**mãy**
hotel	**otɛl**	*rapaz*	**ʀapaz**	*trem*	**trẽy**
mar	**mar**	*país*	**paiz**	*armazém*	**armazẽy**
senhor	**señor**	*boi*	**boy**	*lição*	**lisãw**

• Stem alternants. In the presence of the plural suffix: (a) two ordered
rules apply to stems ending in the minor-syllable **-l**:

Lexical item:	*carrís*	*paúis*	*papéis*	*canais*	*sóis*
Underlying form:	**kaʀil+z**	**paul+z**	**papɛl+z**	**kanal+z**	**sɔl+z**
(1) Final **-l** → **-y**	**kaʀiy+z**	**pauy+z**	**papɛy+z**	**kanay+z**	**sɔy+z**
(2) **-y** → ∅ / after **i**	**kaʀi+z**	...	...	...	...
Surface form:	/kaʀís/	/paúys/	/papéys/	/kanáys/	/sɔ́ys/

We may note that final clusters with coda **-l** do not occur, nor does the
segment **iy; hence the two rules.

At the surface, any originally minor-syllable **-y** or **-w** becomes the semivowel ([α bk]) of an off-glide diphthong whether it is final or nonfinal, as in
ley → /léy/ or **ley+z** → /léys/, **sal+z** → /sáys/, **sɛw** → /séw/ or **sɛw+z** →
/séws/, **dewz** → /déws/, **mãw** → /mãw/ or **mãw+z** → /mãws/.

There are a vast number of stems whose singular forms end in surface
/ãw/, as in *irmão, capitão, coração*. However, such stems appear in one of
three surface shapes in their plural form: /ãw/ in *irmãos*, /ãy/ in *capitães*, or
/õy/ in *corações*. It seems therefore preferable to take each of these divergent
shapes as a direct reflection of the underlying forms and to posit rules which
convert both **-ãy** and **-õy** to /ãw/. Two ordered rules will account for this:

Lexical item:	*irmão*	*capitão*	*coração*
Underlying form:	**irmãw+#**	**kapitãy+#**	**korasõy+#**
(3) [−bk] → [+bk] SC/__#:	...	**kapitãw**	**korasõw**
(4) [−hi][+mid] → [−hi][−mid]/__w:	...	...	**korasãw**
Surface form:	/irmãw/	/kapitãw/	/korasãw/

This alternation is morphologically rather than phonologically conditioned,
because both /ãy/ and /õy/ can occur word-finally, as in the one noun
exception to Rule (3), namely, **mãy+#** → /mãy/ *mãe*, and in the verb form
/põy/ *põe*.

Students of Spanish will observe that these three underlying forms match
one for one the cognate items ending, respectively, in **-ano** (*hermano*), **-an**
(*capitán*), and **-on** (*corazón*). There is, however, some shimmer among the
Portuguese items of masculine gender, which force us to posit up to 25-odd
sets of free variants, e.g.

gwardiãy ~ **gwardiõy** for *guardião* **ʀefrãw** ~ **ʀefrãy** for *refrão*
kortezãw ~ **kortezõy** for *cortesão* **vulkãw** ~ **vulkãy** for *vulcão*

(b) A different rule applies to stems ending in a minor syllable other than

-l, namely, the insertion of an epenthetic **-e-** before the plural suffix, so as to yield a major syllable with the consonant as onset: **mar+z** → /máres/, **profesor+z** →/profesóres/, **voz+z** → /vózes/, **žuiz+z** → /žuízes/, **dewz+z** → /déwzes/.² Traditional grammars of Portuguese offer an alternative analysis for this last group of stems, including also those of 2.2. [*Problem. Look up this solution in case you do not already know what it is, and compare its adequacy to that given here. Consider at the same time the analogous possibilities for Spanish noun stems.*]

2. The second-largest number of noun stems bear stress on their antepenultimate, or next-to-next-to-last, syllable. Such items are marked for stress displaced to the left from the canonical position; hence the stress must be included in the basic notation.³

2.1 In most such items the final syllable ends in one of the nuclei **-a**, **-u** or **-e**, as in the following examples:

sílaba	**sílaba**	*gênero*	**žéneru**	*ênfase*	**éfaze**
lâmpada	**lắpada**	*médico*	**médiku**	*análise*	**análize**
ciência	**siẽsia**	*período*	**períodu**	*hóspede*	**óspede**
história	**istória**	*gáudio*	**gáwdiu**	*série*	**série**

2.2 In addition, many antepenultimate-stressed items end in a minor-syllable consonant, i.e. in **-l**, **-r**, **-z**, **-y**, or **-w**, as in the following examples:

fóssil	**fósil**	*açúcar*	**asúkar**	*ônus*	**ónuz**
réptil	**Réptil**	*líder*	**líder**	*jóquei*	**žókey**
nível	**nível**	*revólver*	**Revólver**	*homem*	**ómẽy**
cônsul	**kõsul**	*lápis*	**lápiz**	*passagem*	**pasážẽy**
mártir	**mártir**	*pires*	**pirez**	*bênção*	**bẽsãw**

• Stem alternants. In the presence of the plural suffix: (a) two ordered rules apply to stems ending in minor-syllable **-l**:

Lexical item:	*fósseis*	*níveis*
Underlying form:	**fósil+z**	**nível+z**
(5) [+hi][−mid] → [+hi][+mid]/___-l	**fósel+z**	. . .
(6) Same as Rule (1) in 1.2:	**fósey+z**	**nívey+z**
Surface form:	/fóseys/	/níveys/⁴

(b) A different rule applies to stems ending in **-r**, or in **-l** after a nonback vowel, namely, **e**-epenthesis before the plural suffix, with the same outcome as noted in 1.2: **mártir+z** → /mártires/, **kõsul+z** → /kõsules/. [*Query. Both this and Rules (1), (2) have an explanation in common; what is it?*]

• Suffix alternant. When added to a stem ending in minor-syllable **-z**, the plural suffix, having identical features, becomes zero at the surface: **lápiz+z** → /lápis/. We must note at once that the absence of an overt plural inflection does not mean that the noun 'has no plural form' like, say, *arroz*. These nouns are countable, and the presence of determiners or modifiers reveals the contrast between singular and plural, as in *um lápis preto, dois lápis pretos*.

3. Finally, there remain a sizeable number of stems stressed on their ultimate—and by the present analysis necessarily open—syllable. This category, of course, includes all monosyllabic stems; and whether mono- or polysyllabic, they are all marked for stress displaced to the right from the canonical position; hence the stress must be indicated in the basic notation. They end variously in all the vowel nuclei (with the minor exception of -ɛ̃) as in the following:

javalí	**žavalí**	*maná*	**maná**	*tu*	**tú**
mercê	**mersé**	*dó*	**dɔ́**	*rum*	**Rṹ**
pé	**pé**	*paletó*	**paletɔ́**	*som*	**sɔ̃́**
café	**kafɛ́**	*avô*	**avó**	*lã*	**lá̃**
chá	**šá**	*baú*	**baú**	*jardim*	**žardĩ́**

4. The morphophonemics of noun-stem derivation by suffix constitutes a description apart from that of noun inflection, and its place is in the lexicon rather than in the grammar. However, just as certain stems have alternants conditioned by the presence or absence of the plural inflection, so also do certain roots vary in accordance with the presence or absence of a deriving suffix. There are, of course, distinct sets of suffixes and rules for deriving nouns from nouns, nouns from verbs, nouns from adjectives, verbs from nouns, and so on. The smallest of samples will suffice us here, namely, the derivation of nouns from nouns with the one suffix **-a** (which as we have seen denotes 'female individual').

4.1 Stems ending in unstressed **-u** or **-e** lose that final vowel before the suffix, thus: **amigu+a** → /amíga/, **meninu+a** → /menína/, **mosu+a** → /mósa/ (*moça*); **mõže+a** → /mõža/ (*monja*), **mɛstre+a** → /méstra/, **ɔ́spede+a** → /ɔ́speda/ (*hóspeda*). This straightforward elision of any stem-final unstressed vowel by any suffix-initial vowel, stressed or not, is known in limited circles (though up to now not in print) as 'Agard's Law' and has been found to be widely applicable in describing the morphophonemics of both derivation and inflection in any Romance language. [*Query. Is it a P-rule?*]

4.2 Stems ending in a minor-syllable consonant simply add the suffix, which becomes the nucleus of that same syllable, thus: **dowtor+a** → /dowtóra/, **pastor+a** → /pastóra/, **žuiz+a** → /žuíza/, **dewz+a** → /déwza/ (*deusa*). In the one case of **señor,** the stressed nucleus shifts from [+hi][+mid] to [−hi][+mid] in the presence of the suffix: /señɔ́ra/ (*senhora*).

4.3 Stems ending in a minor-syllable semiconsonant are subject to three ordered P-rules:

Lexical item:	*irmã*	*órfã*	*capitã*	*aldeã*	*leoa*	*patroa*
Underlying form:	**irmãw+a**	**órfãw+a**	**kapitãy+a**	**aldeãy+a**	**leõy+a**	**patrõy+a**
(7) SC → ∅ /__-a:	**irmã+a**	**órfã+a**	**kapitã+a**	**aldeã+a**	**leõ+a**	**patrõ+a**
(8) Coalescence of [−hi][−mid]	**irmã**	**órfã**	**kapitã**	**aldeã**	. . .	. . .
(9) [+nas] → [−nas]/__V:	. . .	. . .	. . .	. . .	**leo-a**	**patro-a**
Surface form:	/irmã́/	/órfã/	/kapitã́/	/aldeã́/	/leóa/	/patróa/

We note at once that positing of underlying stems ending in three different shapes, pointed to in plural inflection, is further motivated by the data in view here. Thus also, if both /ermitã́/ and /ermitóa/ exist as free surface variants of the same derived stem, then it is precisely because there are freely alternating roots as well: **ermitãw ~ ermitãy ~ ermitõy**.[5]

Notes for Appendix 1:

1. [*Query. What points are there to note here about the marking of stress in Portuguese orthography?*]

2. Exempt from Rule (1) are the stems **mal** and, optionally, **kal, mɛl, fɛl** (*mal, cal, mel, fel*). This 'Minus Rule (1)' feature causes the present Rule of **e**-Epenthesis to apply instead: **mal+z** → /máles/, etc. Cf. the existence of Type 1 stems such as **vale** or **pɛle** (*vale, pele*), which provide a phonemic model for the plurals in view. Note also **kayz+z** → /káys/, as in Appendix 1:2.2.

3. Displaced stress, either to the left as here, or to the right as in Appendix 1:3, is consistently marked in Portuguese orthography.

4. Plural forms /fɔ́sis/, /ʀéptis/ do appear, however, in some dialects; these speakers are applying instead Rules (1) and (2).

5. On *solteirão* (f. *solteirona*), *chorão* (f. *chorona*), etc.: these are nominalized adjectives; we know it because all such 'nouns' have corresponding adjs but not all such adjs have corresponding nouns.

Appendix 2
Inflection of adjectival determiners in Italian

0. The special subclass of Italian adjectives that function as determiners excludes the items *abbastanza, assai, più,* and *meno*. These four quantifiers do not show agreement of either number or gender and are to be classed as adverbs not only because they are uninflected but also because they occur in other syntactic functions associated with adverbs, including the prime one of modifier in a clause. We may proceed to classify the remaining items in the following way.

1. One set consists of the items with underlying stem-final **-o**, namely, the articles and demonstratives; the limiters *alcuno, nessuno, ciascuno*; the quantifiers *molto, poco, parecchio, troppo, tanto, quanto*; and all the specifiers but *tale*. This set displays three different suffixes and thus signals full four-way concord, with the trivial exception of *uno, nessuno,* and *ciascuno,* which simpy never occur in pluralized NPs and therefore have no occasion to copy number. The underlying forms of the three concord suffixes are: fem.sg. **-a**, pl. **-i**, fem.pl. **-e**. When any one of these vocalic suffixes is added, the stem is subject to Agard's Law of Internal Elision, resulting in the following typical concord paradigm:

kwesto	→	/kwésto/
kwesto+a	→	/kwésta/
kwesto+i	→	/kwésti/
kwesto+e	→	/kwéste/

After elision has applied, further surface modifications of the resulting forms are manifested as SANDHI ALTERNANTS conditioned by their phonological environment, in this case the initial phoneme(s) of the head (or specifier) which follows the determiner in the NP. The conditioning is in some instances automatic, in others not.

1.1 Before a word beginning with any onset other than minor-syllable **s-** or onset **c- ʒ- š- y-:**

● Forms of **uno, alkuno, ne=suno, časkuno** truncate final **-o**, e.g. /ungátto/ *un gatto,* /nessúnsénso/ *nessun senso.*

● The non-gender-copying (i.e. nonfeminine) forms of **lo, de=lo, kwe=lo** are shortened in accordance with the following rules:

Lexical item:	*il*	*i*	*del*	*dei*	*quel*	*quei*
Underlying form:	**lo**	**lo+i**	**de=lo**	**de=lo+i**	**kwe=lo**	**kwe=lo+i**
(1) Truncate/Elide:	l	l+i	de=l	de=l+i	kwe=l	kwe=l+i
(2) Prosthetic V/_l-:	il	...	...	...	...	...
(3) Coda = → ∅:	...	...	del	del+i	kwel	kwel+i
(4) -l- → ∅/_V:	...	+i	...	de+i	...	kwe+i
Surface form:	/il/	/i/	/del/	/dei/	/kwél/	/kwéi/

Examples: /ilkáne/ *il cane,* /delformáǧǧo/ *del formaggio,* /kwélǧórno/ *quel giorno,* /ilíbri/ *i libri,* /deipréti/ *dei preti,* /kwéimoménti/ *quei momenti.*

1.2 In other environments—i.e. before minor-syllable **s-** or onset **c- ʒ-**
š- y- ∅:

● The (nonfem.) plural forms of **lo, de=lo, kwe=lo** obey a different rule immediately after Rule 1 (Truncation):

Lexical item:	*gli*	*degli*	*quegli*
Underlying form:	lo+i	de=lo+i	kwe=lo+i
(1)Truncate:	l+i	de=li+i	kwe=l+i
(5) Palatalize -l-/_V:	ʎ+i	de=ʎ+i	kwe=ʎ+i
Surface form:	/ʎi/	/deʎʎi/	/kweʎʎi/

Examples: /ʎiẓíi/ *gli zii*, /deʎʎistudénti/ *degli studenti*, /kwéʎʎišámi/ *quegli sciami*.[1]

- Before a vowel-initial word, all forms of **lo**, **de=lo** and **kwe=lo** except the fem. plural in **-e** elide the final vowel, as in /lórso/ *l'orso*, /dellákkwa/ *dell'acqua*, /kwéʎʎɔkki/ *quegli occhi*.

- Also before a vowel-initial word, the singular but not the plural forms of **uno, alkuno, ne=suno, časkuno,** and **kwesto** elide their final vowel, as in /unánno/ *un anno*, /nessúnáltrapárte/ *nessun'altra parte*, /kwéstóra/ *quest'ora*.[2]

2. A second set of stems comprises the limiters *ogni, quale, qualunque, qualsiasi, qualche,* and the specifier *tale,* none of which ends in **-o**, plus all the cardinal quantifiers from the second on, which end variously. Of these, none shows gender agreement while only *quale* and *tale* show number agreement with the suffix **-i**, e.g.:

    kwale   /kwále/

    kwale+i   →   /kwáli/

However, the remaining limiters occur only in singular NPs and the cardinals only in plural NPs. Therefore it cannot be said that these residual limiters do not copy number; what they fail to signal is gender concord, and in this respect they are like our second set of stems and seem to belong together with them every bit as much as *uno, nessuno,* and *ciascuno* do to the first set. They are uninflected words only by default, as it were, and they are not assignable to the adverbs for the simple reason that they never function as modifiers in a clause—the prime requisite of 'adverbhood'.

Notes for Appendix 2

1. Also, by unique exception, /ʎidéi/ *gli dei*, etc., instead of the expected */idéi/ etc.

2. Except from **lo+a** or **de=lo+a,** elision of **-a** before a nucleus other than **a-** is optional, e.g. /unísola/ *un'isola* or /unaísola/ *una isola*; /kwélletá/ *quell'età* or /kwéllaetá/ *quella età*.

Appendix 3
Adjective inflection in French

0. There are two classes of stems: (1) STRONG stems, which agree in gender and number with (pro)nouns; (2) WEAK stems, which show number agreement but not gender agreement.

1. STRONG stems end underlyingly in a minor syllable (**pətit** *petit*) or in a nucleus other than [−hi] [+mid] [−bk] [+lax] schwa (**žɔli** *joli*). Agreement with a feminine (pro)noun is marked by the suffix **-ə** (**pətit+ə vilə** *petite ville*, **žɔli+ə mɛzɔ̃** *jolie maison*), while—as we say for all our languages—agreement with a masculine (pro)noun is unmarked (**pətit vilažə** *petit village*, **žɔli žardɛ̃** *joli jardin*). In the standard language a phonological rule (P-rule) reduces the concord suffix **-ə** to zero under the same circumstances that any word-final **-ə** is reduced, as in **pətitə vilə** → /ptitvil/.[1] As such an example shows, ə is a systematic phoneme of the French language but not an autonomous phoneme of the standard dialect. To posit the functional reality of the schwa in underlying forms is justifiable not only on basic phonological grounds for the language as a whole (as expounded in 21.2) but also because it affords far and away the simplest rules for the surface contrasts between agreeing and nonagreeing forms of most Class 1 adjectives ending in a consonant, i.e. in a minor syllable. First there is the general rule, valid for all sectors of French morphology, that minor-syllable consonants are for the most part deleted before a following onset or before any open juncture—an environment which we shall call CHECKED POSITION. This applies to bare adjective stems with final consonants as illustrated:

pətit → / pti /[2]	**fos** → / fo /
kɔ̃tɑ̃t → / kɔ̃tɑ̃ /	**gras** → / gra /
frwɑd → / frwa /	**griz** → / gri /
grɑ̃d → / grɑ̃ /[3]	**blɑ̃š** → / blɑ̃ /
lɔ̃g → / lɔ̃ /	**frɛš** → / frɛ /

1.1 Vowel alternations. Bare stems ending in the nasal consonant **-n** are subject to vowel alternations in accordance with the following ordered rules applying before truncation:

Lexical item:	*fin*	*sain*	*brun*	*bon*	*-man*[4]
Underlying form:	**fin**	**sɛn**	**brün**	**bɔn**	**-man**
Nasalize Vowel:	**fĩn**	**sɛ̃n**	**brü̃n**	**bɔ̃n**	**-mɑ̃n**[5]
Lower a [hi] Vowel:	**fɛ̃n**	. . .	**brö̃n**	. . .	. . .
Truncate:	**fɛ̃**	**sɛ̃**	**brɔ̃̃**	**bɔ̃**	**-mɑ̃**
Surface form:	/ fɛ̃ /	/ sɛ̃ /	/ brɔ̃̃ /	/ bɔ̃ /	/ -mɑ̃ /

[*Query. Why could we not as well posit underlying forms with nasal vowel, e.g. *bɔ̃n rather than bɔn?*]

The [−hi] [+mid] vowel ɔ is raised to / o / in the bare stem, e.g. **sɔt** → / sot /

~ /sɔ/ *sot*; **idyɔt** → /idyɔt/ ~ /idyo/ *idiot*. [*Query. Is this a P-rule or is it an M-rule? Why could we not posit underlying* **sot, idyot***?*]

1.2 Retained final consonants. The obstruents **-k** and **-v**, and the resonants **-r, -l** and **-y**, not generally truncated from the bare stem, are nevertheless severally subject to certain rules, some P-rules and some M-rules. As to **-k**, there exist but three items,[6] one of which obeys an M-rule when **-ə** is added. The three are:

Lexical item:	*sec*	*sèche*	*grec*	*grecque*	*public*	*publique*
Underlying form:	**sɛk**	**sɛk+ə**	**grɛk**	**grɛk+ə**	**püblik**	**püblik+ə**
Palatalize /_-ə	. . .	**sɛš+ə**	. . .	. . .	. . .	. . .
Delete Schwa:	. . .	**sɛš**	. . .	**grɛk**	. . .	**püblik**
Surface form:	/sɛk/	/sɛš/	/grɛk/	/grɛk/	/püblik/	/püblik/

As to **-v**, it becomes unvoiced in the bare stem, thus:

Lexical item:	*vif*	*vive*	*sauf*	*sauve*	*neuf*	*neuve*
Underlying form:	**viv**	**viv+ə**	**sov**	**sov+ə**	**növ**	**növ+ə**
Unvoice Final C:	**vif**	. . .	**sof**	. . .	**nöf**	. . .
Delete Schwa:	. . .	**viv**	. . .	**sov**	. . .	**növ**
Surface form:	/vif/	/viv/	/sof/	/sov/	/nöf/	/növ/

[*Query. Is this a P-rule or an M-rule?*]

As to the nonobstruents here, there is general retention without change in the bare stem, as illustrated:

amer **amɛr** → /amɛr/	*seul* **söl** → /söl/
cher **šɛr** → /šɛr/	*vil* **vil** → /vil/
pair **pɛr** → /pɛr/	*egal* **egal** → /egal/
sûr **sür** → /sür/	*tel* **tɛl** → /tɛl/
noir **nwar** → /nwar/	*pareil* **parɛy** → /parɛy/
meilleur **mɛyör** → /mɛyör/	*vermeil* **vɛrmɛy** → /vɛrmɛy/

However, three items in **-r** are caught up in the checked-position truncation, namely, *premier* **prɛmyer** → /prmye/; *dernier* **dɛrnyer** → /dɛrnye/; and the derivational suffix **-yer** → /-ye/ in adjs like *hospitalier, printanier* . . . Actually, there is a single constraint of French phonological structure that will account for both the truncation and the vowel alternation to /ɛ/ in the feminine forms *première* /prmyɛr/ etc. [*Query. What is it?*] On the other hand, a lone **y**-final item, likewise subject to truncation—*gentil* **žãtiy** → /žãti/—cannot be accounted for by a phonological constraint [*Query. Why not?*], even though unique in having the final segment **-iy**.[7]

Finally, four **l**-finals and one **y**-final undergo special checked-position treatment in which the minor syllable is modified, instead of deleted, as follows:

Lexical item:	*mou*	*fou*	*beau*	*nouveau*	*vieux*
Underlying form:	mɔl	fɔl	bɛl	nuvɛl	vyɛy
Final C→[+rnd] SV:	mɔw	fɔw	bɛw	nuvɛw	vyɔ̈ẅ
SV→V [α bk]:	mɔu	fɔu	bɛu	nuvɛu	vyɔ̈ü
[+hi] → [−hi]/_[−bk]V:	...	...	bɛo	nuvɛo	vyɔ̈ö
V → ∅/_V:	mu	fu	bo	nuvo	vyö
Surface form:	/mu/	/fu/	/bo/	/nuvo/	/vyö/

If we are charged with taking a peek at the phonological history of French in order to arrive at this formulation, we shall answer with the claim that irregular synchronic processes are, in fact, known to reflect processes which were phonologically regular at an earlier stage, and that a morphophonemic solution which runs parallel rather than counter to diachrony bids fair to be more elegant and better motivated.

[*Query. Is there any a priori reason to disregard known history in doing synchronic work? If you believe so, what alternative solution would you sooner propose for the data in view?*]

2. WEAK stems end in schwa (**fasilə** *facile*, **ružə** *rouge*, etc.), which is reduced to zero in the normal way: so /žɔnɔm/ *jeune homme* or /žɔnfiy/ *jeune fille*, but with phonetic [ə] retained in, say, *juste mesure*. We are saying that weak stems copy no gender, though this could simply be because the surface mechanism for it is lacking. [*Query: Do you see a possible strategy for combining the two stem classes into one at the basic level? If so, what would be gained by adopting it? At the same time, what objection might there be?*]

3. PLURAL CONCORD. Whether there be two classes of stem or just one, all French adjs copy the plural number of the (pro)noun they modify, by suffixing -z: **nwar+z** *noirs*, **ružə+z** *rouges*. The presence of this marker then creates checked position for any strong stem; and hence before it, as anywhere else in checked position, bare strong stems undergo their expected truncation or modification, as in, say, **pətit+z ami+z** /ptizami/ *petits amis*. On the other hand, feminine stems and weak stems, though losing their schwa at surface as anywhere else, of course retain their minor-syllable consonant as a coda, thus yielding, say, **pətit+ə+z ilə+z** /ptitzil/ *petites îles*, or **žɔnə+z ãfã+z** /žɔnzãfã/ *jeunes enfants*. We must note at the outset, however, that word-final -z itself, like most other minor syllables, is subject to deletion in checked position; hence there is *double* truncation in masc.plur. forms, as in **pətit+z** → /pti/ *petits*, **grãd+z** → /grã/ *grands*, **fos+z** → /fo/ *faux*, **griz+z** → /gri/ *gris*, and so on. The order of deletion seems at first glance immaterial— i.e. we might have either **vɛrt+z** → **vɛrt** → /vɛr/ or **vɛrt+z** → **vɛrz** → /vɛr/ for *verts*. Actually, there is evidence in favor of one order over the other. [*Query. Can you state it?*] Moreover, it is supported by the fact that bare stems ending in -al,[8] which do not suffer modification of the lateral elsewhere, nevertheless are all subject, but before -z only, to the rules which operate on **mɔl, fɔl, bɛl,** and **nuvɛl** in any checked position; thus for example:

Lexical item:	*égaux*	*généraux*	*-aux*[9]
Underlying form:	**egal+z**	**ženeral+z**	**-al+z**
Final **-l** → [+rnd] SV:	**egaw+z**	**ženeraw+z**	**-aw+z**
SV → V:	**egau+z**	**ženerau+z**	**-au+z**
[+hi] → [−hi]/_[bk]V:	**egao+z**	**ženerao+z**	**-ao+z**
V → ∅/_V:	**ego+z**	**ženero+z**	**-o+z**
Surface form:	/ego/	/ženero/	/-o/

Notes for Appendix 3

1. This is to say that in Parisian French the occurrence of a phonetic [ə] is fully predictable in terms of syllable structure. All syllables with underlying schwa as nucleus become minor syllables (i.e. syllables with zero nucleus and onset/coda neutralized) at the surface, with the ə retained as phonetic [ə] under the following four conditions applicable to segments which are either words or phrases:

- the syllable is initial, as in /pti/[pə'ti] (as against /mɔ̃pti/ [mɔ̃p'ti])

- the syllable is medial and preceded by a coda, as in /žüstmã/ [žüs-tə'mã] (as against /žüst/ ['žüst])

- the syllable is medial and consists of a cluster, as in /librmã/ [li-brə'mã]

- the syllable is final, as in /libr/ ['li-brə] or ['libr], with the [ə] in this instance optional.

2. Cf., however, /ptitɔm/ *petit homme*, in which the underlying **-t-** is retained as onset in close juncture before a vowel-initial head in a NP.

3. The stem-final consonant is underlyingly **-d** because of **grãd-ə**, but when retained in the bare form it unvoices, as in /grãtãfã/ *grand enfant*. Contrariwise, underlying **-s** when retained voices, as in /fozami/ *faux ami*. This may perhaps be put down to analogical leveling with the plural suffix **-z** (see Appendix 3:3).

4. Derivational suffix as in *musulman, birman . . .*

5. The reality of this stage, where syntactically possible, is evident in /ãsyẽnami/ *ancien ami* as against /ãsyenami/ *ancienne amie*.

6. The adj. *chic* **šik** uniquely straddles the two classes, being a strong stem which fails to copy gender.

7. On *flatteur, menteur* etc.: these are adjectivalized nouns; we know it because all such 'adjs' have corresponding nouns but not all such nouns have corresponding adjs.

8. With the trivial exception of *naval* **naval**.

9. Derivational suffix as in *national, théâtral . . .*

Appendix 4
Verb morphology in Spanish

0. Stem classes. All Spanish verb stems end basically in a vowel and are classifiable according to that stem vowel, or thematic vowel (ThV), as it is often called: Class 1 stems end in **-a**, e.g. **toma, embia, akomoda**; Class 2 stems end in **-e** or **-i**, e.g. **kome, aprende; abri, dirixi.** All stems have inherent stress in the unmarked position, on what is termed the root vowel; this stress moves to its right under predictable conditions, as will be noted.

Each and every stem exhibits two distinct paradigms: (1) a system of three mutually exclusive suffixes marking the function of the verb within a VP or a reduced dependent clause, (2) a set of inflectional suffixes expressing the tense (±mood) generated in the modality constituent of the clause but carried in the surface structure by the verb. To these inflectional suffixes are added in turn the P/N concord endings.

1. The functional paradigm. The suffixes are three in number: the infinitive marker **-r**, the participle marker 1 **-ado** ~ 2 **-ido**, and the gerund marker 1 **-ando** ~ 2 **-yendo**. Thus, for example:

Inf.	**toma+r** → /tomár/	**kome+r** → /komér/	**sumi+r** → /sumír/
Part.	**toma+ado** → /tomádo/	**kome+ido** → /komído/	**sumi+ido** → /sumído/
Ger.	**toma+ando** → /tomándo/	**kome+yendo** → /komyéndo/	**sumi+yendo** → /sumyéndo/

It is to be borne in mind that all segmental cuts made by the linguist between stem and suffix must be considered arbitrary. The criterion employed—descriptively adequate but no more so than another—is to take (i) the maximal three-way vowel difference at the boundary as indicating a consonant-initial ending added to an untruncated stem, and (ii) any two-way vowel difference at the boundary as indicative of a vowel-initial ending added to a stem apocopated by Agard's Law.[1] As for stress movement, the present description allows for as economical a statement as any, in terms of two ordered rules:[2] in the presence of a suffix, stress

(1) moves to the ThV;

(2) is superseded by any stress inherent in an ending.

Irregular stem and suffix alternations will be noted after Appendix 4.2, covering both paradigms.

2. The inflectional paradigm. There are two sets of suffixes: five tense (±mood) inflections which attach directly to the stem, and five concord markers which attach in turn to the first set.

2.1 The tense (±mood) suffixes. The tense (±mood) suffixes are underlyingly the following:

Present [−subj]: 1 -a ∼ 2 -e, Present [+subj] 2 -e ∼ 2 -a³
Imperfect [−subj]: 1 -aba ∼ 2 -ia, Imperfect [+subj]: 1 -ara/-ase ∼ 2 -yera/yese.⁴
Preterite: 1 -ó ∼ 2 -yó
Present + fut-1 -rá
Imperfect + fut-1 -ria

The following examples are given with no P/N suffix added:⁵

Pres	{[−subj]	toma+a	→ /tóma/	kome+e	→ /kóme/	sumi+e	→ /súme/
	{[+subj]	toma+e	→ /tóme/	kome+a	→ /kóma/	sumi+a	→ /súma/
Impf	{[−subj]	toma+aba→	/tomába/	kome+ia	→ /komía/	sumi+ia	→ /sumía/
	{[+subj] {	toma+ara →	/tomára/	kome+yera →	/komyéra/	sumi+yera→	/sumyéra/
	{	toma+ase →	/tomáse/	kome+yese	→ /komyése/	sumi+yese →	/sumyése/
Pret		toma+ó	→ /tomó/	kome+yó	→ /komyó/	sumi+yó	→ /sumyó/
Pres + fut-1		toma+rá	→ /tomará/	kome+rá	→ /komerá/	sumi+rá	→ /sumirá/
Impf + fut-1		toma+ria	→ /tomaría/	kome+ria	→ /komería/	sumi+ria	→ /sumiría/

2.2 The P/N suffixes. As to the P/N suffixes, we should keep in mind that while it is certainly convenient, and doubtless even necessary, to segment off these markers for purposes of morphophonemic description, the fact remains that tense/mood suffix and concord suffix are morphemically one. There is no contrast among, say, the endings /-ía/, /-ías/, /-íamos/, /-íais/, and /-ían/: these are but five allomorphs of one and the same morpheme, in complementation relative to the nominal subject with which they stand in construction.

The underlying shapes of the concord suffixes vary according to the tense suffix onto which they 'hop'. They are as follows:

● 1st-sg. local on present [−subj]: -o, which triggers a cyclic application of Agard's Law, thus: toma+a+o → *toma+o → /tómo/, kome+e+o → *kome +o → /kómo/, sumi+e+o → *sume+o → /súmo/. On present [+subj], on imperfect [±subj], on present + fut-1 and on imperfect + fut-1: zero (∅), as in toma+e+∅ → /tóme/, kome+a+∅ → /kóma/, sumi+a+∅ → /súma/, and so on after -aba ∼ -ia, -ara ∼ -yera, -ase ∼ -yese, -ré⁶ and -ria.

● 2nd-sg.local on all but preterite: -s, as in tom+a+s → /tómas/, toma +rá+s → /tomarás/, and so on through.

● 1st-pl.local on all: -mos, as in toma+aba+mos → /tomábamos/, toma+ ré+mos⁶ → /tomarémos/, and so on. We note, however, that -mos on present [−subj] yields /tomámos/, /komémos/ and /sumímos/; see just below.

● 2nd-pl.local on all but bare stem or preterite: -ys,⁷ as in toma+ara+ys → /tomárays/, toma+ré+ys → /tomaréys/, and so on. But again we note that -ys on present [−subj] yields /tomáys/, /koméys/ and /sumís/; one way to account for the three-way vowel distinction here and just above is to posit an alternation of the tense suffix to zero before -mos/-ys/-d, i.e. toma+∅+mos etc. A second solution, that of positing alternation of -e to -i before -mos/-ys just in Class 2 i-stems, seems even more ad hoc. Whichever is adopted, the location of stress in present [+subj] **toma+e+mos** → /tomémos/, **kome+a+mos** → /komámos/, **sumi+a+mos** → /sumámos/, and in **toma+e+ys** → /toméys/, **kome+a+ys** → /komáys/, **sumi+a+ys** → /sumáys/ necessitates a third stress rule added to those given in Appendix 4.2, namely:

(3) moves to vowel immediately preceding **-mos/-ys/-d.**

• Plural on all but preterite: **-n**, as in **kome+e+n** → /kómen/, **kome+rá+n** → /komerán/, and so on throughout.

• On the preterite, the concord suffixes not only stray from their basic shapes but also cause variations in the tense suffix itself, to such an extent that there is little point in attempting segmental cuts. If, therefore, we content ourselves with portmanteau morphs in this case, the following set of basic forms emerges:

	1		2	
1st sg.	**-é**	~	**-í**	
2nd sg.	**-aste**		**-iste**	
1st pl.	**-amos**		**-imos**	
2nd pl.	**-asteys**		**-isteys**	
Plural	**-aron**		**-yeron**	

Examples: **toma+é** → /tomé/, **kome+í** → /komí/, **sumi+í** → /sumí/, and so on through.

3. Stem alternants.

3.1 Radical-changing verbs. Said to be RADICAL-CHANGING are those verbs whose root vowel is one of the diphthongal nuclei **-ye-** or **-we-** or, within Class 2, some with radical **-i-**. Let us look first at Class 1 stems and Class 2 e-stems. When the unmarked stress inherent in the radical is moved to the right by Rules 1-3 as given, the respective diphthongs undergo monophthongization to /e/ or /o/ as determined by the phonological feature [±back] on the semivowel (i.e. [α back]). The result is, in effect, that such verbs as **pyensa, pyerde, kwenta** or **kweṣe** show the monophthongal radical throughout the functional paradigm and in all forms of the inflectional paradigm except those of the present tense without P/N **-mos/-ys/-d.**[8]

In Class 2 i-stems, the monophthongization triggered by stress movement is primarily not to the mid vowels /e/ and /o/ but rather to the high vowels /i/ and /u/, again [α back]. As a result, such verbs as **syenti** or **dwermi** show numerous forms with this monophthongal radical, e.g. /sintyéndo, sintyéra, sintyó, sintamos/ or /durmyéndo, durmyése, durmyéron, durmáis/.[9] However, these i-stems together with many (not all!) basic radical **-i-**—e.g. **pidi, sigi, bisti** . . . as against **bibi, permiti, Reṣibi** . . .—are subject to a subsequently applying dissimilation rule which lowers the unstressed radical to /e/ or /o/ ([α back], of course) when the following nucleus is itself an **-i-**. This rule results, for example, in /sentír, sentído, sentía, sentí, sentímos/ etc., and in /dormír, dormído, dormía, dormíste, dormís/ etc., exactly like, say, /pedír, pedído, pedía . . ./.[10] The following matrix graphically illustrates the monophthongization and dissimilation rules in i-stems, using the infinitive and gerund as tokens in the stems **yeri, mweri,** and **sigi**:

Lexical item:	*herir*	*hiriendo*	*morir*	*muriendo*	*seguir*	*siguiendo*
Underlying form:	yeri+r	yeri+yendo	mweri+r	mweri+yendo	sigi+r	sigi+yendo
Apocope:	. . .	yer+yendo	. . .	mwer+yendo	. . .	sig+yendo
Stress Movement:	yerí+r	yer+yéndo	mwerí+r	mwer+yéndo	sigí+r	sig+yéndo
Monophthongi-zation:	irí+r	ir+yéndo	murí+r	mur+yéndo	. . .	. . .
Dissimilation:	erí+r	. . .	morí+r	. . .	segí+r	. . .
Surface form:	/erír/	/iryéndo/	/morír/	/muryéndo/	/segír/	/sigyéndo/

3.2 Velar-final stems in present-tense forms. Many Class 2 stems with a lone **ṣ, l, n,** or **y̆** before the ThV are subject to accretion of a /k/ or /g/ when in contact with a nonfront vowel as the result of Agard's Law. The choice of the particular velar is [α voice]—i.e. the voiceless /k/ after the voiceless **ṣ**, otherwise the voiced /g/. The nonfront vowel is either the present [+subj] tense **-a** or (by virtue of cyclic application of Agard's Law) the local P/N **-o.** The result is, for example, **naṣe+a** → /náθka/, **konoṣe+o** → /konóθko/, **sali+a** → /sálga/, **pone+o** → /póngo/, **oy̆i+a** → /óyga/. Though entirely statable in phonologocal terms, the VELAR EXTENSION is an unpredictable and not an automatically conditioned alternation, for there are several stems of this type not subject to it, e.g. **meṣe, kweṣe, impele, uni, -kluy̆i, -struy̆i, -stituy̆i.**

A few irregular stems are subject to one or another extra rule integrated with the Velar Extension rule. Thus **aṣe** (*hacer*) and **diṣi** (*decir*), after Agard's Law, are further apocopated to **a-** and **di-**, respectively, before Velar Extension, resulting in **aṣe+o** → /ágo/ or **diṣi+a** → /díga/. The stems **tyene** of *tener* and **byeni** of *venir* undergo monophthongization of their radical not only after stress movement but also as a consequence of Velar Extension even under the stress: **tyene+o** → /téngo/, **byeni+a** → /bénga/. To recapitulate Velar Extension graphically:

Lexical item:	*placer*	*decir*	*valer*	*venir*	*oir*	*caer*[11]
Underlying stem:	plaṣe	diṣi	bale	byeni	oy̆i	kay̆e
Add -a/-o:	plaṣe+a	diṣi+a	bale+a	byeni+a	oy̆i+a	kay̆e+a
Apocope 1:	plaṣ+a	diṣ+a	bal+a	byen+a	oy̆+a	kay̆+a
Apocope 2:	. . .	di+a	. . .	. . .	. . .	. . .
Velar Extension:	plaṣk+a	dig+a	balg+a	byeng+a	oy̆g+a	kay̆g+a
Monophthongiza-tion:	. . .	. . .	. . .	beng+a	. . .	. . .
Surface form:	/pláθka/	/díga/	/bálga/	/bénga/	/óyga/	/káyga/

3.3 Apocopated stems in fut-1 forms. A number of Class 2 stems with a lone **b, d, n, l, r,** or **ṣ** before the ThV—many of which have just been noted as subject to velar extension—are apocopated in an environment not covered by Agard's Law, namely, before the **-r-** of the fut-1 inflections **-rá/-ria,** after these suffixes have drawn the stress from the stem, as in /sabrá/ or /sabría/. The apocope in view is accountable in phonological terms, albeit not automatically as by Agard's Law. The required rules figure in the following illustrative matrix:

Lexical item:	*haber*	*poder*	*poner*	*tener*
Underlying form	**abe**	**pwede**	**pone**	**tyene**
Add **-rá**/**-ria**:	**abe+rá**	**pwede+rá**	**pone+rá**	**tyene+rá**
Monophthongize:	. . .	**pode+rá**	. . .	**tene+rá**
Apocope 1:	**ab+rá**	**pod+rá**	**pon+rá**	**ten+rá**
Apocope 2:	. . .	. . .	. . .	. . .
r → dr/ n,L__:	. . .	. . .	**pond+rá**	**tend+rá**
r + r → R:	. . .	. . .	. . .	. . .
Surface form:	/abrá/	/podrá/	/pondrá/	/tendrá/

Lexical item:	*salir*	*querer*	*decir*	*hacer*
Underlying form	**sali**	**kyere**	**di$i**	**a$e**
Add **-rá**/**-ria**:	**sali+rá**	**kyere+rá**	**di$i+rá**	**a$e+rá**
Monophthongize:	. . .	**kere+rá**	. . .	. . .
Apocope 1:	**sal+rá**	**ker+rá**	**di$+rá**	**a$+rá**
Apocope 2:	. . .	. . .	**di+rá**	**a+rá**
r → dr/ n,L__:	**sald+rá**	. . .	. . .	. . .
r + r → R:	. . .	**ke+Rá**	. . .	. . .
Surface form:	/saldrá/	/keRá/	/dirá/	/ará/

Also included in the subset in view are *saber, caber, venir, valer.*

3.4 Truncated bare stems as imperative forms. The following six Class 2 stems with lone **-n-**, **-l-**, or **-ş-** are truncated in another environment not covered by Agard's Law, namely, in word-final position, thus: **pone+#** → /pón/, **tyene+#** → /tén/, **byeni+#** → /bén/, **sali+#** → /sál/, **aşe+#** → /áθ/, and **dişi+#** → /dí/.

[*Queries. What further rules apply subsequent to the truncation in three of the stems listed? To what extent are the resulting forms accountable on phonological grounds? To what other stem alternation are all six of these verbs subject, and which rules apply in both environments?*]

3.5 Stem alternants in the imperfect [+subj] and preterite tense forms. A number of verbs, including two from Class 1, exhibit special stem alternants when followed by the imperfect [+subj] suffix or the preterite suffix. The imperfect alternant is uniformly the Class 2 **-yera** ~ **-yese**, as in **pone** ~ **pus+yera** → /pusyéra/ or **pus+yese** → /pusyése/, even in Class 1 **anda** ~ **andub+yera,** etc. The preterite alternant is also that of Class 2 when packaged with a P/N suffix, as in **tyene** ~ **tub+iste** → /tubíste/, **tub+imos** → /tubímos/, **tub+isteys** → /tubísteys/, **tub+yeron** → /tubyéron/. However, the preterite signal in the absence of any P/N is unstressed **-o**, and when packaged with the 1st-sg.local it is **-e**. Both of these endings being unstressed, the inherent stress remains on the radical with resulting /túbo/ and /túbe/: whence the traditional term STRONG PRETERITE. Since the alternant in question is clearly not conditioned phonologically, it is to be taken as a morphologically determined underlying variant. The following list illustrates the alternants as they appear in the strong preterite:

andar	**anda** ~ **andub**+**o** → /andúbo/	*poder*	**pwede** ~ **pud**+**o** → /púdo/
decir	**disi** ~ **dix**+**o** → /díxo	*poner*	**pone** ~ **pus**+**o** → /púso/
-ducir[12]	**-dusi** ~ **-dux**+**o** → /-dúxo/	*querer*	**kyere** ~ **kis**+**o** → /kíso/
estar	**sta** ~ **stub**+**o** → /estúbo/	*saber*	**sabe** ~ **sup**+**o** → /súpo/
haber	**abe** ~ **ub**+**o** → /úbo/	*tener*	**tyene** ~ **tub**+**o** → /túbo/
hacer	**ase** ~ **is**+**o** → /íθo/	*traer*	**trae** ~ **trax**+**o** → /tráxo/
caber	**kabe** ~ **kup**+**o** → /kúpo/	*venir*	**byeni** ~ **bin**+**o** → /bíno/

The variations of radical and/or stem-final consonant from one to another alternant are evidently unsystematic, and to describe them would be an essentially uninteresting exercise.

3.6 Strong participles. A handful of Class 2 verbs exhibit short alternants of both the stem and the participle suffix (e.g. *muerto* of *morir*). Since it is not possible to identify any phonological environment which determines the shortening of either element, both alternants must be considered underlying rather than rule-governed, including the [−voice] of the suffix onset. In any case, there being no nucleus present to receive right-moving stress, the inherent stress remains on the radical: hence likewise characterized as STRONG. In all instances but the first in the following list, the ThV-less stem undergoes further alternations such as apocope, one or another of which might be accounted for, though awkwardly, as P-rule adjustments. The full battery:

morir	**mweri** ~ **mwer**+**to** → /mwérto/	*abrir*	**abri** ~ **abyér**+**to** → /abyérto/
volver	**bwelbe** ~ **bwel**+**to** → /bwélto/	*cubrir*	**kubri** ~ **kubyér**+**to** → /kubyérto/
escribir	**skribi** ~ **skri**+**to** → /eskríto/	*ver*	**be** ~ **bis**+**to** → /bísto/
romper	**ʀompe** ~ **ʀo**+**to** → /ʀóto/	*decir*	**disi** ~ **dis**+**to** → /díčo/
poner	**pone** ~ **pwes**+**to** → /pwésto/	*hacer*	**ase** ~ **es**+**to** → /éčo/

3.7 Monosyllabic stems. The five verbs *dar, ir, ver, ser,* and *estar,* with the respective basic stems **da, i, be, se,** and **sta,** lack a radical vowel and thus constitute but a single syllable with the stem consonant (or minor-syllable **s**+**t**). These short stems nevertheless have inherent stress, and naturally it is on the ThV. In **da, sta,** and **be,** when the ThV is canceled by the inherently unstressed present tense suffixes, the stress remains in situ and therefore falls by default on the ending, thus: **da**+**a** → /dá/, **da**+**e** → /dé/, **sta**+**a** → /está/, **sta**+**e** →/esté,[13] **be**+**e** → /bé/. Under the stress the local P/N **-o** acquires the diphthongal alternant /óy/, as in **da**+**a**+**o** → /dóy/, or **sta**+**a**+**o** → /estóy/.

Further quirks in these short stems are covered in the following section.

3.8 Highly irregular alternants. The following series of statements is ordered, so that any one may constitute a partial exception to a subsequent, more general one.

(1) The verb *ser* exhibits the following portmanteau forms:

$$\text{Stem } + \begin{cases} \text{Present [−subj]} & \textbf{es} \rightarrow /\text{és}/ \\ \text{Present [−subj]\_\_\_P/N -s} & \textbf{ere} \rightarrow /\text{ére}/ \\ \text{Imperfect [−subj]} & \textbf{era} \rightarrow /\text{éra}/ \end{cases}$$

(2) The verbs *haber* and *saber* show, respectively, /é/ and /sé/ as three-morpheme portmanteaux of stem plus present [−subj] plus local P/N **-o.**

(3) The verb *ser* alone takes a present [−subj] alternant **-o** instead of the regular Class 2 **-e**, thus:

$$\text{se+o} \begin{cases} \textbf{+o} & \rightarrow /\text{sóy}/ \text{ (cf.3.7)} \\ \textbf{+mos} & \rightarrow /\text{sómos}/ \\ \textbf{+ys} & \rightarrow /\text{sóys}/ \\ \textbf{+n} & \rightarrow /\text{són}/ \end{cases}$$

(4) The ThV of *ser* and *ver* is exempt from Agard's Law before nonfront **-a/-o** and before **-ia**, as in **se+a** → /séa/, **be+a** → /béa/, **be+o** → /béo/, **be+ia** → /beía/.[14]

(5) Both the radical and the stem-final consonant of *caber* and *saber* alternate before nonfront **-a/-o** to yield /képa/, /képo/, /sépa/ .

(6) The verbs *ir* and *haber* have the Class 1 monosyllabic stem alternants **ba** and **a** before the present tense suffixes, yielding, respectively, /bá/ and /á/ and so on, with or without P/Ns added; however, for *haber* before **-mos/-ys** we note /émos/ instead of the expected */ámos/—analogical with 1st-sg /é/ or with the regular present suffix which would follow the regular stem **abe**? *Before deciding, note also the failure of the stem to alternate at all in* /abéis/ *where we would look for* */áis/. With just the two stems **ba** and **a** the present [+subj] suffix has the alternant **-ya**, as in **ba+ya** → /báya/ and **a-ya** → /áya/.[15] The verb *ir* further exhibits the portmanteau form /íba/ etc. for stem plus imperfect [−subj].

(7) The verbs *ser* and *ir* have one and the same stem alternant before the imperfect [−subj] and preterite suffixes, namely, **fw**. The resulting forms /fwéra/ ~ /fwése/, as well as /fwí/, /fwíste/, /fwéron/ etc. show the regular Class 2 suffixes, with the underlying **-ye-** monophthongized after **w** by a mere phonological constraint. But to account for /fwé/ rather than the expected */fwó/, it seems necessary to posit an irregular preterite alternant to the **-yó** occurring everywhere else in Class 2. [*Query. What shape of alternant would you propose?*][16]

(8) The verb *dar* unexpectedly takes the imperfect [+subj] and preterite suffix alternants normally associated with Class 2 stems, with resulting /dyéra/ ~ /dyése/, /dyó/ etc.

Notes for Appendix 4

1. There is independent evidence for the apocopation of stems, within both paradigms.

2. Note that Agard's Law applies prior to stress-movement rules.

3. The feature [±subj] corresponds to the traditional 'indicative mood' versus 'subjunctive mood'. The characterization of this distinction as a morphological feature matching the semantic feature [±res] on certain predicates or heads dominating embedded clauses is explained and justified at 13.1. Note the CHIASTIC pattern of marking [±subj] with the present-tense suffixes.

4. The **ra**-final and **se**-final shapes are in noncontrastive and essentially free variation.

5. There is nothing to be gained, descriptively, by trying to separate a segment representing tense from one representing mood in these last two 'package morphs', i.e. portmanteaux.

6. This is a mere alternant of **-rá**, occurring before some (but not all) of the P/N suffixes.

7. When added to the bare stem in the predicate verbal of an imperative clause with subject *vosotros* (see 10.4), the suffix alternant is **-d** as in **toma+d** → /tomád/, **kome+d** → /koméd/, **sumi+d** → /sumíd/.

8. A very small number of Class 1 stems are exempt from the monophthongization rule, e.g. **aʀyesga, deswesa**, derived from nouns (**ʀyesgo, weso**) which themselves never alternate.

9. Included by exception here is the Class 1 stem **xwega** (cf. /xugár/ *jugar*, etc.) and the Class 2 **e**-stem **pwede** in just the gerund /pudyéndo/.

10. Exempt from this dissimilation rule is the prefix-bound stem **-kyeri** in **adkyeri** and **inkyeri** (*adquirir, inquirir*), though not in **ʀekyeri** (*requerir*).

11. If the verbs *caer* and *traer* are taken to have the basic stems **kaye̯** and **traye̯**, then by velar extension **kaye̯+a** → /káyga/, or **traye̯+o** → /tráygo/. [*Query. Why should we include the -y̆- in the basic stem of* oir, -cluir *etc. in the first place? Are the reasons equally strong for including it in* caer *and* traer? *How would you handle* oir, caer *and* traer *without a basic ThC -y̆-?*]

12. A prefix-bound verbal stem, as seen in the items *conducir, producir* etc.

13. The initial unstressed /e/ in all forms of *estar* is strictly a surface phoneme which comes to precede, throughout the language, any initial minor-syllable **s-** at the underlying level. [*Query. What is to be gained by this attribution?*]

14. A peek at the antecedent language Castilian, which had for these items the stems **see** and **vee** instead of **se** and **be,** respectively, might prompt us to posit analogous alternants (**see, bee**) precisely to account for the forms in question. [*Query. But there is a fairly strong counter-argument; can you discern what it is?*]

15. [*Query: Would you see any descriptive advantage in positing a different segmental cut here?*]

16. Incidentally, since *ser* is a linking verb and *ir* an intrans-2, there is rarely any difficulty in interpreting the homonymous forms by context.

Appendix 5
The morphophonemics
of Roumanian clitics

0. The underlying forms of these clitics may be tabulated as follows:

Clitic:	1st sg.	2nd sg.	1st pl.	2nd pl.	m.sg.	f.sg.	m.pl.	f.pl.	Reflex.
Object: **mə**	**te**	**ne**	**və**	**l**	**o**	**yi**	**le**	**se**
Dative: **mi**	**ci**				**yi**		**le**	**ši**

The morphophonemic alternations which these forms undergo have no relation to grammatical function; they are determined entirely by their phonological environment, in some though not all cases obeying actual constraints of phonological structure. For present descriptive purposes, then, we may classify them according to their vocalic nuclei:

1. The items with basic **-ə**, namely, **mə** and **və**, elide before a vowel: obligatorily before an Aux V, optionally elsewhere:

/yél ma vəzút/ *el m-a văzut*, /yéy mar vedẹá/ *ei m-ar vedea*
/yéy vaw vəzút/ *ei v-au văzut*, /yéw vaš vedẹá/ *eu v-aş vedea*
/yéle mə ayútə/ *ele mă aiută* ~ /yéle mayútə/ *ele m'aiută*[1]

2. The items with basic **-e**, namely, **te, ne, le,** and **se,** and the unique item **o,** do not vary at all except for the obligatory elision of **se** before an Aux V:

/yéw team vəzút/ *eu te-am văzut*, /yél nẹar vedẹá/ *el ne-ar vedea*
/yéy sar skulá/ *ei s-ar scula*[2]

3. The items with basic **-i**, namely, **mi, ci, yi, ši:**

• do not alternate before a **ye**-initial form of *a fi* nor before any Aux V, as in

/miye fwáme/ *mi e foame*, /ciye séte/ *ţi e sete*, /yiyerá káld/ *i era cald*[3]

• elsewhere semivocalize the vowel by the general rule **i → /y/__#,** and then:

(i) join phonologically to a vowel-initial Aux V:

/yél mya spús/ *el mi-a spus*, /yá myar spúne/ *ea mi-ar spune*,
/yéy cyau spús/ *ei ţi-au spus*, /yéle cyar spúne/ *ele ţi-ar spune*,
/yéw yam spús/ *eu i-am spus*, /tú yay spúne/ *ţu i-ai spune*[4]

(ii) otherwise delete by another general rule which, however, entails everywhere the incidence of a preceding syllabic nucleus; if such an element is not already available as the final vowel of any preceding word within the VP— i.e. *nu, că, să, ce, a* or some imperative verb (see 10.4)—then the clitic generates its own nucleus in the form of the phoneme /ɨ/. The same is true, naturally, of the wholly vowel-less Clitic l. To illustrate the rule-ordering entailed in this latter environment:

Lexical item:	*nu-mi spune*	*îmi spune*	*că-ţi ofer*
Underlying form:	**nu+mi+spune**	**mi+spune**	**kə+ci+ófer**
Semivocalization:	**nu+my+spune**	**my+spune**	**kə+cy+ófer**
Epenthesis:	. . .	**ɨmy+spune**	. . .
Deletion:	**nu+m+spune**	**ɨm+spune**	**kə+c+ófer**
Surface form:	/ númspúne /	/ ɨmspúne /	/ kəcófer /

Lexical item:	*îţi ofer*	*pune-l*	*îl pune*[5]
Underlying form:	**ci+ófer**	**pune+l**	**l+pune**
Semivocalization:	**cy+ófer**	. . .	. . .
Epenthesis:	**ɨcy+ófer**	. . .	**ɨl+pune**
Deletion:	**ɨc+ófer**	. . .	. . .
Surface form:	/ ɨcófer /	/ púnel /	/ ɨlpúne /

4. When two clitics cooccur in the same verbal, one of them is always a dative and is the one which precedes. The full battery of cooccurrence potential is illustrated in the following tabular display (phonemic above orthographic):

	l	o	yi	le	se
mi	/ mil /	/ mio /	/ mi /	/ mile /	/ mise /
	mi-l	*mi-o*	*mi-i*	*mi le*	*mi se*
ci	/ cil /	/ cio /	/ ci /	/ cile /	/ cise /
	ţi-l	*ţi-o*	*ţi-i*	*ţi le*	*ţi se*
ne	/ nil /	/ nio /	/ ni /	/ nile /	/ nise /
	ni-l	*ni-o*	*ni-i*	*ni le*	*ni se*
və	/ vil /	/ vo /	/ vi /	/ vile /	/ vise /
	vi-l	*v-o*	*vi-i*	*vi le*	*vi se*
yi[6]	/ yil /	/ yo /	/ yi /	/ yile /	/ yise /
	i-l	*i-o*	*i-i*	*i le*	*i se*
ši	/ šil /	/šio/	/ši/	/šile/	
	* şi-l*	*şi-o*	*şi-i*	*şi le*	

Notes for Appendix 5

1. Glosses: 'il m'a vu, ils me verraient; ils vous ont vu, je vous verrais; elles m'aident'. As a visual aid in the (surface) phonemic notation, spaces are added between items wherever a disjuncture can (though need not) occur.

2. 'je t'ai vu, il nous verrait, elles les a vues; ils se lèveraient'.

3. Optionally, **ne** and **və** show basic alternants **ni** and **vi**, respectively, in this particular environment, yielding / neye fríg / ~ / niye fríg / *ni e frig*, / vəyerá fríkə / ~ / viyerá fríkə / *vi era frică*. Glosses: 'j'ai faim (*lit.* m'est faim),

tu as soif (*lit.* t'est soif), il avait chaud (*lit.* lui était chaud), nous avions froid (*lit.* nous était froid), vous aviez peur (*lit.* vous était peur)'.

4. 'il m'a dit, elle me dirait, ils t'ont dit, elles te diraient, je lui ai dit, tu lui dirais'.

5. The verb *a pune* is 'mettre/poner'.

6. The dative plural **le** does not cooccur with a fronted clitic. This being so, a plural dative nominal is not fully reducible when for any reason an object clitic is present; such a dative can at best be replaced by the substitute dative pronoun *lor*, as, for example, in *le-am dat studenţilor → le-am dat lor* 'je les ai données aux étudiants → je les leur ai données'. Cf., however, *am dat-o studenţilor → le-am dat-o* 'je l'ai donnée aux étudiants → je la leur ai donnée', where reduction *is* viable.

Appendix 6
The surface phonemes of
Standard (Bucharest) Roumanian

1. The vowels. All occur both stressed and unstressed. Lack of stress is not marked in the transcription, since in a phonological word this is automatic relative to the one stressed vowel marked with / ′ /. All stressed vowels are relatively tense, and unstressed ones only slightly less so. Except as noted below, all are relatively uniform in length. There are seven contrasting spatial positions, as follows:

1.1 /i/ is a class of high, unrounded front-vowel phones: ['zi] /zí/ 'jour', [mi-li'tàr] /militár/ 'militaire', [tri'mi-tè] /trimíte/ '(il) envoie'. In hiatus before another vowel, the allophones of unstressed /i/ are discretely shorter, nevertheless full vowels in contrast to the semivowel /i̯/: [vǐ'à¢ə] /viácə/ 'vie', ['pe-rǐ-e] /périe/ 'brosse', [so-čǐ'àl] /sočiál/ 'social'. In hiatus after another vowel, or word-initial, or after a velar consonant, the allophones tend to begin with a quasi-semivocalic, homorganic constriction: [gə'i̯i-nə] /gəínə/ 'poule', ['kà-i̯i-lor] /káilor/ 'aux chevaux', ['i̯i-ni-mə] /ínimə/ 'coeur', [i̯n'ki̯ide] /ɨnkíde/ 'fermer'. Careful speakers avoid this tendency word-initially in such items as *inutil, istorie,* or the like.

1.2 /ɨ/ is a class of high, unrounded back-vowel phones: [ˌko-bo'rɨ] /koborɨ́/ 'descendre', ['gɨ-tuˇl] /gɨ́tul/ 'la gorge', [ˌvɨ-nə'tor] /vɨnətór/ 'chasseur'.

1.3 /u/ is a class of high, rounded back-vowel phones: ['tu] /tú/ 'toi', [ˌbu-ku'reštị] /bukuréšti/ 'Bucarest', [ku'su-te] /kusúte/ 'cousues'. In hiatus before another vowel, the allophones of unstressed /u/ are discretely shorter, nevertheless full vowels in contrast to the semivowel /u̯/: [ˌsi-tŭ'at] /situát/ 'situé', [kon'ti-nŭ-ə] /kontínuə/ '(il) continue', [ˌre-lŭ'a̯] /reluá/ 'reprendre'. In hiatus after another vowel, or word-initial, the allophones tend to set in with a quasi-semivocalic, homorganic constriction: [bə'u̯ut] /bəút/ 'bu', ['rĭ-u̯ury] /rɨ́ury/ 'fleuves', ['u̯u-šə] /úšə/ 'porte'. Careful speakers avoid this tendency altogether.

The three high vowels range nondiscretely lower, respectively, in closed syllables: /i/ is [iˇ] in ['viˇn] /vín/ 'vin' or [ko'piˇl] /kopíl/ 'enfant'; /ɨ/ is [ɨˇ] in [ro'mɨˇn] /romɨ́n/ 'roumain' or ['kɨˇnd] /kɨ́nd/ 'quand'; /u/ is [uˇ] in ['duˇk] /dúk/ 'je porte' or ['druˇm] /drúm/ 'chemin'.

1.4 /e/ is a class of mid, unrounded front vowels with range [e]-[ɛ], here transcribed merely as [e]: ['re-ǧe] /réǧe/ 'roi', [a'les] /alés/ 'choisi', [te'ren] /terén/ 'terrain'. In hiatus before another vowel, the allophones of unstressed /e/ are discretely shorter, nevertheless full vowels in contrast to the semivowel /e̯/: [prě'ot] /preót/ 'prêtre', [ˌɨm-pré'u-na] /ɨmpreúna/ 'ensemble'.

1.5 /ə/ is a class of mid, unrounded back-vowel phones with range [è]-[ə], here transcribed merely as [ə]: ['kər-¢i-le] /kə́rcile/ 'les livres', [ˌkuˇm-pə'rəm] /kumpərə́m/ 'nous achetons', ['ka̍-sə] /kásə/ 'maison'.

1.6 /o/ is a class of mid, rounded back-vowel phones with range [o]-[ω], here transcribed merely as [o]: ['žos] /žós/ 'bas', [no'rok] /norók/ 'chance', [ˌfo-lo'si] /folosí/ 'employer'. After unstressed /e/ the allophones of /o/ tend to be central, in the range of [ó]-[ọ̀]: [vrě-ò'da-tə] /vreodátə/ 'quelquefois'.

1.7 /a/ is a class of low, unrounded central-vowel phones: [man'ta̍] /mantá/ 'manteau', [ˌa̍-rə'ta̍] /aratá/ '(il) montrait', ['ka̍-sa̍] /kása/ 'la maison'. After /e̯/, the allophones of /a/ are fronted to [a]: ['ve̯ak] /ve̯ák/ 'siècle'; after /u̯/ or /w/ they are backed to [ɒ]: ['pu̯ɒ-te] /pwáte/ 'peut-être'.

2. The semivowels. There are three contrasting positions.

2.1 /y/ is a class of high, front, unrounded semivowels. In medial position before a consonant or after a nonvelar stop, it runs to a relatively nontense semivocalic [i̯]: ['ha̍i̯-nə] /háynə/ 'veston', ['kui̯b] /kúyb/ 'nid', ['pi̯a̍-trə] /pyátrə/ 'pierre', ['mi̯e-re] /myére/ 'miel'. Elsewhere it tends toward a relatively tense though frictionless semiconsonantal [y]: ['ya̍r-nə] /yárnə/ 'hiver', [yu'bi-re] /yubíre/ 'amour', ['čay] /čáy/ 'thé', ['kye-ye] /kyéye/ 'clef', ['gya̍-¢ə] /gyácə/ 'glace'. In final position after a consonant, the [y] allophones are very short, perceptibly reduced in sonority, and themselves voiceless after a voiceless consonant: [ro'mɨˇny] /romɨ́ny/ 'roumains', ['krezy] /krézy/ 'tu crois', ['luˇpy] /lúpy/ 'loups', [kar'tofy] /kartófy/ 'patates'. For contrast with the full vowel /i/, cf. [vĭ'a̍¢ə] /viácə/ 'vie', ['lu-pi] /lúpi/ 'les loups'.

2.2 /w/ is a class of high, back rounded semivowels; medially next to a consonant, the allophones are a relatively nontense semivocalic [u̯]: ['ka̍u̯-zə] /káwzə/ 'cause', ['a̍u̯r] /áwr/ 'or', ['nu̯ɒp-te] /nwápte/ 'nuit', ['su̯ɒ-re] /swáre/

'soleil'. Elsewhere they are a relatively tense though frictionless semiconsonantal [w]: ['wɒ-ye] /wáye/ 'mouton', [mu'zew] /muzéw/ 'musée', ['zi-wɒ] /zíwa/ 'le jour'. For contrast with the full vowel /u/, cf. [sŭ'àv] /suáv/ 'suave'.

2.3 /ę/ is a class of lower-mid front unrounded semivowels, occurring as [ɛ] only medially before /a/: ['dęal] /dęál/ 'colline', ['tęa-mə] /tęámə/ 'peur', ['be-ręa] /béręa/ 'la bière'. For contrast with the full vowel /e/ in this position, cf. [te'à-tru] /teátru/ 'théâtre'.

3. The consonants. All tend to be relatively fortis when preceding a stressed vowel, and slightly less so elsewhere. There are twenty-two: six occlusives or 'stops', three affricates, seven fricatives, two nasals, one lateral, one flap.

● The stops:

3.1 /p/ subsumes voiceless bilabial stop phones: ['pàs] /pás/ 'pas', ['à-pə] /ápə/ 'eau', ['opt] /ópt/ 'huit'.

3.2 /b/ subsumes voiced correlates of /p/: ['bàl] /bál/ 'bal', ['bàr-bə] /bárbə/ 'barbe', ['slàb] /sláb/ 'faible'.

3.3 /t/ subsumes voiceless apicodental or apicoalveolar stops with range [t̪]-[t], transcribed here merely as [t]: ['tà-re] /táre/ 'fort', ['tà-tə] /tátə/ 'père', ['às-ta] /ásta/ 'ceci'.

3.4 /d/ subsumes voiced correlates of /t/, with range [d̪]-[d], transcribed here merely as [d]: ['dà] /dá/ 'oui', ['strà-də] /strádə/ 'rue', ['uˇn-de] /únde/ 'où'.

3.5 /k/ subsumes voiceless dorsovelar stops with principal range [ḳ]-[k], here transcribed merely as [k]: ['kàl] /kál/ 'cheval', ['và-kə] /vákə/ 'vache', ['koks] /kóks/ 'coke', [ïŋ'kịi-de] /inkíde/ 'fermer'.

3.6 /g/ subsumes voiced correlates of /k/, with principal range [ĝ]-[g], here transcribed merely as [g]: ['gà-tà] /gátə/ 'prêt', ['rụɒ-gə] /ruágə/ '(il) prie', ['merg] /mérg/ 'je vais', ['gyor-gye] /gyórgye/ 'Georges'.

In final position the stops are released. In this environment the voiceless /p t k/, but not the voiced /b d g/, tend to be aspirated by some speakers: [du'làpʻ] /dulэp/ 'armoire', ['pàtʻ] /pàt/ 'lit', ['làkʻ] /lák/ 'lac'.

● The affricates:

3.7 /c/ subsumes (voiceless) apicoalveolar affricate phones: ['¢à-rə] /cárə/ 'terre', ['fà-¢ə] /fácə/ 'face', ['làn¢] /lánc/ 'chaine', ['frà¢y] /frácy/ 'frères'.

3.8 /č/ subsumes voiceless laminopalatal affricate phones: ['čày] /čáy/ 'thé', ['pà-če] /páče/ 'paix', ['biˇč] /bíč/ 'fouet'.

3.9 /ǧ/ subsumes voiced correlates of /č/: ['ǧàm] /ǧám/ 'vitre', ['mer-ǧe] /mérǧe/ '(il) va', ['reǧ] /réǧ/ 'rois'.

• The fricatives:

3.10 /f/ subsumes voiceless labiodental slit spirants: ['fel] /fél/ 'genre', ['ru-fe] /rúfe/ 'linge', ['kàr'tof] /kartóf/ 'pomme de terre'.

3.11 /v/ subsumes voiced correlates of /f/: ['vàl] /vál/ 'val', [ser'viˇč] /servíč/ 'service', [bol'nàv] /bolnáv/ 'malade'.

3.12 /s/ subsumes voiceless laminoalveolar groove spirants: ['sà-re] /sáre/ 'sel', ['me-se] /mése/ 'tables', ['čàs] /čás/ 'horloge'.

3.13 /z/ subsumes voiced correlates of /s/: ['za-hər] /záhər/ 'sucre', [lu'krẹa-zə] /lukrẹázə/ '(il) travaille', ['kàz] /káz/ 'cas'.

3.14 /š/ subsumes voiceless laminopalatal groove spirants: ['šà-se] /šáse/ 'six', [mə'tu-šə] /mətúšə/ 'tante', [o'ràš] /oráš/ 'ville'.

3.15 /ž/ subsumes voiced correlates of /š/: ['žà-le] /žále/ 'chagrin', ['gri-žə] /grížə/ 'soin', [pri'lež] /priléž/ 'occasion'.

3.16 /h/ subsumes (voiceless) glottal slit spirants: ['hày-nə] /háynə/ 'veston', [pà'hàr] /pahár/ 'verre'. Before /i/ or /r l/ or when final, /h/ is fronted nearly or wholly to the dorsovelar position [x]: [xi'mi-e] /himíe/ 'chimie', [xris'tos] /hristós/ 'Christ', ['duˇx] /dúh/ 'esprit'.

• The nasals:

3.17 /m/ subsumes bilabial nasals: ['mà-re] /máre/ 'mer', ['mà-mə] /mámə/ 'mère', ['kuˇm] /kúm/ 'comment'.

3.18 /n/ subsumes nonlabial nasals with range from apicoalveolar [n] back to dorsovelar [ŋ]. Palatal allophones occur before /č ǧ š ž/: ['bəňč] /báňč/ 'bancs', ['miˇn-ǧe] /míňǧe/ 'balle', [diˇs'tiˇňš] /distínš/ 'distingués', [ˌà-ràň'žá] /aranžá/ 'arranger'; velar allophones occur before /k g/: ['baŋ-kə] /bánkə/ 'banc', ['luˇŋg] /lúng/ 'long'. Elsewhere the allophones are alveolar: ['nu] /nú/ 'non', ['kïy-ne] /kíyne/ 'chien', ['buˇn] /bún/ 'bon', [bàny] /bány/ 'argent'.

• The lateral:

3.19 /l/ subsumes apicoalveolar lateral phones: ['làk] /lák/ 'lac', ['sà-lə] /sálə/ 'salle', ['kàl] /kál/ 'cheval'.

• The flap:

3.20 /r/ subsumes apicoalveolar flaps: ['ràs] /rás/ 'ras', ['so-rə] /sórə/ 'soeur', ['mər] /mə́r/ 'pomme'.

Appendix 7
Roumanian orthography

0. As in all the Romance languages that have writing systems, the basic unit within which the orthographic rules operate is the grammatical word as initially defined, but extended to embrace also pronominal clitics in some but not all positions relative to the word they are attached to. (Cf. the hyphen in Appendix 7:3), with similar function in French and Portuguese but not in Spanish and Italian.

1. From phoneme to grapheme in Standard Roumanian.

1.1 The vowels. Stress is not indicated; so, for example, /mína/ 'la main' and /miná/ 'mener' are written identically as *mína*. This is the major UNDER-DIFFERENTIATION in Roumanian spelling.

/i e a o u/ are written with the matching graphemes in one-to-one correspondence; examples follow passim.[1]

/i/ → *î*: /ínkə/ încă 'encore', /píyne/ pîine 'pain', /urí/ urî 'haïr'.[2]

/ə/ → *ă*: /ə́st/ ăst 'ce', /kədeə́/ cădea 'tomber', /másə/ masă 'table'.

1.2 The semivowels

/y/ → *i*: /yárbə/ iarbă 'herbe', /yéry/ ieri 'hier', /yúte/ iute 'vite', /pyérde/ pierde 'perdre', /máy/ mai 'plus', /lúpy/ lupi 'loups'.[3]

/w/ → $\begin{cases} o \text{ before stressed } /á/: /wárə/ \text{ oară 'fois', } /pwáte/ \text{ poate '(il) peut';} \\ u \text{ elsewhere: } /zíwa/ \text{ ziua 'le jour', } /nówə/ \text{ nouă 'neuf', } /muzéw/ \end{cases}$
muzeu 'musée', /ríw/ rîu 'fleuve', /kəwtá/ căuta 'chercher'.

/ę/ → *e*: /sęárə/ seară 'soir', /kafęá/ cafea 'café', /vrémęa/ vremea 'le temps'.

1.3 The consonants.

/p b t d f v s z h m n l r/ are written with the analogous graphemes in one-to-one correspondence; examples passim.

/c/ → *ţ*: /cárə/ ţară 'terre', /pucín/ puţin 'peu', /lánc/ lanţ 'chaîne'.

/š/ → *ş*: /šáse/ şase 'six', /ašá/ aşa 'ainsi', /oráš/ oraş 'ville'.

/ž/ → *j*: /žók/ joc 'jeu', /grížə/ grijă 'soin', /priléž/ prilej 'occasion'.

/č/
/ǧ/ → $\begin{cases} \left.\begin{array}{c} c \\ g \end{array}\right\} \text{ before } /i, e/: /číne/ \text{ cine 'qui', } /zéče/ \text{ zece 'dix'; } /fuǧí/ \text{ fugi 'fuir', } /ǧéme/ \text{ geme 'gémir'} \\ \left.\begin{array}{c} ce \\ ge \end{array}\right\} \text{ before } /a/: /čárə/ \text{ ceară 'cire', } /vóča/ \text{ vocea 'la voix', } /ǧám/ \text{ geam 'vitre'} \\ \left.\begin{array}{c} ci \\ gi \end{array}\right\} \text{ elsewhere: } /čúdə/ \text{ ciudă 'dépit', } /pičwáre/ \text{ picioare 'pieds', } /aíč/ \text{ aici 'ici', } /ǧuvayér/ \text{ giuvaier 'joyau', } /réǧ/ \text{ regi 'rois'.}[4] \end{cases}$

/k/
/g/ → $\begin{cases} \left.\begin{matrix} ch \\ gh \end{matrix}\right\} \text{before /i/: /kímik/ chimic 'chimique', /deskís/ deschis 'ouvert', /gičí/ ghici 'deviner', /gišéw/ ghişeu 'guichet'.} \\[1em] \left.\begin{matrix} c \\ g \end{matrix}\right\} \text{elsewhere: /kál/ cal 'cheval', /stíklə/ sticlă 'verre', /adínk/ adînc 'profond'; /gáta/ gata 'prêt', /négru/ negru 'noir', /lúng/ lung 'long'.} \end{cases}$

/ky/
/gy/ → $\begin{cases} \left.\begin{matrix} ch \\ gh \end{matrix}\right\} \text{before /e/: /kyém/ chem 'j'appelle', /vékye/ veche 'vieille'; /ingyecá/ îngheţa 'geler'.} \\[1em] \left.\begin{matrix} chi \\ ghi \end{matrix}\right\} \text{elsewhere: /kyár/ chiar 'même', /ókyul/ ochiul 'l'oeil', /únky/ unchi 'oncle', /gyácə/ ghiaţă 'glace'; /magyár/ maghiar 'hongrois', /úngy/ unghi 'angle'} \end{cases}$

/ks/
/gz/ → *x*: /tékst/ text 'texte', /ekspórt/ export 'export', /táksə/ taxă 'taxe', /egzákt/ exact 'exact', /egzistá/ exista 'exister'.[5]

2. From grapheme to phoneme in Standard Roumanian.

2.1 The vowel letters. All the vowel graphemes represent indifferently a stressed or an unstressed vowel phoneme. Apart from this all-pervasive ambiguity in the writing system:

a → /a/, and *ă* → /ə/, consistently; examples of both passim.

e before *a* → /e̦/: deal /de̦ál/ 'colline', bea /be̦á/ 'boire', calea /kále̦a/ 'l'avenue'

elsewhere → /e/: sete /séte/ 'soif', and passim.[6]

i betw. vow. & cons.
betw. cons. & vow. $\Big\}$ → ambiguously /y/ or /i/: haină /háynə/ 'veston' vs. găină /gəínə/ 'poule' or băile /bə́ile/ 'les
final after vow. bains'; voi /vóy/ 'je veux' vs. /voí/ 'vouloir'; piaţă /pyácə/ 'place' vs. viaţă /viácə/ 'vie'

initial bef. vow.
between vowels $\Big\}$ → unambiguously /y/: iată /yátə/ 'voilà', ieşi
final after cons. /yešǐ/ 'ṡortir'; nevoie /nevóye/ 'besoin', băiat /bəyát/ 'garçon', ceaiul /čáyul/ 'le thé'; pomi /pómy/ 'arbres', fraţi /frácy/ 'frères', eşti /yéšty/ 'tu es'.[7]

elsewhere → unambiguously /i/: citi /čití/ 'lire' and other examples passim.

î → /i/ consistently: vîrî / virí/ 'fourrer' and passim.[8]

o before *a* → /w/: oameni /wámeny/ 'hommes', toate /twáte/ 'toutes', joacă /žwakə/ '(il) joue'

elsewhere → /o/: acolo /akólo/ 'là' and passim.[9]

u final after vowel
between vowels $\Big\}$ → /w/: ră100u /rə́w/ 'mauvais', beau /beáw/ 'je bois', cadou /kadów/ 'cadeau', steaua /ste̦áwa/ 'l'étoile', două /dówə/ 'deux'.

elsewhere → /u/: Bucureşti /bukurésty/ 'Bucarest' and passim.

2.2 The consonant letters.

● The graphemes *b d f h l m n p r s t v z* stand in one-to-one correlation with the matching phoneme symbols; examples passim.

ce, ge before *a* → /č/, /ǧ/ respectively: ceapă /čápə/ 'oignon', răceală /rəčálə/ 'rhume', acea /ačá/ 'celle-là'; geană /ǧánə/ 'sourcil', degeabă /deǧábə/ 'en vain', legea /léǧa/ 'la loi'

ci, gi before *o, u* or final → /č/, /ǧ/: cioban /čobán/ 'pâtre', fecioară /fečwárə/ 'petite fille', cinci /čínč/ 'cinq'; giugiuli /ǧuǧulí/ 'câliner', strígi /striǧ/ 'tu cries'.

c, g before *e, i* → /č/, /ǧ/: cere /čére/ 'demander', cifră /čífrə/ 'chiffre', răcit /rəčít/ 'enrhumé'; gest /ǧést/ 'geste', înger /ĭnǧer/ 'ange', ginere /ǧínere/ 'gendre', fugit /fuǧít/ 'fui'

c, g elsewhere → /c/, /g/: cum /kúm/ 'comment', crede /kréde/ 'croire', act /ákt/ 'acte', loc /lók/ 'lieu'; gînd /gínd/ 'pensée', găsi /gəsí/ 'trouver', Magda /mágda/ (name), steag /steág/ 'drapeau'.

ch, gh before *e* → /ky/, /gy/: cheie /kyéye/ 'clef', pereche /perékye/ 'paire', ghete /gyéte/ 'bottes', îngheţa /ĭngyecá/ 'geler'

ch, gh elsewhere → /k/, /g/: chibrit /kibrít/ 'allumette', rochia /rókya/ 'la robe', vechi /véky/ 'vieux'; unghii /úngi/ 'les angles'

j → /ž/ consistently: jos /žós/ 'bas', grajd /grážd/ 'écurie', Cluj /klúž/ (place)

ş → /š/ consistently: şapte /šápte/ 'sept', şti /ští/ 'savoir', oraş /oráš/ 'ville'

ţ → /c/ consistently: ţine /cíne/ 'tenir', cărţi /kə́rcy/ 'livres', braţ /brác/ 'bras'

x between initial *e* and a vowel → /gz/: examen /egzámen/ 'examen', exemplu /egzémplu/ 'exemple';

x elsewhere → /k/: fix /fíks/ 'fixe', lexicon /leksikón/ 'lexique', explica /ekspl009ká/ 'expliquer'.

3. The hyphen.

In addition to its regular, generalized use as a divider of a word broken at the end of a textual line, the hyphen serves to bind pronominal clitics into single phonological words with the verbs to which they are attached.

3.1 Before a verb, wherever one of the clitics has a nonsyllabic allomorph,[10] it is hyphen-linked to the verb, or to a preceding clitic or functor in the same construction: *s-a sculat* /saskulát/ '(il) s'est levé', *mi-au spus* /myawspús/ '(ils) m'ont dit', *ne-a văzut* /nĕavəzút/ '(il) nous a vus', *ţi-l va da* /cilvadá '(il) te le donnera, *că-i schimbă* /kəyskímbə/ 'qu'(il) les change'.

3.2 After a verb, any clitic is hyphenated to the verb, whether syllabic or nonsyllabic: *scuzaţi-mă* /skuzácimə/ 'excusez-moi', *culcă-te* /kúlkəte/ 'couche-toi', *am găsit-o* /angəsíto/ 'je l'ai trouvée', *spune-mi* /spúnemy/ 'dismoi/', *dîndu-mi-le* /dɨndumile/ '(en) me les donnant'.

[*Project. From Phoneme to Grapheme, and/or From Grapheme to Phoneme, in any of the other four languages under study. (Note: In describing the orthography of French it will prove eminently preferable, when dealing with the fact that the word /dwa/ is written* doigt *(or whatever), to assume the existence of nonrepresentational graphemes and to dismiss their use as nonsystematic ornamentation. You can then be content to state that /wa/ is written* oi, *or that* oi *alone represents /wa/, and so on.)*]

Notes for Appendix 7

1. There is one exception here: word-final /i/ is written *ii* as in /táci/ *taţii* 'les pères'. This serves to differentiate /i/ from the semivowel /y/ in the same position, as in /tácy/ *taţi* 'pères'. In this situation involving noun inflection, the orthography is based uniquely on the underlying rather than the surface phonemics: *taţii* represents underlying **tat+i+i**.

2. A marginal OVERDIFFERENTIATION: the phoneme in view is written *â* instead of *î* in the word /romɨn/ *român* 'roumain' and its derivatives (e.g. *România*).

3. In vowel-initial forms of the verb *a fi* 'être', and in the substitute pronoun forms /yél, yéy, yéle/ 'lui, eux, elles', the /y/ is not written at all—e.g. /yéste/ *este* '(il) est', /yerá/ *era* 'était', /yél/ *el* 'lui' etc. For the pronoun /yá/ 'elle', the spelling *ea* matches the other members of the paradigm, and at the same time differentiates the pronoun from its verbal homophone /yá/ *ia* '(il) prend'. There is one other equally minor overdifferentiation for the sake of a morphological distinction: the fem.sing. form of the demonstrative pronoun *acela* 'celui-là' is written *aceea*, and the masc.plur. form *aceia*, although both are phonemically /ačéya/.

4. There is underdifferentiation here, because the sequences /čio čiu ǧio ǧiu/ are also written with these same graphemes in words like *serviciu, religiune, religios* etc.

5. Clearly there is underdifferentiation here, although in fact /ks/ and /gz/ are in complementation: /gz/ occurs between initial /e/ and a vowel, and /ks/ in other environments only.

6. A very minor ambiguity, with next to no functional significance: *ea* represents the sequence /ea/ rather than the diphthong /ĕa/ in a few items such as *teatru* /teátru/ 'théâtre' or *realiza* /realizá/ 'réaliser'.

7. In this particular environment a double *i* is used for /i/, including

postvocalic instances like *caii* /kái/ 'les chevaux' or *copiii* /kopíi/ 'les enfants'. The *ii* may also represent /íy/, as in *ştii* /štíy/ 'tu sais'.

8. The writing *â* in *român* /romín/ could be said to represent an ALLO-GRAPH of the grapheme *î*, since the two graphic symbols are nowhere in contrast.

9. A very minor ambiguity, with essentially no functional load: *oa* represents the disyllabic sequence /oa/ rather than the diphthong /wa/ in a very few items such as *oază* /oázǝ/ 'oasis'.

10. Although the morphophonemic rules producing these allomorphs are irrelevant here, they are set forth in Appendix 6.

Bibliography

Note. The majority of important works on Romance linguistics being altogether or in part historically oriented, they are essentially irrelevant to the content of the present volume; the following titles are principally limited to those of representative grammars of the sort constituting one of the author's sources of data as enumerated in the Preface. A more plentiful general bibliography is provided in Volume 2.

French:
Fraser, W. H., J. Squair, and A. Coleman. 1921. New complete French grammar. Boston: Heath.
Grevisse, M. 1969. Grammaire française avec des remarques sur la langue française d'aujourd'hui. 9th ed. Paris: Hatier.
Valdmann, Albert. 1976. Introduction to French phonology and morphology. Rowley, Mass.: Newbury House.

Spanish:
Alarcos Llorach, Emilio. 1961. Fonología española. 2nd ed. Madrid: Gredos.
Alonso del Río, J. 1963. Gramática española. Madrid.
Ramsey, M. M. 1964. A textbook of Modern Spanish as now written and spoken in Castile and the Spanish American republics. Revised by R. K. Spaulding. New York: Holt, Rinehart and Winston.

Portuguese:
Cunha, C. 1970. Gramática do português contemporâneo. Belo Horizonte: Alvares.
Hills, E. C., J. D. M. Ford, and J. de S. Coutinho. 1944. Portuguese grammar. Revised by L. G. Moffat. Boston: Heath.
Mattoso Câmara, Joaquim. 1977. Para o estudo da fonêmica portuguesa. 2nd ed. Rio de Janeiro: Padrão.

Italian:
Hall, R. A., Jr. 1971. La struttura dell'italiano. Rome: Armando.
Lazzarino, G. 1979. Da capo: A review grammar. New York: Holt, Rinehart and Winston.

Lepschy, A. L. and G. Lepschy 1977. The Italian language today. London: Hutchinson.

Regula, M., and J. Jernej. 1965. Grammatica italiana su basi storiche e psicologiche. Bern: Francke.

Roumanian:

Agard, F. B. 1958. A structural sketch of Romanian. Supplement to Lg. 34 [Monograph 26]. Baltimore: Linguistic Society of America.

Cazacu, B., M. Caragiu, C. G. Chiosa, and V. Guţu R. 1969. A course in contemporary Romanian. Bucharest: Editura Didactică şi Pedagogică.

Graur, A., M. Avram, L. Vasiliu, et al. 1966. Gramatica limbii române. Bucharest: Editura Academiei Republicii Socialiste România.